THE NATION'S NEWSBROKERS

THE NATION'S NEWSBROKERS

VOLUME 2:
*The Rush to Institution,
from 1865 to 1920*

RICHARD A. SCHWARZLOSE

Northwestern University Press
Evanston, Ill.

Published by Northwestern University Press
Evanston, Illinois 60201
Printed in the United States of America

Composition by Point West, Inc., Carol Stream, Illinois

Library of Congress Cataloging-in-Publication Data
(Revised for vol. 2)

Schwarzlose, Richard Allen.
    The nation's newsbrokers.

    Includes bibliographical references.
    Contents: v. 1. The formative years, from
pretelegraph to 1865—v. 2. The rush to institution, from 1865 to 1920.
    1. News agencies—United States—History.
2. Journalism—United States—History. 3. Press—
United States—History. 4. Journalists—United States—
Biography.   I. Title.
PN4841.A1S34 1989   070.4'35'0973   88-37160
    ISBN 0-8101-0818-6 (v. 1)
    ISBN 0-8101-0819-4 (v. 2)

To Daniel and Rebecca with love

Contents

CONTENTS

PREFACE

This volume and its predecessor describe and analyze the origins and growth to maturity of newsbroking as a social institution and a cultural force in the United States.[1] Less than two years after Samuel F. B. Morse opened his first experimental telegraph line to traffic, a pattern of journalistic behavior began to emerge in conjunction with that new technology that was novel and, as it turned out, enduring. That behavior was the daily collection and distribution of general news dispatches via communication systems among journalists in several communities, a process controlled by an agent or agency, in other words, a newsbroker. The previous sentence serves as a definition of newsbroking in this two-volume work.

All but two elements of this definition could also apply to related journalistic activities. The "daily collection and distribution of general news dispatches," for example, could also refer to newspaper publication. The movement of dispatches "among journalists in several communities, a process controlled by an agent or agency" might also describe the activity of special correspondents and feature syndicates. But "general news" eliminates feature syndicates, and "daily," except in moments of unusually high volumes of news, eliminates special correspondents. Likewise, "via communication systems" points squarely at newsbroking's historic use of telegraph, telephone, radio, and now satellite communication, distinguishing it, at least until recently, from transportation-bound feature or supplemental services.

This communication-transportation distinction is a major theme in newsbroking's early development as described in Volume 1. Despite repeated journalistic attempts at intercity movement of news via the transportation system before the arrival of telegraphy in the United States, no regular and enduring newsbroking pattern materialized. Rather than being newsbroking's simple and singular cause, telegraphy contributed new forms and organizing concepts to journalistic practices and enabled previously unfulfilled journalistic needs to be met. The telegraph advanced ongoing intercity news movement from its casual, sporadic, expensive, and unsatisfactory condition in transportation to a system of speed, continuity, permanence, and power. Even though all newsbroking is intercity news movement and historically relies on communication technology, intercity news movement encompasses newsbroking and much more by relying on both communication and transportation systems.

In Volume 2 the scene shifts from newsbroking's early reliance on emerging technology to the political and economic struggles that led to formation of a newsbroker institution controlled by publishers rather than by independent entrepreneurs or by the telegraph companies. The post–Civil War period witnessed repeated attempts by telegraph executives, their journalistic agents, or independent journalists either to wrest control of existing newsbrokerages from the publishers or to replace these journalism-controlled agencies with ones wedded to forces outside of journalism. Two decades of such threats led to national cooperation (some aboveboard, some collusive) among publishers' newsbrokerages in the 1880s, to the democratization of the Associated Press in the 1890s, and to the appearance of substantial competition for AP by 1920. What new technology had made possible in the 1840s, journalism had organized and refined by 1920 into the newsbroking institution we know today. This post–Civil War political and economic maturation in the face of external threats is the subject of the present volume.

This narrative ends with 1920 for several reasons, chief among which is that newsbroking, the author has contended for many years,[2] attained institutional maturity by that time, leaving newsbroking's story of the nearly seventy years since to be told only in terms of continued technological progress and of relative prosperity. In addition, the source materials suggest 1920 as a stopping point. The simple fact is that reliable primary source materials that can sustain a narrative of this detail do not exist for periods beyond 1920.

An emphasis on the nineteenth century brings the present work into direct competition with Victor Rosewater's *History of Cooperative News-Gathering in the United States*,[3] which, unlike the saccharine house histories of the Associated Press[4] and United Press,[5] is a formidable adversary, still regarded in the field as the authority on news-gathering history up to 1930. Rosewater was a newsbroking insider.[6] His father, Edward, founded the *Omaha Bee* on June 19, 1871, joined the Northwestern Associated Press after a short membership in the American Press Association, and was deeply involved in the AP of Illinois, serving briefly on its board of directors. Victor, armed with an AP franchise, ran the *Bee* from 1906, when his father died, until 1920, when he sold the paper to fuel magnate Nelson B. Updike. The younger Rosewater was chairman of AP's nominating committee in 1916, becoming embroiled in a controversy over the representativeness of AP's board of directors. Between them, father and son experienced nearly fifty years of news-gathering history.

Rosewater's work was the first book-length history of newsbroking that was not also autobiographical. The Rosewater family papers reveal that he labored at length in several Eastern libraries and collections researching his history, and the book's foreword acknowledges that Rosewater's research "extended over many years" and included access to internal corporate documents. Surprisingly, however, the book's narrative does not reflect the intimacy Rosewater and his father obviously had with newsbroking. Moreover, all but about half a dozen of Rosewater's bibliographic entries could be easily located and examined in public depositories. There was disappointingly little in the family papers that cannot be found on public shelves or in other collections.

Although the principal purpose of the present project is to draw together and examine all significant information on the early years of newsbroking in the United States, an important byproduct of this endeavor has turned out to be correcting false and misleading accounts of the subject that now reside in the literature. Because neither historical completeness nor objectivity was the goal of newsbrokerages' house histories, to undertake a point-by-point adjustment of their narratives would be to set up a straw man. Many of the corrections in or additions to the historical record proposed in this volume, however, are at Rosewater's expense. He was, it should be noted, a good scholar, handicapped by not having union lists of manuscript collections, accessibility of microfilm, and his own book as a starting point.

* * * * *

Newsbroking is viewed in these volumes as a techno-journalistic system of policies, structures, political-economic functions, and news content, developing among and interacting with other technological and journalistic systems. The present research seeks to trace newsbroking's growth from inception to maturity as a separate institutional and cultural entity in society, a goal first pursued tentatively by the author more than twenty years ago.[7] In large part such separateness will be measured by the changing dynamic and inter-actional relationships newsbroking shares with adjacent institu-tions. Changes in relationships among systems or their components, it is assumed, signify meaningful history. Walter J. Ong lends to this perspective the commonsense tone it deserves:

> Open-system thinking is interactional, transactional, devel-opmental, process-oriented. Terms such as these have by now operated in the discourse about human activity at almost all levels. . . . There had never been any closed system anyhow and the basic insights offered by open-system models were at root even banal. The assertion that everything interacts with every-thing else is hardly news.

Ong observes that ''it has become urgent to exploit this insight''[8]—essentially, it seems to the present author, because behavioral ap-proaches or causal historical models have failed to comprehend and illuminate the magnitude and complexity of history. Progressivist or leftist revisionist perspectives or historic determinism based on great men, economic factors, technological innovations, or com-munication media to the contrary notwithstanding, historians re-main in the final analysis bounded by and only as good as the evidence available to them.

The test of research now, as always, is the publication of sources and replicability of findings, not a project's kinship to some episte-mological labels or trends currently fashionable in the discipline. Stuart Bruchey states the problem well:

> Perhaps there will someday be elaborated a ''general theory of society—specifically some sort of sociology of change''. . . that will be inclusive of economic and all other major sources of change. Until the dawn of that doubtful day, only the total re-sources of the historian, critical and narrative, can succeed in weaving the thread of growth into the richer pattern of human change. His data may often prove unquantifiable, but history is likely to remain the art of weighing the imponderable. . . . It will always be true that a Collingwoodite immersion in the uniqueness of the particular may disclose differences that may be justified as more important than similarities. Certainty is un-attainable, and we may mince nearer the throne only by shuf-fling between the particular and the general, man and his whole environment, cause and effect.[9]

In general, the chapters of this work present the development of newsbroking in the United States chronologically, while material within each chapter is arranged under topical headings. Because the chapters attempt multidimensional approaches to relatively complex relationships, even though in reasonably short time periods, they are uncommonly long. In addition to the topical subdivisions, the reader may find assistance in the discussion sections at the end of each chapter.

* * * * *

The reader will be spared the reasons why newsbroking and its news report are significant forces in society. They should be obvious to all who know the names Associated Press and United Press International. In the nearly quarter of a century that this research has been in progress the author has benefited greatly from the assistance of several research and library colleagues. Among the numerous researchers who have helped this work, several deserve special thanks. They are Catherine L. Covert and Henry F. Schulte of Syracuse University; John D. Stevens and Marion Marzolf of the University of Michigan; Carol Smith of the University of Iowa; Tom Reilly, founder of *Journalism History,* of California State University, Northridge; and Peter R. Knights of York University. From the start of this adventure, Knights has been extraordinarily generous with his time, research materials, and suggestions. His unselfish commitment to another's research project defines collegiality in uncommonly kind and professional terms and traces a rare dimension of friendship.

Kenneth Smith at United Press International good-naturedly put up with the author's many questions and requests during several extended visits and permitted the author to prowl through his files for early International News Service and United Press memoranda. Mrs. Wesley P. Wilmot graciously permitted the author access to her privately held papers on Frederic Hudson.

Without many librarians and their staff members, access to obscure and scarce historical resources would have been impossible. While they may claim to be merely doing their jobs, librarians are indispensable, silent partners in all humanistic research. Special thanks are due to the patient and professional staffs at the Northwestern University Library, especially to Marjorie L. Carpenter and R. Russell Maylone, and at the University of Illinois-Urbana Library, especially to Eleanor Blum.

Released time and financial assistance for this work have been provided by the Purdue University Research Foundation and Northwestern University's Research Committee, Office of Research and Sponsored Programs, and Medill School of Journalism, received with the assistance of Russell Cosper, Benjamin H. Baldwin, Sig Mickelson, Elizabeth S. Yamashita, Edward P. Bassett, and I. W. Cole. For the efforts of the readers, editors, and craftspeople who have labored over these volumes for the Northwestern University Press, the author expresses his gratitude. Special thanks go to the Press's Managing Editor, Susan Harris, for her patience and to Sally Serafim, whose editing saved the author numerous times in this manuscript.

I have drawn strength and encouragement from Edwin and Michael Emery and their historical text, from Tom Reilly and his pioneering spirit, and from Peter R. Knights and his generosity. Despite the obvious toll such an undertaking as this exacts on family and friendships, Sally, my wife, has remained understanding, supportive, and protective throughout, and our children, Dan and Becky, have been blissfully indifferent to, and I hope unscarred by, this endeavor. Heartfelt thanks to all of you.

Chapter 1
POSTWAR PROTECTIONISM

When [the Associated Press] becomes virtually a department of the Western Union Telegraph Company, and the great dailies are merely an expression of the wishes and fears of Mr. Orton and Mr. Simonton, it assumes the shape of a national calamity.

"The Great Monopoly," **The Spirit of the Times**
(July 17, 1869)

The charge that the Western Union Telegraph Company and the New York Associated Press together control the news of the world, and that the former can put a muzzle on the press. . . is utterly groundless.

William Orton, testimony before
Committee on Post-Offices and Post-Roads of U.S. Senate
(January 22, 1874)

What is it that we monopolize? Nothing. . . except our own machinery . . . the product of our own brains which no power on earth can take from us . . .

James W. Simonton, testimony before
Railroad Committee of U.S. Senate
(February 17, 1879)

Such was the war of words that developed after the Civil War and continued into the twentieth century between the Associated Press–Western Union complex and its growing army of detractors. Volume 1 of this work, *The Nation's Newsbrokers: The Formative Years, from Pretelegraph to 1865,* traces the growth of AP's power to gather and deliver news to a broadening field of newspapers. Despite occasional attempts at newsbroking competition by factions in

1

the telegraph fraternity, the Associated Press had, from its mid-1840s origins to the end of the Civil War, gradually established a national journalistic significance, leading to the status of semi-official organ of the Lincoln administration during the Civil War.

How could it be, then, that the AP, an organization that in the 1850s eagerly enlisted newspapers in droves and brought the world's news to many grateful publishers, was becoming the object of journalistic wrath and congressional inquiry in the postwar period? The answer is to be found both in the changing and uncertain conditions of post–Civil War newspaper publishing and in the forging of a mighty telegraphic monopoly that many Americans resented, but that the AP could not ignore if it wanted to survive. Rebel capitulation failed to restore financial normality, but it did trigger a rash of new newspapers whose appearance, in turn, caused the established press to assume a protectionist posture. A major battleground of this journalistic confrontation was newsbroking, where AP memberships became scarce and new news agencies sprang to life.

Peter R. Knights characterizes the newspaper industry in the years immediately following the war as "fluid [and] mixed."[1] Knights's research reveals that newspapers' costs of raw materials, especially rag paper, jumped 100 to 150 percent and labor costs climbed about 50 percent during the war. In general prices in the North hovered at an index level of 175 in 1865 (1860 = 100) and were still inflated to an index level of 154 in 1868. (On the telegraphic front, however, the nation's newspapers appear not to have felt the sting of inflation in their AP assessments. The New York AP in 1860 had annual expenses of about $200,000, of which roughly half was paid by members and customers in New York City.[2] Total telegraphic and incidental expenses for the New York AP in 1865 were $153,082.95, according to general agent Daniel H. Craig's annual report to AP's executive committee. Annual revenues that year, which were $1,720.70 less than these expenses, came in in slightly greater percentage [51.8 percent] from the "outside press," that is from all papers outside the seven newspaper partners of the New York AP.[3])

Although the general picture alarmed established publishers after 1865, the postwar rush of new newspapers into the marketplace posed an even more serious threat to them. In the 1850s dailies increased by 52.4 percent to an 1860 total of 387. In 1870 that total had risen to 574, an increase of 48.3 percent, but most of that growth had occurred in the five postwar years of the decade. The 1870s saw an increase of 69.2 percent in dailies.[4] Knights notes that the first three years of the postwar growth included the beginnings of trends toward evening publication and "independent" political affiliation among newspapers. Growth in "basal" competition (competing papers, regardless of publication field or political affiliation, drawing on the same market area for readers and advertisers) among dailies was "an outstanding characteristic of the post–Civil War press," says Knights.[5] Of the nation's 497 dailies in 1868, 89 percent found themselves in basal competition, Knights attributing this finding to the fact that the daily in 1868 "was primarily an urban phenomenon."[6] Interestingly, whereas states in the lower Mississippi Valley showed the highest rates of increase between 1865 and 1868 (owing to small totals in the former year), the Middle Atlantic states of New York, New Jersey, and Pennsylvania (where newspapers were already the most numerous) added forty-three new papers to their 1865 total of ninety-nine, the largest jump in absolute terms nationally in these three years.[7]

In addition to inflation and new competitors on all sides, however, Northern editors emerged from the Civil War contemplating the peacetime puzzle of holding on to readers attracted by and addicted to dramatic war dispatches. For the editor who had grown wealthy and secure on the war's sensations the problem was to keep the reader from jumping to some upstart journal while offering bland peacetime news. One solution for AP newspapers was to exploit their newsbroker affiliation—hold fast to it, pour money into it to improve its news report, and severely limit additional memberships. For existing AP papers at war's end their newsbrokerage offered strength and protection, and for strong young papers in regions not yet dominated by AP news, forming a regional AP organization and affiliating with the eastern AP crowd secured a position on the ground floor in their area.

The Associated Press was thus turned into a fortress by member editors to repel hordes of newcomers and to hedge against an uncertain future. While the stonework consisted of the nation's established journals, the mortar was the new Western Union telegraph monopoly, which transmitted AP's reports exclusively as long as AP and its members spoke well of Western Union and used its lines exclusively. Although it was an edifice of many regional factions, not immune to internal squabbling, Associated Press was becoming an exclusive club, sought after or despised by outsiders. For the non-AP press, which represented a majority of the nation's newspapers soon after the war, the only option was a series of rickety newsbroker lean-tos that barely protected editors from the winds of an existence without telegraph news reports. Not until 1882 did United Press begin to erect a brokerage of sturdier stuff.

This chapter and the next one describe these developments both in and out of the AP during the first ten years after the Civil War. The first chapter describes the emerging telegraphic monopoly, a technological and corporate inevitability for U.S. newsbrokers, and explores AP's postwar factionalism and franchise protectionism. Chapter 2, covering roughly the same period, introduces AP's regional structure, describes the drama of realignment between the New York City and Western publishers, and notes the tentative beginnings of competing newsbroking. Since much of newsbroking's postwar development might have been quite different in the absence of Western Union's new monopoly, we must begin with telegraphy's postwar metamorphosis.

WESTERN UNION'S EMPIRE

How magnificently laissez faire was Hiram Sibley of Rochester, N.Y., and Western Union's president from July 1856 to July 1865! An organizing and negotiating genius, Sibley presided over the complex of mergers and territorial incursions necessarily preparatory to confronting and overwhelming the American Telegraph Company in 1866 and thus forging a national telegraphic monopoly. Volume 1 describes Sibley's handiwork in the Six-Nation Alliance of August 10, 1857, which wrested telegraphy from its first-generation organizers and imposed exclusive territories and traffic exchange provisos on that competition-ridden industry. The resulting North American Telegraph Association, while seeming to protect member companies from each other and from upstart telegraph lines, effectively froze the industry's major companies in their place. Sibley was thus positioned to conquer his own generation of telegraph leaders, one at a time.

Hemmed in by other association members on the east, south, and west, Sibley's Western Union had clear title only to Ohio, Indiana, Michigan, Wisconsin, a corridor into Chicago, and Pennsylvania west of Pittsburgh and Erie. Sibley's mission was twofold: (1) to leapfrog the territory locked up by the association agreements and enter the Western frontier and (2) to seek a separate peace with any association partner who agreed to be merged with, or leased by, Western Union. Association territory stretched from the Atlantic coast to the western boundaries of Minnesota, Iowa, Missouri, Arkansas, and Louisiana and from the Gulf of Mexico to the Canadian border, with the American Telegraph Company holding rights to New Brunswick, Nova Scotia, and Newfoundland in anticipation of a successful Atlantic cable. Logic told Sibley that Western Union should concentrate on constructing a transcontinental telegraph line from Omaha to California through uncontested western territory and should examine the possibilities of pushing a land line through the Northwest and across the Bering Strait and the Russian expanse, linking the United States with European telegraphic systems at St. Petersburg.

Bold ventures? Perhaps, but both promised the leverage Sibley needed to gain the whip hand among his colleagues. Moreover, after Cyrus W. Field's ill-fated Atlantic cable-laying expeditions in the late 1850s (see Volume 1), many doubted the technical feasibility of a three-thousand-mile submarine cable. As Sibley saw it, the successful completion of either Field's Atlantic cable or his own Bering Strait link with Russia would foreclose efforts to complete the other, given the expense involved in either project. By 1860 Sibley viewed the matter largely as a race between telegraphy's two giants in which the first to establish contact with Europe would automatically rise to control of the industry. But even if the Bering Strait project never came to fruition, Sibley's immediate goal was to link the Pacific Coast with Omaha, both as a first step toward Europe and because telegraph construction in California threatened to upset his applecart.

Transcontinental telegraph proposals[8] dated from the mid-1850s, but two companies, spurred on by California state stipends, were actually erecting lines eastward from San Francisco in 1860, one plotting a course south to Los Angeles and then east through the New Mexico Territory and Texas to link up with the lines of Sibley's enemy, the American company, at New Orleans. The other company, whose route suited Sibley's purposes better, pushed straight east from San Francisco and by the end of 1860 had strung lines into the Stillwater Mountain range some ninety miles east of the California-Nevada border. Sibley secured an amendment to a U.S. Senate bill granting a federal subsidy to the northern route he favored, and although the U.S. House eliminated mention of a specific route and substituted open bidding on the subsidy before passing the amendment, Sibley's bid for support of the northern route was mysteriously the only one on file when the contract was let in the fall of 1860.

A variety of contractors participated in the transcontinental project, but they were all allies of Sibley's Western Union. By July 1861, crews were pushing east from Carson City, west from Omaha, and both directions from Salt Lake City. Even though most predicted the project would take two years to complete, the work was so well organized that the first message passed over the line from San Francisco to Washington, D.C., through Omaha on October 24, 1861. With a corridor from Omaha to the Pacific, Western Union might have moved ahead immediately with the Bering Strait project had the Civil War not been under way for six months when the transcontinental line was completed.

The war forestalled both Sibley's land line to Europe and Field's transatlantic cable, but in most other respects Western Union benefited handsomely from the hostilities,[9] placing its officers in key governmental positions to oversee the North's nationalized telegraph system, receiving large revenues from the heavy volume of wartime military and journalistic traffic, swallowing several other telegraph companies, and generally rising to the leadership of the North American Telegraph Association. Perhaps Western Union's greatest asset was its safe location behind Union lines. The American company, as volume 1 notes, was sliced in half on the Potomac River bridge at the start of the war, and contact between Washington, D.C., and Richmond was not reestablished until April 3, 1865, when General Grant's forces moved into the Confederate capital.

Likewise, the Southwestern Telegraph Company, occupying the territory south of Louisville in the lower Mississippi Valley to the Gulf of Mexico, was torn to pieces, first taken over by Confederate forces and then cut to shreds by protracted military activity in its territory. As Union forces slowly claimed real estate in the Mississippi Valley, remnants of the Southwestern's lines came into Northern jurisdiction, falling under the control of the U.S. military telegraph's superintendent, Anson Stager, who was also the general manager of Western Union. "Early in 1864," says Robert Luther Thompson, "Western Union had launched a determined campaign" to bring the Southwestern company under its control. "One proposal after another was made, but . . . in spite of continued pressure by Western Union during the ensuing months, . . . the Southwestern Telegraph Company stood firm and united."[10]

Although Western Union's efforts to absorb the Southwestern company were, for the moment, stymied, Sibley and his associates had far better luck in the East, where they shopped for all-important links between their eastern termini at Pittsburgh and Erie and the Atlantic Coast. Here they gained control of two of the seven members of the North American Telegraph Association. One was the venerable old New York, Albany & Buffalo Telegraph Company, the only original Morse-Kendall franchisee still recognizable in its earliest form and the line along which the nation's first newsbrokerage had developed 17½ years earlier. (See Volume 1 for details.) On January 1, 1864, Western Union leased the old company's lines between its own at Erie and New York City for ten years in a stock-exchange agreement that freed New York, Albany & Buffalo officials of some troublesome new telegraphic competition in their territory and gave Western Union a clear passage through American Telegraph Company territory to New York City.

The other association member that yielded to Western Union's overtures was the Atlantic & Ohio Telegraph Company, with a territory embracing Pennsylvania east of Pittsburgh and portions of Maryland and Virginia as far south as Washington, D.C. On April 15, 1864, a ten-year lease of these lines gave Western Union access to Philadelphia, Baltimore, and Washington, D.C. By the end of the Civil War, therefore, Western Union controlled the transcontinental telegraph from Omaha to San Francisco and significant, high-volume circuits between Chicago and all major Atlantic coast cities except for Boston and those south of Washington, D.C. A crucial link in Western Union's plan for telegraphic supremacy was the circuit between Omaha and Chicago. Owned by another association member, the Illinois & Mississippi Telegraph Company, this line resisted Western Union takeover until 1867, only a few months after the Western Union's triumphal assimilation of the American company.

AN ATLANTIC CABLE

With the transcontinental line and a corridor to the Atlantic in place, with the public eager to invest in the Western Union goldmine, and with Civil War fortunes swinging slowly toward the Union forces, Western Union's directors in March 1864 gave the green light to the overland project to link California with Europe via the Bering Strait and Russia. By this time Western Union representatives had conducted preliminary surveys of the Russian territory and persuaded the Russians to construct a line east from St. Petersburg into south central Russia, where it would be spliced to the Western Union line running southwest from the Bering Strait. The Russians had completed about three-fourths of their section in 1864. In Congress, Western Union secured an act granting a right of passage through territorial areas, military protection, and naval assistance in laying cable and surveying. The law, signed July 1, 1864, by President Lincoln, also stipulated that no newspaper or news agency could receive preferential or exclusive treatment on the proposed Russian-American line. The company issued 100,000 shares of stock at $100 each to finance the project; the entire issue was immediately purchased.

By the fall of 1865, with the Civil War settled, a force of several thousand workers was surveying in British Columbia and Alaska and along the Anadyr River in Siberia. The following spring, poles and lines began going up along the proposed route, but not without numerous problems, setbacks, and delays. While Western Union pumped substantial sums into its Russian-American venture, Cyrus W. Field in the summer of 1865 organized his first postwar cable-laying project in the Atlantic. After three cable failures in the 1850s totaling losses of $2.5 million for Field and his British-based cable company and the wartime hiatus during which experiments had yielded improved methods of constructing and laying the cable, Field confidently believed he would link Europe and the United States before Western Union could.

One of Field's improvements was to enlist the steamer *Great Eastern* to lay the cable.[11] In the 1850s he had used two ships, which met in mid-Atlantic, spliced their cables, and steamed off in opposite directions. Two ships were necessary because one was too small to carry the 1,400 nautical miles of cable needed to link the two continents. The *Great Eastern*, however, with a width of 120 feet and a length of nearly 700 feet and with a steam propulsion system able to generate 11,000 horsepower, was comparable to twentieth-century liners and equal to Field's task. The brainchild of I. K. Brunel, who thought he was designing and building a ship that could carry enough fuel for the round trip between England and Ceylon and thus monopolize that trade route, the *Great Eastern* was launched into the Thames River on January 31, 1858, to begin a life of ocean-going failure, unable to attract large enough loads of passengers or cargo to offset its massive operating expenses.

When Field contracted in 1864 to use the *Great Eastern* for laying cable, the ship already had bankrupted three owners and registered losses of $5 million in a four-year period, but the contract was to Field's liking. The ship's owner, Daniel Gooch, proposed that if the cable failed, Field would owe him nothing for the mission, but if the cable worked, Gooch wanted $250,000 in cable stock. In July 1865, riding low with the weight of newly wrapped cable, the *Great Eastern* steamed westward out of Valentia Bay on the Irish coast, paying out cable day and night at a steady six miles per hour. With only a few hundred nautical miles remaining and the crew attempting to splice cable sections together, the free end slipped from the ship into the ocean, and nine days of grappling failed to retrieve the lost cable. A buoy was anchored at the site, and the *Great Eastern* returned to England in defeat.[12]

On July 13, 1866, the great ship again departed from Valentia Bay with a fresh cargo of cable, this time landing its precious strand at Heart's Content on Trinity Bay, Newfoundland, on July 27. In the previous couple of days Field, aboard the *Great Eastern* and in constant telegraphic contact with Europe, asked Valentia for the latest European news, which could be transmitted to Canadian and U.S. newspapers when the cable was landed. That dispatch, composed of several brief items, cabled during the previous week to Field, appeared in several extra editions of the New York City papers on Sunday, July 29, exhibiting the brevity and sketchiness that would characterize cabled news in the first few years of cable operation. It would, in fact, be several years before telegraphed transoceanic news dispatches would largely replace clips from British and Continental newspapers in American news columns.

Meanwhile the *Great Eastern* returned to the buoy planted in 1865 and, after thirty attempts, grappled up the 1865 cable and found it still in working order. After a trip to England for more cable, the ship completed laying the 1865 cable. From a venture that had eaten up millions in investment capital for a decade without more than three weeks of successful operation in 1858, Field within a month found himself the proprietor of the only two operating transatlantic cables. Such a monopoly was bound to be challenged, and on July 23, 1869, the *Great Eastern* neared St. Pierre Island, off the Newfoundland coast, laying a cable for a French and British company connecting North America with Brest, France.[13]

At home the news of Field's successful cable, while received with cautious optimism by the press and public, was greeted in the Western Union boardroom with a mixture of joy and sadness. Clearly the company's overland Russian-American telegraphic project was doomed by the cable's success. Although the company maintained a public posture of pursuing the venture until March 1867, the work had foundered during the summer of 1866 as crews found the going extremely arduous in British Columbia. At the first news of the cable's success, North American crews and supervisors scattered in all directions searching for less taxing livelihoods. The Siberian crew, directed by George Kennan, worked on until a ship finally brought Kennan news on May 31, 1867, of Field's success.[14]

A TELEGRAPH-NEWSBROKER MONOPOLY

Field's victory, however, was by no means a serious blow for Western Union. While the *Great Eastern* lumbered through the North Atlantic in the summer of 1866 laying cable, the telegraphic map of the United States was changing rapidly.[15] Emerging from the Civil War, U.S. telegraphic interests coalesced around the "big three," the American Telegraph Company, Western Union, and a newcomer, the United States Telegraph Company. The last named was a merger formed on August 3, 1864, of several smaller state or regional lines in the North that were furnishing vigorous competition along several key routes of the American and Western Union. Figures from *Telegrapher* magazine in 1865 showed Western Union leading with 44,000 miles of line, American second with 23,000, and the United States with 16,000.[16] While there were still numerous smaller independent systems and vestiges of the old North American Telegraph Association,[17] the dance for telegraphic supremacy would be among the "big three," but more likely between the "colossal two." As telegraph historian James D. Reid put it,

> The colossal [American and Western Union] interests had already largely absorbed most of the telegraph organizations of the country. . . . They could be splendid friends and magnificent enemies. . . . [S]ome passage of arms between these telegraphic armies would soon decide the future status of the American Telegraph.[18]

Armed with a skilled and conservative management,[19] and retaining its connection through Cyrus W. Field to the Atlantic cable project, the American company rapidly recuperated from its Civil War bifurcation and emerged by late 1865 the solidest of the "big three." It was this public impression of dependability that led American to absorb the Southwestern company in January 1866, and thus thwart Western Union's long campaign to acquire the latter company. The North American Telegraph Association was thus reduced to four members. The United States company, on the other hand, the darling of investors early in 1865 because of its vigor and daring, had by mid-summer come under a cloud as stockholders began inquiring pointedly and publicly why large revenues yielded small profits and why company officials and an inside ring of stockholders seemed to be living exceedingly well. Under such pressure its president, James McKaye, resigned, replaced by William Orton, who was called from his federal post as commissioner of internal revenue to set the company back on the track. After three months of efforts for the United States company, Orton, however, found that a Western Union merger proposal was his company's best course of action. That merger, signed February 27, 1866, made Orton a vice-president of Western Union under Jeptha H. Wade, who had replaced the ailing Hiram Sibley as Western Union president seven months earlier.

With the acquisition of United States lines that stretched throughout the nation irrespective of the territorial exclusiveness that was set up in the North American Telegraph Association agreements, Western Union could now repudiate that association and operate in direct competition with the American and Illinois & Mississippi companies. For the American officers, the writing was ' on the wall. Protracted negotiations between the two giants followed, culminating on June 12, 1866, with consolidation of the two under the name of the Western Union. Even though independent lines continued to operate, and others would appear from time to time, this was the nation's first national monopoly, embracing 37,380 miles of telegraph routes over which 75,686 miles of line were strung among 2,250 offices.[20]

The significance of this merger and its potential impact on national communications was not lost on Congress, which on July 24, 1866, passed a resolution that (1) gave government messages priority on the nation's telegraph lines, (2) granted the postmaster general power to fix rates for government messages sent by telegraph, and (3) permitted the federal government after the act had been in force five years to purchase the lines and property of the private telegraph companies for a price to be set by a five-member commission.[21] The resolution arose in the wake of the merger announcement and while the Senate was considering a bill to establish under governmental sponsorship a National Telegraph Company. The next Congress, the Fortieth, entertained three bills, two proposing national postal telegraph systems, one to be run by the federal postal service and the other to be run by an outside corporation under contract to the Post Office, and the third bill proposing federal supervision of lines to be constructed between Washington and Boston.[22]

The nation thus embarked upon thirty years of debate over the propriety and profitability of installing some form of postal telegraph, either as competition to the Western Union monopoly or as a replacement for it. Alvin F. Harlow counts nineteen times before 1900 that congressional committees examined the issue of government versus private monopolies in telegraphy, and seventeen times these committees reported favorably on government ownership.[23] Although the debate raged on in committee hearings, floor debate, pamphlets, and magazine articles, Congress was unconvinced of the need either to establish a postal telegraph system or to provide even modest competition to the ever-expanding Western Union system.

The postal telegraph debate revolved around, on the one hand, the proper role of representative government in the free enterprise system and, on the other hand, the effects of a private monopoly upon the consumer. Western Union, the first and for a decade the nation's most obvious monopoly, faced a constant barrage of criticism, some well founded and some exaggerated or dishonest, and fought back, often with the help of a friendly AP newspaper press, with its own version of the facts. To the disadvantage of those trying to form an informed opinion on the issue, the debate became mired in rhetoric rather than fact. Even the seemingly clear-cut case study offered by England, which had nationalized its telegraph system in February 1870 and thus presented statistical data representing the same system under private and governmental control, was perceived by participants in the postal telegraph debate in wholly different ways.[24]

Newsbroking, of course, also became embroiled in the debate. There was no escaping the mutual business reliance of AP and Western Union. The telegraph company reported that $521,509 of its total $6.6 million in revenue during 1866 came from "transmitting regular press reports on contract" with AP. Western Union estimated that those regular reports totaled 294,503,630 words, in addition to which it transmitted 75,359,670 words in special press reports in 1866.[25] But beyond paying tolls for a contracted service, the AP, as a national news disseminator, could assist its telegraphic ally with carefully shaped news reports of congressional proposals, even though such coverage might fuel the attacks regularly mounted by critics of the Western Union–AP alliance. The regional Western Associated Press's executive committee in 1873, at a moment when Western Union seemed ready to abandon its exclusive contract with the AP system, noted that "during the nearly six years" of the existing contract Western AP had paid the telegraph company at least $1.6 million in transmission charges, adding,

> And to this immense patronage must be added [Western AP's] powerful influence actively exerted in supporting and defending the franchises of the [Western Union] Company against propositions strongly advocated in Congress, of transferring the Telegraphic business to the direction and control of the Post Office Department, and which undoubtedly would have been carried into effect before this time, but for the opposition of the Press.[26]

Government and private critics of Western Union's monopoly seldom missed an opportunity to assail the Associated Press also, linking the two enterprises in a darkly sinister scheme of mutual support and protection. And other newsbrokerages formed later were also criticized for becoming allied with such upstart telegraph companies as the Atlantic & Pacific Company and the Postal Telegraph Company. Newsbrokers' need for regular, dependable telegraphic service is obvious, and following standard business practice they contracted with telegraph companies for special rates, specified transmission times, and lengths of news dispatches. It was also standard practice at that time to write exclusive contracts that guaranteed the newsbroker a continuing telegraphic service at reduced rates in exchange for the newsbroker's exclusive patronage and loyalty. The critic, however, was also justified in viewing these contracts as collusive and adding indignantly that one of the parties exercised extraordinary power over the public's opinion of monopoly via its manipulation of news dispatches.

In the final analysis, while AP and Western Union "were firm allies," as Harlow observes, "Western Union naturally held the whip hand."[27] AP derived most of the leverage its members wielded over outside newspapers from its contract with Western Union. On the other hand, Western Union had become a stunning national monopoly by its own efforts and, outside of occasional publicity blurbs in the AP news report, could have survived quite well without AP.

NEW YORK CITY FACTIONALISM

New York City's AP newspapers were barely recognizable after four years of Civil War. That cozy collection of seven journals that for two decades or so had set the course for U.S. newspaperdom from a handful of newsrooms in lower Manhattan prior to 1860 emerged from the war unequal and in disarray. The *Courier and Enquirer* was dead; the *Journal of Commerce* and *Evening Express* had settled into unassuming journalistic roles. The pioneering penny *Sun* had lost its zest and sparkle. The *Tribune* and *Herald*, on the other hand, rode the crest of war reporting enterprise into national postwar journalistic leadership. The *World,* the *Courier and Enquirer's* replacement in AP, skyrocketed from oblivion to lusty success after Manton Marble grasped its helm in 1862. Meanwhile, the *Times* faltered, caught on the horns of political dilemmas concocted in its own editorial columns.[28]

Additionally most of the guiding spirits of these journals—the men who in their youth had struggled to convert their concepts of journalism into practical, paying news sheets—were nearing retirement. Most were in their forties or fifties when the war ended and either had already turned over the reins of their papers to younger men or were about to do so.[29] Frederic Hudson retired at age forty-seven in 1866 as the *Herald's* managing editor, and James Gordon Bennett left the editorship of the *Herald* to his son in 1867. The elder Bennett died in 1872. Moses S. Beach sold the *Sun* in 1868 to a consortium headed by Charles A. Dana, formerly a *New York Tribune* managing editor. William Cowper Prime and David M. Stone had replaced Gerard Hallock at the *Journal of Commerce* in 1861. Henry J. Raymond died in 1869, and the *Times* came under the direction of his partner, George Jones, who "had had no experience in the supervision of editorial policy," says Elmer Davis.[30] The *Tribune's* Horace Greeley, who would die in November 1872, had relied heavily on managing editors for years, and in 1866 acquired John Russell Young for that post. Young was succeeded three years later by Whitelaw Reid, who then followed Greeley in the editor's chair of the paper. The Brooks brothers at the *Express* maintained an ever-lower journalistic profile, distracted by political affairs. James died in 1873; Erastus sold the *Express* to a consortium in

1877, staying on only as a writer. Manton Marble sold the *World* in 1876.

Despite these many changes in personnel and newspaper ownership in AP's ranks, the newsbrokerage's first postwar moves implied business as usual. AP's executive committee issued a circular in the fall of 1865 announcing that the AP contract with the American Telegraph Company would expire on October 31, 1865, and that S. H. Gay of the *Tribune* would receive bids from all interested telegraph companies by October 1.[31] The record contains responses from Western Union on October 9 and from American on October 20. Western Union proposed

> simply, that the present arrangement for transmission of regular and special reports over our lines be continued for five years, with the understanding, that the Press receiving such reports shall as heretofore use our lines exclusively, except of course when we cannot do the business promptly.[32]

The American company was

> willing to renew the present contract for five years, with the exception of applying the sliding scale to our existing tariff, instead of the one attached to the contract. We are also willing to modify any of the clauses of that agreement, which may have been found not conducive to mutual interest.
>
> As no proposal in writing can be made to cover all the questions of importance . . . we would like to have a committee of your Association meet a committee of this company to discuss the whole subject.[33]

Whether the proposal to continue the present arrangement with Western Union was accepted is not known, but AP and the American penned an agreement on December 22, renewing the old pact for another five years. American pledged (1) not to "become pecuniarily interested in . . . any association or arrangement formed for the purpose of competing" with the AP "for the reporting of Foreign and Domestic News," and (2) to prohibit its employees from collecting and transmitting general news in towns where "special reporters for Newspapers" were located.

AP agreed to use American's lines exclusively within the company's territory for "all telegraphic messages which may relate to the News, or to the business of the Newspapers" of the AP.[34] A printed tariff schedule attached to the contract suggests that these rates were below regular commercial rates. Either party could give three months' notice of termination of the contract.

Despite such contract renewals, all was not business as usual at AP. George Wilkes, a founder of *The Spirit of the Times* and its sole proprietor since 1858,[35] used this sports and political journal in 1869 to survey AP's operation and assert that four New York City AP papers hid behind the agency's protective shield. The *Express* "lives by grubbing," said Wilkes. "It lives along in its free, careless, gypsy way, finding a ribbon here and an old hat there, and remnants of silk and lace shreds and rags and patches." The *Journal of Commerce* "has no ambition in news gathering. Its owners report the markets and the arrival of ships, and there stop!" The *Sun* "merely wants the news dispatch. The briefer it is the better. The space is limited. It cannot afford to take a page or two of dispatches."[36] Wilkes saw the *Times* as a special case. By 1869, *Times* partner and former correspondent James W. Simonton had replaced Craig as NYAP's general agent, and Wilkes saw the paper (which, when Wilkes wrote the following, had been operating without Raymond's guiding hand for a month and a half) as wielding "a vast influence in the machinery of the Association." Wilkes explained that

> One of [the paper's] owners is [AP's] General Agent. Another owner is the Associated Press Director of the Western Union . . . and one of the Executive Committee. A former employee is the London Agent, another a Havana Agent. Nor have these owners and employees of *The Times* been unmindful of their newspaper in the service they render to the Association.[37]

Wilkes pointed out that this weak foursome as a majority in the NYAP hemmed in and fed upon AP's three aggressive members—the *World*, *Tribune*, and *Herald*.

> While every interest advances, the Press stand still. It is because in some unaccountable way, Mr. Greeley and Mr. Bennett have allowed themselves to be hedged in and curbed by a monopoly which began with an economical expedient twenty-five years ago.[38]

Saying that a "blight seems to have fallen upon" the New York AP papers, Wilkes observed that "if any member of it ventures to show special enterprise or industry, the whole advantage must be shared with journals who have borne nothing of the expense."[39]

16

Thus, Mr. Bennett may send a man to Russia at great expense, and Mr. Greeley may have his emissary in Cuba, and any news they send *must* be given to the *Sun, World,* and *Times* for a little more than the share of tolls! All expense of outfit, time, salary are borne by themselves. The advantage is shared all around.[40]

Wilkes here points out AP's greatest postwar drawback. In addition to being a device to eliminate costly news-gathering competition among New York papers, AP had developed into a protection for the weaker members and an impediment to stronger members. All three of the strong papers noted by Wilkes had shown signs of restlessness within AP. As we shall see in the next chapter, when Craig was fired by AP in 1866, the *World* eagerly followed him out of the association for about five weeks. "Once or twice James Gordon Bennett had threatened to take the Herald out" of the AP, says Augustus Maverick,[41] one of them on June 29, 1867.[42] The *Tribune,* either because of indifference to, or malice for, AP, was a haven for reporters and editors working against the AP. On April 27, 1869, the *New York Sun* accused *Tribune* managing editor Young of telegraphing AP dispatches to the *Philadelphia Morning Post,* a paper he had an interest in although it was a non-AP paper. The charge was true, and within a month Young had left the *Tribune* and was in Philadelphia helping to organize an opposition newsbrokerage.[43]

Then there was George H. Stout, called an "able and longtime employee" of the *Tribune* by Bingham Duncan,[44] who in 1869–70 assisted competitors of AP while a *Tribune* staffer. After an extended exchange with AP general agent Simonton, *Tribune* managing editor Reid fired Stout on February 18, 1870. Reid had been reluctant to act, insisting on his autonomy as a managing editor, and even after the firing, Stout believed himself on firm enough ground to attempt to get his *Tribune* job back.[45] There is evidence that in the first few months after Reid became managing editor, the *Tribune* at times received and published news from organizations opposing AP.[46]

Moreover, the New York AP partnership seemed at times on the verge of collapse under the weight of its strong-willed members. At the surface were the obvious political tensions (*Times, Tribune,* and *Sun,* after Dana's takeover, were Republican voices; *World* and *Express* were in the Democratic camp, the *Herald* as the group's mugwump; and the *Journal of Commerce* generally eschewed politics), but lurking beneath were the explosive and erratic personalities of leading publishers, who were accustomed to having things their own way and striving through journalism's various avenues to attract an audience. Dana's recent acquisition of the *Sun* and his consequent need to turn the paper's politics around and redirect its circulation appeal, for example, made him the partnership's spoiler by the early 1870s. It was Dana, as noted above, who blew the whistle on Young's trafficking with non-AP journalists while the *Tribune*'s managing editor. A personal friend and strong supporter of Ulysses S. Grant in the 1868 campaign, Dana soon turned on the Grant administration, finally breaking the Crédit Mobilier scandal story while Grant was seeking reelection in 1872. The exposé discredited AP partner James Brooks, a proprietor of the *Express*, and Schuyler Colfax, Grant's first-term vice-president and a candidate to replace Horace Greeley as *Tribune* editor. Dana, while nominally supporting Greeley's 1872 presidential bid as a Liberal Republican in opposition to Grant, simultaneously poked fun at Greeley, whose *Tribune* Dana, as managing editor, had abandoned early in the Civil War because of differences with Greeley.

When Greeley died in late November of 1872, soon after his presidential campaign loss to Grant, Dana among others blamed *Tribune* managing editor Reid for breaking the old warrior's heart by ruthless editing and suppression of Greeley's post-election editorials. In this instance, Dana snared himself, the *Tribune*, and factions of his own Republican party in his own trap by linking Colfax, one possible Greeley replacement, with Crédit Mobilier, and by viciously attacking Reid, the other candidate for Greeley's chair, an attack that backfired on him in some party circles. Reid within a month had secured the financial backing to acquire a majority of the *Tribune* stock and Greeley's position.[47]

Author Royal Cortissoz describes how Reid and Dana were finally brought together over a matter of pressing New York AP business some years later (presumably the creation, described in Chapter 3, of the joint executive committee of AP late in 1882). "Reid's ancient feud with Dana," says Cortissoz, ended when "he and his old foe met around the Associated Press table for the first time in ten years."

> They had not set eyes upon one another in five or six [years]. The situation was droll. Without any greeting they solemnly and scrupulously transacted their business. Presently Reid had some odd experiences with contracts to tell. Dana let out a

laugh. Before he knew it he was insisting that Reid was particularly fitted to serve on a sub-committee that was found necessary.... As the meetings multiplied the ice was melted. Dana and Reid reached a point of friendly co-operation, in which, for the nonce, their historic enmity, the soreness of the Greeley days, was submerged if not forgotten.[48]

While there might have been room for a mellowing of relations by the 1880s, New York's AP during and soon after the Civil War underwent strenuous, self-imposed tightening of controls on its partners. Changes in the organization's bylaws since their adoption in 1856 (see Volume 1, chapter 5) reveal a drift toward protection both from outside journalism and from fellow New York AP partners, a reflection of the partnership's drift into the strong and weak factions Wilkes notes above. Following is a chronology of all AP bylaw changes between 1856 and 1874 still in force in 1874:[49]

March 26, 1856—"The impropriety of members publicly assailing [the AP's] agents and reporters was discussed, but without action save an understanding that the latter would not be indulged in."

October 21, 1857—"The members...agree to publish no complaint against Mr. Craig or other...agents without first submitting the same to the Association, and also that Mr. Craig be instructed to make no publication reflecting upon members of the Association...without first submitting the same to the Association."

June 30, 1859—AP resolved not to furnish news to any newspaper outside of New York City that uses the reports of a rival organization.

November 20, 1861—"Official documents from the Departments or members of the Government at Washington or Albany ...if received by telegraph [by one member are to] be sent around" to other members.

1861—The expense of gathering "news of movements connected with the war, in different parts of the country" will be borne by all members, even if one member declines to use such news.

January 6, 1863—AP's news may not be sold to any parties in New York City "other than those who now receive it."

September 11, 1863—"It was understood among the members that the proceedings of the Association be considered private—except portions necessary to be made public."

May 17, 1866—The first Tuesday in each month, at 2 o'clock, was designated as AP's regular meeting time.

August 1, 1866—"Each member of the Association [will] instruct the Telegraph Company, in writing, to send every special telegram for foreign news which may be sent to any newspaper, not to the office of that newspaper, but to the office of the Associated Press, there to be manifolded and distributed at the same time to all the members of the Association."

November 9, 1866—The executive committee was expanded to three members.

June 3, 1867—"Upon all Domestic special dispatches hereafter sent around to the members of the Associated Press, there shall be charged *pro rata* to such papers as may make use of the same an addition of twenty per cent upon the Telegraphic cost."

December 9, 1867—Although receiving six votes, the following failed for want of a unanimous vote: "No member of the Association shall denounce or assail through the columns of the Press, the business management of the Association or the acts of its regularly authorized Agents in the performance of their duties" but rather appeal to AP's executive committee "to remedy the evil complained of" and failing that, report to the association as a whole.

January 5, 1869—"Five Dollars shall be paid to each member of the Association who shall be in his place at the hour named in the call."

July 2, 1869—The bylaw reading "Dispatches received from a resident Editor, or resident Reporter, of any one particular paper connected with or supplied by the Association, can be used by that paper for its own sole use" was construed to mean editors and reporters reporting within New York City, and does include those "employed . . . to procure and transmit by telegraph news out of" New York City.

December 14, 1869—The punishment for AP employees disclosing AP news to parties not entitled to have it was upgraded. The employee would be dismissed after the first, rather than the second, offense.

October 11, 1870—The principle was reasserted that "specials are not the property of the paper to which addressed."

November 1, 1870—"Printed 'slips' of Specials do not meet the requirements of the rule, but the original copy must be sent to the General Agency."

There is a clear business propriety in not openly criticizing either one's partners or the mutually created organization, and in not revealing a partnership's deliberations. There is business wisdom in seeing that one's product does not reach the hands of those unauthorized to receive it and in swiftly punishing employees who traffic with the competition. And there is business necessity in sharing the contingencies of war coverage. But one can find only mutual suspicion and self-protection in rules requiring foreign news specials and domestic specials originating outside of New York City, even though addressed to one member, to be delivered to AP's offices for distribution to all partners. In 1874 we find the forced sharing among AP partners of individual papers' enterprise journalism imposing a mediocrity on all seven papers by boosting the weaker papers' news reports and discouraging stronger papers' initiative. At the outset of this chapter the AP structure was likened to a fortress, a bulwark against the hordes of "outside" newspapers. We find, in these rules, that inside the fortress the generals had also formalized ways of protecting their flanks from their comrades in arms.

George Wilkes's observations in *The Spirit of the Times,* cited above, begin to have the ring of truth after one examines AP's rules. A comment in *The Nation* in 1870 about the press fraternity generally suggests a context in which AP's rules may have seemed appropriate to the partners.

> The members of the press deal with each other, in all business matters, not simply at arm's length, as ordinary business men do, but as blacklegs or professional gamblers may be supposed to deal with each other, with pockets buttoned tight, a revolver within easy reach, and with ready access to a window looking out on the street. Now, nobody would perhaps have a right to ask the gentlemen engaged in this wretched business to mend their manners if they did not preach so much; but their preaching. . .makes their mode of transacting business rather ludicrous.[50]

THE ASSOCIATED PRESS "FRANCHISE"

If the "inside" papers thus regarded each other with suspicion and barely disguised enmity, the "outside" papers regarded the AP establishment with abhorrence, privately mixed with envy. The New York AP and the emerging regional and local auxiliary APs (discussed in the next chapter) all clung tenaciously to their printed news report, admitting new members and subscribers sparingly and only where such admissions would not threaten existing AP papers. This was the origin and impact of the famous AP "franchise" so frequently applauded in AP literature over the years and not eliminated from AP lore until the agency was forced to do so in antitrust litigation in 1945. With a variety of phrases and terms, the franchise right was repeated in rules and bylaws throughout the AP system. In New York City, AP's bylaws since 1856 said, "No new member shall be admitted to this Association without the unanimous consent of all the parties thereto. . . ."[51] Article 11 of the Western Associated Press bylaws as of 1867 said:

> No journal not now receiving and paying for the news of this Association, shall be permitted to receive the same without the consent of all the newspapers receiving the dispatches, in the town where it is to be published.[52]

The Kansas and Missouri AP bylaws in 1883 said:

> No new member shall be admitted without the unanimous consent of the member or members in the city or town, or within five miles of the corporate limits of the city, where the business is to be carried on.[53]

And Article 16 of the bylaws of the Northwestern Associated Press said, "No new member shall be admitted without the unanimous consent of the members in the city or town where his business is carried on."[54]

Such were the barriers facing "outside" papers that wanted the AP news report, and although the outsiders rancorously attacked the AP club publicly, many would have given much to have had that membership and news report. As the postwar years passed and even though more new papers came on the scene, AP's national membership continued to represent roughly only one-third of the nation's total of dailies. S. N. D. North's census of newspapers and periodicals estimates that "over 200 daily papers" were served by AP in 1872. Compared with the nearest U.S. census report of total dailies, 574 in 1870, two hundred dailies is 34.8 percent. North precisely reports the situation in 1880: 355 out of 971 dailies received AP dispatches, or 36.6 percent of the total.[55] (See table 1 in the Appendix for state and regional breakdowns of the 1880 AP membership.) An indication of the morning slant of the membership is found in the fact that in 1880 52.1 percent of the nation's morning papers belonged to AP, whereas only 23.8 percent of the evening papers did.[56]

A case study of how the established press controlled AP's membership and resisted encroachment by newcomers is the Northwestern AP, formed at a meeting in Chicago on February 22, 1867, and covering portions of Illinois, Iowa, and Nebraska. Prior to its formation, the Northwestern AP's newspapers "produced their telegraphic news by individual contracts or agreements with the Western Associated Press,"[57] an organization described in chapter 2 as forming in 1865 and representing primarily big-city papers between Pittsburgh and St. Louis, the Great Lakes and the Ohio River Valley. Organization by the smaller papers making up the Northwestern AP was "the best leverage for concessions," from the Western AP and the telegraph companies, according to Victor Rosewater.[58] It was also encouraged by the Western AP as an efficient means of dealing with the smaller papers without admitting them to WAP membership.[59]

Thirty newspapers[60] combined to form the Northwestern AP in 1867, three-quarters of which had been founded before 1861.[61] The new agency incorporated in Illinois with a capitalization of $20,000 and issued a $25 share to each daily in the agency's territory "who shall desire to become subscribers."[62] In 1879 during new incorporation proceedings, involving recapitalization at $100,000, only twenty of the original newspapers had survived to purchase new stock. Only one new member had been added to Northwestern AP's rolls in those first twelve years, the *Sioux City* (Iowa) *Journal*.[63] According to Winifred Gregory's union list of newspaper files, six of the papers withdrawing from membership were still publishing in 1879 and even in 1887, when the newsbrokerage observed that "some of the papers which withdrew have since purchased of the Northwestern Associated Press news on yearly contracts."[64] Of the remaining four that disappeared from the agency's membership, three appear to have suspended publication prior to 1879, and the fourth had an irregular publication history prior to 1879, according to Gregory.

Like the other AP auxiliaries, the Northwestern AP limited its membership. Thirty established members in 1867 had dwindled to twenty in 1879 and stood at twenty-two in 1887. Similar to New York City's AP, founded by the leading and established journals that seemingly had no thought of expanding their membership rolls or territorial reach, Northwestern AP papers wanted safety in numbers, as long as the numbers were confined to the old crowd that published stable newspapers, at least when the newsbrokerage was getting under way.

During the 1870s and 1880s an AP membership caused a newspaper's value to soar. The literature is sprinkled with accounts of how young editors guaranteed their journalistic futures by purchasing a newspaper with an AP affiliation. Unlike the 1830s and 1840s, when a Benjamin Day or a Horace Greeley had a fair chance at success if his news and opinions concepts were novel and saleable, journalistic success after the war was measured, in part, by one's ability to get hold of the AP news reports. North, noting that admission to the New York City AP as a partner "has long been regarded as impossible," estimated that in 1884 the AP franchise held by each New York partner was worth one-quarter of a million dollars.[65]

A case in point is Edward Rosewater, who founded the *Omaha Bee* on June 19, 1871. The Northwestern AP, founded four years earlier, included only the *Herald* and *Republican* (later the *Tribune and Republican*) in Omaha as two of its thirty charter members. The *Bee* struggled along outside of the AP for from eight to sixteen years[66] owning stock in the American Press Association, AP's chief competitor, after September 11, 1875.[67] Rosewater's paper was one of only two joining the Northwestern AP in the twenty years following the newsbrokerage's founding in 1867. One may surmise that the *Bee* could not join AP's ranks until the *Republican* withdrew, since, as noted earlier, membership in the Northwestern AP required "unanimous consent of the members in the city or town where his business is carried on."[68]

Three weeks after Rosewater purchased APA stock in 1875, the APA changed its name to the National Associated Press Company, and a year later Rosewater was on NAP's board of directors. A fellow director in the fall of 1877 was Melville E. Stone, publisher of the struggling young *Chicago Daily News*, another "outside paper."[69] This is the same Stone whom the AP called on sixteen years later to lead an assault on competing newsbrokerages and attempt to establish a national Associated Press (see chapter 5). Stone turned out the first issue of the *News* on December 23, 1875, his chief roadblock to an AP membership being the evening *Chicago Post and Mail* (which Stone had helped merge in 1874). Inexplicably, although the *Post and Mail* received AP's news report, it habitually stole news items from Stone's *News*, the latter eventually trapping the former in an act of thievery. As Stone describes it, the *Post and*

Mail "was literally laughed to death." Stone, now sharing the *News*'s direction with Victor F. Lawson, bought the *Post and Mail* in 1878 for $15,000.[70] The *Post and Mail* equipment and plant were disposed of, Lawson and Stone salvaging its only asset—the dead paper's AP membership, which Lawson's biographer calls one of the "chief benefits derived from the purchase."[71] Lawson at the time of the purchase was anticipating the membership's advantage, writing, "We should then have the whole field of evening journalism secured against any future competitor and should have only one paper—the *Journal*—to divide business with. It is a golden opportunity beyond a doubt."[72]

Joseph Pulitzer and Charles A. Dana are other noteworthy examples of editors who shopped around for AP franchises. Pulitzer was a kind of dealer in WAP franchises in St. Louis. The *Missouri Democrat*, an AP member, had repeatedly blackballed efforts by its chief rival, the *Globe*, to secure AP news. Pulitzer at a bankruptcy sale bought the *Missouri Staats-Zeitung* and its AP franchise for "a few thousand dollars," ran it one day, dismantled the property, and sold its AP franchise to the *Globe* for a sum variously reported as "about $27,000" and "a little in advance of $40,000."[73] Four years later when Pulitzer finally purchased the *Dispatch*, this too at a bankruptcy sale, he made sure it had an AP franchise. As a Pulitzer biographer comments, the franchise "Pulitzer knew very well had a value of its own."[74]

After two years of struggling to make a success of an underfinanced *Chicago Republican*, Dana, disgusted with Chicago, its journalism, and its Republicans, returned to New York City in 1867 bent on founding a new paper. Organizing a high-powered consortium of backers, Dana pushed toward introduction of the *Evening Telegraph* late in 1867. But the much-rumored paper never materialized, leading in turn to rumors about the delay. Frederic Hudson explains that

> It was then ascertained that, owing to the opposition of two or three members of the Associated Press, the new paper could not have the telegraphic news of that institution, and without that news the contemplated paper could not succeed; indeed, it would be folly to bring out the first number.[75]

Dana next scouted NYAP's partners for a newspaper seller and found one in Moses S. Beach, who at age forty-five desired "rural enjoyment" more than operating the nation's pioneer penny paper.[76] Dana and his syndicate purchased the *New York Sun* for $175,000 on January 1, 1868. A moment's reflection on this sale indicates the value of that AP franchise to Dana. He would rather purchase an AP paper, even though its political and journalistic traditions were alien to his own, than found a paper in his own image. Hudson says,

> the *Sun* of Moses S. Beach had set, and the *Sun* of Charles A. Dana had risen....In this way the first penny paper of the country, after a prosperous existence of over thirty years with its democratic tendencies, became an independent organ of the Republican Party....[77]

The franchise privilege of blackballing competitors seeking entry into AP was only the most extreme and obvious means by which the outside press was kept in its place. Occasionally AP papers and their news association received generous assistance from their ally, the Western Union telegraph company, in dealings with both inside and outside newspapers. Both the AP and Western Union insisted publicly that their relationship was only business, that they were indifferent to each other's successes and difficulties. Western Union president William Orton, for example, acknowledged in testimony before a Senate committee that the two associations enjoyed a steady, but platonic, affair.

> The relationships between the press and the telegraph are necessarily constant and intimate. The former are valuable customers of the latter, and each contributes in no small degree to the prosperity of the other. Years of business intercourse between men whose daily dealings are mutually satisfactory can hardly fail to produce, if not warm friendships, at least mutual respect; and he must be a poor student of human nature who expects to disturb such relations, much more to break them up, by proclaiming their impropriety merely because one of the parties declines to make war on the other in the interest of a stranger....[78]

But other sources describe the relationship as more than "friendship" or "mutual respect." Daniel H. Craig, AP's general agent until late 1866, said in 1883 that "For seventeen years previous to 1867, it was an unwritten law of the N.Y. Associated Press and the Telegraph Co....that neither should do anything to the prejudice of the other's interests." Craig explained with the following example:

The only morning journal in one of the largest of the interior cities of [New York state] commenced to take news reports over a competing telegraph line. This was an offense to the officers of the W.U. Co., though the editor continued to publish and pay for my Associated Press reports. After learning the Company's wishes, I notified the editor that he could not have the Association's reports unless he ceased to patronize the opposition line. He continued his business with it, and the following day we entered into negotiation with an evening journal in his city to publish a morning edition, pledging to him free and exclusive reports for a year. This movement coming to the ears of the unruly editor, he quickly dropped the opposition line, and begged to be reinstated in the Associated Press.

"Had [AP's editors] assented to my wishes," asserts Craig,

the Western Union Telegraph Company would have been buried in its infancy, or, if permitted to live, it would have been as the tail to the Associated Press' kite, instead of the Association's being in that relation to the Western Union Company, as it is, and has been [since 1867].[79]

Illustrating AP's deep fear of ruffling Western Union feathers, an 1867 circular from the Western AP's executive committee demanded that the agency's members scrupulously adhere to a clause of a new contract with Western Union "which forbids us to encourage or support any opposition or competing Telegraph Company." The circular explains that the "clause was to the Telegraph Company a valuable consideration for the favorable terms upon which they contracted with us."[80]

AP–Western Union intimacy involved cohabitation as well as cooperation. About a year after the June 1866 merger of the American and Western Union companies, *Telegrapher* magazine described the consolidated offices of the merged concern at 145 Broadway in New York City, saying:

Entering the large room on the ground floor, from Broadway, we find ourselves in the department devoted to the reception of messages from the public. This occupies about one-third of the entire room. . . . The remainder of the room is now being fitted up for the accommodation of the New-York Associated Press, which is at present occupying temporary quarters in one of the rear buildings.[81]

Looking back over nearly a decade of "oppressions" by these two "gigantic monopolies," the *New York Graphic*, a paper outside of AP, was eighteen months old when on September 15, 1874,[82] it asserted that Western Union

> finds in the New York Associated Press its best customer and natural ally. The success of each depends mainly upon the aid of the other. The one collects, the other transmits the news of the world. The president of the telegraph company is a trustee of the [New York] Tribune, and the publisher of the [New York] Times is a director of the telegraph company.[83]

Believing that "no paper can sustain itself as a first-class daily without [AP's] reports" and that Western Union "can raise or depress its prices to any paper at its will," the *Graphic* concluded that

> every paper must support and uphold these two organizations upon which its very existence depends. Such a power over the press has hardly been possessed by any despot or censor of the press at any time or in any country.[84]

In support of these allegations the *Graphic* cited four instances of AP–Western Union oppression, each widely discussed and debated in print when they occurred. The *Petersburg* (Va.) *Index*, an AP paper, after criticizing AP's news report and exclaiming "away with this humbug," lost its AP report. "One of the conditions of our service," explained AP's management, "is that supposed causes of complaint shall be presented by *letter* to the executive committee or general agent, in lieu of public assault...."

The *St. Louis Globe*, as noted above, was unable to sustain itself with American Press Association news reports and was forced to purchase a German newspaper with an AP franchise in order to obtain AP's news. The *Alta California* in San Francisco lost its AP report under orders from Western Union because it vigorously supported the postal telegraph movement. Western Union raised telegraph tolls for the news report delivered to the *San Francisco Herald*, whose editorial policy seemed inappropriate to the telegraph company, from seven to fifteen cents a word and lowered tolls at the same time for the same report to other California AP papers from 2.4 to 1.2 cents per word.[85]

DISCUSSION

"Socially and industrially the North was more active and prosperous" during the Civil War than ever before, says Emerson David Fite. "Both capital and labor were alive to their respective interests and made definite advances...."[86] As the war entered its final month the *New York Sun* chirped,

> There never was a time in the history of New York when business prosperity was more general, when the demand for goods was greater, and payment more prompt, than within the last two or three years....In short, New York has shown no evidence of business prostration...and there is, as yet, no sign of the "grass" in the streets, as was gravely predicted by the rebels.[87]

But recapturing peace brought change and uncertainty, a new promise of profits and the peril of new competitors. The post–Civil War years witnessed the first signs of a new industrial society, consisting, as Joseph Dorfman notes, of "the growth of large-scale business enterprise and the development of monopolistic practices, . . . the formation of labor unions, . . . a speculative stock market, and . . . a new economic order emerging in the South." Government's role in this new setting remained unclear for many years, "but already it was being pulled in two directions," says Dorfman, one to promote industrial enterprise and the other to limit high-handed business practice.[88]

The "new orientation" in business and manufacturing George Rogers Taylor identifies as existing by 1860[89]—an integrated, increasingly self-contained, national system of commerce based on burgeoning transportation and communication systems—not only prospered safely north of Civil War battle lines, but sought to expand and eliminate costly competition once peace was restored. Although never able to rid itself wholly of competitors, some of which were conceived to be adopted by it, Western Union controlled the bulk of telegraphy's postwar traffic, exemplifying a wartime boom industry successfully resisting postwar competition. Bristling with lines to most communities, operating multiple circuits among commercial centers, opening the first transcontinental line, and controlling the American end of the first two transatlantic cables, Western Union became the prototype for subsequent electronic communication monopolies, teaching the importance of absorbing serious competitors, controlling and developing key patents, occupying as much of the national and international markets as early as possible, be-friending key news media voices, and vigilantly fighting govern-ment ownership or intervention.

Less obvious, but potentially more dangerous to democratic prin-ciples, was the monopoly the Associated Press sought to establish after the Civil War among the nation's leading and well established newspapers. Made possible through its exclusive alliance with the Western Union, AP's policy of selective self-protection rested on a twenty-year-old principle among New York City papers that sharing a common news dispatch was less odious than failing to control and limit the flow of news from important news centers. It was probably press agentry, and not ignorance of AP's growing telegraphic power, that prompted James Parton to write in 1866:

> We in America have escaped all danger of ever falling under the dominance of a [news]paper despot....Twenty years ago the New York news and the New York newspaper reached dis-tant cities at the same moment; but since the introduction of the telegraph, the news outstrips the newspaper, and is given to the public by the local press. It is this fact which forever limits the circulation and national importance of the New York Press....[90]

The Midwestern editor, however, knew well the folly of Parton's comment. The advantage that the New York editor had yielded to the local press when telegraphy appeared he shortly reacquired by capturing control over the flow of European and Washington news and by warding off a series of newsbrokers who threatened that control.

A majority of four New York City AP partners, in league with their general agent and Western Union after the Civil War, shaped the day's news, punished editors who criticized the news report, and withheld or offered the news report according to the advantage they or their colleagues would realize. As makeshift telegraph com-panies and newsbrokerages and new newspapers kept springing up after the war, AP retreated from Daniel H. Craig's prewar dream of a news monopoly for all American newspapers and settled for con-trol over news flowing to a minority of quality newspapers, whose franchise in the AP "club" would counteract local competition.

The conditions described in this chapter—accommodation with a telegraph monopoly, New York City factionalism, and national pro-tectionism from "outside" papers—barely begin to reflect the Associated Press in the first ten postwar years. Other forces were afoot to reinforce the monopoly, factionalism, and protectionism described above, and they included, as chapter 2 describes, rising regionalism, Craig's departure from AP, and new competition.

Chapter 2
POSTWAR FRAGMENTATION

It seems to me clear that no business which, like that of the [Associated Press], is made up almost entirely of details, sudden emergencies, conflicting wants and ever-changing phases, could have been successfully managed with much less than dictatorial authority on the part of the General Agent, and to this power, which was cheerfully conceded to me, do I ascribe, in the main, my success.... But my [recent] recommendations have not seemed to meet the views of a majority of the Association, and hence, ...I have, very reluctantly, concluded to retire at an early day from my present position.

Daniel H. Craig, printed circular, Manton Marble Papers
(November 1866)

Mr. D. H. Craig, the former Agent of the Associated Press, having stated in a card that he had not been discharged from such agency..., it becomes proper for us to state that...he was discharged by a vote of the Association.

Executive Committee of AP, "Card from the Associated Press,"
Telegrapher
(December 15, 1866)

By introducing this chapter with the above quotes, the author engages in tawdry news reporting. "Before a series of events become news," observes Walter Lippmann, "they have usually to make themselves noticeable in some more or less overt act. Generally too, in a crudely overt act."[1] In light of his fifteen-year reign as newsbroking's absolute monarch, Daniel H. Craig's dismissal in late-1866 by the seven publishers of the New York Associated Press was a "crudely overt act." But it was an act that, like the visible tip of the iceberg, signified a mass of hidden forces at work below the surface of intercity news movement.

This chapter describes the most important of these forces—rising regionalism and creeping competition—as they developed during the ten years following the Civil War. This chapter, therefore, adds the dynamics and specifics of newsbroker politics to the backdrop of broad postwar conditions in telegraphy and the Associated Press outlined in the previous chapter. Before the action can begin, however, a catalogue of the AP organizations operating after the war will set the stage.

THE ASSOCIATED PRESSES

The post–Civil War growth of state and regional Associated Press organizations sprang from newspapers' desire to protect themselves from local competition by monopolizing the nation's only stable and relatively complete news report, a report sustained and protected by its exclusive transmission over the circuits of the Western Union monopoly and by its exclusive news exchange contract with Reuters News Company in London. Additionally through weight of numbers these organizations sought leverage in dealing with one another and with the telegraph company. In general, however, they were far more successful at fighting local competition than in gaining equity among themselves or equality with Western Union.

Sitting atop the AP heap was the New York AP, supplier for the entire system of all foreign news received over the transatlantic cable, most standard Washington, D.C., news, reports from the leading Eastern markets, and New York City's news. NYAP was also the clearinghouse through which AP dispatches traveled from one auxiliary AP to another. The leverage enjoyed by controlling foreign cable news cannot be overemphasized. The NYAP still held contracts for use of the overland telegraphic corridor from Halifax to New York City when Field brought the first successful Atlantic cable ashore at Newfoundland in July 1866. By January 31, 1870, the NYAP had penned a contract with Reuters, in effect making itself an appendage of the British agency, but thus gaining U.S. distribution rights for the combined world news reports of Reuters, France's Agence Havas, and Germany's Wolff News Agency.[2]

In addition, the New York AP claimed the right to control the domestic news gathered not only by its own staff but, through contracts, the news gathered by its auxiliary APs as well. For example, Martin W. Barr, who assembled the news report in Washington, D.C., for distribution to the Southern AP members and who was responsible for forwarding Southern news to the New York AP, was a New York AP employee and "only a nominal agent of the Southern Association," as F. W. Dawson of the *Charleston* (S.C.) *News* put it in 1869.[3] Indeed, the Southern AP observed in 1869 that its contract with the New York AP reserved to the latter the right "to admit, and has admitted, papers to the benefits of the Southern news system, without the consent of the Southern Press Association," which additionally "has no control whatever over the appointment of local agents."[4] From the New Yorkers' viewpoint such leverage was necessary to guarantee a full telegraphic news report for their own daily editions; it was of only secondary interest to the New York papers that this same report could then be transmitted (frequently returned) to members of auxiliary organizations.

The AP of New York City had eight auxiliaries, five formed prior to the Civil War and two more formed later in the West and Southwest to outflank Midwestern AP editors. The eighth auxiliary was the Western AP, which, although relying on the NYAP for much of its key news in the early postwar years, strove to become NYAP's equal as the years passed. The Western AP, in turn, had five relatively small auxiliaries in the Midwestern and Plains states. Excluding the Western AP, there were seven auxiliaries of the New York AP:

THE NEW ENGLAND ASSOCIATED PRESS. An outgrowth of the prewar Boston Associated Press, it was by 1872 paying $4,350 per month to the NYAP for a news report delivered to papers in New Haven, Hartford, Norwich, Springfield, Worcester, Boston, and Providence. The New England association designated which papers were to receive the report.[5] It gradually expanded its territory, reaching a peak of 103 papers in New England, and even including New Brunswick and Nova Scotia.[6] As subsidiaries of this AP auxiliary, the Maine newspapers maintained a separate organization and got their news from the New England AP, and fifteen or twenty Connecticut papers had their own group until mid-1896, when they allowed themselves to be absorbed by the NEAP.[7]

THE NEW YORK STATE ASSOCIATED PRESS. The nation's first newsbrokerage, this organization retained its separate identity from its inauguration in the summer of 1846 (which is described in detail in volume 1) until 1897, incorporating in New York on April 24, 1867,[8] to represent the interests of AP papers in the state outside of New York City and Brooklyn.

THE SOUTHERN ASSOCIATED PRESS (also sometimes called the Southern Press Association). Dating from 1847 and suspended during the Civil War, it began to reappear when the War Department on September 18, 1865, assented to AP's transmission of a 100-word daily news report from Washington, D. C., to August and Mobile. Within a month "the whole South has been thrown open to the Associated Press," *Telegrapher* reported.[9] The Southern AP was organized in 1866 as a subordinate branch of the New York AP, with William Barr as its principal agent. Addressing his executive committee at the start of 1866 AP general agent Craig reiterated New York's determination to "resist, at all points" any "association similar to our own.... Our policy," he explained, "is to submit to no division of power in news matters. Whil'st we deal directly with individuals or with small local associations, we shall avoid the bad policy of building up a consolidated power, which might prove ruinous to the peaceful rule of the New York Association."[10] Although by February 1869 the Southern AP listed thirty-four newspaper members in Alabama, Georgia, North and South Carolina, Mississippi, Tennessee, and Kentucky, it had no independent governing apparatus, relying totally on the goodwill and power of the New York papers. It "functioned merely as a fellowship society," says Victor Rosewater, until growing conflict among various regional organizations caused it to incorporate on November 16, 1892.[11]

Some idea of the casualness of the Southern AP's pre-incorporation days may be gleaned from reminiscences offered by Adolph S. Ochs at a dinner in 1921 celebrating twenty-five years of Ochs's control of the *New York Times.*

> I began as a client of the New York Associated Press at Chattanooga, Tenn., paying all—perilously near more than the traffic would bear— [of] $25 a week paid in advance to the manager of the local Western Union office;—and have had the experience of having the meagre report delayed in delivery until the *quid pro quo* was in hand.
>
> I was one of the organizers of the social club called the Southern Press Association—membership confined to the clients in the Southern States of the New York Associated Press. We held annual meetings devoted principally to junketing and sight-seeing (free transportation and free feed) and the joy of an address from some of the big wigs of the New York Associated Press on the early history of co-operative news-gathering.

> We were frankly told that we should be thankful to the associ-
> ated New York newspapers for the news we received . . . .[12]

THE PHILADELPHIA ASSOCIATED PRESS. Growing up alongside the
New York City AP as a local association of newspapers receiving and
protecting their interests in New York's news report, this AP seems
to have remained a partnership, like the New York AP, throughout
its history. One source substitutes "Pennsylvania association" for
Philadelphia AP in a list of auxiliary APs, leaving the suggestion
that Philadelphia papers may have extended their territory into
portions of the state after the Civil War.[13]

THE BALTIMORE ASSOCIATED PRESS. Like the APs in New York City
and Philadelphia, this was a local partnership that protected Baltimore newspapers' AP franchises. There is no evidence that it ever
incorporated or extended beyond Baltimore proper.[14]

THE TEXAS ASSOCIATED PRESS. Territory competed for by the New
York and Western APs after 1866, Texas was recognized in 1875 by
Western AP as "always claimed by, and hitherto conceded to, the
New York Associated Press."[15] Although this organization is some-
times referred to in correspondence as the Southwestern AP, the
prestige of Texas newspapers made the state the leading force in
Southwestern AP affairs. The Texas AP was chartered under the
laws of Texas on February 7, 1879.[16]

THE CALIFORNIA ASSOCIATED PRESS. Its nuclei were the *San Francisco Evening Bulletin* and the *Morning Call*, one of whose owners
was James W. Simonton, New York AP general agent after late 1866.
From his New York seat of power Simonton controlled the flow of
news to and the membership in the California AP,[17] which initially
included California, Oregon, Washington state, Montana, Idaho, Wy-
oming, Colorado, Utah, Arizona, and New Mexico.[18] Characterized
by one trade journal as a rival at its inception to the WAP, the California AP was a stock company; it ran into financial trouble and
went out of business in June 1890.[19]

(Simonton additionally refers to the Canadian Associated Press
as an auxiliary agency.[20] In reality the NYAP sold its news report to
the Canadian Pacific Railway at Buffalo, which operated a telegraph
system in conjunction with its rail traffic and chose items from the
NYAP report that it thought would interest Canadian readers for
transmission to Canadian newspapers. Meanwhile the Great North-

western Telegraph Company, a subsidiary of the Grand Trunk Railway, operated a domestic newsbrokerage for Canadian papers, generating a news report compiled by its district telegraph agents. Railway telegraphic control of Canadian news movement continued until 1907, when newspaper publishers began organizing three regional newsbrokerages, which were combined in 1910 to form the Canadian Press.)[21]

The remaining six regional APs of the postwar period—the Western AP, Northwestern AP, Kansas and Missouri AP, Trans-Mississippi AP, Colorado AP, and Northern AP—formed an island in the middle of the nation. Created by a sharp conflict between the New York AP and Western AP late in 1866, this island owed its existence to some startling concessions made by the New Yorkers to the Western AP in January 1867, concessions that New York never made to another organization. In the aftermath the WAP, although still relying on the NYAP for much of its important news, had a freer hand than other APs in admitting members, arranging for its own news-gathering system, negotiating with telegraph companies, and resisting the New Yorkers' occasional attempts to dominate the relationship. The New York–Western clash and WAP's origins will be examined later in this chapter.

The Western AP was incorporated under the laws of Michigan on March 21, 1865,[22] and included the territory from the Great Lakes to the Ohio River Valley and from western Pennsylvania (including Pittsburgh) to the Mississippi River and St. Louis. Its seventeen member newspapers in 1866 grew to fifty by November 1, 1867.[23] Its strength, deriving principally from publishers in Chicago, Cincinnati, Louisville, and St. Louis, allowed it to control the territory on its western flank through five auxiliary organizations. Auxiliary agencies, William Henry Smith explained many years later, were preferable to membership in WAP.

> To avoid the annoyance of dealing with individual newspapers of uncertain financial standing in a new country, Mr. [Joseph] Medill encouraged them to form sub-associations. . . . This made convenient dealing. . . . [24]

The five WAP auxiliaries were:

THE NORTHWESTERN ASSOCIATED PRESS. Organized on February 22, 1867, and including thirty small dailies in downstate Illinois, Iowa, and eastern Nebraska, it incorporated under the laws of Illinois on

June 9, 1879.[25] The Northwestern AP purchased its news from WAP and could not admit new members without first gaining permission from the WAP, according to a contract dated May 9, 1873.[26]

THE KANSAS AND MISSOURI ASSOCIATED PRESS. Granted a charter in Kansas on October 11, 1868, it included morning papers in both states, excluding St. Louis.[27]

THE TRANS-MISSISSIPPI ASSOCIATED PRESS. Consisting of evening papers in the same territory as the Kansas and Missouri AP, it was incorporated on October 21, 1875, in Kansas and was an auxiliary of both the Western AP and the Kansas and Missouri AP.[28]

THE COLORADO ASSOCIATED PRESS. In 1877 the Western AP, without interference from the New York AP, assisted the Colorado papers to form the Colorado Press and News Association. After two years the New York AP attempted to add Colorado to its California AP and succeeded only in dividing Colorado's newspapers into two camps, the Colorado AP, which received its news from the WAP, and the other, a faction of the California AP, fed news by the New York AP.[29]

THE NORTHERN ASSOCIATED PRESS. Formed during the summer of 1882, this organization included the newspapers in Minnesota and North and South Dakota. There is no record that it was incorporated.[30]

A WESTERN UPRISING

Thanks to a historian's proclivity for preserving official letters and documents, WAP general agent William Henry Smith left two extensive collections of papers that, with WAP's published annual *Proceedings*, give us a reasonably clear picture of Western AP between 1866 and 1892.[31] Since Smith and Peter R. Knights have written extended treatments of the origins of the WAP and the 1866–67 reorganization of New York AP–Western AP relations,[32] these episodes will receive only brief treatment here.

Even as Rebels were firing on Fort Sumter in April 1861, Midwestern editors were complaining about the news report fed to them by the New York AP, threatening "to shake off this humiliating vassalage," as Smith later put it.[33] The *Chicago Tribune* referred to the "meagerness of information brought us by the arrangement";[34] the St. Louis *Missouri Republican* complained of receiving "the merest skeleton synopsis of the dispatches published in the New York . . . and all other papers of the East";[35] the *Chicago Journal* spoke threateningly of "a movement" against "that greatly mismanaged but extremely exacting and exorbitant monopoly, the Associated Press of New York."[36] Midwestern anger over AP's news, obviously prompted by an impending civil war, was also a regional jealousy about the Eastern press's occupying the driver's seat. The New York AP report was condensed for transmission west of Buffalo, but an even more tender point in the West was that the westbound night report closed between 11 and 11:30 P.M., Buffalo time, and, as William Henry Smith later observed, "Comparison with the New York papers showed that the news of greatest importance was received after that hour and did not reach the West until the day following."[37]

Joseph Medill of the *Chicago Tribune* is credited with sending the "discreet letter" that summoned Midwestern editors to Indianapolis late in 1862 to meet and organize "quietly, so as not to make the New Yorkers suspicious," as John Tebbel puts it.[38] Publishers from nine cities[39] attended the meeting, which seems to have been prompted by simultaneous increases in telegraph tolls and New York AP assessments.[40] But the meeting was not quiet enough. Craig told his New York editors at the end of the year, "I deemed it advisable to send one of our Western Agents to meet the Editors at the Convention." Feeling he had extinguished this Western brushfire, Craig reported to his patrons that after a "full understanding of the whole question" the editors "expressed the most perfect satisfaction, both with the [NYAP] and the Telegraph Companies."[41]

But the fires smoldered on, fanned by continuing regional resentment and the unprecedented value of Civil War news, only a fraction of which trickled west out of New York in good time. The Western editors met again in Dayton during 1863 and in 1864 in Cincinnati, where it was decided to place Thomas M. Knox in New York City to gather and transmit a supplemental news report for the larger Midwestern papers. Permitting Knox in its news room was the first of many concessions the New York AP would have to make to the Western group. The leaders of the Western movement were the wealthy metropolitan papers, who wanted and could afford more news from the East. Their needs, however, conflicted with those of the smaller Midwestern papers, which already received and were content with the existing report. In the compromise that allowed the Western AP to encompass large and smaller papers, all Midwestern AP papers would continue getting the standard report relayed from Buffalo, but the larger papers could receive an "extra report" averaging 2,000 words per day at a cost per paper of $2,000 per month. Knox assembled this "extra report" and transmitted it directly from New York City.[42]

Also at Cincinnati the editors decided to formally organize as the Western Associated Press and adopt "some rules which would not disturb the Associated Press of New York or arouse the suspicion of its amiable agent," as Medill later described it.[43] Incorporation under Michigan law was on March 21, 1865, and the editors of fifteen papers gathered in Louisville on November 22, 1865, to approve incorporation papers and adopt bylaws.[44] Listing its purpose as the "procuring [of] intelligence for the newspaper press, from all parts of the world, by telegraph," Western AP issued 100 $10 shares of stock.[45]

The bylaws called for a board of directors, elected by members (one vote per share), to govern the organization, but up through 1876 directors were meeting only once a year, immediately after the annual meeting of the membership, leaving the actual management of the far-flung newsbrokerage to a three-director executive committee.[46] (See table 6 in the Appendix for lists of WAP's directors and officers. (The board elected a president, vice-president, secretary, and treasurer; appointed the executive committee; employed agents as needed; set assessments for the news report; and by a two-thirds vote suspended members for nonpayment or for "acts which the Board may deem injurious to the best interests of this Association." Admission to membership required "the consent of all the members receiving the dispatches, in the town where" the prospective member published.[47]

New bylaws, adopted in 1874, preserved this structure and introduced tighter controls on WAP members. After 1874, membership was identified by possession of one share of stock in WAP, with only one share permitted to each member; stockholders were entitled to one vote each in WAP elections; and persons leaving newspaper publishing or the WAP service were required to surrender their stock certificates. Additionally, a member's privileges would be suspended if he

> furnish[ed] the news of this Association in advance of publication to any person who is not a member [or] furnish[ed] local or special news to any newspaper or combination of newspapers

not having a membership in this or in any Associated Press organization. . . .

In 1883 WAP attempted to prohibit members from receiving news from non-AP organizations,[48] but was advised that it probably could not expel a member for trafficking with opposition newsbrokerages.[49] (A similar prohibition, successfully enforced by AP between 1893 and 1915, was a source of AP strength and of not insignificant litigation and criticism, as we shall see.)

In this new WAP, Western editors created a force demanding negotiation and hopefully equality with the New York AP and the telegraph company. It was hoped in the Midwest that some of Eastern journalism's arrogance could be blunted. There was a lot of that to blunt. James Parton, for example, an occasional New York newspaper contributor, commented in 1866 that

> The grand reason why the New York papers have national importance is, that it is chiefly through them that the art of journalism in the United States is to be perfected. They set daily copies for all editors to follow. . . . New York is first in the field . . . and it therefore devolves upon the journalists of that city to teach the journalists of the United States their vocation.[50]

But Eastern egos were only a fraction of the Westerners' problems. Even with a brand-new Western AP, Midwestern papers still contracted individually or as city groups with the New York AP for the news report, much as the Southern AP members were still doing for many years after the war.[51] For example, Chicago's AP papers—*Tribune, Post, Times, Journal,* and *Illinois Staats-Zeitung*—received their news report through a contract with the New York AP that prohibited other Chicago papers from receiving the report without the written consent of all Chicago AP papers *and the New York Associated Press.*[52] The upstart Western AP would not begin to realize its potential power until it could negotiate a single contract with the New York AP on behalf of all its Midwestern members.

CRAIG'S DEPARTURE

When they convened in Detroit on August 7, 1866, for their fifth annual meeting, the Midwestern editors were aware that "trouble was brewing in the New York Association," as Smith reports, "and the true policy of the Western Press was to take advantage of division in the ranks of the opponents."[53] The "ring of four . . . papers of less enterprise and influence''[54] in the New York AP (namely the *Times, Express, Journal of Commerce,* and *Sun*), Smith noted, had pulled the reins and purse strings of AP's operation so tight that discontent extended not only to the *New York Herald, Tribune,* and *World,* as we have seen, but also to the AP papers in the rest of the nation. The immediate cause of discontent was sparse and expensive news reports received over the new Atlantic cable. Smith says,

> The murmurs of discontent. . .which had merely served to keep up a gentle and apparently harmless agitation among the clients of [the New York AP], by midsummer grew into a loud and angry roar, which encouraged the Western leaders in their work of independence.[55]

But discontent was not confined to press circles. If the four weaker members of the New York partnership could bring national newsbroking to the brink of revolution with stingy, self-serving news policies, Western Union's press revenue could be threatened by the resulting discord in AP's ranks. While AP bickering grew, Western Union's managers resurrected prewar plans for a telegraph-operated newsbrokerage and approached New York AP general agent Daniel H. Craig, as he later explained it, to ''form a general news company and give [Western Union] one share more than one-half of it.'' Western Union promised Craig to keep hands off the news report, to convert its office managers into news correspondents for Craig, and to provide ''a special wire to all the main points of the country, both to receive and to send news reports.'' Craig and Western Union also discussed plans to organize a national commercial news system ''to which all bankers, brokers, merchants and speculators would be forced to subscribe,'' Craig later reported.[56]

The New York AP learned of the scheme, fired Craig on November 5, 1866, appointed James W. Simonton as general agent,[57] and addressed a notice to the nation's newspapers saying that ''the change of the New-York Agent will prove beneficial to the entire newspaper press.'' Sounding conciliatory, the NYAP notice continued,

> We have no interest not in harmony with the press outside of New-York, our only desire being a union of newspaper interests, which should be identical all over the entire country. We can assure the entire press of the country that the quality of the Association's news shall be improved, and the expenses kept within

proper limits. Let the press be a unit in this business and all will be well.[58]

Western editors, however, noted with interest that the *New York World* had not signed the notice.

Characteristically, Craig fought his own termination aggressively. New York AP president William Cowper Prime and secretary Joseph P. Beach telegraphed a dispatch to all AP papers the afternoon of November 5 stating that Craig "has been discharged. . .by the unanimous vote of the members." Later that night Craig filed his own dispatch claiming he had "not been discharged unanimously or at all," owing his job not to the AP membership but to the executive committee. Craig's dispatch then asserted that his resignation had been in the committee's hands "for several weeks" and that he would retire "at the end of this week" under any circumstances. He said,

> It is true that I have for some weeks past headed a movement here to remodel and improve our Association, as you will learn from my printed circular, now on its way to you, and it is also true that all these arrangements are completed and will go into effect next Monday.[59]

AP executive committee members Samuel Sinclair and Manton Marble, however, ended any speculation on November 7, stating that Craig had been "employed by and responsible to the Association and not the Executive Committee, and that he was discharged by the vote of the Association."[60]

The sense of the matter from the New York AP viewpoint was expressed at the end of November by the *New York Tribune.*

> Mr. Craig was dismissed. . .for endeavoring, while receiving pay from the New York Associated Press, to subvert it, and make a new organization which would make him the arbiter of news in America—with power to keep or print it, use it as he pleased in commercial operations and give it to the press when he thought proper. He would become the Reuter of America. He arranged all his plans. They were discovered. He was instantly, unanimously and ignominiously dismissed from our service. . . .[61]

Craig pushed ahead with his plans for an independent newsbrokerage, to be called the United States and European Telegraph News Association and utilizing telegraph companies outside of Western Union, the latter having broken off negotiations with Craig when his scheme was discovered and publicized. On November 5, Craig announced his expectation of launching his new agency on November 12. In fact, the U.S. and European's first news report moved on November 25 from headquarters at 145 Broadway, Western Union's building.[62] In the shuffle Craig took with him "most of the agents and all the clerical force" of the New York AP, including agents Oliver M. Bradford and Amos F. Learned in New York and John Hasson in Philadelphia.[63]

While Craig was putting his newsbrokerage together, the Western AP board, sensing that the shake-up in New York afforded it an unparalleled opportunity to gather and assert organizational strength, met in Cincinnati on November 19. In a series of resolutions designed "to maintain relations of amity between [the Western and New York] Associations if it could be done on a footing of equality," the board set forth the radical proposal of replacing contracts between the New York AP and individual Midwestern papers and cities with a single contract between the New Yorkers and all the Midwestern AP papers, as represented by the Western AP. WAP's executive committee, consisting of Murat Halstead of the *Cincinnati Commercial* and C. D. Brigham of the *Pittsburgh Commercial*, augmented by Horace White of the *Chicago Tribune*, was empowered to go to New York City and offer this proposal to the New York AP. The board further stipulated that if "these resolutions were not agreed to by the New York Associated Press, the Committee were empowered to make such other arrangements as they should deem advisable."[64]

Here was a thinly veiled threat of jumping to Craig's new brokerage if the New York AP would not recognize Western AP's right to represent its members collectively. But Halstead later hinted at Western AP's true feelings, saying Craig's "news agency would be useful only so far as it might enable [the Western AP executive committee] to make better terms with the New York Associated Press."[65] Brigham was unable to participate, leaving Halstead and White to take WAP's case to New York City. On November 25, the same day Craig began service on his U.S. and European system,[66] the two associations' representatives met for the first time. Halstead and White offered WAP's proposal, asserting WAP's right to act on behalf of its full membership. The New Yorkers said this "could not be considered," because to do so "would imply that the Western Associated Press was to be treated by the New York Association as an equal; and that, in the view of the New York gentlemen,

45

would be an intolerable humiliation to them," Halstead later wrote.[67]

At a second meeting the following day, the New Yorkers "urged upon us," says Halstead, "that the essential thing to be accomplished was the unity of the press of the country" and that New York's AP was committed to staying in the newsbroking business and "could sell us just the article we wanted." Agreeing to "unity" but not "at the expense of the continued centralization of authority," the Westerners proposed "a republican form of government." Halstead later reported the next exchange as follows:

> The time had come, in our judgment, when the New York Associated Press [had] outlived its usefulness. . . . We told the gentlemen of the New York Associated Press that we represented more money invested in the newspaper business. . . than they did. . . . The gentlemen of the [New York] Association would not give any consideration to our revolutionary ideas. They believed themselves in possession of great power, and proposed to hold it.[68]

On November 27 at a third meeting the Western AP offered a compromise proposal: that the West continue to take the regular report from the New York AP and "appoint an agent in New York who should collect news from all accessible sources. . . ." New York responded that it would permit no newspaper receiving its news "to obtain intelligence from any rival Association," said Halstead, continuing, "We asked. . . whether. . . if we accepted their news, and our agent bought an item from Craig, and sent it to us, our news supply would be cut off by them." The New York answer was yes, leading Halstead to observe:

> So it appeared not only that there remained in the New York Association after Mr. Craig's connection with it ceased, the old and well-known despotic exclusiveness and intolerance, but that there had been added a hitherto unknown and most offensive stupidity.[69]

White and Halstead asked for twenty-four hours, ostensibly to survey the situation, but in fact to seek out Craig, who offered "the only opportunity we have ever had. . . of establishing *competition* in news gathering in New York," Halstead said. Craig promised the Westerners in writing to develop a full newsbrokerage in opposition to New York and promised that, when completed, it would be turned over to the nation's press with Craig acting as its general agent. Returning to the New Yorkers on November 28, "I had the satisfaction of telling those gentlemen," Halstead reported, that

> it would best serve the interests of the Western Press we repre-
> sented, to aid in the establishment of an opposition in the news
> business in New York, and that we were ready to supply our-
> selves with news without any further assistance from them.[70]

A New York AP news dispatch later that day announced that Hal-stead's *Cincinnati Commercial* and White's *Chicago Tribune* had been cut off from New York news service and asserted that the West's executive committee had sought special advantage for the papers in St. Louis, Chicago, and Cincinnati at the expense of the smaller Midwestern AP papers.[71] The New York AP papers, while publicly asserting that AP continued to do business as usual,[72] pri-vately tried the divide-and-conquer tactic in the West. Meanwhile Halstead and White, who were not empowered to sign a contract with Craig, rushed back and endeavored to sell their handiwork to a hastily called special WAP membership meeting.

Smith reports that nearly all of AP's agents in the West and Southwest stayed with Craig,[73] although the "three veteran re-porters" he sought to handle his Washington report remained loyal to the New York AP.[74] The *Baltimore American, Buffalo Commer-cial Advertiser, Troy Times,* and *Philadelphia Press* joined Craig on November 29, and there were signs of tilting toward Craig's plan in the New England and New York State APs. The Western AP received both New York AP's and Craig's dispatches, as the two agencies waged a "fierce and hot" battle for the West's affections. "Craig and Simonton," Smith says,

> published cards with great frequency, and instructed the same
> agents with commendable energy. One night the "boys" were
> informed at 10 o'clock that they must recognize Craig as the
> Agent of the Press, and in half an hour later that Simonton was
> the only true agent.... [75]

Thus the roughly thirty-three[76] Western AP newspapers received two "complete reports of the news collected at extraordinary ex-pense," Smith says.[77]

THE EAST-WEST ALLIANCE

"There was an unpleasant feeling in the [New York] Associated Press" in 1866, recalls Hudson;[78] it arose, in addition to Craig's treachery and the Western AP's challenge, from the completion of the Atlantic cable. As we have seen, each New York AP paper was required to share special foreign or domestic dispatches with its partners, who, in turn, paid a portion of the transmission costs, but not the expenses, of the paper's correspondent in the field. The *Herald, Tribune,* and *World* especially felt oppressed by this rule, a feeling exacerbated by the opportunities for foreign enterprise offered by the new cable.

George T. McJimsey observes that the *Herald*'s extensive use of special cables in the summer and fall of 1866 riled *World* editor Manton Marble, who "ever since he assumed control of the *World*. . . had sought to challenge the *Herald*'s place in New York journalism."[79] Unable to pay for the *Herald*'s specials, to set up his own foreign correspondence, or to get the AP rule changed, Marble saw in Craig's new agency and the revolt in the West an opportunity to "gain the support needed to put the *Herald* in its place," says McJimsey.[80] Showing an inclination to support the Westerners' demands, the *World* was expelled from the NYAP on November 28 but later that evening was reinstated.[81] On December 3, however, the *World* announced it would not "consent to be hampered by the inferior enterprise of rival newspapers" and would take its news from whomever it pleased.[82] The following day the New York AP expelled the *World*,[83] leaving the paper "alone in its glory in the metropolis," says Hudson.[84]

Back in the West, the resolve of Midwestern editors and the correctness of Halstead's and White's dealings with the New York AP and Craig were tested when the Western AP members convened in special session in Chicago on December 12 and 13. In the wake of events in New York City some Midwest editors feared the loss of all news reports and cable dispatches, and J. E. Scripps, managing editor of the *Detroit Advertiser and Tribune,* an AP paper, even echoed New York's propaganda of "a conspiracy" by some Chicago, Cincinnati, and St. Louis papers "to prostitute the machinery and influence of the Association to the promotion of their own individual interests." To Scripps, the issue was

> whether it is better to submit to the mild tyranny of a distant and hence impartial master. . . or whether we shall place ourselves in the clutches of a Western monopoly, whose interest will ever lie in tampering and crushing us for their own aggrandizement.[85]

The Chicago meeting featured impassioned pleas by New York AP's Erastus Brooks to preserve the old arrangements and by the *Chicago Tribune*'s Joseph Medill to break with New York and assert independence. Angrily, even daringly, rising to the occasion, Medill called the New York AP "one of the most pernicious and crushing monopolies that ever existed," asking, "How much longer shall we play the part of menials to autocratic masters?" He declared, "For the first time in our lives we have a chance to assert our rights, and to have a voice in the control of our dispatches."[86]

Despite much artful parliamentary opposition and some genuine fears that independence might result in isolation from Eastern news, Medill carried the day with a 21-to-11 vote confirming the executive committee's actions in New York City.[87] The way was thus cleared to dispatch committees to negotiate a new contract with the Western Union and to seek rapprochement with the New Yorkers. Meanwhile the battle between Craig and Simonton for clients and superiority continued. The New York State AP edged toward Craig, but finally yielded to reportedly great concessions offered by the New York AP. The New England AP papers likewise eventually sided with New York. On the other side, Craig acquired the papers in Raleigh and New Bern, North Carolina; Chattanooga; Atlanta; and New Haven.[88] On the eve of the Chicago WAP meeting in mid-December, the *New York World* reported Craig's list, which, in addition to the WAP, included the majority of papers in Arkansas, Mississippi, and Texas, all but one paper in Louisiana, all but three or four papers in Virginia, all in North Carolina, four-fifths of the papers in Georgia, all the Washington, D. C., papers, half of the Baltimore papers, eight of thirteen Philadelphia papers, two of three Newark papers, all the papers in Brooklyn, and three of the nine New York City papers formerly receiving the AP news.[89] One observer reported that in addition to "principal papers" in most cities outside of New York City, Craig signed up "the greater proportion of the 'country journals.' "[90]

As both camps enlisted recruits in December in what was developing as a standoff, Craig capitalized on a Simonton miscalculation, tipping the scale in the direction of his U.S. and European company. Simonton, a former *New York Times* correspondent in Washington and without experience managing a newsbrokerage, dispatched Alexander Wilson of the *New York Times* to London to begin filing New York AP's European dispatches, which Wilson was to assemble from the London press. This was cheaper than paying the three thousand pounds per year that Reuters News Company was then asking for same-day delivery of the news in London. The one-day delay caused by waiting for Reuters news to appear in the London press seems not to have bothered Simonton. Craig's many years of flying homing pigeons, monopolizing telegraph lines, and chartering horse and steamer expresses told him, especially in light of the Atlantic cable's newness, that one day made a difference to American editors. He consequently sought out Reuters's New York agent and on December 17 announced an exclusive news-exchange agreement between his U.S. and European agency and Reuters, beginning January 1, 1867.[91]

Craig's capture of the Reuters contract made the situation precarious for New York; an announcement of same-day foreign news direct from Reuters could start a stampede of papers to Craig's agency. Knights speculates that the Western Union, whose circuits may have been clogged with competing news reports, may have "forced peace upon the press association."[92] William Henry Smith, on the other hand, says "The New York people were the first to cry out for peace" by stating that "if some of the 'old heads' were sent down with the 'young men' of the [executive] committee, a treaty could be formed that would be acceptable to all concerned." Medill, WAP president H. N. Walker of the *Detroit Free Press*, and Richard Smith of the *Cincinnati Gazette* were the "old heads" who accompanied White and Halstead to New York for "several weeks" of negotiations, "characterized by a brilliant display of diplomacy on both sides."[93]

The end of hostilities—and of Craig's U.S. and European company—came on January 11, 1867, when the NYAP, WAP, and Western Union penned three contracts among them. In a joint statement NYAP president Prime, the *World*'s Marble, and WAP's R. Smith, Halstead, and Medill had the "pleasure" of announcing that their "differences...have been adjusted satisfactorily to all parties." The Reuters contract was transferred back to AP, the *World*'s NYAP membership was restored, and a contract for a "mutual exchange of news" was signed by the NYAP and WAP.[94] With modifications for changes in territories, in news report size, and in cable news costs, these contracts were still in force in 1875.

In a private circular to Western AP members, announcing the new contracts, Halstead commented that the contract with the NYAP establishes the independence of the Western Associated Press; its complete control over its own affairs: the collection, compilation, and transmission of news, and over the news agents within its own lines. The Western newspapers are able now to give authoritative directions as to the make-up and distribution of their news reports.[95]

According to the NYAP-WAP contract, WAP's territory was delineated[96] but NYAP's was not; a WAP agent in New York City received access to all news received by the NYAP, and a NYAP agent in Chicago had access to WAP's news; WAP delivered NYAP's news to the Southwestern AP to fulfill a NYAP contract obligation, and WAP had access to the California news, which the NYAP was collecting and transmitting eastward; each agency could send special correspondents into the others' territory to cover news; both agencies agreed to serve only newspapers receiving AP news and not to enter into agreements with any "rival news association"; and WAP agreed to pay NYAP $8,000 per year for general news, 22 percent of the cable news costs, and 20 percent of the cost of California news.[97]

Limits on the size of the news reports were set not by the newsbrokerages' contract, but by their separate contracts with Western Union and by the ability of each agency to pay for additional news. WAP paid $60,000 per year for a daily report (excluding Sundays) of 6,000 words, divided as follows: a 500-word morning report and a 300-word noon report both filed from Buffalo, a 3,200-word night report from New York City (for Pittsburgh, Cincinnati, Indianapolis, Louisville, St. Louis, Chicago, Detroit, Toledo, Cleveland, and Milwaukee),[98] and a 2,000-word report originating from cities within WAP's territory. WAP agreed to use Western Union "exclusively to transmit. . .all telegraph messages relating to the news or newspaper business" and not to "encourage or support" any competing telegraph company. Western Union agreed not to sell news in WAP's territory (reserving, however, the right to sell "strictly commercial news or market reports and quotations") and not to "transmit news to or for any rival news association on more favorable terms" than those granted WAP in the contract.[99]

In the aftermath of hostilities the newsbrokerages agreed, "in order to put out of sight forever the personal grievances of the agents," as Smith put it, "that Mr. Craig should retire from the news business."[100] Although unceremoniously dumped by the press, Craig, backed by Western Union, developed a commercial news system. "After I had that business well developed," Craig later said, "the Western Union Co., aided by four of the seven members of the Associated Press wrested it from my control—the Western Union Co. forming an alliance. . . with the New York Associated Press."[101] William Aplin, an AP staffer, writing in *Putnam's* magazine in mid-1870, explained that the merger was intended as "a new source of revenue" and to halt "false news, fraudulent quotations, and stock-jobbing 'despatches' [that] deceive and defraud."[102] The giant of newsbroking's formative years, Daniel H. Craig, that irascible despot whose flinty pen, shrewd investments, and boundless energy had forged AP's monopoly, was consigned at age fifty-five to the quiet backwaters of business. He declared bankruptcy in the late 1860's, helped promote the ill-fated National Telegraph Company in 1869, attempted for many years to find a buyer for a high-speed "automatic" telegraph system, organizing the American Rapid Telegraph Company in 1879, and pamphleteering on behalf of his "machine telegraphy" during the 1880s and early 1890s.[103] In a shaky hand Craig, still brimming with schemes but sadly out of touch, wrote William Henry Smith in 1894, offering his telegraph system for use on AP's circuits, apparently not knowing that Smith, too, had been deposed the year before.[104] Craig died January 5, 1895, in his home in Asbury Park, N. J. The last entry on him in R. G. Dun & Company's credit ledgers, dated July 21, 1885, says, "Craig is of g[oo]d char[acter] & ability, but financial responsibility cons[idere]d light."[105]

Western AP set up headquarters in Cleveland and hired George B. Hicks as its general agent at $60 per week. Before the 1866 confrontation between NYAP and WAP, Hicks had been NYAP's agent for filing the report to Midwestern AP papers.[106] Bradford was named WAP's night reporter in the New York office but was replaced by Charles A. Boynton of Cincinnati on December 1, 1870.[107] Learned became WAP's day man in New York but was replaced on January 1, 1870, by John H. Howell, the New York City agent for the New York State AP.[108] The roughly thirty-three original WAP members rose to fifty by November 1, 1867, the total membership not again being recorded in the *Proceedings* for a decade.[109]

Within three years the WAP underwent major alterations. The members moved their headquarters from Cleveland to Chicago in January 1870.[110] Hicks was replaced by William Henry Smith of the *Cincinnati Chronicle* on November 1, 1869,[111] and revisions in WAP's two contracts increased its daily news report from 6,000 to 8,700 words and combined WAP's separate payments for domestic,

California, and cable news into a $42,000-per-year obligation to the New York AP.[112] From then until the mid-1870s, monthly expenses for WAP averaged about $15,000, running slightly behind revenues to create a cash reserve of about $40,000 by October 31, 1875.[113] Between September 1869 and 1874–75, while the $42,000 assessment by the NYAP remained the same, telegraph tolls rose from $80,000 per year (or 53.5 percent of total WAP expenses) to $111,378 per year (or 61 percent of all expenses).[114] This occurred in spite of Smith's efforts to reduce the words per daily report by using a cipher for market quotations.[115] (Table 3 in the Appendix presents all available WAP expenses.)

Meanwhile, as they came into existence, WAP's five auxiliary agencies made arrangements with the WAP similar to the latter's arrangements with the NYAP. In 1873, for example, the Northwestern AP paid WAP $77.80 per week for a sampling of WAP's daily report, delivered to a Northwestern agent in Chicago.[116] The Kansas and Missouri AP in 1877 was paying WAP $40 per week for a daily report of from 2,500 to 3,500 words,[117] and the evening papers in the Trans-Mississippi AP in 1878 paid $375 per month for a daily report of 1,100 words.[118] Such interlocking agreements, accompanied by separate contracts between each agency and Western Union, held the AP system together in a loose confederation having as its primary purpose the processing of each day's news into a marketable product saleable to members' readers and protecting members from competitors.

AP's Aplin, describing AP's New York headquarters in the Western Union building,[119] reported in 1870 that twenty manifold copies of the New York AP report were written as the news dispatches arrived—thirteen copies for the local newspapers entitled to the report,[120] six copies for agents of auxiliary APs who had desks at the New York headquarters (the APs of New York state, Boston, New England, Western, Southern, and "Far Southern," presumably referring to the Texas or Southwestern AP), and one copy for the office record. Using a special manifold paper developed exclusively for AP, the headquarters in 1870 moved 150 sheets of news per day, which at 233 words per sheet came to a total of 35,000 words passing daily through the New York office.[121] Western Union's telegraphers, located across Liberty Street from the main offices, received the dispatches for transmission beyond New York City on one of three "miniature elevated railroads" which "trundle[d]...across [Liberty] street...to the apparent bewilderment of humanity below."[122] Sixteen telegraph lines fanning out from New York City were needed each night to transmit and receive AP's news.[123] The extent of the news-gathering network in 1869 is suggested in the following passage by Augustus Maverick, a *New York Times* staffer:

> Through a complete system of agencies, all the news of the world is received daily at the General Office,—by the Atlantic Cable, by the Cuba Cable, by the lines of land telegraph, by ocean steamers, and by ships which fly to and from the South American ports. Agents are stationed in London and Liverpool, and in all the principal cities and towns of the United States.... [124]

AP agents stationed in major U.S. cities received $25 to $35 per week, and those in smaller communities were paid $50 to $60 per month.[125]

AP's daily office routine early in Simonton's regime is outlined by W. F. G. Shanks in the *Harper's Monthly* for March 1867.

> Business begins about eleven o'clock in the morning, and, with an interregnum of a few hours in the afternoon, lasts until two o'clock in the morning.... The first duty of the day is to serve the afternoon papers...with the news of the morning. The first telegraphic copy for New York afternoon papers must be delivered by or before one o'clock, and then as rapidly as possible until the several editions which each paper issues every afternoon have been struck off. Nothing more is then delivered until perhaps ten P.M., when the copy is sent to the offices of the morning papers.... The telegrams received [from correspondents] are elaborated from the abbreviated form which all agents employ, and copied on "manifold paper."... [T]he news from all points, which is being delivered to the New York evening papers, is also being delivered at the same time to the country evening papers, thus securing its simultaneous publication all over the country. The process is repeated at night for the benefit of the morning papers, the only difference being that the labors of the night are heavier.[126]

A COMPETITOR OF SORTS

Although Western Union is widely recognized as the nation's first industrial monopoly, at no time did Western Union stand alone in the field, as new telegraph patents and companies continued to appear after the Civil War. Some of the independent ventures were formed with the sole purpose of being absorbed by Western Union. This steady stream of postwar independent telegraphy provided the circuits over which newspapers outside the AP system gradually organized and reorganized a sequence of newsbrokerages that provided a modest news competition to the Associated Press. The Franklin and the Atlantic and Pacific telegraph companies, both organized in 1865 and, Alvin F. Harlow hypothesizes, both "intended to flirt with the Western Union," were in their day the principal conduits for non-AP newsbroking. The Franklin was an aggressive New England company that spread its lines through the crucial central Atlantic states. The Atlantic and Pacific, a rapidly expanding network, had linked New York and San Francisco via Chicago in the early 1870s. Eventually leasing the Franklin system, the Atlantic and Pacific operated 17,759 miles of telegraph routes by the start of 1877.[127]

The movement to oppose AP had its origins in Philadelphia, and can first be detected in January 1866, when John Hasson, AP's agent in that city, addressed the Philadelphia Press Club on telegraphy and newspapers. Hasson's speech, describing his experiences as an AP Civil War correspondent with the Army of the Potomac, "gave rise to a lengthy and warm discussion of the merits and demerits" of the AP, according to a contemporary account.[128] Hasson was apparently still with the AP in Philadelphia when late in 1868 Henry George came east from California attempting to get an AP membership for the recently revived *San Francisco Herald*. After stopping off first in Philadelphia to see his family, George, accompanied by Hasson, a boyhood friend, went on to New York City, where, it will be recalled, the California AP news report was controlled by NYAP general agent Simonton, an owner of the *San Francisco Evening Bulletin* and *Morning Call*. Testifying before the Senate Committee on Education and Labor in 1883, George described his attempt to get NYAP news.

> When I came on and called upon [Simonton] he received me very courteously, but he said, "You can't get the news, Mr. George. I hold this position at a salary of $5,000 a year; I would not work for $5,000 a year; I am simply here to keep yours and any other papers from getting the news."[129]

George and Hasson returned to Philadelphia and set up Hasson's News Association to serve the *San Francisco Herald*. Occupying "a little coal office...on Third Street, almost opposite St. Paul's church,"[130] Hasson acquired the special dispatches of the *New York Herald* and employed John J. Kiernan, who had begun his newsbroking career as an AP "attaché" under Craig and later ran a stock quotation system in New York and the Wall Street Financial News Bureau, a department of Western Union's Gold and Stock Company.[131] The California-bound Hasson report was sent in code over Western Union lines, until the AP protested about Western Union's handling of Hasson dispatches. As George later explained it, although Western Union would not make a written contract, it informally agreed to transmit 500 words a day from the East for $900 per month. But when the AP in San Francisco found that Hasson was beating them with the news, Western Union insisted that the Hasson agency be moved to New York City. "Their idea in moving me from Philadelphia," George later said, "was that I could not get the news as well in New York; but I did get the news...." At that point the telegraph company raised the monthly toll of the Hasson report to $2,000.[132] George protested the toll increase but to no avail. The higher rate forced Hasson to cut his report to a fraction of its original length.

During this time, mid-May 1869, it will be recalled, John Russell Young lost his post as *New York Tribune* managing editor for sending AP dispatches to the non-AP *Philadelphia Morning Post*, in which Young had an interest. Young subsequently went to Philadelphia and helped to organize a news service opposing AP. Meanwhile George returned to California, armed with a contract from Young to write articles for the *Tribune* describing his trip west on the new transcontinental rail line.[133] Young's hasty departure precluded publication of George's series, but the Young-George-Hasson triumvirate was in place and would resurface the following year, when Hasson's bureau was reorganized as the American Press Association. Mrs. George, living in Philadelphia and writing her husband in California in August 1869, indicated the closeness of this trio.

> Mr. Hasson spent two or three hours with us this afternoon. He is a firm friend and an ardent admirer of yours.... He says that John Russell Young is going to start a hundred thousand dollar paper in the fall [the *New York Standard*, founded in 1870], and will want your services, as he thinks there is no one like you. Hasson says that Young told Greeley that when he let you go he let go the very man he had been looking for for two years.[134]

During this same period New England publishers, voicing "general dissatisfaction" with the nature and cost of telegraphic news, met in New Haven, Conn., on January 27, 1868, formed the Eastern Press Association, and agreed to utilize the Franklin Telegraph Company lines. Although the association was characterized as a New England movement, which was expected to "lead to the establishment of news agencies all over the country" and to the "employment of various facilities for the collection of the news," all the original officers were representatives of New Haven or Hartford newspapers.[135] The rapid growth of the Atlantic and Pacific company's telegraph system by 1870 and completion of the French transatlantic cable in the summer of 1869 encouraged new and non-AP papers to believe that a national newsbrokerage could be organized to duplicate the AP–Western Union alliance. Thus the American Press Association was organized at a meeting in mid-January 1870 with John Russell Young, publisher of his just-started *New York Standard*, elected president.[136] Hasson was retained as general agent although not without a fight from George H. Stout, who, it was noted earlier, had been on the staff of the *New York Tribune*. Stout had sent circulars to U.S. publishers prior to the APA organizing meeting announcing his intention of starting a news agency rivaling the AP. He also appears to have been involved in marketing foreign dispatches arriving over the new French cable.[137] When Hasson was retained as general agent of the new APA, apparently by an election, Stout was encouraged to stay with APA,[138] but he hovered outside waiting for a chance to unseat Hasson.[139] By September 11, 1871, however, Stout was manager of the New York News Association at 119 Nassau Street, which offered a domestic news report and foreign dispatches from the French cable.[140] It cannot be determined how successful this agency was.

George, who joined the *Sacramento Reporter* after the *San Francisco Herald* failed, was named APA's California agent.[141] One of Hasson's assistants, George H. Sandison, later replaced Hasson as APA's general manager.[142] Publishers, in addition to Young, involved in APA's beginnings were Joseph Howard, Jr., of the *New York Star*; Francis Wells, *Philadelphia Bulletin*; and Thomas Kinsella, *Brooklyn Daily Eagle*.[143] Walter P. Phillips, general agent of the old United Press, a descendant of the APA, commented in 1891 that the APA "was conducted as a bureau of the Franklin and Atlantic and Pacific Telegraph Companies, and . . . was essentially a news and telegraph enterprise combined."[144] The contract, dated June 1, 1870, between the APA and the Atlantic and Pacific company, gave the telegraph company APA's business exclusively west of Philadelphia. The morning report was limited to 500 words each from New York and the western cities combined; the noon report was limited to 200 words in the aggregate, regardless of origin; the night report from the West was limited to 2,000 words. There was no limit on the night report from the East, containing the foreign dispatches. Atlantic and Pacific telegraph operators were instructed to ''transmit all important intelligence.'' Eighty percent of the assessments from APA newspapers were allotted to the telegraph company and 20 percent to the APA. The APA was to maintain ''competent agents'' at the news centers of Europe and in New York, Philadelphia, Baltimore, Washington, D. C., Cincinnati, Louisville, St. Louis, Chicago, and New Orleans.[145]

On April 28, 1871, the APA was incorporated in Pennsylvania ''to collect, receive, and distribute news to the newspaper press, and to persons or corporations for public or private use,'' its list of fourteen incorporators exhibiting the beginnings of a national clientele.[146] About ''thirty or forty newspapers, some of them being important journals which had grown up after the war,'' Phillips says, constituted APA's original list of customers,[147] but two-thirds of the 200 shares of stock , at a value of $100 per share, was purchased by the *Star, Evening Mail, New Yorker Journal, Demokrat,* and *News* in New York City; *Evening Bulletin* and *Star* in Philadelphia; *Germantown Chronicle; Pittsburgh Evening Leader; Providence Morning Star;* and *Boston Herald.* William Roche was APA's agent in New York (it is not known whether Hasson had left APA or moved back to Philadelphia), and James McLean was the agency's London manager.[148] In 1872 Frederic Hudson reported that the APA served eighty-four dailies in the United States.[149]

The APA received considerable attention in AP circles. NYAP agent Simonton, writing to Whitelaw Reid, observed, ''The opposition is sleepless, active, untiring and *unscrupulous,*'' and commented that Young ''is President of the 'opposition' avowedly in the hope that he may find therein opportunity to punish the Ass[oci-ate]d Press for causing his retirement from the Tribune.''[150] Writing WAP's William Henry Smith, Simonton asserted that APA's ''President and General Agent are men who have been convicted of dishonest practices; the latter was a manifolder in our office at Philadelphia and was discharged because he was untrustworthy and dissipated.'' The APA, Simonton continued, has only two or three *bona fide* agents, and for the rest depend[s] upon the operators of opposition telegraph lines to supply the news. They appropriate and send in their reports to news-papers, as *news*...all items published in our evening papers.[151]

To which Smith added in his report to the WAP membership, "Day after day, have [APA's] dispatches been made up almost exclusively of what they would filch from our reports." Smith said that such APA pilferage had been detected at Harrisburg, Pittsburgh, Cincinnati, and Chicago.[152]

Such Associated Press characterizations no doubt stretched the truth, but clearly AP's well-oiled and practiced system easily surpassed APA's faltering first steps. Such disparities did not stop the *New York News* from boasting, however, that the APA has "furnished to its members many of the best items of news that ever transpired, far in advance of the older press association."[153] Another APA client, the *New York Evening Mail*, commented on May 13, 1871,

> The dependence of the large morning Associated Press papers upon the American Press Association evening papers of the day previous, and their continued omission of proper credit to the [APA], are subjects of general comment among newspaper men in this city.[154]

But as we have seen, defections from APA to AP, such as Edward Rosewater's and Melville E. Stone's, described in chapter 1, occurred whenever aspiring publishers could accomplish them. Perhaps the shakiness of APA's early service can be exemplified by the view at the *Boston Globe*, an APA paper when Charles H. Taylor took it over in 1873. Taylor's biographer, James Morgan, says,

> There never could be any certainty that [APA's] service had not been scooped on the biggest piece of news of the night, until the anxious night editor, by hook or crook, had obtained a copy of the first edition of some other paper that was in the Associated Press. To capture that copy, before the final edition of the Globe went to press, required swift and furtive work in some gray dawns on old Newspaper Row.[155]

DISCUSSION

Competition from the new guy on the block or the hungry outsider with a new idea to peddle has historically enriched the marketplace in our open system. The Hassons, Georges, and Stouts in the American scheme of things have always managed to upset the establishment's apple cart. What is surprising about the post-Civil War Associated Press is that it permitted so many regional and local organizations to operate and, thus, potentially to threaten the New York City overlords. Competition from the "outside press" was to be expected, but to breed a confederation of auxiliaries tempts revolution—an especially dangerous form of competition. What is even more surprising, however, is that only one such regional auxiliary actually mounted a successful challenge to the New Yorkers. And here success was defined as clear-eyed, pragmatic business accommodation. It is far from obvious that the Western AP would have tried to survive indefinitely with Craig's U.S. and European news service if the New York AP had been more stubborn. But, of course, New York had to back down after only a month. Repeatedly in this narrative superior Washington, D.C., coverage, voluminous Eastern news, or timely foreign dispatches are seen as the keys to success or to settlement in the newsbroking game. With these cards, your hand will win; without them, you must neutralize the player who holds them. When Craig drew the Reuters service card, New York was forced to team up with the Westerners who had been keeping Craig in the game.

How many other attempts were made by auxiliaries to renegotiate contracts with the New York or Western APs over the years cannot be guessed. We know that the South unsuccessfully sought an independent agency for many years, but what about the New York State or Kansas and Missouri APs? It is a measure of the importance of New York's news reports that the city's AP could control a far-flung confederation of auxiliaries from a few rooms tucked away in the Western Union building on Broadway. But more important, such control is a measure of the alliance the New York AP had forged with Western Union. Simply because we have no evidence, beyond his own words, that the huge telegraph monopoly supported Craig's efforts to overcome factionalism in the New York AP with a new newsbrokerage does not mean that such support did not exist. The next chapter depicts Western Union officials taking drastic action deep within the New York AP to defuse this same kind of factionalism in the early 1880s. The company's national telegraphic network was technological clout at its best, but additionally the company's officers busied themselves preserving the health of their premier news customer whenever disturbing symptoms appeared. Volume 1 depicts a telegraphic industry occasionally on the verge of taking over newsbroking before the Civil War. After the war, although a takeover was still possible, telegraphy concentrated on maintaining harmony in journalism so that newsbroking would continue.

The news reports of newsbrokers generally remained modest affairs in the decade following the Civil War, and newsbroking structure, outside of a few news centers, was detectable only in terms of the allied circuits and operators of Western Union or one of its competitors. Nonetheless, newsbroking had acquired presence enough in journalism to classify newspapers according to their newsbroking affiliation. AP's exclusionary and self-protective policies and the movement of reaction known as Hasson's News Agency and the APA, led to a brisk trade in newspaper properties, journalistic self-consciousness, news competition, and the steady practice of plagiarism among newsbrokerages and local news competitors. The news report, in gradually enlarging dimensions, continued to flow daily from the Eastern offices of newsbrokers, but for those newspapers affiliated with Associated Press, the assembling and transmitting of news had been joined by the equally obvious function of assembling and protecting regional groups of newspapers qualified to receive AP's news. Indeed, as one reads the postwar record, it is difficult to decide which AP "service" its regular members valued more, protection or a news report.[156]

The "powerful national drama" after the Civil War, according to Thomas C. Cochran, was business growth and exploitation. "Material success became the highest goal,... and ...politics and social morality adjusted to the needs of the grand process."[157] Consistent with the prevailing pragmatic morality of business survival and conquest, AP made no secret of its exclusionary policies, as the following bold testimony of William Henry Smith before a U.S. Senate committee in 1884 illustrates.

> QUESTION: No person wishing to start a paper within the territory of one of these local [AP] associations can get the news reports of the Associated Press without the consent of the association of that locality?
>
> SMITH: Not without the consent, if you please, of the paper in that locality whence the application comes. That is the universal rule....
>
> QUESTION: Then, so far as the news that is furnished is concerned, it is restricted at the demand of the parties who are now receiving it?

SMITH: They have a right to elect whether they will admit new partners or not.... No reasonable application is ever refused. There are a great many foolish people who want to start newspapers. You can find them every two weeks in almost every town or city in the land.... [158]

Five years earlier James W. Simonton had stated AP's position even more bluntly to another Senate committee: "We are not in the newspaper business as missionaries or philanthropists, but in pursuit of bread." [159]

The postwar decade found newspaper publishers forming state press associations in record numbers to battle outside forces, [160] while ironically at the same time they organized themselves along AP and "outside" lines to battle one another. Thanks in part to newsbroking's struggle over control of the national flow of news, newspaper editors found themselves entangled in local competitive fights for survival. Like much of post–Civil War business, newspaper journalism had been plunged into costly combat, a brutal, decisive battle that only the fittest could survive. The stage was set in journalism, as well as in business generally, in the late 1870s for the discovery that cooperation and combination were preferable to ruthless competition. In newsbroking AP first had to rid itself of divisive regional hostility within the ranks, as we shall see in chapter 3, and then when a virile new competitor challenged AP, the two followed contemporary practice and formed a trust, as chapter 4 describes.

Chapter 3
REGIONALISM CONQUERED

The immediate social effect of the big company . . . was to produce a small but new social strat[um] of well-paid, and generally well-educated [managerial] careerists. They were not usually rich, but were influential in the business community because of the power of their corporations.

Thomas C. Cochran, **Business in American Life: A History**
(1972)

Our [NYAP] Ex. Committee sends you a letter today in regard to the interminable disputes growing out of our several "Agents" and as I believe wholly unnecessary. I wish your [WAP] Ex. Committee could restrain your man as we would ours and let matters go on as long as we act together without these "Tempests in Teapots" eternally arising.

George Jones to Joseph Medill
(December 30, 1879)
William Henry Smith Papers, Ohio Historical Society

Matthew Josephson called them "unscrupulous men" and "robber barons." The contract, the cartel, the corporation, the trust, and the stock market were merely toys to the late-nineteenth-century captains of industry, men of immense and previously unthinkable wealth. But to the managers and operators just below the top rung, these toys were the tools by which power and reputation, if not a fortune, could be forged. The quest for a safe haven from competition by whatever means presented themselves was a tolerated national spectacle after the Civil War and a grim business reality. In the shallows of postwar business's turbulent stream two newsbroker managers vied for supremacy—New York Associated Press's James W. Simonton and Western Associated Press's William Henry Smith. Bearded and dapper chieftains, letter-writers capable of syrupy cajoling and flinty indignation, they circled each other like wary wrestlers for more than a decade, each looking for a chance to infiltrate or overwhelm the other's empire, while exchanging news dispatches daily for a gradually expanding AP news report on which they both depended for their power. This chapter sketches Simonton and Smith, describes their relations and Smith's ultimate triumph only after Simonton had left the scene, and traces newsbroking's steady growth within a socio-economic setting that condoned cartels, crafty business intrigue, and money's power to set policy.

SIMONTON AND SMITH

Daniel H. Craig had set the standard for newsbroking agents during fifteen years of fighting off competitors, consorting with telegraphers, and making his news reports indispensable to newspaper publishers. He marketed dispatches distinguished for their unimaginative, flat factuality, dependable rather than daring, and held together a techno-journalistic system that lent credibility to his dry, routine news product. When his scheme to hijack the AP news monopoly for his own and Western Union's benefit led to his forced retirement in early November 1866, Craig left behind a noticeable vacuum in AP's operation. A replacement with standing in journalism and the stamina to endure the newsbroking grind was needed, and quickly. The "ring" of four weaker New York AP papers, which, as we have seen, controlled the agency after the Civil War, led by the *New York Times*, called on one of its own to fill Craig's shoes.

Simonton,[1] forty-three years of age when called to the helm of the New York AP, had already distinguished himself in New York journalism and was living off the fruits of wise investments in California. Born into a poor family in rural New York state on January 30, 1823, Simonton moved with his family to New York City as a youth and, after a brief apprenticeship as a tailor, became at twenty-one a court reporter for the *American Republican* in New York City. Within a year or so he joined the *New York Courier and Enquirer*, which soon assigned him to congressional coverage in Washington, D. C., alongside Henry J. Raymond, who was also with that paper. His dispatches were widely respected, earning him a permanent assignment to cover Congress for the paper, a task he fulfilled until November 1850, when he quit the paper and headed for California with the idea of starting a Whig paper in San Francisco. Finding one already successfully operating, the *San Francisco Courier*, he spent three months on its staff before returning to New York City and rejoining the *Courier and Enquirer* as night editor under Raymond.

When Raymond founded the *New York Times* in 1851, Simonton was briefly the new paper's night editor before returning to Washington as the *Times*'s congressional correspondent. His weekly dispatches, entitled "The History of Legislation," were acclaimed for their thoroughness and insight. In January 1857 a Simonton dispatch exposed a scheme among several congressmen to give away large chunks of the Minnesota Territory to a group of lobbyists (ostensibly for railroad construction) in exchange for money. "A wonderful amount of virtuous indignation displayed in the House of Representatives," according to Benjamin Perley Poore, greeted Simonton's assertions, followed by the convening of an investigating committee, "disposed to treat Mr. Simonton as a terrier treats a rat."[2] His dispatch failed to name the guilty congressman, and, summoned before the committee to tell what he knew, Simonton testified that although he had no personal knowledge of corruption, he knew of it from private conversations with House members who had been approached with corrupt propositions and who had approached him for information about exchanging votes for money. But claiming a right to protect his confidential sources, Simonton refused to name those who had talked to him.

Reporting these matters to the full House, the committee's chairman moved to direct the sergeant-at-arms to bring Simonton before the bar of the House to respond to a charge of contempt. Simonton, who was in the chamber, surrendered voluntarily, was granted permission to speak, and reiterated his charges, "moral convictions," and the right to a newsman's privilege. AP's Washington bureau chief, Lawrence A. Gobright, reports that

> An exciting debate followed. It was soon understood among members, that evidence had already been elicited, tending to disgrace several of their number, and a sort of panic seized a majority of the House, each man seeming to fear that he might be suspected of trying to cover up corruptions, if he should fail to vote for whatever the "Corruption Committee" might ask.[3]

The House detained Simonton and reasked its questions, and he again refused to answer. He was released after three weeks in custody when four congressmen were permitted to resign rather than face expulsion stemming from the corruption charge. Congress relieved Simonton of the contempt citation but also excluded him from the House floor as a reporter.

So ignominious a conclusion to the episode left Simonton vulnerable to later misinterpretations of his role and motives in the affair. One anonymous pamphleteer in 1873 reprinted the committee and House transcripts interlaced with insinuating subheadings, and in introductory remarks called Simonton

> an unscrupulous man, devoid of all regard for truth and justice, filled with prejudice and hatred growing out of punishment inflicted upon him and bent upon building or tearing down the reputation of individuals by reckless misstatements scattered broadcast throughout the land. . . .

Charging him with being a "hired lobbyist," a slanderer, and perjurer, the pamphlet describes its intent as being to arouse the public "to the real character of this small and vicious tyrant who prepares for the public the only telegraphic record they can have."[4]

In the spring of 1857 Simonton was in Utah for the *Times* covering a Mormon war that never materialized and traveled on to San Francisco where he bought a one-half interest in the *San Francisco Evening Bulletin*, for which he worked until 1860, when he resumed his employment for the *New York Times*. Retaining his holdings in the *Bulletin*, Simonton and his California partners eventually gained control of the *San Francisco Morning Call*. (Simonton also owned an interest in the *New York Times*.) Through the *Times*'s AP membership, he secured the New York AP's news report for his San Francisco papers (the start of the California AP, as noted in chapter 2), presumably first delivered via the pony express, which was launched in 1860, and then delivered via the transcontinental telegraph, which was completed October 24, 1861.[5]

Two months before he replaced Craig as the NYAP's general agent, R. G. Dun & Co. ledgers revealed that Simonton

> Is a young man of excel[len]t char[acter] formerly correspondent of the Times in Washington and is now interested in the paper owning 5 shares in it for wh[ich] a party w[oul]d give him $25,000. Owns 1/3 of the San Francisco Bulletin besides his house in Staten Island and other p[ro]p[ert]y. Parties think he w[oul]d be good for any contract he might make.[6]

Known among journalists as an "exceptionally good descriptive writer," according to his obituary in the *New York Times*, Simonton also had "the facility of sharp incisive writing in a marked degree which made him especially obnoxious to such as deserved and received castigation from his pen." His letters show Simonton to be generally a conciliator, who sometimes appealed to correspondents' loyalty to AP, personal friendship, or their sympathy for his burden of having to keep his NYAP papers in line. Responding to a *New York Tribune* complaint and attempting to soften a complaint lodged by another NYAP paper against the *Tribune*, for example, Simonton wrote Whitelaw Reid in August 1870,

> I write you now this personal and unofficial note, to ask you frankly to inform me what has happened to impair the personal relations of mutual confidence and regard which has [sic] marked our intercourse ever heretofore. I have counted fully on your cordial support of my administration in a delicate and difficult time.[7]

Three days later Simonton was still trying to win Reid's support through understanding.

> My position is an exceedingly delicate one,—being compelled as I am to stand between converging fires, unable to judge for myself between our members, obliged by duty to present the complaints of either against the other and unable, with propriety, to relieve myself of responsibility by stating who it is that has complained.[8]

In making his own complaint about a *Tribune* violation of an AP rule, Simonton's touch was delicate.

> You have on former occasions manifested such ready disposition to conduct your office so as to avoid any embarrassment to the Associated Press organization, that I am sure you will allow me to make a suggestion for your consideration without suspecting me of obtrusive purpose to interfere unnecessarily.[9]

Although often sounding meek or cloying, Simonton, rather than being weak, habitually relied on indirect and mild language even in his most aggressive moments. When the *New York Tribune* "was made the medium for spreading vile calumnies of me" by carrying an article signed "G. H. Butler," Simonton's threat to institute libel action was couched in measured, temperate terms:

> I am earnestly seeking some available mode of redress, and hope to get it through your friend's disavowal of the libel and a statement of Mr. Greeley's personal knowledge of my character.

> If you disappoint this hope, what can I do but appeal to the courts for vindication? I know Mr. Greeley too well to think of intimidating him and you will not suspect me of presuming to threaten when I pledge my word of honor to pursue my legal recourses unless you can aid me to a better and readier redress. . . .
>
> Herewith please find rough draft of such a paragraph as the *Tribune* might publish conspicuously on its Editorial page without humiliation. . . . [10]

While Simonton earned his stripes covering and being badgered by politicians, William Henry Smith[11] launched his career as a political reporter and a politician. Smith was born December 1, 1833, in Columbia County, New York. When he was still an infant, his family moved to Homer, Ohio. While a young schoolteacher and tutor, Smith met Rutherford B. Hayes at a Free Soil meeting, joined that group, and in May 1855 moved to Cincinnati. He joined the staff of the *Cincinnati Commercial* on January 1, 1858, and covered state government in Columbus for that paper using "Paul Crayne" as a pen name until early in 1859, when he moved to the staff of the *Cincinnati Gazette*, again covering political affairs. Covering the Antioch College commencement exercises in June 1859, Smith first met Whitelaw Reid, who was covering the exercises for his own *Xenia* (Ohio) *News*. By the spring of 1861 Reid was city editor of the *Cincinnati Gazette* and was heading into the field for the first Civil War skirmishes, writing under the name of "Agate." Thus, between the ages of twenty-one and twenty-five Smith acquired the friendship of four notable Republicans, all of whom would figure prominently in his later career—Hayes, elected president in the contested 1876 election; Murat Halstead, a rising force in the *Cincinnati Commercial* and later in the Western Associated Press; Richard "Deacon" Smith, proprietor of the *Cincinnati Gazette* and a WAP leader;[12] and Whitelaw Reid, later publisher of the *New York Tribune* and instrumental in getting Smith appointed NYAP general agent in 1882.

An enthusiastic young Republican during the Civil War, Smith, according to Reid, "threw himself heart and soul into the work" of opposing the Ohio gubernatorial candidacy of Clement L. Vallandigham, who had been banished to the South by President Lincoln.[13] Smith's candidate, John Brough, was elected in 1863 and Smith became his private secretary. The next year Smith headed the Republican ticket as candidate for secretary of state and swept into office on an impressive 56,000-vote majority. Re-elected two years later, Smith resigned in January 1868 shortly before his second term expired, vowing never to hold public office again. His premature departure appears to have been prompted by reaction to his overly exuberant efforts while in office to support Hayes's bid for the Ohio governorship. (Hayes, meanwhile, was elected governor, a post he held for three terms, making him a contender for the Republican presidential nomination in 1876.)

Out of political life at the tender age of thirty-four, Smith went back to Cincinnati, where he was already planning with several others, including R. H. Stephenson, to launch the *Cincinnati Chronicle*.[14] Smith became editor-in-chief of the new paper in March 1868 in its infancy. The new paper shortly became a member of the Western AP upon payment of a $6,000 bonus, and purchased its evening competitor, the *Times*, for $138,550 at auction upon the death of the *Times*'s owner, merging the two as the *Times and Chronicle* on April 29, 1871, at which point the owners held two WAP franchises.[15] The burdens of starting a new paper affected Smith's health, and by mid-1869 he had to retire from active work for several months.

Meanwhile, Smith had other irons in the fire. Back in November 1868, Richard Smith on behalf of the Western AP had offered Smith the position as WAP agent in New York City at $3,500 per year. Writing Reid, who only months before had replaced John Russell Young as the *New York Tribune*'s managing editor, Smith asked for advice.[16] Wiring immediately "Take it," Reid followed with a letter saying the WAP agency in New York City

> has, I think, some incidental income (of wh[ich] the Western people know nothing) & at any rate on $3,500 you can live in Brooklyn very well. Besides the N.Y. Assd. Press agent is to be chgd. before very long & there might thus be an opening for advancement.[17]

Despite such enticements (and Reid's wishful thinking about Simonton being replaced as NYAP agent), Smith rejected the low salary and the expense of living in New York City. Outwardly, however, Smith's colleagues at the *Cincinnati Chronicle* were saying he could not be spared as editor in chief.[18]

Sometime during 1869 the WAP found it necessary to replace its general agent at Cleveland, George B. Hicks, and Smith filled the post on October 26, 1869.[19] There is no record of whether Hicks's departure may have been prompted by a shortage of about five thousand dollars in the books Hicks kept,[20] or by an involvement with the National Telegraph Company that linked him with Craig.[21] After only two months in office, Smith was moved by his new employers to new headquarters in Chicago, specifically a third-floor room in the Chicago Tribune building. Biographer Edgar Laughlin Gray reports that Smith, a shrewdly economical organizer and a man who attracted confidence, quickly paid off an $18,000 debt, began amassing surpluses, hired stronger agents, badgered the telegraph company for better service and operators, and improved the quality of the news report.[22] In February 1871 Richard Smith wrote Reid that William Henry Smith "is indispensable to W. A. P. All our trouble with N.Y.A.P. was brought about by Simonton and there will not, I presume, be smooth sailing while he remains."[23]

Smith had been stationed in Chicago only ten months in the fall of 1871, and an exciting fall it was, thanks to journalism. Henry M. Stanley, on assignment for the *New York Herald*, was trekking through central Africa, still searching for the missionary David Livingston. Meanwhile, the nation watched to see if Boss William Marcy Tweed would be arrested as a result of the "Tweed Ring" exposés begun by the *New York Times* on July 8.[24] In Chicago the *Tribune* on October 8 reported a lumberyard fire that high winds had whipped into a million-dollar disaster. It was the thirtieth fire in as many days, the paper noted, reiterating editorially its plea of several months' standing that the Chicago city council establish a construction code reducing the threat of fire.[25] October 8, 1871, was a Sunday, and the *Tribune* (and Smith's WAP headquarters) occupied a new four-story "fireproof" building. At 9:30 that night, a spark from an overturned lantern (according to conventional wisdom) touched off the Great Chicago Fire, engulfing a one-by-four-mile strip of the central city, including the *Tribune*'s building. Writing Reid on October 20, Smith described the disaster from a newsbroker's viewpoint.

> When the connections were severed in the heart of the city the obstacles in the way of reaching the outside world seemed insurmountable. Gen. [Anson] Stager [of Western Union] and his assistant worked with great energy and kept a way open for us.... [W]hile I kept four experienced men collecting material, I permitted nothing to go over the wire, not carefully verified. Especially careful was I to prevent a general panic in the country....

Our Assn. is crippled thru the Chicago Press—temporarily of course. If the Tribune and Times had the facilities for printing, their receipts would be quite as large as formerly. The Journal is all right. I think the Republican's obituary might be written now....I fear the Evening Post is without resources, also the Staats Zeitung.

[The *Tribune*'s Joseph] Medill's loss will reach $250,000, but he has as much left....

I had the balance for Association in bank of about $20,000, and for two or three days I was in doubt about it. We shall get it all, I think. My personal loss is—stock rendered worthless—$1250; valuable books recently purchased $60. But our house was untouched, and our lives spared, and for this we are profoundly grateful, I trust, and shall never cease to thank the Lord. The desolation and misery that now surrounds us will continue to remind us of our own blessings for a long, long time.[26]

At the height of the fire, WAP's local Chicago agent, S. V. R. Hickcox, carried "the most valuable of the books and papers" of the WAP from his office in Western Union's building to Smith's in the Tribune building, supposing they would be safe there. In all, Smith calculated the loss at $2,720.80 in office furnishings and books, loss of Chicago assessments, and "extraordinary expenses." Assessments of Chicago papers were temporarily suspended, and other WAP papers were asked to make up the difference in the interim. Four weeks after the fire all Chicago papers were again paying assessments, except for the *Republican*, which paid half-rates until November 25, when it again assumed its full obligation. At its next annual meeting, in June 1872, the WAP thanked Western Union "for the prompt action and aid extended" during the fire, and it thanked Medill for "offering to make good any loss the Association might sustain."[27]

While Simonton was to R. G. Dun & Co. "a shrewd money making man" with investments in various newspapers, property, and the Russian Baths in New York City totaling between $250,000 and $300,000 by mid-1875,[28] Smith, "a reserved but kindly man in speech," according to one employee,[29] seems to have lived more modestly, preferring to blend managerial chores with a lifelong pursuit of historical research and writing. While he was Ohio's secretary of state, Smith devoted considerable effort to gathering, organizing, and preserving the archives of the Northwest Territory.

This led to an Ohio legislative commission for Smith to edit the papers of Arthur St. Clair, a general in the French-English-Canadian and Revolutionary wars, president of the Continental Congress, and the first governor of the Northwest Territory. This collection was published in two volumes in 1882.[30] Meanwhile Smith gathered and prepared material for *A Political History of Slavery*, which was nearly completed at the time of his death in 1896. Published posthumously in 1903 with an introduction by Whitelaw Reid, this work sought to shift the spotlight on the anti-slavery movement away from New England, the East, the boisterous abolitionists, and anti-Constitutionalists and toward the Midwestern free soil and Republican Party movements of which he had been a part.[31]

Smith's revisionist study of the history of slavery arose from research conducted preparatory to undertaking another project. President Hayes had named Smith his literary executor, charged with writing Hayes's authorized biography. Still largely unfinished when Smith died, the biography was completed by Smith's son-in-law, Charles R. Williams, editor of the *Indianapolis News*, in 1914.[32] Smith also wrote a few journal articles.[33]

THE UNEASY ALLIANCE

Simonton, the man of modest wealth who was once quoted as implying that he was NYAP's general agent only to protect the flow of news to the California newspapers in which he owned an interest,[34] and Smith, who while describing the Chicago Fire to the governor of Ohio felt it necessary to say, "I had also about $60 worth of valuable historical books in a wardrobe in the office, which disappeared in the smoke and flames,"[35] might seem to have been an uneven match. To *The Journalist*, a trade weekly that in the mid-1880s vigorously supported United Press fortunes against Smith's AP, Smith was no match for Simonton, who

> did the best he could for the association over which he presided until his death. He was a monopolist *incarne*, to the very backbone, but at the same time he was a good newspaper man, and though he failed to advance with the times, he rendered services that made the years of his dotage forgivable.

Smith, on the other hand, according to the magazine,

> does not know the difference between a piece of news and a bar of pig iron. Since he has had charge the Associated Press

ing day, however, WAP's agent, Charles A. Boynton, was given "a closet 9 9/12 × 15 feet, accessible only through the [NYAP's] manifold room," as Smith described it. "After some friction" the company gave WAP a room on the fifth floor, and Simonton announced that he would advise the NYAP to cut off news to the WAP because NYAP did not want to deliver its news outside of its own rooms.[41]

NYAP's executive committee (Erastus Brooks, George Jones, and David M. Stone) protested that a separate WAP room violated the 1867 contract between the NYAP and WAP. The WAP committee (Richard Smith, Murat Halstead, and Joseph Medill) claimed the "privilege" and accepted the responsibility under the contract to operate out of a separate room.[42] The correspondence on both sides was vitriolic, New York claiming that WAP's Boynton was creating the controversy to better his own position, Smith claiming that Simonton and the *New York Times* "ring" wanted to control the nation's news.[43] In April reason finally prevailed in the person of the *Cincinnati Gazette*'s Richard Smith, who after a visit to the New York facility advised Medill not to push the quarrel because the fifth floor room was inconvenient and the WAP was well cared for in the new AP complex. "There is no desire on the part of the N.Y.A.P. or of Simonton to quarrel with us," R. Smith wrote to Medill. "Jones says a fight would be a bad thing for both parties and we ought not and *must* not fight."[44] "A little concession on each side," defusing a "temporary misunderstanding" with the NYAP, was how the WAP board described the resolution later in the year. Otherwise, said the board, "there has scarcely been a ripple on the surface of our affairs to disturb the calm monotony."[45] From examining the extant correspondence on this matter, one cannot escape the impression that both executive committees may have been urged into a temporary hostility by the barrage of antagonism streaming from William Henry Smith's and Boynton's pens at a time when Simonton's position with the NYAP may have been in jeopardy.[46]

Efforts by both agencies or their agents to court the support of auxiliary APs periodically surfaced in the correspondence for a decade and a half after the 1867 contract. Smith had replaced Oliver M. Bradford and Amos F. Learned as WAP agents in New York City, the implication being that they were suspected of being too friendly to the NYAP. In the fall of 1871 both NYAP and WAP sought ties with the New England AP by offering their New York representatives to serve as the New Englanders' agent. Smith's New York man, Boynton, was offered to New England, but the New Englanders "proved weak in the knees," as Smith reports, and at Simonton's insistence hired Bradford and Learned, a "precious pair" of "corrupt, bad men," in Smith's words.[47] Two years later Boynton wrote Smith confidentially that "the bulk of the New England Press are favorable toward an ultimate union" with the WAP, except for the *Boston Herald*, which was seeking full membership in the New York AP partnership.[48] There were also periodic WAP overtures for an alliance with the Southern AP in opposition to NYAP, but such ventures proved fruitless.

Another periodic source of conflict was control of the news transmitted to papers beyond Nebraska, Kansas, and Missouri. Simonton's interest in the *San Francisco Evening Bulletin* and *Morning Call* formed the basis, it will be recalled, for the California AP as an appendage of the NYAP. Charles and Michel de Young's *San Francisco Chronicle*, born in 1865, was by the early 1870s a serious threat to Simonton's newspapers in that city. Although unable despite many attempts to gain membership in the Simonton-dominated California AP, the *Chronicle* had risen in popularity via good local coverage and a mixture of American Press Association reports and specials until in the spring of 1876 it was a formidable West Coast voice, again insisting on an AP membership. The New York AP partners took up the *Chronicle*'s request on March 14, 1876, with Simonton privately urging rejection of the paper's application, writing Reid, "We cannot consent to any sort of union with the *Chronicle*, because that would be lending our strength to their weakness."[49] Deliberations in New York dragged on until mid-July, when Simonton's cause was rejected and he was forced to announce that the NYAP had agreed to provide the *Chronicle* at New York and Chicago with a report that differed from that transmitted to the California AP.[50] The de Youngs chose William H. French, a WAP agent in Smith's Chicago office, to act as their agent to ensure that their news report differed from the one the NYAP's agents were sending to the California AP.

Abandoned by his New York patrons, Simonton commented that "while I consent to hold my position as 'General Agent,' I must in good faith and earnestness support whatever policy the Association has determined." Simonton could only look forward hopefully to "a square victory, on an open fight" between his California AP and the *Chronicle*'s separate AP report being handled by Smith's office.[51] It was a serious wound to Simonton, one which Smith could aggravate by balking at handling the *Chronicle* report. And Smith did balk, based on his and WAP's view that the NYAP unjustly assumed that all the news available in Chicago, including that gathered by the WAP, was New York's property to sell wherever it pleased.[52] Simonton pleaded with Smith that "if you persist in refusing, . . . it will leave our Committee in a bad scrape, and de Young will try to make them believe that I am responsible for it."[53] The *Chronicle* finally got its report as requested, and Smith had his moment of superiority over Simonton.[54]

Also in 1876 the NYAP abruptly claimed the right to serve some of the newspapers in Texas, a state previously served by Western Union, which had purchased the WAP report at St. Louis for delivery in Texas.[55] Smith hoped to acquire Texas papers as a WAP auxiliary, but Simonton claimed the 1867 NYAP-WAP contract reserved Texas as NYAP territory.[56] Simonton's interpretation carried the day, leaving Smith to rant to WAP's membership that

> The New York Association claims the sole right of selling news on the American Continent, not only of its own news, but of the news collected and paid for by the Western Press. It proposed to come into our territory, take our news at any accessible point, and sell it. . . .[57]

A similar problem arose over delivery of the news report to Colorado newspapers. As with Texas, a WAP report had been sold to Western Union, which then sold it in Colorado. All went well until the spring of 1879, when, as Smith reports,

> Mr. Simonton suddenly appeared upon the scene and endeavored to take possession of the territory. Notice was served upon me to withdraw from the field, as it belonged of right to New York.[58]

This was followed by Western Union's notice that it would no longer deliver the WAP report at the old rates. The Colorado papers, which had earlier formed the Colorado Press and News Association at Smith's suggestion, announced that the association "desires to remain in the Western Press Association, and prefers its reports to any other."[59]

The Texas and Colorado conflicts resulted from frontier development. As long as the Colorado area boasted only a few newspapers, both agencies left the area's meager profits to the telegraph company, but the growth of Colorado journalism eventually attracted the attention of both agencies. According to the 1867 NYAP-WAP contract, Colorado belonged to the NYAP, but as Smith later observed, in 1867

> the country west of Omaha and east of the Rocky Mountains
> was uninhabited and its future development was unknown to
> either party. It was not taken into consideration by the Western
> Press people. . . . The people of Colorado hold such relations to
> the people and business interests of Chicago and St. Louis, as to
> render a service by New York very objectionable. . . . This is the
> first time New York has ever made a claim on that territory.[60]

While New York could turn to the 1867 contract to assert its rights
in Colorado,[61] Smith had to rely on a decade of indirect WAP service
through the telegraph company in the area to support his claim to
the area. "Every time a question has been raised," Smith wrote Medill of WAP's executive committee, "the Western Press has yielded,
so that now the N.Y. people entertain a very contemptible opinion
of the Western papers." He frustratedly asked Medill, "must there
not occur a time when the Western Press should assert their supremacy, or sh[oul]d demand a recognition equal with that of the
N.Y. Press?" Attempting to convince Medill of the rightness of his
position, Smith asserted,

> we must have a fair division of the territory of the United
> States in accordance with the new order of things; and that if
> this is done peaceably we shall continue to cooperate, but if not
> we are prepared to enter the entire field as competitors.[62]

Smith persisted and several months later was reproached by WAP
president Murat Halstead, who wrote Smith, "You have a most
charming way of ignoring facts." In 1867 when WAP secured its "independence of the N.Y. Ass[ociate]d Press," Halstead continued,

> we defined our territory—we built a fence around ourselves.
>   All outside of that belongs to the N.Y. Press. There never has
> been any doubt about that. We have nothing to do with Colorado. [Richard] Smith and Medill perfectly agree with me about
> this.
>   Therefore the Colorado war policy is totally baseless. I think
> it should be frankly abandoned and that all the contention
> caused about it should be abandoned also.[63]

This flowed from Halstead's pen one month after George Jones of
the New York AP executive committee had written Medill, "I wish
your Ex. Committee could restrain your man as we would ours," sin-

gling out Smith and Simonton as the causes of "these 'Tempests in Teapots' eternally arising."[64]

As matters turned out, the NYAP offered Colorado its California news report to be transmitted from Cheyenne, Wyo., and the WAP offered its report at Kansas City, both at the same rates. The Colorado press was thus forced to divide into two camps, leaving Smith to console himself that "the strongest of the papers remain with the Western Press."[65]

Smith, eager to promote the power of his WAP against what he perceived as the unjustified superiority of the ruling NYAP clique, kept running up against the 1867 contract and a conservatism among WAP members and officers who placed more importance on receipt of the daily news report and its attendant local protection from competition than on the relative strength of the two APs. Although general agents Simonton and Smith periodically met on the field of verbal battle, Simonton's ulterior motive was protection of his San Francisco newspaper interests, leaving Smith to seek his journalistic stature solely through the fortunes of a newsbrokerage in which he held no stock and could not vote. Smith's aggressiveness reflected both a conscious strategy and a personal frustration. Writing in 1890, he said,

> The correspondence between me and Mr. Simonton . . . would fill volumes. When our relations became strained through the aggressive policy [I was] pursuing, there would be meetings between the Executive Committees of the two associations to try to bring out harmony. Some concessions would be made, but there was never cordiality. . . . These were preliminary to the final contest with the New York Associated Press in 1882.[66]

Smith might have wearied of his vulnerability and snail's pace and might have left WAP service had the Western Union and Jay Gould not provided him with the opportunity to mount an assault on NYAP on behalf of WAP's equality.

PRELUDE TO THE "FINAL CONTEST"

Waged during the second half of 1882, "the final contest" between WAP and NYAP, as Smith refers to it above, arose from complex and changing conditions in both newsbroking and telegraphy, principally over a six-year period. Superficially control of journalism on the frontier, aggravated by the out-of-date 1867 contract, was the issue embroiling the two agencies. Less obvious, but more important as factors propelling NYAP and WAP toward the "final contest" were (1) persistent newsbroking competition, fostered by a parade of independent telegraph companies; (2) changes in NYAP's management and membership that sharpened Western Union's interest in cooperating with WAP; and (3) a series of corporate mergers that left Western Union controlled by Jay Gould, who then momentarily interested himself vastly in the national news movement business.

The wheels grinding inexorably toward the 1882 contest were set in motion on September 30, 1876, when the National Associated Press Company arose from the wreckage of the American Press Association. The APA and its predecessor, Hasson's News Association, as noted in chapter 2, owed their existence both to a growing number of newspapers outside the AP organization and to the Atlantic & Pacific and Franklin telegraph companies, operated since 1865 in opposition to the Western Union. By January 1, 1877, A&P had leased the Franklin circuits and was operating a transcontinental line, 17,759 miles of routes, and more than twice that mileage in lines. During the previous few years Gould had amassed a controlling interest in A&P, enticed Thomas A. Edison and his quadruplex transmitting device away from Western Union (which was operating a duplex system developed by Joseph B. Stearns in 1873), and convinced Thomas T. Eckert to quite as Western Union's eastern division superintendent and become A&P president in January 1875.[67] One of a parade of telegraph companies in the 1870s poised to fight, or sell out to, Western Union,[68] A&P, once offered to Western Union and rejected, was now a formidable telegraphic force, especially with its Gould connection.

Not so formidable, however, was A&P's American Press Association ally. "After a career of varying fortunes," according to Walter P. Phillips,[69] the APA was dissolved on September 30, 1876, replaced by the National Associated Press Company. The transformation was prompted by the fact that Robert Johnston of the *New York Evening Mail* had acquired a majority of APA's four hundred shares of stock, and, according to the *New York Tribune*, was "able to defeat the measures of the other publishers for elaborating and improving their system of news collecting."[70] Specifically Johnston had blocked an increase in APA's stock issue by one hundred shares, which would have undermined his control, and he adopted a resolution halting a suit by APA against him for $1,800 that the agency claimed he owed it. The changeover occurred when the APA was abandoned by the *New York News, New York Graphic, Providence*

Star, Pittsburgh Leader, Boston Globe, and APA manager William B. Somerville. The same papers and manager then created the National AP at the same meeting.[71]

The new agency, a stock company with holdings limited to five shares per newspaper, was governed by a board of nine directors elected by stockholders. According to the new bylaws, "for their mutual protection and to the end that the value of their respective interests in [the NAP] may be enhanced," members agreed to allow the company to supervise the distribution, transfer, and redemption of stock, obviously an attempt to avoid a repetition of the Johnston episode.[72] Somerville continued as general agent until joining the Western Union in 1879 as superintendent of press transmission. James H. Goodsell, publisher of the *New York Graphic*, and NAP president throughout the company's six-year history, managed the NAP after Somerville left, causing NAP membership "dissatisfaction with its reports which...constantly increased," says Phillips, until the United Press superseded the NAP in 1882.[73] The record preserves only one set of NAP directors, those elected October 3, 1877, the board being controlled largely by evening and Eastern papers.[74]

With a stable, if mediocre, NAP in tow, the A&P telegraph company moved early in 1877 to challenge Western Union with a rate war orchestrated by Gould. This David-and-Goliath confrontation looks ludicrous on paper,[75] until one considers on the one hand Gould's ability to lose vast sums of money in the short haul in quest of a more lucrative goal and, on the other, Western Union's propensity to cave in and absorb any competitor showing the slightest spunk. Within a few months Western Union had capitulated and purchased the A&P system and Gould's A&P interests, making Gould a substantial, but not the controlling, stockholder. The merger sent shock waves through the Associated Press. In Western Union's 1867 contract with the NYAP and WAP, the telegraph company was prohibited from transmitting the reports of rival news agencies, but, by assuming the contract obligations of A&P in 1877, Western Union was now transmitting NAP's news reports—in some places at rates below those charged the AP by Western Union. William Henry Smith observed in his mid-August 1878 report to WAP's membership that Western Union "has disregarded the terms of our contract and the best interests of old and useful clients. It is right to demand reparation."[76]

In addition to taking official and disapproving notice of Western Union's broken promise to avoid "unfair competition with other Associations in the transmission of news,"[77] the WAP membership resolved to seek new contracts with Western Union and NYAP, and authorized its board

> to procure from Congress a special enactment conferring upon the Western Associated Press, and such other similar associations as may be invited to combine with it in this enterprise, a permanent charter, granting authority to construct, maintain and operate *telegraph lines* within. . .the United States. . . .[78]

The idea of a national charter, including telegraphic operations, was later deemed "inexpedient,"[79] but a modification of WAP's contract with Western Union in September 1878 allowed WAP a reduction of roughly $10,000 in annual toll charges, a trifle in light of the company's duplicity toward press organizations. Richard Smith, reporting for WAP's executive committee, was pessimistic about getting Western Union to halt transmission of NAP's news reports. If the NAP were charged AP's rates, he said, the NAP "could not exist," but WAP members "help to keep alive the [NAP] by purchasing its news in violation of our rules." He left the matter for the full membership to thrash out.[80] William Henry Smith's accompanying report expressed similar frustration over the situation.

> Gentlemen, I have exhausted the English language, as well as all the resources that I am possessed of, to carry out your instructions. . . . Nothing has been accomplished. We stand to-day, in respect to the National Press, where we did one year ago.[81]

Regarding WAP's relations with the NYAP, matters seemed equally bleak, unless extreme measures could be undertaken. Constant bickering over control of news flowing into Colorado, California, and the Southwest, a WAP suspicion that it was paying NYAP excessively for its European cable reports, a general dissatisfaction with the report from the East, and the continuing antagonism between Simonton and Smith—all had brought relations to the point of a "costly and unsatisfactory warfare," as Whitelaw Reid later described it.[82] Melville E. Stone later pointed to the absence of a WAP voice in the management of the Eastern news-gathering apparatus as the chief cause of WAP's eventual "revolt."[83] In February 1879 WAP notified NYAP of its intention to sever relations, although subsequent events revealed this to have been a bluff.

In May 1879 WAP representatives were seen in Washington, D. C., meeting with representatives of the Southern AP and William B. Somerville of the NAP. The plan being contemplated by these three agencies, according to gossip, was to unite and to invite other state and regional APs into a national confederation that would exclude the New York AP.[84] Such proposals were not new in 1879. Three years earlier APA's Somerville had urged William Henry Smith to "come right into the East, take the A.P.A. papers as a nucleus and run your own service independent" of the NYAP. "You can make immediate inroads on the NYAP," Somerville observed, leaving "the NY Assd. Press in a position that competition with you would be out of the question."[85] Nothing came of these overtures, and again in 1879 the Washington meeting came to naught. Richard Smith, addressing the WAP membership in early September 1879, expressed the gloomy outlook for NYAP-WAP relations.

> No concessions of any kind are to be expected from the N.Y. Associated Press, except through an abrogation of the contract. . . . Of one thing you may feel assured, the N.Y. Associated Press is for itself; it apprehends, if it does not desire, a rupture, and is fortifying at every point.[86]

WAP's mid-May meeting with the Southern AP and NAP may have been prompted by the appearance nine days earlier by a new challenger to the Western Union monopoly. Fathered by Gould, the American Union Telegraph Company, born May 15, 1879, was an innocent effort, Gould later testified to a congressional committee, to find a place for a good friend in telegraphy. Having joined the Atlantic & Pacific company at Gould's insistence in 1875, Thomas T. Eckert was denied a position in the new amalgam when Western Union and A&P merged in 1877. The American Union, Gould told legislators, was set up for Eckert, who became the company's president on January 1, 1880. Subsequent events, however, revealed the American Union to be a pawn of Gould's final drive to gain control of Western Union. Matthew Josephson catches the flavor of the scheme. Gould's purported act of friendship toward Eckert, Josephson says, was discovered too late as part of "an imperial plan to capture strategic sections of the country's industrial system." Gould, says Josephson,

> would be as one who deals out marked cards in the game of buying and selling capital, since he would be fully able to fore-

see the "nature, magnitude and incidence" of all the risks he created. His system could no more fail than loaded dice.[87]

On the surface, the appearance of a new and potentially powerful challenger to Western Union would have encouraged WAP officials to push NYAP harder, a large part of the New Yorkers' strength arising from a new contract between NYAP and Western Union that relieved the NYAP from sharing Western Union facilities with NAP.[88] Already controlling numerous railroads, especially in the West, Gould threw Western Union off several key rail rights-of-way and installed his own American Union. He formed an alliance with the French cable company to force down Western Union's transatlantic cable rates,[89] and put an end to rumors and some evidence that the three existing cables fixed rates jointly.[90] Rates and management of the cable had been sources of continual dispute between press and cable operators since the novelty of same-day telegraphic news dispatches from Europe had given way to the pain of arbitrary rules and sustained high rates for use of the cable.[91]

In April, May, and June of 1867, AP averaged only eighty-four words per day over Field's cable,[92] the total held down by ruinous rates, which started at ten dollars per word in 1866, took two years to fall to $1.58 per word, and took another two years to reach seventy-five cents per word.[93] With each reduction in rates, the volume of special and newsbroker dispatches proportionately increased, although news still came abbreviated and in code. One estimate had the NYAP paying nearly $17,000 during August and September of 1870 for cable dispatches,[94] a daily average of $283. Without cable competition in the Atlantic, Simonton had to limit his foreign news transmission, even though the NYAP could expand a brief dispatch in code into a column or two of type each day by 1870.[95] By 1878–79, according to one source, AP's cable tolls averaged $500 per day, at times reaching $2,000 per day.[96] Gould's lease of the French cable provided some relief for the press—and pressure for Western Union.

Gould's assault on Western Union, in other ways, may not have been so consoling to the press. In mid-July 1880 the American Union took steps to organize a newsbrokerage, president Eckert writing Reid that he was "just taking up the subject of furnishing a press report to the various parts of the country" and asking for the *Tribune*'s market reports "if consistent with the obligations of the paper."[97] It, of course, was not consistent with the paper's obligations to the NYAP, and, although there is no record of an American Union news service actually operating, Eckert had found a way to threaten potential Gould involvement in journalism. Elsewhere in New York City, Gould's journalism was more obvious. In 1879 he had acquired the *New York World*[98] and was using its news and editorial columns to attack the management and operations of Western Union, driving down the value of the company's stock in the process.

If Gould was not enough, Western Union also faced a showdown with a rising telephone business. Alexander Graham Bell's telephone patent application of 1876, although contested immediately and periodically thereafter, led on July 9, 1877, to creation of the Bell Telephone Company. Belatedly realizing that it had better get into this new form of wired communication, Western Union created the American Speaking Telephone Company in 1877, based on the telephone patents of Amos E. Dolbear and Elisha Gray. When Bell's chief attorney, Gardiner G. Hubbard, convinced Theodore N. Vail to leave the superintendency of the U.S. Railway Mail Service and become the Bell company general manager, Bell's operations were placed on a firm corporate footing. Bell sued the American Speaking Telephone Company for patent infringement in September 1878, and Western Union backed out of the telephone business the following summer, desiring to negotiate the issues out of court. On November 10, 1879, Western Union formally promised to stay out of the telephone business in exchange for Bell's promise to stay out of telegraphy and to absorb the American Speaking Telephone Company.[99]

With Gould pushing forward on all fronts and with the Bell company strenuously entering the field of wired communication, Western Union was staggering by the end of 1879, the kind of unsettled climate from which WAP believed it could capitalize. Calling together representatives of the NYAP, the New England AP, New York State AP, the Philadelphia AP, and its own leadership, WAP proposed, at a meeting on November 26, 1879, in New York City, a "news clearing house" to be administered jointly by the leading APs. The proposal suggested a "National Associated Press,"[100] controlled by the five represented APs and managing news gathering in Washington, Europe, and the Eastern seaboard in the interests of all five organizations.[101]

One representative from each of the five APs was chosen to discuss the proposal further at a meeting on January 23, 1880, in Philadelphia.[102] Although uninvited, Simonton also attended the New York meeting,[103] and the proposal and meeting were doomed by NYAP's unwillingness to accept a proposal that, in effect, would have reduced it to the level of some of its auxiliaries. On the eve of the Philadelphia gathering, the NYAP executive committee fired off an abrasive bill of particulars to Medill, complaining of a "real grievance" the NYAP had with a recent William Henry Smith order withholding Chicago specials from the NYAP. Noting that before the Philadelphia meeting "it was important, if possible, to arrive at some understanding upon questions of right and duty" on the Colorado service, the committee played NYAP's old tune.

> Colorado is our territory under the contract; and we are willing to refer the fact, upon the record, to any justifiable arbitration. It is ours also from ten years use and practice in the collection and distribution of news from that region....[104]

Clearly, WAP was moving too boldly and brashly for the New Yorkers, whose defense, as always, consisted of reasserting the provisions of a contract now thirteen years old and still preserving NYAP's superiority. In the end WAP's idea of a "news clearing house" crumbled under regional fears of losing NYAP's news, and Richard Smith could only report to WAP's membership that "it was concluded best to continue our relations with the New York Associated Press, and upon the terms at present existing."[105] Except for a partially successful attempt at modifying its contract with the Western Union, WAP could only preoccupy itself during most of 1880–81 with housekeeping chores and await a more propitious moment for reform or revolution.[106]

Meanwhile in telegraphy events were moving rapidly toward a climax. A steady barrage of *New York World* criticism had forced Western Union's stock down to 1850s levels. By the start of 1881 Gould's American Union operated 2,000 offices, 10,000 miles of routes, and 50,000 miles of wire. Western Union, reeling under months of mounting pressure, finally broke on January 9, 1881, when its leading stockholder, William H. Vanderbilt, sent a note requesting "a few moments" of Gould's time. Negotiations produced an agreement on February 15 by which Western Union absorbed Gould's American Union and Gould captured Western Union, adding to his shares from the A&P merger those of the American Union consolidation and another block he had quietly bought when, with the help of his *World*, Western Union dropped sharply in the market.

As the company's largest stockholder, Gould promptly claimed fifth floor office space in the Western Union building, just three floors below AP's newsrooms, uncomfortably close to newsbroking facilities, some reasoned, but not as close as Gould would later get, as we shall see. Dr. Norvin Green, who had replaced William Orton in 1878 as Western Union president, continued in office. Gould's friend Thomas T. Eckert now finally found his place in the Western Union organization—director, vice-president, and general manager—where he remained until 1893, when he became the company's president.

Perhaps the most tangible reaction to Gould's takeover of Western Union was the creation of the Postal Telegraph Company on June 21, 1881, which pinned its hopes on a harmonic telegraph instrument developed by Elisha Gray and a new steel-and-copper telegraph wire devised by Chester Snow. The company grew rapidly, capturing enough of the telegraph market to be out of debt by the summer of 1883, when it attracted a one-million-dollar investment from John W. Mackay, who had gained his wealth by tapping the Comstock Lode in the Virginia City silver and gold fields. Mackay immediately became Postal's president. In September 1883 Mackay and *New York Herald* publisher James Gordon Bennett, Jr., formed the Commercial Cable Company,[107] which during 1884 laid two Atlantic cables, one to England and the other to France. Although occasionally experiencing rough financial sledding in its competition with Western Union, Postal survived past the turn of the century and in 1903 was the first concern to link the United States and Asia with a transpacific cable that passed through Hawaii and Midway.

Meanwhile Gould at the head of Western Union was not content with the Atlantic cable situation. Two lines were British-owned and the third was French, and, although Western Union controlled the American end of the British cables through Cyrus W. Field and of the French cable through Gould's American Union lease, Gould would not feel secure until he could install his own, American-owned cable. This he accomplished during the first summer he controlled Western Union; the cable opened for service on August 15, 1881, with Gould announcing lower rates on it than its British and French competitors.[108] Within hours of its inauguration, however, Gould's cable broke, and, during the several months required to restore service, negotiations led to an agreement among all cable operators that divided traffic and revenue (87.5 percent to European companies, the remainder to Gould), reestablishing the pre-1881 practice of rate fixing.[109]

Even with the Postal company and the Mackay-Bennett cables serving as competition, "nothing Mr. Gould ever did in his life," says biographer Trumbull White, "so arrayed public sentiment against him as this creation of the telegraphic monopoly."[110] A Western Union monopoly for the past fifteen years was bad enough in the minds of many, but now it was controlled by "The Evil One." A mob surrounded the Western Union building calling for Gould's blood, the Anti-Monopoly League filled its date book with protest meetings, a rash of magazine articles argued again the merits of government and private ownership of the telegraph,[111] and there was a resurgence of postal telegraph proposals in Congress, requiring several past and present newsbroker managers to testify about the telegraph-newsbroker alliance.[112]

The postal telegraph question, dating from Western Union's emergence as a monopoly in 1866, had become a double-edged sword for publishers, who, on the one hand, profited from news delivered under exclusive contracts with telegraph monopolies but, on the other hand, had to acknowledge the success of government telegraphy in Europe and the increasing public disenchantment with the U.S. telegraphic monopoly. The following tightrope-walking act was performed editorially by the *New York Tribune* in early 1877 in response to a letter from a reader.

> There is no doubt that the mismanagement and extortionate charges of the telegraph companies have greatly stimulated public feeling in favor of a postal telegraph. Neither is there any doubt that the postal telegraph experiment in England . . . has now proved in many respects a great success, and has been of especial advantage in lowering rates. The press in particular have profited enormously by the change, and the press rates in England are now absolutely trifling when compared with the most favorable rates obtained by newspapers in this country. Nevertheless, a system of Government telegraphy would be exposed to especial dangers here, and we still believe that the original objections urged against it are likely long to have weight. . . .[113]

The forces favoring government ownership renewed the charge that AP's relationship with Western Union drew the newsbrokerage into a monopolistic web detrimental to press freedom and enlightened public opinion. One writer argued that the AP and Western Union did not "often exercise the power which they possess," but

> The fact that it exists is sufficient, and, consciously or unconsciously, influences the publisher and editor of every journal dependent on their reports. The press is not free.... Such a power over the press has hardly been possessed by any despot or censor of the press, at any time, or in any country.[114]

After examining several instances in which criticism of AP's reports by AP papers had brought a cutoff of AP service, this author observed that

> There is not a branch of service, governmental or private, not a single officer of government nor corporation, nor any individual, public or private, that the press can not and may not attack, save the New York Associated Press.[115]

Such adverse publicity sporadically surfaced throughout the 1870s and early 1880s, compounded by the appearance of Jay Gould, not only at the helm of Western Union, but also within the membership of the New York AP. Indeed, several changes in NYAP's membership had shifted the balance of power in the partnership by mid-1881, making it vulnerable to criticism because of its capitalist connections.

The post–Civil War "ring" controlling NYAP consisted of the partnership's four weakest papers—the *New York Times, Journal of Commerce, Sun,* and *Evening Express.* Their control, as chapter 1 explains, blunted the journalistic enterprise of the three stronger partners—the *Tribune, Herald,* and *World*—by forcing the latter to share their specials with the ring of four in exchange for only a portion of the transmission tolls. By the start of 1882, however, Charles A. Dana's *Sun* had risen to a more prominent position among the seven, and the *World* was slipping. The papers least affected by the passage of time were James Gordon Bennett's *Herald,* as feisty, independent, and popular as ever, and the *Journal of Commerce,* still seeking modest circulations with limited mercantile content. Co-owner William Cowper Prime was editor-in-chief of the *Journal of Commerce,* and therefore NYAP president, from 1861 to 1869, when Prime's partner, David M. Stone, assumed the paper's editorship and the NYAP presidency, holding both until 1893. Whitelaw Reid's *Tribune* also steered a successful course, mixing political Republicanism and journalistic independence.

George Jones, one of Henry J. Raymond's partners at the founding of the *Times*, had been the largest stockholder in the paper
when Raymond died in 1869, and after 1876 he owned a majority of
Times stock. The paper, despite occasional and highly acclaimed exposés of government corruption, had grown old fashioned and less
successful under Jones.[116] The *World*, which under Manton Marble
had attained remarkable and rapid success during and after the
Civil War, passed into the hands of Thomas A. Scott, president of
the Pennsylvania Railroad, after Marble became disgusted with the
outcome of the contested 1876 presidential election. Scott wanted
the paper as "a propaganda vehicle for his own stock enterprises,"
says W. A. Swanberg, but while unloading some railroad holdings on
Jay Gould in 1879, Scott threw in the newspaper. Already known as
a "pawn of capitalists," in Swanberg's words, the *World* was now
turned to the promotion of Gould's schemes, even though Gould's
ownership was widely known, "a stigma not even a good paper
could survive," comments Swanberg.[117]

Meanwhile the *Evening Express*, never an outstanding newspaper, faced a fate similar to the *World*'s. Erastus Brooks, the sole
surviving founder of the paper, relinquished control of the *Express*
in June 1877 to John Kelly, Augustus Schell, and others, but continued to write occasionally for its columns. Under its new owners the
Express "became a hack party organ," according to Brooks's obituary in the *New York Times*.[118] Late in 1881 Cyrus W. Field, of Atlantic cable fame, acquired both the *Express* and the *New York
Evening Mail*,[119] producing the first number of a consolidated *New
York Evening Mail and Express* on December 5, 1881, and benefiting
from the *Express*'s old NYAP membership. One biographer calls
Field's move into journalism "impulsive," based on a lifelong envy
of men like Horace Greeley and William Cullen Bryant, "who had
made themselves instruments of power through the printed
word."[120] Like Gould's *World*, Field's *Evening Mail and Express* was
suspected, probably with justification, of being turned to the service of its owner's various investments and stock market forays.
Field and Gould had collaborated on numerous Wall Street schemes,
and, when their financial power was joined overtly early in 1881
with Gould's conquest of Western Union and the later price-fixing
arrangement among Atlantic cable operators, the AP's *World* and
Evening Mail and Express became publicly suspect.

A third NYAP paper also had a Gould connection. In order to
wrest control of the *Tribune* from another Republican faction in

1872, Reid had turned to Gould for financial assistance to assemble a controlling block of stock. Added to a similarity of political views between Reid and Gould (which some perceived as affecting coverage of crucial elections in favor of Republican candidates who were acceptable to Gould), this link suggested that the *Tribune* belonged to the capitalists' *World* and *Evening Mail and Express* axis.[121] Here were three NYAP papers presumed by some to support not only a capitalists' image of the Republican Party, but the interests of a handful of monopolists led by Jay Gould. If one more NYAP paper of this ilk materialized, a new ring could hand the NYAP over to Gould interests.

Of the four remaining papers, Dana's *Sun* was seen as the most likely candidate to fall under Gould's influence. Dana exhibited "a mere hodge-podge of jingo programs, an irrational bundle of personal prejudices and private interests," says Vernon L. Parrington, that amounted to ruthless individualism, imperialism, and extreme capitalism of the Manchester school.[122] To some it was clear enough that, as Josephson asserts, Gould "exercised a remarkable control over the press in general through the Associated Press."[123] Another millionaire-watcher, Gustavus Myers, states the supposition more forcefully. A highly "successful and insidious method of influencing public opinion" was through Western Union and the AP.

> Distorted, misleading or false news dispatches were manufactured or artfully colored and supplied to the public press. These not only gave Gould superior underhand facilities for influencing the course of the stock market, but they were also used in favor of capitalists and against labor and radical movements at every opportunity. The public was fed on grossly perverted news accounts of strikes and labor and political movements....[124]

While some members of the New York AP were "demoralized by having Jay Gould and Cyrus W. Field [as] members," as Smith later phrased it,[125] Smith and Reid basked in the opportunity afforded by the telegraphers' presence in the NYAP. Correspondence during the first half of 1882 reveals the courtesy and harmony of comradeship among Reid, Smith, Dr. Green, Eckert, and Somerville, but beneath the surface a conspiracy to overturn the NYAP management was brewing. In New York City the *Herald* and *Times* were the most outspoken NYAP members magnifying the Gould threat. Bennett, as a matter of principle growing out of long-standing exasperation over high cable tolls, "fought Jay Gould with unrelenting ferocity," says James Creelman. Bennett once had the satisfaction of printing a ten thousand–word attack upon Bennett's personal life, an attack that Gould had sent to all the New York papers but the *Herald*.[126] In the case of the *Times*, hatred of Gould seems to have been the result of paranoid fear. The Republican paper with a penchant for exposing government corruption had occasionally been the target of those who wished to silence it in retaliation for its attacks on them or their friends. One such instance, the Tweed Ring exposés in 1871, saw the paper coming perilously close to falling into nonjournalistic hands, one pair belonging to Gould.[127] For Smith the issue of Jay Gould served as a barometer of NYAP alliances and majorities, and eventually was the factor that isolated the *Times* in the NYAP and cleared the way for the "final contest" by which a new "ring" reorganized the AP.

THE "FINAL CONTEST"

For a year and a half since early 1880 the Western Associated Press had sat on the sidelines, finding no chink in NYAP's armor and awaiting resolution of the turmoil in telegraphy. Gould and a renewed Western Union and Atlantic cable monopoly, while expensive to all newsbrokers, were not as threatening to WAP as the 1867 contract, which the NYAP refused to renegotiate and, indeed, at times hid behind. The lack of strong alternatives precluded WAP's unilateral breaking off of relations with NYAP. Potential newsbroker allies, the National AP and some of the regional AP auxiliaries, were too weak or frightened to mount a revolt, and the months-old Postal Telegraph Company was too young and small to replace Western Union as a news mover. One possible break in NYAP's fortifications came unexpectedly on September 17, 1881, when NYAP's general agent, James W. Simonton, abruptly retired. Having spent fifteen years in the post, thus equaling the tenure of his predecessor, Daniel H. Craig, Simonton moved to California to supervise his West Coast newspaper holdings and to oversee a large, recently acquired tract of land in California's Sacramento Valley. Fourteen months later, on November 2, 1882, Simonton died in Napa, worth about $200,000.[128]

Simonton's departure by itself might not have shaken the NYAP, but how he was replaced suggests that the organization had given little thought to a successor. Simonton was followed by a two-man committee consisting of James C. Hueston and "manager ad interim" Erastus Brooks, assisted by George A. Leach.[129] At forty years of age, an AP staffer since the end of the Civil War and a former AP London agent and assistant to Simonton, Hueston appears to have been properly qualified. But the fact that AP buttressed Hueston with the aging, semiretired Brooks, a member of NYAP's executive committee, suggests a lack of confidence in Hueston. Perhaps the fact that Hueston had always worked in Simonton's shadow and had had no other journalism experience made a two-headed management seem necessary to AP. A native of Baton Rouge, La., and an 1861 graduate of Princeton University, Hueston entered AP's service in 1865 after wartime service in the Confederate army.[130]

William Henry Smith watched closely to see when he could capitalize on the change of command in New York, finding, at least, that he could deride Hueston in correspondence with his WAP principals. A recent letter from New York, Smith wrote Richard Smith, was "a fair specimen of the impertinence of Hueston."

> For two days he made [Charles A.] Boynton's life a burden, by talking to him about this same thing and speaking in censorious terms of me. This was while I was in New York. He followed up his impudence there by writing [a] letter to [W. H.] French.... He thus attempts to make mischief with our subordinates.
>
> I am losing my patience at the arrogance and impudence of the three fellows who run the New York Assd. Press and claim to own the press of the whole country.... Boynton and Gallagher in the New York office are under espionages every moment. They are under lock and key, and no one is permitted to visit them without first passing the guard.... [They] live in constant dread, and never dare to speak above a whisper....
>
> Is it not time...[to] improve the present opportunity—the best that will ever offer—to clip the wings of the four N.Y. papers and assert for the great newspapers outside of New York their just share of influence?[131]

The "present opportunity" Smith referred to was an "invitation" extended to Smith by Gould and the Western Union hierarchy in May 1882 "to take charge of a large news service designed to supplant that of the New York Associated Press to all of its clients," as Smith later phrased it.[132] Harboring growing frustration with Hueston and bitterness toward three or four NYAP papers—the *Times,* the *Journal of Commerce,* the *Herald,* and possibly the *Sun*—Gould meant to break up the NYAP and saw Smith and the Western AP as useful allies in that endeavor. Through Reid and William Henry Hurlbert, Gould's editor-in-chief at the *World*, Smith was drawn in the spring of 1882 into close contact with Western Union leadership and was much impressed by the treatment they accorded him, as the following report to Walter N. Haldeman of the WAP indicates:

> Mr. Gould and General Eckert treated me handsomely and sought for and listened to advice. They pledged themselves to us, and come what may our territory is secure. But they wish to go further, and place us in possession of New Orleans, Texas, Colorado, and the Pacific Coast.
>
> I counselled delay, patience, conservative action and peace if an honorable one could be obtained....

From his new position of intimacy with the New York scene, Smith went on to characterize the pending fight over the future of the NYAP as between pro- and anti-Gould factions. Three NYAP papers—the *Tribune, Evening Mail and Express,* and *World*—he said "are openly against" the NYAP management, and "Mr. Dana told Mr. Hurlbert in my presence that the Sun was also against it."[133] Replying two days later, Haldeman confirmed Smith's rosy view of Gould's amity toward the WAP. Norvin Green, Western Union president, "has been here recruiting," Haldeman reported, and

> thinks we should have all of Alabama, Louisiana, Texas, Colorado and the Pacific.... He is much irritated against the New York Associated Press and is ... excessively angry at Hueston and declares it impossible to get along or deal with him.[134]

Nine years later Smith wrote that he "waive[d] all personal advantage involved in" the invitation, in favor of unifying WAP and NYAP, which he felt to be in "the true interests of the American press."[135] Smith's hindsight, however, launders a grimy conspiracy among Smith's WAP, Western Union's hierarchy, and the pro-Gould faction in the NYAP. The developing scheme exploited the growing friction within NYAP over the post-Simonton management and was urged on by earnest moves by the non-AP press to rejuvenate their newsbrokerage in opposition to the AP. While all of the conspirators feared new or reasserted newsbroking in opposition to the Western Union–AP axis, Gould seized the moment to attempt to wrest control of the NYAP from his enemies at the *Times, Herald,* and *Journal of Commerce,* and Smith saw his opportunity at least to elevate WAP to an equal footing with the NYAP, and perhaps to assume personal command over the entire AP system. The conspiracy within AP burst forth in June 1882, just when the opposition agency was reorganizing.

Regardless of how weak or ineffective it might be, a competing newsbrokerage was always on AP's mind. The potential for serious competition was always there, and, although unsuccessful, Smith's overture to the National Associated Press Company in May 1879 to establish an alliance that would exclude the NYAP indicates his respect for the NAP and the role it might play in his game plan. In the three years since that overture, however, the NAP had deteriorated rapidly. As a last-ditch effort, its president, James H. Goodsell, applied to Western Union for service in the spring of 1882, offering the support of the two hundred papers receiving NAP news. When Western Union rejected Goodsell's bid, NAP member Arthur Jenkins of the *Syracuse Herald* called a meeting of non-AP papers to attempt to inject new life in newsbroking outside of AP. The result was the United States Press Association, organized June 19, 1882, as a stock company under the management of Jenkins and F. X. Schoonmaker. The USPA purchased the NAP and in December 1882 leased circuits from the Mutual Union Telegraph Company. The new association underwent a total revamping in March 1883, as we shall see shortly, and sometime in the first two months of life the USPA shortened its name to the United Press.[136]

With these ominous rumblings outside AP's fortress as background, Gould, through his Western Union lieutenants and with the prior knowledge of William Henry Smith in the West, fired off an unsolicited proposal at his enemies controlling the New York AP. To "effect the most harmonious and profitable solution of the present issues," the proposal called for a tripartite "American News Association," governed jointly by Western Union, NYAP, and WAP, with a board consisting of two directors from each partner. The proposal guaranteed continued news service to present NYAP and WAP newspapers, but said that news reports could "be sold without discrimination to responsible newspapers not in the Association" with the understanding that reports "shall be sold as extensively as possible." Profits would be divided equally among the telegraph company, NYAP, and WAP.[137] While it is not clear whether Gould initially was serious about dealing Western Union into the newsbroking business (the company and other telegraphers had periodically made similar moves over the past three decades), the proposal was calculated at least to elicit NYAP's negative responses to both the sale of news to non-AP papers and a partnership with Gould's Western Union.

Smith, who had seen the proposal before it was delivered to the NYAP, replied tactfully but firmly for the record that any reorganization of news arrangements must protect AP members' franchises and "the independence of the press." His counterproposal suggested the sale of news "at all new points" where AP franchises did not exist, but did not oppose Gould's suggestion of a tripartite directorate and distribution of profits, in effect tacitly accepting the possibility of a partnership between his WAP and Western Union. Observing that NYAP's power historically had existed solely through an alliance with the telegraph company, Smith told Gould that "Without such a compact the press outside of the city of New York will not be constrained to buy the wares of the N.Y. Assd. Press, but will be free to make such combinations and contracts as they choose."[138] Within a week Gould assured Smith that the telegraph company would remain a common carrier and newspapers would continue to supervise newsbroking.[139]

By the end of June NYAP leaders predictably rebuffed Gould's proposal, offering their own, which was merely a modification of the existing 1867 contracts among Western Union, NYAP, and WAP, and thus preserved NYAP's ring of leaders and WAP's subordinate position. It would not have mattered how New York responded. Gould and Smith were simply observing the amenities of gentlemanly preliminaries, and now, with NYAP's response in hand, Western Union and the Western Associated Press notified NYAP that they intended to terminate their contracts with it, effective October 1, 1882. Simultaneously WAP and Western Union announced their agreement to write a contract, leading to the delivery of a news report after October 1 without the assistance of the New York AP.[140] Obviously enjoying himself, Smith described to Reid the serving of WAP's termination papers on the New York people. NYAP president David M. Stone and Hueston, Smith wrote,

> endeavored to stay action on our part by endeavoring to persuade Richard Smith that General Eckert and myself were seeking to betray the Western Press into the clutches of the Western Union.... Richard with dignity and delicious coolness informed Mr. Stone that there was no intrigue and that our Board in voting to terminate the contract had done so after perusing the contract proposed by [the NYAP].[141]

Stone saw Western Union behind the termination. WAP "is very unfriendly," Stone wrote to Hurlbert, "but the Western Union in encouraging that organization to take such a stand against us had gone a great way in forfeiting all claims to respect."[142] Hurlbert, Gould's editor at the *World*, sought to convince Stone that, rather than a conspiracy against NYAP, the move would damage both NYAP and WAP equally,[143] but Stone saw only "measures hostile" to the NYAP in the contract terminations and the separate Western Union–WAP agreement.[144] Stone was, of course, correct. Hueston's thought at that moment was that, in Eckert's words, the WAP "is but a rope of sand which he can separate." Hueston wanted to travel the Midwest stealing newspapers from WAP, but president Stone blocked this plan as being beyond Hueston's authority.[145] NYAP's executive committee, meanwhile, sought in vain to examine the new WAP–Western Union contract. Struggling against a rising feeling of isolation, chairman Brooks observed that neither Gould nor Norvin Green "felt at liberty upon a very earnest request from me to say that in the event of a possible disagreement between [WAP and NYAP, the Western Union] could consent to occupy a strictly impartial or neutral position."[146]

To the old ring in New York, the situation was desperate. A general agent for less than a year, Hueston had neither experience nor temperament to be relied upon. The executive committee's two members had quite different perspectives—Jones of the *Times* saw Gould's hand in the breakup and wanted to fight to the death, whereas Brooks, the semiretired representative of Field's *Evening Mail and Express*, found his loyalties divided between protecting the old ring and serving the new pro-Gould management of his own paper.

The New Yorkers, however, knew or surmised only half of the WAP–Western Union strategy aimed at them. Armed with the telegraph company's secret code and a pledge to provide all the circuits necessary, Smith quietly set out to organize an independent news service embracing Washington, the East, New England, the Pacific Coast, and Europe. When WAP's notice of termination took effect on October 1, Smith announced that he shortly would not need NYAP's news and would be prepared to sell news to New York. "Their Ex[ecutive] Com[mittee] were incredulous," Smith recalled eight years later.[147] It was the jolt that brought NYAP to its senses and at long last initiated earnest negotiations.

Earlier efforts at negotiation, during the summer and early fall, had failed because NYAP had attempted to deal with WAP from a position of superiority while undergoing internal power shifts. A new pro-Gould ring, attempting to unseat the old NYAP ring, saw its opportunity in late summer when the *Times*'s Jones, the anti-Gould leader of the old ring, was absent from the city. At a special meeting on August 12 the NYAP in Jones's absence transferred the task of reestablishing relations with the telegraph and the WAP from the executive committee of Jones and Brooks to a special committee composed of the *Tribune, World, Journal of Commerce,* and *Sun.*[148] Gould's friends were the *Tribune* and *World.* Stone of the *Journal of Commerce* as NYAP president was obliged to act as an honest broker. Everyone, however, held his breath to see which way the unpredictable Charles A. Dana of the *Sun* would jump. With WAP's executive committee, consisting of Richard Smith, W. N. Haldeman of the *Louisville Courier-Journal,* and William Penn Nixon of the *Chicago Inter Ocean*, and with William Henry Smith close at hand for guidance,[149] the two agencies agreed to meet on September 14, necessitating postponement of WAP's annual meeting.[150] "Our committee should be [in New York] the day before" meeting with NYAP, Smith advised Haldeman, "so as to have time to confer with Dr. Green and General Eckert."[151]

THE JOINT EXECUTIVE COMMITTEE

At the NYAP-WAP meeting in September, a Whitelaw Reid resolution carried, attracting affirmative votes from all but Stone. It proposed a joint board of control, consisting of NYAP's seven members and WAP's seven-director board, to take charge of both agencies' news-gathering, news-selling, and contract negotiations.[152] Two days later, however, at a NYAP meeting Dana offered a substitute resolution calling for a joint five-man NYAP-WAP executive committee composed of two representatives from each agency and a chairman chosen by the NYAP. Dana also proposed that no change in telegraph rates or existing NYAP and WAP territory be made by this committee "without the assent of both associations." Dana's proposals were tabled temporarily.[153] Reid sought equality between the agencies with overarching power granted to a large joint board of directors, but at the price of splitting the super board down the middle between representatives of the two agencies. Dana sought a smaller, more manageable joint executive committee, numerically favoring the East and subordinated to the wills of the two agencies' existing governing apparatus.

Dana's earlier support of Reid's proposal for equality between the agencies, followed two days later by his own (which seemed to preserve vestiges of the old order), singled out the *Sun*'s editor as the one equivocating New York partner, whose vote needed courting by each side. The *Times, Herald,* and *Journal of Commerce* on September 23 printed howls of outrage at Dana's vote on September 14 for a special committee, attempting to shame Dana by asserting that he had fallen in with the Gould crowd. Calling Gould ''a sharper who spares neither friend nor enemy,'' the *Times* asserted that

> if the central news association of the country, which Mr. Gould aspires to control, becomes a mere bureau of the Western Union Telegraph Company...there would not only be a few hundred newspapers ready to publish news with a Gould twist or color, but there would remain hundreds of others to which these in turn dispense the same news in more or less compressed form.[154]

Without referring to AP business, Dana privately wrote Jones defending Gould six days after the *Times* blast, saying that ''The people would a thousand times rather have [the telegraph] in Gould's hands than to have it a gov[ernmen]t monopoly in the hands of any political administration.''[155] After some backstage maneuvering in late September, Smith, Reid, and Hurlbert believed Dana had been won to their cause by an offer to make him permanent chairman of the five-man executive committee he had proposed.[156] But at an October 7 meeting of the NYAP Dana unexpectedly voted with the old ring to have the original NYAP executive committee push toward a separate contract with Western Union.[157] Dana had retreated, disbelieving that Smith and the WAP could move into New York City and set up its own national news operation.[158] Momentarily negotiations were back on square one, with Dana holding the key to the solution.

Ten days later the annual WAP meeting in Detroit produced resolutions approving the board's past actions against the NYAP and granting the board ''discretionary power to establish a full national news service,'' including invading NYAP's territory if the latter invaded WAP's area. The WAP also resolved that

> no contract shall be made with [NYAP] that shall not recognize
> and concede the territorial extensions southward and westward
> . . . and that shall not give this association an equal voice and
> control in determining expenses and in the management of all
> Associated Press matters. . . . [159]

There would no longer be any doubt in the East that WAP's membership stood behind Smith and the WAP executive committee in defiance of NYAP's old management and ring. Indeed, by October 20 Smith was arranging for a New York City office and a foreign news service.[160]

In the face of this resistance in the West, a flurry of proposals and options swirled in NYAP meetings on November 1 and 8[161] before a memorandum of agreement between NYAP and WAP emerged from behind closed doors for New York's approval on November 15. The memorandum said:

> Unite the two Associations for a term of five years, terminable after one year by a six months' notice from either party, under one joint committee, organized under the plan of Mr. Dana's resolution, which shall have entire control of rates, of the collection of news and the distribution of the same to papers now entitled to receive it, and of the whole service.
>
> *Provided*, That any new assessment of expenses shall be levied upon each association as a whole.
>
> All existing contracts of either association to be scrupulously carried out by the joint committee.[162]

At NYAP's meeting the *Herald* and *Times* voted against the memorandum, and president Stone, who abstained from the vote, ruled that failing a unanimous vote, the resolution lost. Reid appealed Stone's ruling, and only the *Herald* and *Times* sustained Stone, who again abstained. The resolution was adopted by the *Sun, World, Tribune,* and *Evening Mail and Express,* and the same four papers went on to elect the *Sun* as permanent chairman and the *Herald* and *Tribune* as members of the new joint executive committee.[163] Dana had been enticed back into the pro-Gould camp with promises of the chairmanship and adoption of his proposed five-man committee structure, tempered with the oversight super powers that Reid had proposed. Meanwhile WAP's executive committee was deciding that its own members, minus president William Penn Nixon, would occupy the West's two seats on the new committee.

Later on November 15 Whitelaw Reid, Charles A. Dana, Thomas
B. Connery (representing James Gordon Bennett's *Herald*), Richard
Smith, and Walter N. Haldeman sat down for the first time as AP's
new joint executive committee. For the next decade only the representative of the *Herald*'s self-exiled Bennett would change from
time to time. During early November, while the NYAP groped for a
plan by which it and WAP could accommodate one another, Royal
M. Pulsifer, secretary of the New England AP, having gotten wind of
a joint committee in the making, telegraphed Brooks that "In any
arrangement for Associated Press consolidation or Joint Board of
Control, the New England Press demands that it be consulted and
included." The demand was ignored.[164] Although included in WAP-
inspired meetings in 1879 and 1880 looking to a national news
"clearing house," the APs of New England, New York state, and
Philadelphia now found their fortunes dictated by the joint NYAP-
WAP committee rather than by the NYAP alone. Excluded from the
new committee, New England's AP began experiencing defections
to the burgeoning United Press, which Reid later observed "had already made serious inroads in the New England field."[165] Such con-
tributions to UP's strength set the stage for a secret AP-UP cartel
that, as the next chapter describes, arose in the mid-1880s.

The new joint committee, although favoring NYAP three members to two, was a delicately balanced instrument. The chairmanship was offered to, and accepted by, the *Sun* in exchange for Dana's
support of the new committee. "The high position of the *Herald* as a
newspaper suggested the nomination of Mr. Bennett as a member,"
Hurlbert later recalled. Reid's long association with William Henry
Smith and Cincinnati journalism satisfied WAP people "that Western interests would be safe" in Reid's hands, Hurlbert said. The
WAP was permitted to select the NYAP representatives, outside of
Dana, in exchange for a smaller representation, Hurlbert recalled,
adding, "It is absolutely certain. . .that without such pledges [the
WAP] would never have consented to accept a minority representation on the Joint Committee. . . ."[166] Finally, the *Herald* represented
the three anti-Gould NYAP papers, the *Tribune* represented the
three pro-Gould papers, and Dana represented himself and the independent course he had steered between NYAP's two camps.

At its first meeting the new joint executive committee called for
copies of each agency's contract obligations and for costs and details of existing cable news services.[167] The following afternoon the
committee (1) continued WAP's California service, eliminating

NYAP's separate service to Simonton's papers and friends in California;[168] (2) continued WAP service to Colorado and Texas, dropping NYAP's parallel service in those areas; (3) ordered the temporary extension of the contract with Reuters News Company for foreign news; (4) eliminated the duplicate Washington services then operated by the two agencies; and (5) called for meetings with the Western Union leading to a new telegraph contract.[169] The committee had economy of operation and peace on its mind, although the *Times, Herald,* and *Journal of Commerce* afterward "still threaten[ed] war and bloodshed," as Smith put it, adding "and they are encouraged by some of our own papers publishing the foolish lies of the *Herald.*"[170]

Although the new joint committee had until February 1, 1883, to negotiate a new contract with Western Union,[171] extreme pressure from the telegraph company[172] rushed the document through to execution on December 22, 1882, to take effect the first day of 1883. In exchange for favorable rates and a $15,000-per-year leased wire linking New York City, Pittsburgh, Cincinnati, and Chicago, the AP committee agreed to use Western Union exclusively and to furnish exclusively to Western Union's Gold and Stock Company all of AP's "commercial news, reports, [and] market quotations." Western Union also protected its right to fulfill contractual obligations to auxiliary AP organizations and to continue handling news reports of AP's competitors but at the same rates as AP's. Finally the telegraph company reserved the right to gather and transmit news "of disasters or events of great public interest" from locations where AP did not have agents or members and to collect "such sporting news, election news, and marine news," all to be sold piecemeal to the AP.[173]

Obviously the AP system benefited from joint action, not only by facing the telegraph company as a united force, but also by putting "an end to all causes for jealousy and wrangling" between NYAP and WAP, as R. Smith phrased it.[174] But joint action would be jeopardized as long as the agencies retained separate general agents. R. Smith asserted early in 1883 that "the intention from the first was to put our general agent in control in New York."[175] Although it may have been the "understanding" of the inner circle that William Henry Smith would be appointed joint general manager,[176] it was desirable to secure Bennett's approval[177] and necessary to convince Erastus Brooks, who wanted to continue as AP agent, that he could not do so and serve in the New York General Assembly at the same time.[178] Hueston dropped from the scene abruptly at the time of the reorganization. His obituary a decade later says he resigned in 1882 because of ill health.[179] Writing on January 10, 1883, Reid notified Smith that the joint executive committee had granted Brooks a leave of absence and had named Smith "for the present. . .to assume general charge of the whole business."[180] Four months later the NYAP abolished its office of general agent, releasing Brooks and implicitly giving Smith full charge of its affairs.[181]

Smith, although bouncing back and forth between Chicago and New York City for the next ten years, retained his home in Lake Forest, Ill., a community on Lake Michigan twenty-nine miles north of downtown Chicago, until early in 1886, when he found himself spending two-thirds to three-fourths of the year in New York City.[182] William H. French, Smith's assistant in Chicago for many years, went to New York City to oversee AP's new "Eastern Division," and Walter W. Neef, twenty- five years old and Smith's secretary in Chicago since 1876,[183] assumed the duties in Chicago of assistant general manager for the "Western Division."[184]

The Chicago office Neef inherited from Smith consisted of "two rooms in the Western Union building," according to a reporter Neef hired in 1883. The rooms were

> jointly occupied by the press association and a court stenographer, whose name and calling were painted on the two large windows facing on La Salle street, while the modest sign of the Western Associated Press was inscribed, in small lettering on the dust covered transom window over the doorway entrance to one of the rooms.[185]

Smith retained the NYAP's chief of the Washington bureau, David R. McKee, in that post[186] to please his new New York employers. But now that Smith was in New York City regularly, he moved his eyes and ears in New York for many years, Charles A. Boynton, to Washington, D. C., to keep tabs on AP affairs in the capital.[187] Boynton would be chief of the AP's Washington bureau from 1892 to 1908.[188] In addition, Smith sent George A. Leach to London as AP's agent, bowing to sentiment in the NYAP.[189] Meanwhile the New York AP attempted to placate the *New York Times*'s George Jones by electing him its president, thus breaking with the thirty-five-year tradition of automatically naming the *Journal of Commerce* editor its president.[190]

The equality gained by WAP through the new joint executive committee had its price. Only two members of WAP's executive committee actively participated in the final negotiations leading to the joint committee and the contract with Western Union. The third member, Joseph Medill, who was also WAP president for the 1882–83 term, was not even partially informed of the creation of a new joint committee until R. Smith wrote him in later January 1883. R. Smith began by saying that William Henry Smith "incidentally informs me that you have not been fully advised as to the details of the arrangements made with the New York Associated Press." R. Smith went on to say that he intended to call a meeting of WAP's board as "the best way to inform the [WAP] Directors. . . . The story is too long for me to write to the several members."[191] WAP's directors, and in turn the agency's members, thus found themselves an additional step removed from the seat of power in the AP organization.

There is no evidence that this arrangement was secret, nor is there evidence of the membership's response to being represented, at least for five years, by two specific members on a super committee on which they were outgunned three-to-two. Neither Peter R. Knights nor the author has been able to locate a copy of WAP's *Proceedings* for 1883—which is where initial membership reaction would have been recorded. The inner circle may have found it helpful to their reorganization scheme to neglect to print the minutes of WAP's next annual meeting. Previously WAP's officialdom had exhibited inclinations toward secrecy. Annual reports, often lengthy, from the executive committee and Smith, which had been mainstays in the *Proceedings* since 1869, disappeared in the 1882 volume, which was published sometime between the October 17, 1882, annual meeting and the end of that year. They did not reappear until 1891, when the old guard of Smith, Haldeman, and R. Smith were under attack for their secret cartel with United Press. The members learned at the 1886 meeting that "the Board of Directors had decided that these reports shall not be printed, on grounds of expediency."[192]

The minutes of that 1886 annual meeting give the first signs of serious membership dissatisfaction with WAP's management since the formation of the Western AP. A changing and expanding membership, indications of an evasive management, and a distancing of the seat of power from the members and their votes may be measured by the following sequence of parliamentary moves at the 1886 annual meeting: (1) objections were voiced "to the frequent custom of instructing the Secretary to cast the unanimous vote of the Association for Directors"; (2) concerned that the associations' fiscal year and the auditing committee's report were out of synchronization with the annual meetings, thus making the auditors' reports well out of date before the members saw them, members moved to change the date of the annual meeting and the responsibility of the auditing committee; and (3) a motion was offered instructing the general manager to have his annual report printed. The officers acquiesced on the first item, permitting the votes to be tallied as cast. On the other matters I. F. Mack, of the Sandusky (Ohio) Register, WAP's vice-president, who occupied the chair in the absence of president Medill, ruled the motions out of order as infringing upon the executive committee's powers. He was twice overruled on an appeal of the chair's decision, and once a substitute motion was presented. Mack, incidentally, was overruled in his decision that publishing annual reports was within the jurisdiction of the board of directors. When the motion for Smith to print his annual report was made again, it was tabled twenty-to-sixteen.[193] In the two previous annual meetings the same resolution had been offered and adopted by the membership. It read:

> Resolved, That the thanks of this Association are due, and are hereby tendered to the Board of Directors, to the Joint Executive Committee, and to the General Manager, for their efficient management of the business of the Associated Presses during the past year.[194]

No such resolution was attempted in 1886. A time bomb had, instead, begun ticking within the WAP organization that would explode in 1892. Representative association and self-governance had yielded to the joint executive committee and the need to retain R. Smith and Haldeman in its membership. These two, in turn, determined policy in collaboration with the three New York members, rather than in regard to WAP's votes and resolutions. While they no doubt observed Western interests scrupulously, at least as they perceived those interests, Smith and Haldeman operated now on a national plane, which suggested other interests to them as well. The subtle, yet definite, differences between their regional and national allegiances become obvious when the joint executive committee attempted to deal with the competition of United Press, as the next chapter describes.

DISCUSSION

With calculated daring, William Henry Smith orchestrated an assault upon contractual obligations that were subordinating his Western Associated Press to its New York counterpart. Periodically stirring the caldron with innuendos and assertions, Smith drew James W. Simonton and their respective APs into an escalating conflict based on little more than regional jealousies, fears of conquest by the other party, and exaggerated depictions of motives on both sides. The success of this bold strategy, however, rested on the friends Smith could muster within NYAP and telegraphy and on the timely departure of Simonton. Ten years of following this game plan had shown that for all its boldness, the plan could not beat the New York AP unless Smith could find allies of strength and cunning beyond his own organization.

NYAP defectors and the awesome new management of Western Union tipped the balance in favor of Smith, who now found himself a co-conspirator, armed with a secret code and able to make grand boasts of independence that his new friends would back up. It was a classic case of post–Civil War businessmen who, say Thomas C. Cochran and William Miller,

> had but to sit in their offices in great cities and press the proper buttons, call the proper clerks, dictate the pertinent letters, and their wishes would be transmitted to the proper subordinates . . . a hundred, a thousand, three thousand miles away. No village was too distant to escape the influence of New York, Chicago, St. Louis or San Francisco.[195]

And, it will be recalled, at stake in this showdown, beyond metropolitan egos, were vast territories in the West and Southwest, dotted with young villages and their struggling new dailies, which both Chicago and New York wanted to service with a news report. The warfare was forced by the AP organization with the most to gain, and while the conflict disrupted AP's internal affairs increasingly until late in 1882, one is urged to conclude that the 1882 resolution ended a power struggle that had subordinated AP's news function and would have made AP vulnerable to serious competition, had any existed.

The success of the Whitelaw Reid–William Henry Smith–Jay Gould axis to establish a joint executive committee with overarching powers to direct AP's operations (although it robbed both the New York and Western APs of a large measure of independence and self-government) was necessary if the newsbrokerage hoped to function effectively on a national scale. The bulk of AP's papers remained controlled through their regional auxiliaries' contracts with the two major APs, which in turn relied on a delicately balanced mix of joint executive committee members. The singularity of voice represented by the committee was necessary if newspaper-supervised newsbroking was to withstand Western Union's recurring desire to absorb newsbroking.

Finally, the NYAP-WAP compromise embodied by the new committee reflected the prevailing business belief that cooperation with allies was the only way to counteract aggressive competitors. Addressing the Indiana Press Association in 1873, Henry Watterson extolled the virtues of cooperation in business.

> All considerable eminence springs in a measure out of that which is called in common life the co-operative system. We are living in an epoch not of miracles but of mechanics; of multitudinous social, scientific, and professional complexities; and instead of its being true that a man of parts gets on faster and fares better without assistance and encouragement, the reverse is true. One mind aids another; one hand holds up another; one heart cheers another; and, as a man is really an able man, the greater need and use he has for his supports, for that reserved force, without which battles could never be won, nor great edifices constructed, nor political organisms set in motion, nor newspapers made up and issued. [196]

The joint executive committee and Smith's ascendancy to the general managership of the entire AP operation were major strides toward AP's structural maturity. A single policy-making committee—affecting AP's entire news apparatus and membership, forestalling divisive internal strife, and presenting a unified front to newsbroking competition and telegraphy—gave the Associated Press a strength that in the next ten years, as we shall see, permitted expansion of the news report, a wave of technological innovations, and at times an arrogant usurping of members' prerogatives. Never again could a newsbrokerage challenge AP from a merely regional base of strength; future competitors, beginning with the old United Press in 1882, would need a technological reach and a journalistic support that extended throughout the nation.

In addition to the daily packaging and moving of a news report, AP functioned to protect its members from local competitors. As noted in the previous chapters, this protectionist policy, which emerged with the formation of APs in various Eastern cities in the 1840s, encompassed the AP system nationally in the financially uncertain years following the Civil War. But in 1882, when AP finally acquired its national unity and stood ready to battle competitors under one banner, this protectionist policy hobbled AP's natural and necessary inclination to expand. If, as Watterson said, "an able man [has] the greater need and use . . . for his supports," AP could succeed, in large measure, by vigorously expanding its membership among the many "outside" papers willing, if not eager, to pay AP's prices.

Contracts and bylaws, however, officially prohibited an open-door policy until nearly halfway through the twentieth century, even though members began informally and voluntarily waiving their protest or franchise rights before 1920. The diverging perceptions of members seeking strength and protection behind AP's closed door and of a management seeking strength and protection by expanding AP's membership would clash increasingly in the decade following 1882, as we shall see. AP, therefore, was still several years away from setting a course independent of its newspaper membership, which had subordinated the newsbrokerage's fortunes to its own interests since the mid-1840s. United Press, although immature in 1882–83, was poised to offer a national news report without the entanglements and self-limitations of membership. UP's success with this commercial policy over the next decade would draw AP's leadership into cartel and trust arrangements that would threaten AP's internal harmony.

Meanwhile, although Western Union's leverage was pivotal to setting up the joint executive committee at AP, the emergence of that committee, in turn, served notice on telegraphy that newsbroking would likely remain the province of newspaper journalism. And in the area of technology, as the next chapter indicates, both AP and UP during the 1880s acquired leased lines and their own telegraph operators to an extent that the agencies' reliance on telegraph companies diminished dramatically. While newsbroking would not shake off its tangled interdependence with the newspaper institution for another three decades, by 1882 it was poised politically and technologically to chart a course independent of telegraphy.

Chapter 4
GROWTH AND A TRUST

Theoretically, [the New York Associated Press papers] are joined for the purpose of obtaining news from all parts of the world; but, practically, they are an association of customers, who receive whatever their agents decree. The agents of the Associated Press are really the masters of the Associated Press.

> ***Thompson Westcott, "The Mystery of the Associated Press," an***
> ***address***
> (February 15, 1869)

For the two columns of dispatches from all quarters in 1859, we now have page after page printed, and sometimes as much more remorselessly thrown into the waste basket—sent by telegraph and paid for, but not used, merely because the columns will not contain it.

> ***Whitelaw Reid, "The Practical Issues in a Newspaper Office," an***
> ***address***
> (June 17, 1879)

Had the newsbroker tail begun to wag the newspaper dog? Thompson Westcott's remark above, made to the Press Club of Philadelphia,[1] was probably a premature assessment by an outsider hoping to discredit AP. But when his comment finds kinship ten years later in the observations of one of those New York Associated Press "customers," one might wonder whether AP had set a journalistic course independent of, and not wholly approved of by, its members. Whitelaw Reid, however, possessed an especially critical perspective of journalism's practice, a view couched in a keen understanding of the practical pressures facing newspapers. In three recorded speeches[2] given during a thirty-year period Reid sagaciously examined these pressures, revisiting over time some of his pet notions, one of them being that too much was written about too many news

109

events to serve either the reader or the editor well. He laid this shortcoming, in part, at the door of telegraphic news-gathering.

With the advent of telegraphy the "journalist, at one leap, took the whole world for his province every morning," Reid said, asking "Why should the busy man read the history of yesterday at a greater disadvantage than the history of a hundred years ago?"[3] In historical accounts, he said in 1879,

> You are not forced to read the official documents, to burrow among the dry reports, to study with minute and painstaking care the *disjecta membra*. You are not loaded with facts that are useless, particulars that give no form or color to the picture. . . . Thousands of pages are searched to give you one, but that one is all you need to know.[4]

Returning to this theme at Yale University in 1901, Reid continued his assault on "large and long-winded papers."

> Even routine news, casual city reports, and the Associated Press dispatches from remote and unimportant points are often stretched out to an inordinate length and with wearisome detail. Far more miscellaneous news is collected than ever before—far more, in fact, than the most prolix of newspapers is ever able to print. Tedious as the published reports are, nearly every New York newspaper still throws into the waste basket, every night, masses of "copy" which the Associated Press brings it.[5]

Reid's comments struck at the heart of an AP enterprise that his dear old Ohio friend William Henry Smith had painstakingly built up for over twenty years in Chicago and New York City. The last third of the nineteenth century witnessed a steady growth in newsbroking facilities in the United States. Not only did Smith's AP system crank out ever-larger daily news reports in an increasingly complex technological setting, but Smith's United Press competitor steadily grew to fearsome proportions. Reid the editor disparaged precisely what Smith the newsbroker valued as the overt expression of his competitive and technological success.

Telegraphy's continued expansion and innovation after the Civil War gradually armed both AP and UP with the technical power to offer unified national news services to the nation's publishers and to battle each other for supremacy. As newsbrokers rushed to expand and keep each other at bay, individual publishers found their franchises in AP or UP losing value as a protection from local competition. Finally came the disheartening discovery that AP news reports, meticulously gathered, jealously protected, and expensively financed by AP editors, were being handed by AP officials to the UP, which transmitted these same reports to local non-AP competitors. Moreover, these AP officials were also exposed as holders of UP stock.

Unimpeded technological growth, attended by modest economies in transmission tolls, catered to newsbrokers' desires for fuller news reports as a way of supplanting newspapers' special reporting and making the newsbrokerage indispensable to the local editor. Expanding AP and UP news reports heightened competition between the two agencies, and, although there was clearly room for two newsbrokerages on the national scene, the resulting glut of telegraphic news dispatches led newsbroking to adopt the prevailing response of the business community to competition—the gentlemen's agreement to partition the work and the territory, followed by a stock trust that firmly shackled the competitors. This chapter traces the technological innovations and the resulting news report developments between 1875 and 1891 and examines the covert methods used by AP and UP between 1882 and 1891 to limit each other's threat. Chapter 5 picks up the story at the point at which the collusion is discovered and traces efforts at reform, restructuring, warfare, and resolution, all between 1891 and 1897.

TECHNOLOGICAL IMPROVEMENTS

Acquisitions and continual expansion caused Western Union's miles of wire to increase tenfold from 76,000 miles in 1866 to 769,000 miles in 1893.[6] Together with the Postal Telegraph and the Baltimore and Ohio Telegraph companies, Western Union afforded newsbrokers a continuously expanding horizon for reaching members and clients. Not only did circuits penetrate newly settled Western territory and finally reach small towns bypassed by earlier telegraph construction crews, but existing routes received additional lines as traffic demands grew.[7] Telegraph growth put newsbrokers in touch with more newspapers while multiple circuits on high-traffic routes permitted newsbrokers to lease wires for delivering their daily news reports with their own operators.

The earliest recorded attempt to secure a leased wire for news purposes occurred in September 1850, when Frederic Hudson of the *New York Herald* and William M. Swain, president of the old

Magnetic Telegraph Company, exchanged letters on the subject. Swain's company then operated four lines between Washington, D.C., and Jersey City, N.J., two of which continued on to New York City. If the other two lines could be extended across the Hudson River, Swain wrote, Hudson might get his wire.[8] There is no record that Hudson ever got his wire. In 1876 Western Union offered the *New York Tribune* a wire from Washington, D.C., to New York City between 5 P.M. and 2 A.M. for $5,000 per year, connected to the paper's offices in each city.[9]

This *Tribune* offer followed by more than one year AP's first leased wire, installed in 1875 between New York City and Washington, D.C.[10] "I am happy to say that the success of our experiment of leasing a wire and working it for ourselves, on the Washington circuit, has been complete," general agent James W. Simonton reported to the New York Associated Press early in 1876. His total expense for running the leased wire during 1875 was $43,090, which, when compared to the $92,118.57 expense of the Washington service the previous year, is a reduction of 53.2 percent.[11] (To understand this savings within the context of total New York AP expenses, see table 2 in the Appendix.) Supervised by Walter P. Phillips, who was then the telegraph and manifold manager for the AP, the leased line was later extended to Boston. In addition to Phillips, the early operators of the line were Joseph Christie, Thomas R. Taltavall, Fred N. Bassett, Wilfred Gove, W. H. C. Hargrave, H. A. Wells, and E. C. Boileau. These eight telegraphers were the first of a growing, and much romanticized, breed of operators who handled the taxing job of sending press dispatches as employees of newsbrokerages. Phillips, Hargrave, Wells, Christie, and Gove while on a Sunday outing during the summer of 1875 discussed ways of expediting news delivery on the new leased wire. The result of this discussion was the Phillips code, which was subsequently used extensively in press telegraphy until Teletype printers began replacing telegraph sounders and operators in newspapers offices just before World War I. The code, copyrighted by Phillips and available in pamphlet form after 1879, provided a standard set of abbreviations for words commonly found in press dispatches.[12] Below, as an example, are the first three sentences of a dispatch filed to the *Chicago Times-Herald* during the 1896 presidential campaign, in Phillips code on the left and in published form on the right.

N.Y., Aug. 14–Sar Gorman who is to b t actual mgr f Popocratic campaign, bvs Mr. Bryan wb eld President f U S nx Nov. If Mr. Gorman did n bv ts he wd n be so eager to identify hsf w a cause whose principles he cannot support. T fact tt Mr. Gorman bvs in Bryan's success dz n signify mh, for t Md Sar, w all his shrewdness & sharp pix, was nv counted a campaign prophet.

New York, August 14–Senator Gorman who is to be the actual manager of the Popocratic campaign, believes Mr. Bryan will be elected President of the U.S. next November. If Mr. Gorman did not believe this he would not be so eager to identify himself with the cause whose principles he cannot support. The fact that Mr. Gorman believes in Bryan's success does not signify much, for the Maryland Senator, with all his shrewdness and sharp politics, was never counted a campaign prophet.[13]

The author of the above example, reporter Walter Wellman, had put his story into code before handing it to a telegrapher for transmission, thus expediting the filing of his dispatch. Mastery of the Phillips code by both correspondents and telegraphers became a necessary talent for most newsbroker employees after the 1870s. As newsbrokerages hired more telegraphers to operate their leased wires, correspondents and editors were increasingly drawn from the ranks of telegraphers because of their experience in transmitting news copy and knowledge of the press code. Edwin M. Hood, for example, who later distinguished himself as AP's State Department reporter and briefly as chief of AP's capital bureau, began on December 20, 1875, in the Washington, D.C., bureau of AP as a manifolder and messenger with telegrapher aspirations. He could not attain satisfactory speeds as an operator, but armed with the code he gradually slipped into reporting on Capitol Hill and in the departments.[14] For every Hood, however, there was probably a newsbroker reporter who was better suited to be a telegrapher. Many years later Melville E. Stone, looking back on AP in the 1870s and 1880s, observed that, "Unfortunately...too many of the employees were chosen because of their familiarity with the technical side of the telegraph business, and were incapable of writing the news in interesting fashion."[15] By 1887 Western Associated Press was paying $136,612 per year for the lease of two wires and their operation.[16] As footnote c of table 3 in the Appendix points out, however, although this outlay was 51.4 percent of WAP's total telegraphic expenditure for the 1886–87 year, it had caused a reasonably small increase in WAP's percentage of telegraphic costs over the years. Although earlier figures are not available for comparison, WAP employed seventy-eight persons, who were paid an annual total of $85,412 for the year ending June 30, 1887.[17] A sizable percentage of these employees, it may be supposed, were occupied with the growing business of transmitting news on WAP's leased wires.

AP's leased wire system, however, was modest when compared to United Press's. According to Phillips's testimony before a Senate committee early in 1884, by which time Phillips was UP's general manager, UP itself had very few contractual arrangements with the various telegraph companies. Many of the metropolitan newspapers served by UP, however, leased their own wires from New York to receive UP's reports, he said, citing the case of the *Boston Globe*, which bore the entire expense of a leased wire to deliver UP to Boston. UP's use of Western Union wires in 1884, according to Phillips, extended from Pittsburgh to Columbus, Cincinnati, Louisville, St. Louis, Chicago, and Milwaukee, and into parts of Iowa, Michigan, Wisconsin, and the Dakota Territory. This arrangement, however, was between the UP newspapers and the telegraph company, Phillips told the senators.[18] Two years later Phillips could boast of UP's new "Wonderful Wire," 2,635 miles of circuit meandering between New York City and Chicago, all but 600 miles of it leased from the Baltimore and Ohio Telegraph Company. Operated from New York and employing automatic repeaters at Grafton, W. Va.; Newark, Ohio; and Cincinnati, the line carried 10,000 words of UP news copy daily between 6 P.M. and 2 A.M.[19]

One trade journal discussion of newsbrokers' use of leased wires indicates that in mid-1896 AP and UP regularly used 64,000 miles of

Western Union line, 35,000 miles (or nearly 55 percent) of which was leased, the remainder reaching newspapers "off the main lines, where there are not papers enough to warrant. . .a leased wire."[20] Leased wires expedited transmission of the news report, brought its transmission under newsbroker control, and added substantially to the agencies' personnel rosters and expenses by the late 1880s, as table 3 in the Appendix shows.

Other technical steps also expedited the movement of news following the Civil War. First came the automatic repeater, which retransmitted an incoming telegraph message onto the next circuit without the intervention of a human operator. Noting that during the winter of 1869–70 WAP's "reports had dragged along in a provoking sort of way," AP's William Henry Smith hailed the repeater in 1871. "Transmitting five or ten thousand words of news report over a line. . .2,700 miles long without rewriting was unprecedented" until the repeater was introduced, said Smith. With the repeater the report was "received in good time. . .more uniformly, more accurately, and a greater amount of news is received before twelve o'clock than formerly," Smith reported.[21] Human retransmitting of the report between New York City and Chicago was eliminated by the mid-1870s.

Improvements in telegraph printers and registers and the durability of telegraph wire also enhanced telegraphic service. But the greatest breakthrough was Joseph B. Stearns's duplex, introduced generally on Western Union circuits in the mid-1870s and followed within a few years by Thomas A. Edison's quadruplex system. Duplex telegraphy permitted messages to be sent simultaneously over the same wire from opposite ends and allowed the wire to be operated at faster speeds than older systems had permitted. "On some long lines," an observer noted in 1875, "as many messages are transmitted over a single wire [by duplex] as were sent over three wires, on the same lines two years ago."[22] Thus, AP's first leased wire could be carrying domestic and foreign dispatches to the newspapers in Philadelphia, Baltimore, and Washington, D.C., while delivering congressional news to the New York City press. Quadruplex was less useful to newsbroker service. Permitting four messages on a wire simultaneously, quadruplex was found to be more useful in public and commercial traffic than in news transmission, in which news reports and dispatches radiated from hub bureaus.[23]

One other innovation that substantially improved the movement of news during the last third of the nineteenth century was the introduction of the typewriter on the receiving end of the dispatches. John Paine, WAP telegrapher at Nashville, reportedly was the first to use the typewriter, or "the mill" as press telegraphers came to call it, for news reception. Paine started experimenting with a typewriter in 1883, and AP adopted a policy of universal typewriter reception in about July of 1885. In newspapers throughout the country AP's was the first typewriter to appear in the newsroom; the trend it started in journalism needs no explanation here. A fast typewriting receiver could copy sixty-five words per minute, twenty more than a receiver using a stylus and manifold paper,[24] but reception normally ran at forty words per minute. Both in bureaus and individual newspaper offices where news was received, the operator, seated by a telegraph sounder, would translate the Morse code sounds of the Phillips code into full words and sentences on a typewriter simultaneously as the sounder clicked away, the sounder often amplified by an overturned tin can placed over the device. Transmission continued uninterrupted for fifty-five minutes, and the operator was given a five-minute break each hour.[25]

While seemingly tedious work, typewriter transcribing of the news report was, for the operators, a vast improvement over taking the report longhand, pressing hard with a stylus on a stack of manifold sheets. New England Associated Press agent in Boston, L. E. Beard, petitioned the agency's president early in 1887 to introduce two typewriters in the office.

> For some months past, our Boston operators have been seriously complaining because they are compelled to make so many manifold copies of the report, and they find the pressure required, is bringing on writer's cramp, so that they can hardly write at times.

Enclosing a sample of an experimental typewriter-taken news report done in his office, Beard commented that the report in the West is taken by typewriter in most places and "in the New York office, they are almost exclusively used." Beard's operators were making ten or twelve manifold copies per night of five to six columns of copy. "No man can stand a pressure like this for any length of time," Beard observed. With a typewriter the "receiving operator easily keeps ahead of the sender, as the receiver can write forty words, while [the] sender cannot make better time than thirty, and sometimes twenty five words per minute."[26]

Summing up nine years of AP technological development, AP's joint executive committee reported that in 1891 leased wires were

> operated by the most skillful men obtainable, covering New England, the state of New York, on the Atlantic sea-board as far as Norfolk, to the southwest as far as New Orleans, west as far as Denver, and northwest to St. Paul and Minneapolis. Extensions have been made recently to Grand Rapids and Omaha. Two wires extend from New York to Washington, and from New York to twelve of the principal western cities. Neatly printed copy is now supplied directly from Morse instruments by means of typewriters manipulated at the rate of 40 words a minute—a revolution in the method of handling the report. . . . It is interesting to note that all improvements in machinery and in carbonized and manifold paper. . . were made by employes of the Associated Press.[27]

Except for the introduction of leased wires, efficient codes, typewriters, and in-house telegraphers, AP's method of moving news remained generally unchanged during this period.[28] Most of the news still funneled into New York City, where reports for New York papers and the Western press were assembled and the dispatches made available to agents of the various auxiliary APs. The combined management of NYAP and WAP under the joint executive committee and Smith, however, served to centralize supervision of AP's news operation even more. On the other hand, the leased wire system permitted continuous interacting among AP's domestic agents, thus permitting extraordinary news bulletins to move immediately throughout the AP system from any bureau on a leased wire. Indeed, sometime prior to 1890 AP had instituted a "call 95," which when transmitted by a bureau signaled the network that it had a priority bulletin to file.[29] Some trust was, thus, extended by the management to its bureau chiefs.

Although all of these innovations might have cut the costs of telegraphing messages and press dispatches (and did in the 1870s),[30] Western Union's dominance in the field by the early 1880s freed the company of competitive pricing, allowing it to concentrate on high profits and dividends and the rising threat of a labor movement among its telegraphers. Even with special contractual rate reductions, newsbrokerages regularly sought lower rates or larger daily word allowances. WAP's original 1867 contract with Western Union provided for 6,000 words per day at $60,000 per year (3.2 cents per word).[31] The next year the report expanded to 8,700 words per day at $80,000 per year (2.9 cents per word). The addition of Memphis and Nashville to WAP's 8,700-word-per-day service in 1871 brought the annual rate up to $95,000 (3.5 cents per word). Strenuous negotiations in 1878 resulted in a $10,000 reduction for the 8,700-word-per-day report (3.1 cents per word). And during 1880–81 the report was increased to 10,000 words per day at the old $85,000-per-year rate (2.7 cents per word).[32] With the appearance of the joint executive committee and the joint NYAP-WAP contract with Western Union, signed December 22, 1882, the arrangement was placed on a different footing. The option of WAP's first leased wire at $15,000 per year was added to NYAP's leased wire between New York City and Washington, D.C. (The leased wire between New York City and Boston was under a separate contract with the New England AP.) Otherwise, AP's tolls for dispatches transmitted beyond the leased wire network were at a per-word rate that was a fraction of commercial rates.[33]

Table 3 in the Appendix reveals several facets of the WAP-telegraph relationship. First, the annual payments to Western Union usually exceeded contractual amounts up through 1881–82 because WAP's demand for news regularly exceeded the daily word allotments, throwing WAP's telegraphic expenses into a per-word rate, generally totaling about $10,000 per year above contracted rates. WAP generally confined its telegraphic tolls to about 60 percent of total expenses, while the agency's contribution to Western Union's revenues gradually declined and never amounted to much. (The telegraph company clearly benefited from these contracts more through editorial support than through revenue.) The introduction of leased wire service after 1883–84, however, caused the telegraphic portion of WAP's expenses to rise dramatically, resulting in deficit years for WAP more frequently and boosting WAP's contribution to the telegraph company. The index of expenses for the two concerns in table 3 emphasizes how WAP's growth rate caught up with Western Union's during the 1880s, surpassing the latter finally in 1891–92, based in part on WAP's expanding commitment to leased telegraphic service. As footnote c in table 3 notes, however, only 50 or 60 percent of the growing telegraphic expense was due to leased wire service. Throughout the system, more was being spent to move a larger news report to members.

A BROADER NEWS REPORT

Writing to New England AP president W. W. Clapp in the fall of 1890, Smith boasted that

> The Associated Press is growing in strength every day. We are just contemplating extending our wire system largely, and expending a large additional sum of money for improvement of the service. Of course, New England will share in these benefits, but without being called on to pay anything additional.[34]

In 1891 Smith said the news report on the leased wires averaged over 40,000 words per day, 45 percent of which originated in the West and the remainder east of the Alleghenies.[35] This is nearly three times the daily average of 14,459 words of news report moved just ten years earlier by WAP.[36]

Other parameters of the news report's growth are also significant. Between 1882 and 1891 copy going into New York from Washington, D.C., Baltimore, and Philadelphia grew from 9,000 to 15,000 words per day.[37] As for cable news, according to Smith, comparative annual totals of words received in 1882 and 1891 were as follows: general news, 362,821 and 525,647; shipping news, 16,739 and 64,346; markets cabled in open English as part of the general news in 1882, 23,735, and none in 1891, and markets cabled in code, 26,280 and 18,342, giving a total of 405,840 words in 1882 and 632,070 in 1891. Smith pointed out that since each item of cable news "is sent as closely condensed as possible," each cabled word was the equivalent of at least five words of news copy and each code word equaled fifteen words, yielding in 1891 2,650,000 words of general news, 322,000 of shipping news, and 395,000 of market news for a total of 3,367,000 of actual news copy from cable dispatches.[38] While it must be assumed that most of AP's 1882 cable news originated in the Reuters-Wolff-Havas cartel, with which AP had an exclusive contract, part of the 1891 cable news was coming from AP correspondents stationed in various foreign news centers. Although AP in 1891 still had only the one foreign bureau in London, where the cartel news was handed over, part of the latter year's cables came from AP men temporarily assigned to such places as Paris, Rome, and Berlin.[39] After the turn of the century, as chapter 7 notes, AP's foreign news staff grew rapidly, even though the cartel continued in effect.

In Washington, D.C., AP had shifted its mission between 1882 and 1891. For many years, as Washington Bureau chief David R. McKee observed in 1891, "there was no trust or confidence expectant that the Associated Press would furnish from Washington a first-class report. . .on any given subject outside the barest routine." Newspapers' special correspondents prowled the capital unearthing many of the major stories, often giving them political slants consistent with their employers' editorial policies. AP concentrated on stenographic accounts of congressional floor debates and verbatim texts of speeches, documents, and presidential messages.[40] AP's status as recorder of congressional proceedings, in fact, was assured when its representatives alone received desks on the floor of the House on February 26, 1866, and of the Senate on March 12, 1873.[41] Newsbroker reporters late in the nineteenth century, however, began discovering where the real Washington news was lurking.[42] McKee notes that the regular AP capital coverage in 1891 included

> reports of executive sessions of the Senate, secret committee meetings, caucuses, . . .interviews with selected men of prominence. . .and well-planned, elaborate, and well-written descriptions. . .of such notable events as a Presidential inauguration, . . .a wedding at the White House, a great military funeral, . . .the sudden death of a Chief Justice, a Secretary of the Treasury or a United States Senator.[43]

Edwin M. Hood recorded an AP staff of fourteen reporters and editors in the Washington bureau in mid-1888.[44]

The quadrennial presidential nominating conventions drew special effort from the AP, which in 1872 began providing gavel-to-gavel coverage of "every point of interest and interests diverse being developed, so as to meet every variety of taste and opinion," said William Henry Smith,[45] who maintained that AP's

> descriptions of the scenes occurring in the halls during sessions of the various conventions were made with such photographic accuracy as to give the readers of the newspapers in distant cities a clearer idea of what was said and done than was possible to most persons who were actually present.[46]

By 1876 AP carried a running report of conventions for afternoon papers and a full verbatim report for morning papers.[47] AP was employing this system of dual convention reports in 1888, when it had a force of twenty reporters covering each convention.[48] Smith in

1892 reported that the total cost of maintaining reporters and operators to cover four national conventions that year was a mere $4,053.73.[49]

Even a casual reading of AP newspapers between 1875 and 1895 reveals the growing presence of newsbroker copy in newspaper columns. The volume of foreign news increased steadily during this period, as did the amount and diversity of Washington news. The effect of the cable is apparent in previous-day datelines on foreign stories, and the increased effort to serve evening papers is seen in the larger number of same-day datelines in these papers' columns. Susan R. Brooker-Gross, sampling selected newspapers between 1839 and 1899 for trends in time lag between a news event and its publication, found dramatic reductions in time lag after the Civil War in domestic and foreign news, with the former reaching one-day lags in 1879 and approaching a half-day in 1899. Foreign news reached roughly a $1^1/_2$-day lag between 1874 and 1884, later inexplicably retreating to levels between $2^1/_2$ and four days.[50] Concurrently large newspapers' reliance on special correspondence and foreign letters and the previous widespread use of clips from exchange papers diminished during this period. Newsbrokerages, however, still attributed some of their news items to newspaper accounts, especially in the foreign field.

While one still finds many short one- or two-paragraph news items about crimes, new laws, accidents, and the like, reminiscent of the pre–Civil War news reports described in volume 1, the late-nineteenth-century newsbroker's reports also contained many longer and more detailed stories, especially on political, governmental, and military subjects. The topics covered in the post-1866 news reports do not differ appreciably from pre–Civil War reports, newsbroking's preoccupations having been established very early, but the emphasis, as measured by quantity and detail, was shifting to topics of genuine national interest. One new feature of the report after the Civil War, however, was the growing coverage of sports events, looming quite prominently by the end of the century. Boxing, yachting, and horse racing were among the very earliest sporting events covered by AP, but by the early 1890s demand in some quarters for baseball coverage had thrown AP a curve. Members of the New England AP in 1890 requested full box scores of games in both the National and Players (or Brotherhood) leagues, and William Henry Smith reluctantly obliged,[51] but only after his alternative plan to supply scores by innings and a brief game summary

121

was overruled in New York City. Full scores for games played in the farflung leagues occupied two hours each night on AP's circuits,[52] explaining AP's desire to send only abbreviated coverage. Smith, nevertheless, reported in 1891 that "The racing and sporting news has been largely increased; the total per night during the season, of this class of matter, being from 5,000 to 6,000 words, which is an increase of over 40 per cent as compared with the service of last year."[53]

Brevity remained a virtue in newsbroking copy, because even though the technical capacities and the size of the news report increased, the agencies increased the number of stories in their reports. Clipped and reconstructed language (such as "smorning" for "this morning"), cablese, and codes helped economize on telegraph time and costs, but correspondents were regularly admonished to strip their dispatches to essential facts and to file brief first stories or bulletins and await further instructions before sending more copy. A sheet of instructions to New England AP agents in 1883 says,

> Sharp condensation, without omitting essential facts, is eminently desirable, and the efficiency and value of an agent are largely measured by his capacity and skill in this direction: *"Get the most and clearest ideas into the smallest space,"* is the modern journalistic injunction. To get *all the news* is the first and foremost thing, but to get it economically is of scarcely less importance.[54]

Twenty years later AP was telling its correspondents that

> When the news is of extraordinary character, or very sensational, file at once a bulletin of one hundred words, and await instructions before sending the details... A story should be told as briefly as consistent with an intelligent statement of the facts. The news should be given in the first paragraph, details following.[55]

One finds in such instructions a description of what twentieth-century journalists call the summary lead and the inverted pyramid story structure.

Not all newsbroker copy was routine and formularized. As the network expanded, the agencies increased their news staffs and, thus, their capacity to cover more news events directly, even in remote regions, rather than relying on members' coverage, and to bring them to the public's attention more rapidly. Opening this network to descriptions of the blizzard of 1888 or the Johnstown flood or the assassination of President James A. Garfield and the subsequent trial and hanging of Charles J. Guiteau propelled such events onto a national stage instantly, forcefully, and with a single first-day account for newspaper readers throughout the nation. An exception was coverage of the western Indian Wars, in which newsbrokerages took a subordinate role to newspapers' special correspondents, as was the case in the Civil War.[56]

Meanwhile newsbrokers were discovering that the right combination of correspondent, writing, and news event could capture not only the public's attention, but the profession's admiration. John P. Dunning, for example, produced what may have been AP's first truly memorable piece of writing. In March 1889, Dunning of AP's San Francisco bureau was covering an international dispute over control of the Samoan Islands when a hurricane struck the harbor at Apia, where German, British, and U.S. warships were anchored. All but a British vessel were destroyed, the loss of life was heavy, and efforts by natives, who braved their own disaster to rescue surviving sailors, were heroic. Dunning's lengthy and graphic eyewitness account, datelined March 30, took two weeks to reach San Francisco by mail, appearing as a copyrighted AP story in U.S. dailies on April 13 and 14. It was, despite its lateness, a milestone in newsbroking reporting. Melville E. Stone later wrote that the story revealed that

> an Associated Press man might not only be capable of securing exclusive news, but might also be able to write it in a creditable way. . . .
> Mr. Dunning's graphic story . . . will long be accepted as a masterpiece of descriptive literature. . . . It was a revelation to those who had long believed the organization incapable of producing anything more exciting than a market quotation.[57]

Although space does not permit reprinting the entire story here (which the reader can find published in New York's *Times* and *Tribune* and in an edited form in the *New York Herald*, all on Sunday, April 14, 1889), the following excerpts give the flavor of Dunning's writing.

> Apia, Samoa, March 30—The little group of Samoan or Navigators' Islands, which a few months ago attracted the attention of the civilized world by a fierce civil combat between two native factions, and the consequent possibility of serious complica-

tions between the great Powers of the United States and Germany, has been visited by a disaster more appalling than all of the wars ever waged here. . . .

The most violent and destructive hurricane ever known in the South Pacific Ocean passed over these islands on March 16 and 17, and as a result a fleet of six warships and ten other vessels were ground to atoms on the coral reefs in the harbor, or thrown on the beach in front of the little city of Apia; and 142 officers and men of the American and German navies sleep forever under the reefs, or lie buried in unmarked graves, thousands of miles from their native lands. . . .

The beach is strewn with wreckage from one end of the town to the other. Over 900 American and German sailors are quartered in Apia, and for a few days after the storm subsided the greatest confusion existed everywhere. A large number of men on the . . . vessels were badly injured by falling from the rigging and being thrown about decks by the terrible seas, and it was necessary to provide a temporary hospital for them. A great many men from the wrecked vessels became intoxicated as soon as they reached the shore. Every one was drenched with the rain, but stood shivering in the storm, prepared to render whatever assistance might be possible.

The force of the storm was never equalled in this part of the world before. The barometer had been falling steadily for several days previous to the storm and the wind began to blow Friday afternoon, March 15, and continued until Sunday morning. The rain fell in torrents during the whole time, and great clouds of sand swept over the town. Hundreds of people stood on the beach and watched the awful spectacle in the harbor. The vessels all had a full head of steam on, and three or four anchors out. Their yards and topmasts were down, and every precaution was taken to insure the safety of the ships, but the wind constantly shifted from northeast to northwest. The force was so great that the vessels dragged their anchors all over from one side of the bay to the other, and came into collision a dozen times. . . .

Political Campaign Reporting

Postwar newsbrokers, and especially AP, with its ties to the Western Union monopolists, grew to be obvious targets of the criticism that they manipulated election returns and unduly influenced the electorate. One celebrated AP dispatch just before election day in 1884 has, for example, been often cited as causing the defeat of Republican presidential candidate James G. Blaine. One week before the election and favored by two to one to beat Grover Cleveland, Blaine attended a meeting arranged to show ministers' support for his candidacy. One speaker, the Rev. Samuel Dickinson Burchard, ended his otherwise mundane political address with: "We are Republicans, and do not propose to leave our party and identify ourselves with those whose antecedents have been rum, Romanism, and rebellion." The AP's Frank W. Mack, possibly the only newsman covering the meeting, focused on those last four words in his dispatch, which moved throughout the AP system. Burchard's well-intentioned remark backfired, and, as the polls opened a few days later, Cleveland, the eventual winner, was favored by ten to nine.[58] The consensus has been that Mack's attention to this phrase and AP's decision to cover the meeting in the first place influenced the election's outcome.

"Rum, Romanism, and rebellion" is only the best-remembered instance of a string of quadrennial accusations that either AP or Gould's Western Union or both tampered with presidential elections. Suspicions of the power of the press to influence voters and election outcomes, although always fuel for political debates, began to embrace the Associated Press in 1872 when several AP editors were prominent in the Liberal Republican movement to unseat Ulysses S. Grant. Most prominent, of course, was New York Tribune editor and NYAP partner Horace Greeley, the eventual candidate of the Liberal Republicans and Democrats. But serving as convention moguls and the tools of Greeley's nomination in Cincinnati in May 1872 were members of the famous Quadrilateral, a handful of AP editors—Samuel Bowles, Horace White, Murat Halstead, Henry Watterson, and Carl Schurz—whom Whitelaw Reid, Greeley's floor manager and managing editor, later joined. Commenting on the Cincinnati convention, Watterson later wrote, "One might have mistaken it for an annual meeting of the Associated Press."[59]

Whether AP's coverage favored Greeley's candidacy was a roundly debated matter at the time, even among supposedly knowledgeable newspaper editors, as the following exchange in late July of 1872 reveals.[60] It began with an item in the Pittsburgh Mail, a non-AP paper, which said,

> If any reader has any doubt as to the political bias of the Associated Press telegraph reports, let him read them carefully as

they appear in the [Pittsburgh] *Post* and *Chronicle*. The editor of the reports for the Western newspapers is in the employ of the Western Associated Press, but, of course, depends for his news on the New-York Press, which, just now, is conducted, with two exceptions, in the interest of the Tammany Liberal candidates.

One of the "Tammany Liberal" partners of the New York AP, the *Express*, hastened to defend AP's news coverage.

This is but a sample of the falsehoods afloat. The General Agent of the Associated Press is Anti-Greeley and Anti-Democratic, and Pro-Grant; while the *New-York Times*, with the *Herald* and *Express*, make up the Executive Committee of the New-York Association. Partisanship is carefully eschewed in receiving or sending news.

To this, one of the "Pro-Grant" NYAP partners, the *Times*, demurred.

Without at this moment entering into the above discussion, we may say that the remarks of the *Express* as to the Executive Committee of the Associated Press may be technically correct, but at this moment they are calculated to create a false impression. The *Times* takes no part in the direction of the Association, owing to the temporary absence of its publisher. The Executive Committee is, therefore, in the hands of gentlemen favorable to the "Tammany Liberal candidates," as the *Pittsburg Mail* says.

Such seemingly endless debates were pursued vigorously in postwar campaigns because the last third of the nineteenth century witnessed some of the nation's closest presidential elections, accompanied by the longest sustained peak of voter participation in the nation's history.[61] High voter interest both situated newsbroking at the center of the quadrennial spectacle and increased public sensitivity to newsbroking's performance. The highest voter turnout ever, 81.8 percent, was registered in the contested Hayes-Tilden race of 1876, a race that found William Henry Smith and others in the Western AP in the thick of the political battle. In 1875 Rutherford B. Hayes, just re-elected governor of Ohio for a third term, was already receiving favorable notices in the AP's report in anticipation of the Republican national convention, a year away.[62] Smith, it will be recalled, had been Hayes's staunchest supporter back in Smith's pre-WAP days in Ohio, and now, from a seat of press power in Chicago, Smith was watchful and expectant, eager to assist Hayes's star to ascend over the Midwest. The WAP general agent is viewed in history as "Hayes's closest personal friend,"[63] and as "one of his closest friends and advisers. . . . This friendship was warm and personal and Hayes had no secrets from Smith whose advice he often sought and whose opinions he respected."[64] A contemporary spoiler's attack of Hayes puts an interesting twist on this old Ohio friendship. "William Henry Smith was governor as well as secretary of state. . . . [T]he good and gushing Rutherford B. Hayes merely played the part of a dumb Indian at the door of the great Ohio tobacconist."[65]

The record is clear that Smith and some WAP editors and cronies orchestrated some key steps leading to Hayes's presidency.[66] Smith intimated to Hayes his use of the news report for political purposes.

> I have never asked a favor of anyone for myself. I have studiously kept in the back ground while pushing others to the front. With all the means for advertising under my control, I have forbidden it for myself.[67]

Being, as Harry Barnard says, "a potent behind-the-scenes political manipulator,"[68] Smith generally worked overtly through the circle of Republican publishers and correspondents available to him through the WAP. At two crucial moments—when nomination-rival Blaine's bubble needed bursting in the spring of 1876 and when in December 1876 the South had to be scoured for a few electoral votes—a clutch of WAP people quietly swung into action. The names are all familiar: William Henry Smith; W. R. Holloway, *Indianapolis Journal,* a WAP director in 1868–69; Richard Smith, *Cincinnati Gazette,* a WAP board and executive committee member for twenty-two years; Murat Halstead, *Cincinnati Commercial,* two years a WAP director and seven years its president; Andrew J. Kellar, *Memphis Avalanche,* a WAP director for six years; Henry Van Ness Boynton, national correspondent for Richard Smith's *Cincinnati Gazette* and other papers and the older brother of William Henry Smith's New York City agent, Charles A. Boynton; and, tangentially, Joseph Medill, *Chicago Tribune,* WAP board and executive committee member for twelve years and its president for three years.[69] The particulars, more political than journalistic and readily available elsewhere,[70] need not concern us here, except for the fact that the Western AP was the host agency for these machinations.[71] A week after election day, as the three-month ordeal of resolving the contested election was just commencing, Hayes wrote Smith, "Perhaps I ought to say a word how much I am obliged to you. No correspondence during the 144 days has been so valued as you, and my debt dates before and is likely to grow after that period."[72]

AP's operations were unaffected by this adjunct political activity, but Smith was rewarded for his efforts with an appointment as Hayes's collector of the port of Chicago. To Hayes it seemed appropriate. Hayes later wrote his daughter, Fanny, that Smith was "my old friend and staunchest and most efficient political supporter."[73] The appointment also seemed appropriate to Smith, who served efficiently as collector throughout the Hayes administration without relinquishing his position with the Western AP. But the appointment seemed improper to Joseph Medill, who, having been surprised by both Hayes's offer and Smith's acceptance, privately expressed his opposition to the whole affair. In a long, bitter note Medill told Smith,

> You should have explained to me how it would be possible to hold both offices without interference or trenching on the General Agency business, how you could avoid getting into conflict with the Democrats while holding a Federal office. . . .

Medill then reveals a personal motive, asking how the *Tribune* can escape the Democrats' "vengeful blows" with Smith in the custom house.

> I have a fresh and lively recollection of what I suffered at [the Democrats'] hands last campaign on account of alledged [sic] partisan unfairness in respect to reports of meetings sent or suppressed by the General Agent.[74]

Hayes notified Smith of his appointment as collector on September 4, having noted that the post was not equal to Smith's "merits," and after Smith had turned down a foreign mission.[75]

The *Toledo Blade* reported, "For once all the papers have united in approving a Presidential appointment. . . . Make a note of this, for another centennial will elapse before such a phenomenon is again witnessed." From the *Chicago Times*:

> The press, republican, independent, and democratic, is united on William Henry Smith. No appointment of the president was ever so universally endorsed. It must be as good as the privilege of reading one's obituary notice for . . . Smith to peruse the kind words said of him by all the papers.

Medill's *Tribune* permitted itself only to quote the *Philadelphia Times*, which said

> It is gratifying to learn that...Smith...will still continue to discharge the duties of Agent of the Western Associated Press. This is especially pleasing to newspapers who have had occasion to notice the non-partisan and independent manner in which William Henry has fulfilled his duties.[76]

Smith resigned from the custom house position in December 1881 because of "private business" and his health.[77]

After Jay Gould acquired control of Western Union early in 1881 and in light of that company's insistence throughout the 1880s on being free to gather and compile election returns beyond AP's reports, it became the practice to suspect Western Union of tampering with the unofficial voter tally on election nights. And since AP relied in part on the telegraph company's figures, it too was suspected. In 1884, figures compiled by Western Union and used by AP showed James G. Blaine as carrying New York state. When AP and Blaine papers began correcting their figures two days after the election, giving New York (and the presidency) to Grover Cleveland, the *New York World,* sold the previous year by Gould to Joseph Pulitzer, charged that

> During the past two days Gould, by false reports of election figures through his telegraph agencies has been executing his share of the plot by preparing Republican partisans for a fraudulent claim that the vote of New York has been cast for Blaine and Logan.

The *World*'s charge sent a furious crowd into the streets, first threatening Whitelaw Reid's *New York Tribune* and then calling for Gould's scalp at the Western Union building. Swift police action protected the two establishments.[78]

Pulitzer, with memberships in both the Western and New York APs, proved to be a constant political thorn in Smith's side. Responding to an editorial criticism of AP in Pulitzer's *St. Louis Post-Dispatch* in mid-1884, Smith wrote Pulitzer that

> the only relation the Associated Press holds towards the W.U. Tel. Co. is one of antagonism. As to Cyrus W. Field, he is the proprietor of a paper as is Mr. Bennett or Mr. Pulitzer, but he has not sought to control anything that I know of.[79]

Again in early October of 1884 a Pulitzer letter prompted this reply from Smith.

> You know very well that there is no partizanship [*sic*] in the management of the Associated Press. The records of our office will show an impartiality and a faithfulness never excelled by any judge of any court of the land.[80]

And after the 1884 election, when Smith was pressured by a barrage of *World* criticism into firing William H. French for having telegraphed Blaine with an opinion that the latter was carrying New York state, Smith appealed to Pulitzer to cease.

> I have always believed and do believe that you are a generous hearted man. Yet the way in which the *World* pursues poor French suggests that the nervous strain of the last year has sealed up the door to your heart....[Y]ou not only refuse to show him mercy, but you jump upon him when he is down.
>
> This is not like the Joseph Pulitzer I once knew; and if he is to be forever lost, I shall never cease to regret the share I had in bringing him into this wicked New York world.[81]

In the wake of the 1884 election a committee composed of Walter N. Haldeman and Charles A. Dana found AP's election coverage to have been "managed with judicial fairness and with a conscious regard for the rights of all parties," as Smith put it. "The violence of the attacks on the Associated Press in partisan newspapers," Smith observed, "has been equalled only by the untruthfulness."[82] To UP partisans, the uproar was an opportunity. *The Journalist,* a trade weekly, dubbed the Dana-Haldeman report "a mass of lies," "a falsification of the facts," a "whitewashing [and] fraudulent report." This publication, however, had earlier revealed its bias, calling Smith "a tiresome old fraud who is kept where he is, probably, because of the thorough harmony between himself and the age-worn and failing institution of which he is the paralytic head." Calling AP's election returns "weak, vacillating and uncertain," *The Journalist* described AP as "a gibbering, tottering old wreck. Like a superannuated old virgin, it is fit for nothing but to gossip idly about its neighbors and spread injurious rumors based upon little else but imagination."[83]

THE FIRST UNITED PRESS

Walter Polk Phillips was born on a farm near Grafton, Mass., in June 1846. As a boy he was attracted to telegraphy, first as a messenger and then as a telegrapher whose speed in receiving by sound won contests and recognition in telegraph circles. At the age of twenty-one, attracted to journalism, he reported for the *Providence Journal* and later was city editor and managing editor for the *Providence Herald*. In 1871 he went to New York City as a reporter for the *Sun*, and after short stints with Western Union[84] he became, as we have seen, one of eight operators on AP's first leased wire in 1875. This made Phillips an AP employee, and a valuable one given his previous journalism experience. Within two years he was summoned to New York City from Washington, D.C., to assist general agent James W. Simonton with administrative duties.[85]

Dissatisfaction with AP's Washington bureau's coverage developed, principally in the WAP, early in 1878. At sixty-one and chief of the bureau for at least two decades, Lawrence A. Gobright was finding it harder to meet the post–Civil War demands for more news that would satisfy a wider spectrum of regional interests and journalistic tastes. William Henry Smith and Simonton conferred in Washington, and Gobright hired "Hayes and Devine, the two best reporters in Washington," as Simonton later reported to Smith. But problems continued. Finally sometime prior to early June 1878, Simonton sent Phillips back to Washington to take charge of the agency during the remainder of the session.[86] A nineteen-year-old messenger and manifolder in AP's Washington office, Edwin M. Hood, noted in his diary on July 8 that "Mr. Gobright has been deposed and succeeded by Phillips. Likewise [William] Barr has been succeeded by Holland and Mudd"[87] as agents for Southern AP papers. Gobright's retirement was announced in August 1879,[88] and he died May 14, 1881.[89]

Four years later and still Washington bureau chief, Phillips encountered the widening political rift within the New York AP membership, prompted by the rise of Jay Gould and his associates (William Henry Hurlbert, Cyrus W. Field, and Whitelaw Reid) in the agency. During congressional foreign affairs hearings in the spring of 1882, Phillips permitted several witnesses to read and correct AP reports of their testimony, including James G. Blaine and NYAP's Hurlbert, before they were transmitted to newspapers. Especially to the *New York Times*, extending this privilege gave Blaine and Hurlbert undue political advantage. Phillips admitted that Blaine

> read and corrected every line of [his testimony in AP's report] making many changes some of them verbal, some of them evident errors of the reporter, and some of them involving such considerable alteration in the phraseology that they were rejected, and we adhered to our own version.

Stating that this had been a long-standing AP practice, that such privilege was permitted under the rules of evidence in the District of Columbia, and that he was attempting to quiet numerous complaints that the report had not fairly represented the hearings, Phillips stood by his actions, which were referred to the NYAP's executive committee, dominated by anti-Blaine papers. New York AP's general agent at this time, James C. Hueston, consequently fired Phillips as of May 13, 1882, replacing him with David R. McKee. Hood, who by this time had begun doing some reporting for AP under Phillips's tutelage, told his diary, "The entire office is completely demoralized. My feelings I don't care to express." Phillips appealed to Hurlbert and Reid, but to no avail.[90]

At this point, it will be recalled from the previous chapter, the WAP with the help of Gould's Western Union was making a show of splitting off from the NYAP to force a change in the latter's management. William Henry Smith as part of this display contracted for separate European news service and established WAP bureaus throughout the East. At this juncture, about November 1,[91] Phillips reappeared in AP's Washington office, along with P. V. DeGraw, another former NYAP capital reporter, representing the WAP for Smith. Before Phillips and DeGraw could get fairly under way in their new posts, the NYAP and WAP realigned under the new joint executive committee, and Smith released both men on November 21.[92] Such mistreatment at the hands of AP pushed Phillips and De-Graw into the waiting arms of United Press. Late in 1882 Phillips became UP's Washington bureau manager and early in 1883 its business manager in New York. On October 1, 1883, Phillips became UP's general manager, replacing F. X. Schoonmaker, who had held the post from the time it absorbed its National Associated Press Company predecessor in June 1882.[93] DeGraw was named UP's Washington bureau chief in November 1883.[94]

Letting Phillips go may have been Smith's worst blunder at AP, because Phillips's experience in both telegraphy and journalism was precisely what a struggling young newsbrokerage like UP needed to get its operation in motion. Phillips was a master at finding economical telegraphic routes outside the Western Union system. His staff, though thin, could at times beat the AP news machine. After nearly a decade and a half of half-hearted, inferior competition for AP, stretching back to Hasson's News Association in 1869, here at last was a news competitor with a manager strong enough to shake AP's confidence.

Listing barely one hundred subscribers in mid-1882, UP had grown to 166 papers in two years. Table 1 in the Appendix breaks this total down by state and region and compares UP's 1884 figures with AP's total of 425 in 1883. It is clear from these figures that Phillips suffered principally from a lack of telegraphic facilities. The Mackay Postal Telegraph Company, it will be remembered, was still building in 1884 and was largely an Eastern concern, and this was where Phillips could reach his customers, as table 1 indicates. He registered between 50 and 60 percent of AP's membership in New England, the Middle Atlantic States, and the East North Central region, and he had a third of AP's totals in the Plains and Southern states. But in the Southern, Mountain, and Pacific regions he needed circuits, which Western Union was willing to provide but for which Phillips refused to sign an AP-style all-or-nothing contract. Underlining his reliance on alternative circuits, Phillips in early 1884 told a Senate committee, "I cannot see any future for an opposition press association unless there is an opposition telegraph company." [95]

The mainstays of the UP service in the early 1880s were the *Boston Globe* and the *Chicago Herald.* Both substantial papers outside of AP, they paid, because they could, much more than other UP papers for the same news report. Indeed, Phillips, writing Stephen O'Meara of the *Boston Journal* in 1890, commented that

> it was the stupidity that was shown by the Associated Press in keeping out such papers as the Boston Globe in New England and the Chicago Herald in the West, that made it possible for The United Press to grow up into the solid institution that it is to-day. [96]

The *Globe,* founded in 1872 by Maturin Ballou, was dying when Charles H. Taylor took it over after its first eighteen months. Because it was too new and shaky at the start and later under Taylor too aggressive and successful, the *Globe* was denied AP member-

133

ship by its Boston competitors, forcing it to establish its own staff of New England correspondents and to seek alternative newsbroking service. In February 1882 the *Globe* was the only Massachusetts client of the National Associated Press Company, which replaced the American Press Association in 1876 and preceded United Press.[97] In spite of second-class newsbroking service, the *Globe* was immensely successful in Boston because, as one Taylor biographer put it, it was "the paper that was different."[98] A less approving appraisal of Taylor's journalism is provided by Oswald Garrison Villard, who charged that Taylor "led the profession downward" in Boston with "sensational headlines and 'played up' crime."[99]

The *Chicago Herald* was another recent entry in a field crowded with AP papers. Founded in 1881 by James W. Scott, the *Herald* had within a decade, according to Frank Luther Mott, "become one of the handsomest papers in the country, had gained the second place among Chicago papers in circulation, and had erected a fine building."[100] But it could not get the AP service because some much weaker Chicago papers that were AP members would not permit it. Scott would later figure prominently in the conversion of UP into an Illinois stock corporation, a step that would bind AP and UP together. Both the *Globe* and *Herald* were on UP's board of directors in 1884.[101]

A few steps north of UP's offices along Broadway,[102] the Associated Press was satisfied with its new joint executive committee. Reporting to Medill in January 1883, William Henry Smith said, "All partizan [*sic*] feeling with [the New York AP] has disappeared. There is some soreness with one or two of the N.Y. Assn., but it is thought time aided by judicious counsels, will heal that."[103] After only eight months Smith's joint agency had accumulated a surplus of about $35,000, which by September 1883 was duly returned to the New York partners in the form of a dividend,[104] the first on record for the AP and aimed at healing the "soreness" within the New York partnership. Over nine years, while the rebates were paid, all seven NYAP members received a total of $810,700 in dividends.[105] No similar payments were being made to Western AP officers or members. In 1893 when the joint executive committee was being replaced by a new AP of Illinois, Smith confided in Whitelaw Reid (who apparently was unaware of what Smith had been doing) that

I have paid the New York Associated Press large sums without formal approval of the Western Associated Press. . . . The fact is,

> I endeavored to make the N.Y.A.P. a great success, and to conquer the malignant members of it for the benefit of you and Mr. [Charles A.] Dana through enormous profits. To do this I had to contend with our Western people, who protested I was making an unfair division. . . . [106]

The executive committee tackled the UP competition by seeking an eight-hour copyright law from Congress in the winter of 1884. Committee member Walter N. Haldeman dispatched his editor, Henry Watterson, to Washington, D.C., on what the latter called "a fools' errand. . . . In all my life I have never passed so delightful and useless a winter." [107] AP had found its news reprinted in the columns of its members' competitors in editions timed to take advantage of AP papers' first editions. An eight-hour protection would have eliminated the reprinting problem and helped preserve the value of AP franchises. [108] Although many in Washington were interested in the project, Watterson found that because he was seeking "nothing less than the creation of a new property" exclusively for the use of newspapers, Congress would not vote for it. Finally a lawyer pointed out to Watterson several English rulings covering the matter, and AP lived by those rulings until a 1918 Supreme Court decision upheld a copyright specifically for news dispatches. [109]

AP's joint executive committee, created by its own five members for five years, was approved by majorities of NYAP's membership and of WAP's board of directors. [110] Thus, theoretically by consent of only four New York papers and four Western papers, these five men guided the newsbroking service of over four hundred AP newspapers. And when the committee's first five-year lease on life neared expiration in 1887, its renewal was again decided by a handful of newspaper representatives, the decision to renew merely announced to WAP's membership in their annual meeting in October 1887. [111] Additionally, although the members of NYAP and WAP each contributed $7,500 toward William Henry Smith's salary as general manager after 1887, [112] Smith's allegiance was to neither organization, nor to both, but to the joint executive committee. Chairman Charles A. Dana made this perfectly clear in a note to Smith early in 1888.

> There shall be no misunderstanding on your part, that no member of either Association have any right to instruct you. The

only instructions which should be authoritative with you are those of the Joint Committee.[113]

SHUNNING COMPETITION

Without such concentration of power in the joint committee it is doubtful that AP's fateful entanglement in the affairs of the United Press would have occurred. Indeed, it was precisely the birth of the joint executive committee that set the events in motion that eventually required the committee to deal intimately with its competitor. It will be recalled that as the committee was being created, the New England AP's Royal M. Pulsifer, principal owner since 1869 of Boston's leading daily,[114] demanded to be included and was ignored. Two years later Smith said that in 1882 Pulsifer "expressed the opinion that he ought to have been made a member" of the executive committee.

> He said if that were done there would be no trouble with New England. He then presented [his Boston] Herald as the New England Assn. and Mr. Pulsifer as its representative. I saw no way to bring this about...and Mr. Pulsifer has been cross and revengeful ever since.[115]

Newsbroking confederates of the New York AP since the early days of the telegraph, Boston's press had formed the same kind of loose AP partnership that one found in those early days in New York City, Philadelphia, and Baltimore. Likewise, up in Utica, N.Y., S. N. D. North, editor of the *Herald*, was aware that the New York State AP, of which he was a member, was older than both the Western and New York APs.[116] But the Upstate crowd was also dealt out of the new committee. The New York City partners had turned their backs on fellow Easterners, forming a union that while excluding old regional colleagues profoundly affected the news service those old friends received.

Because those long-standing New York state and New England allies felt the rejection of the new committee setup more than other AP groups, they became fertile territory for Phillips to travel in search of clients for his United Press.[117] The second part of table 2 in the Appendix shows the value of New England patronage to AP. Of the three APs represented there, New England, by virtue of its proximity to New York City, paid the smallest percentage of its expenditures for telegraphic service and the largest for a news report,

136

and it would have been a portion of the latter Phillips would have gained if he could have pried loose some of AP's members. As noted above, table 1 in the Appendix shows UP serving better than half as many papers as AP in New England in 1884 (56.1 percent), and in New York state UP papers numbered 62.5 percent of AP membership during 1883–84.

Exacerbating the competitive situation for Smith and the AP was the fact that many Eastern AP members actually believed in the exclusiveness and protectiveness of the AP "club," staunchly resisting growth of AP membership generally and flatly prohibiting such growth in their own communities. New England AP members, notoriously conservative on such matters, refused to admit newer papers to AP, not even on the payment of large bonuses to existing members. The persistent efforts of the *New Haven News* to get into AP,[118] as one example, were met by the following response from the *New Haven Register*, an AP paper:

> I can not see the value of membership in the association, if the business development of any one member is to be restricted by taking from him the advantages he would otherwise receive from exclusive control of the territory he occupies. If, in fact, all competitors are open to the same privileges, I can not appreciate the value of the one association over the other.[119]

Surveying this impasse, NEAP executive committee member S. A. Hubbard of the *Hartford Courant* wrote Pulsifer, "If admitting the *News* should *drive old members out* we should gain nothing."[120] But the committee did eventually admit the *News* and in two months the *Register* had dropped AP for UP,[121] and AP's other New Haven member, the *Union,* was asking the NEAP,

> Will you tell me what the *Union*'s status is in the New England association? If the Executive Committee can give the news to a paper without the consent of the members, why cannot it take the service away from the papers now receiving it . . . ?[122]

Meanwhile the Boston publishers refused to admit the wealthy *Globe,* even though AP's joint executive committee urged it as a way of deflating UP in the Northeast. New England AP's membership was forty-one in 1883, compared with UP's twenty-three subscribers. In March 1887 NEAP membership was down to nineteen,[123] and although there are no 1887 UP totals, one must assume that some of the AP losses over those three years ended up in UP's ranks.

A combination of New England conservatism and vengeful withdrawal from AP in reaction to the indifference of Pulsifer, the NEAP committee, and NEAP agent L. E. Beard to members' franchises brought the New England AP dangerously close to dissolution by 1887. From New York's vantage point Pulsifer seemed as willing to deliver the NEAP into UP's hands as to retain his alliance with AP. Smith reports that when Vermont's AP contingent was about to jump to UP, he roused Beard to attempt to save them for AP only by threatening to take steps from New York to hold on to the state.[124] The Vermont incident foretold the route to resolution in New England: interposing the power of the New York AP in the controversy. NEAP's effort to get a reduction in its payment for its news from New York opened the way for New York to begin suggesting its solutions to New England's problems. The joint executive committee turned down an NEAP request for lower rates in March 1885, observing that

> If the New England Associated Press, which complains of our bills as onerous, will strengthen itself by the addition of The Boston Globe, which is now obviously a strong and well established competitor, we will be glad to [make] a payment of $5,000 as a bonus for their admission.... [125]

AP did not tell New England, however, that Smith had already opened talks with Taylor looking to the *Globe*'s eventual inclusion in AP, either with or without NEAP's approval.[126]

Denied a rate reduction, a large number of NEAP members, principally the "way" papers outside of Boston, threatened at this point to abandon AP and join UP, not knowing that AP had already blocked this path by tying up Phillips (probably during 1885) with a mutual assistance agreement[127] apparently prohibiting UP from serving the "way" papers. The full scope of this first covert link between AP and UP is, understandably, not recorded, and in fact a WAP investigating committee with full access to AP records as it sought to untangle AP-UP relations was unable to unearth the details of working arrangements between Smith and Phillips between 1885 and 1888.[128] We do know, however, that on May 29, 1886, Smith reminded Phillips

> that the agreement was that no new paper should be started without the consent and cooperation of the A.P. [and this] should be kept in view as a cardinal principle. There is safety in first consulting us in all cases, such as franchises.... [129]

Only through general references in subsequent AP-UP contracts do we, and did the WAP investigators, get a sense that AP was supplying certain types of news to UP in exchange for UP's pledge not to raid AP organizations. We shall examine those subsequent contracts below.

After 1885, New England matters continued to deteriorate for AP, and in March 1887 NEAP mounted another effort to strike a bargain with UP.[130] At this point Smith and the joint executive committee intervened, and after two months effected a three-way checkmating accord that preserved the New England AP in the AP camp and limited UP's growth in New England. Executed May 1, 1887, this "tripartite agreement," as it came to be called, was signed by the New England AP, AP's executive committee, and UP. Phillips later called this "a copartnership" between UP and the NEAP, "whose interests are identical," failing to mention the involvement of AP's governing committee.[131] The tripartite agreement required:

- AP to furnish UP with New England news, congressional and New York legislative reports and cable news, in abbreviated form handed over in New York City;
- NEAP to supply news to all AP and UP newspapers in New England, including the *Boston Globe*, in exchange for a guaranteed annual payment from UP to cover the cost of servicing UP papers;
- UP not to serve newspapers in communities with AP papers without the consent of the joint executive committee.[132]

A patchwork quilt, this agreement was far from universally accepted. Smith indicated that the joint committee agreed to the pact "with much difficulty," Smith commenting to Clapp of Boston that "our committee have gone a long way to help you in New England."[133] Not all in New England agreed that they had been helped. From John S. Baldwin of the *Worcester Spy* came word that

> the union of the United Press with our service was opposed by both representatives of the N. E. Association here. . . . It is nothing less than a blow at the Spy from an Association which is bound in all honor to stand by its old and faithful members.[134]

Hubbard at the *Hartford Courant* wrote, "Your plan is not a proper one in any of its features. How much do you propose to charge the *Telegram* [a former UP paper in Hartford] per month for having the benefit of our dispatches? And of our leased wire."[135] Symbolically, this solution to the New England conflict was reflected at a major

Boston event nine days after the tripartite agreement took effect. On May 10, 1887, the *Boston Globe,* having just moved into a new building, hosted a dinner honoring publisher Charles H. Taylor. Prominent among the two hundred guests were both William Henry Smith and Walter P. Phillips.[136]

Competitive turmoil in New England, and its possible repetition in Upstate New York, had been only one factor, however, in Smith's and Phillips's desire to draw their agencies into binding news exchanges and allocations of service among newspapers. Another factor was a new wave of hostility emanating from Western Union's highest officials. Beginning early in 1886 and aimed at AP, the telegraph company's growing arrogance suggested either a marked increase in AP tolls and wire leases or possible entry into the news business in competition with AP and UP. Growth of the Baltimore and Ohio Telegraph Company in the mid-1880s had provided UP with the sufficient telegraph circuits to challenge AP across the country. But when Western Union absorbed the Baltimore and Ohio in October 1887 and expanded its hostilities to UP as well, the newsbrokerages both recognized the telegraph company as a common enemy, against which unity was the only defense.[137]

Indeed, "the unfriendly attitude of the Telegraph Company and rumors of consolidation with other Companies" were viewed by Western AP members at their annual meeting on October 26, 1887, as sufficient reasons for rushing to renew the joint executive committee contract with the New York AP for another five years.[138] Unknown to most WAP members at the time, renewal of the committee contract also preserved the source of AP's growing covert entanglement with UP. Although it ultimately proved harmless, the Western Union threat over two years had sent AP and UP scurrying for the protection of each other's organization.

To protect themselves from each other and from the telegraph company through news exchanges and the avoidance of head-on competition in local newspaper markets, AP and UP devised a gentlemen's agreement, a common post–Civil War apparatus by which business shunned competition and averted destruction. But when United Press upped the ante with a stock issue that involved AP's joint executive committee in the joint ownership of AP's competitor, the two agencies' leadership, recognizing the fallibility of gentlemen's agreements, sought iron-clad enforcement for their articles of collusion. The stock exchange was a standard business vehicle for eliminating competition and holding a contract together by the 1880s, but the AP-UP pool was a rare example in journalism.

The added dimension of stock-pooling in AP-UP relations was introduced by John R. Walsh, who had acquired controlling interest in UP's stalwart *Chicago Herald* in 1883. Facing a ruinous libel judgment, the *Herald* owners had released the paper's stock to Walsh in exchange for his payment of their libel liability. James W. Scott remained publisher of the paper.[139] President of the Chicago National Bank and the Western News Company, a newspaper and magazine distribution firm, Walsh brought a financier's mind to UP operations. While AP characteristically—and journalistically—sought through covert news-exchange agreements to counteract and absorb UP's growth, UP took the riskier, but potentially domineering, businessman's route of overwhelming AP officers with investment and cooptation.

The first trust agreement involved stock in UP's New York corporation and was executed on October 1, 1885. By its terms UP officers pooled 480 of the total 800 UP shares and placed that pool in Walsh's hands, who then sold half of the pool to AP joint executive committee members Dana, Reid, R. Smith, and Haldeman at a face value of $25 each. One-third of the shares bought by R. Smith and Haldeman were, at their request, issued in the name of William Henry Smith. Smith was included because as active head of AP he was in a position to keep an eye on UP's operations and protect the AP.[140] Several years later, when questioned about his involvement in the stock pool, Haldeman said AP officials participated in the pool in the hope of acquiring enough UP stock to eventually control their competitor. He also indicated that he, and probably R. Smith, had no hand in setting up the pool, that arrangements had been made for him to participate before he learned of the scheme and actually received UP stock, and that he did not know who had worked out the plan with United Press.[141] The other half of the pool was retained by UP's officers: Phillips; Charles R. Baldwin, of Waterbury, Conn.; Robert S. Davis, of Philadelphia; and Scott, of Chicago. Shortly after the pool was distributed, UP declared a 100 percent dividend on the pooled stock, and the AP and UP officers were thus reimbursed in full.[142]

To sweeten the pot for AP, and to tighten UP's grip on AP's hierarchy, Walsh and Phillips next incorporated a United Press in the state of Illinois with 10,000 shares representing a capital of $1 million. This Illinois UP, organized August 16, 1887, then entered into a trust agreement with the old UP in New York on September 19, 1887, by which the new UP bought the old company's stock at par, guaranteeing an annual 6 percent dividend and agreeing to operate the newsbrokerage business of the old company. The 480 pooled shares of old UP stock were redeemed at face value (AP's officers thus had their total investment repaid a second time), and 6,000 shares of new UP stock were pooled, out of which half was distributed, without further payment, to AP joint executive committee members. Again R. Smith and Haldeman had one-third of their stock issued in William Henry Smith's name. Annual dividends of 4 percent were then paid on the new stock. All told, the two Smiths and Haldeman between 1885 and 1891 each received $6,500 beyond their total original investment of $6,000 for 240 shares of old New York UP stock.[143] All of this pooled stock was issued in the names of AP and UP officers rather than in the names of their newsbrokerages.

While AP was dragged deeper into the financial affairs of UP, the pool to which AP officials belonged was producing dividends for the individuals. This, clearly, was information the two Smiths were not anxious to have their AP colleagues know. Although it is not known how Dana and Reid reacted to owning UP stock, WAP's representatives on the joint executive committee, especially after the dummy UP corporation appeared in Illinois, were nervous and wondering what had happened to them. R. Smith could not remember consenting to a second pool arrangement. He and Haldeman wanted to look into UP's finances, and R. Smith also wanted to know "what kind of a contract or arrangement they proposed to make with the Associated Press." Asking that a joint AP-UP meeting be scheduled, R. Smith wrote, "I do not propose to go it blind or to get into any trade that I could not explain to the association I represent."[144]

"The U.P. is little more than a blackmailing business," Smith wrote Reid in February 1888. "It is controlled by Walsh, who is not over scrupulous, P[hillips], & Baldwin, and is more for their individual ends." Smith's letter displays apprehension over UP's aggressiveness and AP's inability to control the situation it found itself in.

> If we are not threatened in New York today, we are at some
> other point in the country tomorrow. Each time a new excuse is
> given and more blood required. Seeing this, Mr. Haldeman gave
> notice some time ago that he sh[oul]d decline to approve any
> further concessions.

When we admitted the Boston Globe, the U.P. was floored, and but for our lifting it up, would have gone rapidly to the bad. Here was mistake No. 1. When the W.U. took in the B. & O. their Gen. Eckert offered to help kill the U.P., if we would take firm measures. That this has not been done is mistake No. 2. The question is, Shall the Assd. Press go on building up this concern which is now a leech, & which may become strong enough to be wholly independent & aggressive?[145]

In response to an inquiry from Clapp in Boston, Smith said, "The United Press of Illinois is a scheme gotten up by [Walsh, Scott, Phillips, and Baldwin] to make money for themselves. The whole thing is a fraud." Smith then engages in a little deception of his own.

The parties to [the UP scheme] hope by its means to work the Chicago Herald into the Assd. Press without it costing Walsh anything to the other Chicago papers, and complicate matters for the Associated Press.

Capital stock of the U.P. of Illinois $1,000,000, all of which has been paid for by a worthless patent owned by Phillips!![146]

What must have unnerved Smith was correspondence from UP people like the following sequence of threats and offers penned by Phillips the day after the second trust agreement was signed.

The question of making a closer alliance between [AP and UP] has been in the minds of several persons of late and yesterday one of them suggested the idea of making a purchase outright of the AP business.

Phillips then observed that after pool stock and individual shares in the Illinois company had been distributed, UP would still have $195,000 in treasury stock left, on which Walsh, the banker, could lend from that amount up to a quarter of a million dollars. "Sometimes, when influential men are interested in bringing about a combination, that is in the interest of everybody concerned," Phillips continued, "a good deal can be done with a hundred thousand dollars in cash." Then came another Phillips threat.

Before I've decide[d] to pass out that Treasury Stock free gratis to the [New York] State and New England for the sake of getting them in, on a basis that will give The United Press a profit out of it, would it not be well to consider what can be done with the money . . . by using it . . . with the two Associations which, with us, absolutely control the situation.[147]

Phillips must have relished this moment of dominance over an AP which had fired him five years earlier.

The new AP-UP stock pool was followed eight months later by a new "working contract," signed May 28, 1888, in a Cincinnati meeting of the joint executive committee and UP's Phillips and Scott. Preserving provisions of the two earlier trust agreements involving UP stock and the 1888 tripartite agreement among NEAP, NYAP, and UP, this new contract added four restrictions on UP, concessions in exchange for the stock pool:

- UP would not serve present or recent AP members without AP's consent and only at higher rates than AP's;
- UP would not serve competitors of AP papers for less than what the AP papers were charged;
- UP would, at AP's request, furnish news it had received from AP to any papers designated by AP; and
- UP would furnish all news to AP from territories not covered by AP's leased wires.[148]

Facing the other's competition, each of these two national newsbrokerages had during three or four years baited its hook with its strongest asset in order to reel the other into entangling agreements and pools. AP was forced to share its superior news-gathering apparatus and news report with UP in order to keep its promise to long-standing members of protection from local competition. A measure of UP's need for better news facilities is offered by Theodore Dreiser, who as a young and inexperienced man seeking a newspaper job in Chicago in 1890, was advised to "go to the editor of the City Press Association or the United Press, where the most inexperienced beginners were put to work at the rate of eight dollars a week."[149] UP, on the other hand, was forced to limit its seemingly boundless growth potential and to share its profits with AP leaders in order to secure the AP news needed to bring its report up to running speed. For both agencies the parade of gentlemen's agreements and stock pools had warded off damaging, perhaps destructive, competition, and this final 1887–88 flurry of a second trust agreement and a new working agreement brought the two newsbrokerages to a standoff.

DISCUSSION

Were it not for such enterprises as the American Newspaper Publishers Association, various state press associations, the management of large newspaper chains in recent years, or the governing apparatus of newsbrokerages, very few publishers would have had professional avenues for projecting themselves onto the national stage. Beyond a handful of politically active or obvious metropolitan publishers, the lords of the press are primarily local nobility, ruling editorial and economic fiefdoms extending only to the limits of their circulation zones. Newsbroking, however, was an early opportunity for publishers to share a national identity, while turning that affiliation to protection from local competition. For many years such protectionism had impeded AP's natural growth, setting up a delicate equilibrium between newsbrokerage and members. New, aggressive competition from United Press after 1882 exacerbated the inherent conflict in AP's structure between the interests of the local publisher and those of AP leaders, who struggled to preserve AP's existence nationally.

A growing business ethic of the time, if invoked secretly, might sustain AP's and UP's identities at both the local and national levels. AP's joint executive committee, facing UP, a worthy competitor arising at last from the wreckage of a succession of relatively impotent agencies stretching back to Hasson's in 1869, needed extraordinary strategy to minimize the threat of competition. The business climate at the time counseled the "gentlemen's agreement" as the opening gambit to contain a competitor, and AP complied, initiating a news exchange arrangement with UP to recapture lost regional membership strength. Calling such agreements "imperfect and unreliable," however, Thomas C. Cochran observes that "every large group included many who could not be counted on to behave as gentlemen."[150] UP, also taking its cue from prevailing business practice, directed the next gambit by entangling AP leaders in a UP stock trust, later sanitizing the maneuver by setting up a separate stock holding company for the trust in which it had ensnared AP's joint executive committee.

Meanwhile as the newsbrokerages' reckless game of gentlemen's agreements and stock pools began to make participants, especially at the AP, uneasy, newsbroking was gradually asserting itself more forcefully in technological areas of its operation. Dramatic growth in leased wires and newsbroker-employed operators, and the introduction of typewriter transcription of the efficient Phillips code, freed newsbrokerages from daily reliance on telegraph companies during the 1880s and 1890s. The constant availability of circuits to a growing number of newspapers meant that newsbrokerages could expand their news reports at will, and work the circuits with greater flexibility if the news situation dictated.

The pace quickened on the news circuits, the newsbrokerages casting their light on disasters, government crises, military and foreign affairs, crimes, and even sports events more rapidly, with greater intensity, and through the growing use of bulletins and new leads. Expanded and constant technological capacity also gave the agency flexibility to call on remote correspondents and bureaus to file their breaking news directly to the entire network, headquarters serving less as a collection point and more as a traffic cop who retained ultimate control over the agency's news values but dispensed with the benefit of seeing all the copy firsthand. Such technical flexibility speeded up and diversified the news report, but within news definitions imposed by the manager and his subordinates, definitions inclined to be more rigid, perhaps more superficial, if order and consistency were to be preserved in the system.

The power, therefore, of William Henry Smith and Walter P. Phillips to shape the picture of the world delivered to editors and their readers grew, ironically, as more communities became able to interact with the network and as less raw copy was centrally edited before delivery to newspapers. Already freed of telegraph company restrictions and alliances, newsbrokers in the 1880s stood on the brink of generating a news report exceeding local news copy with its seeming significance, speed, and diversity. While it was obviously *different* from local news reporting and commentary, it is far from certain that it was *better* than local copy. And yet its difference, as measured by speed, geographical reach, and perceived excitement, increasingly attracted the attention of editors and readers alike.

"Rational reporting," in Joseph M. Webb's terminology,[151] was finally challenging the locally generated "romantic reporting," which had been gradually losing ground since its zenith during the Civil War. It was a trend toward "facts that are useless, particulars that give no form or color to the [news] picture" that Whitelaw Reid detected in 1879 and was still bemoaning in 1901, as we saw at the start of this chapter. Technologically enhanced and centrally controlled newsbroker reports were forcing their way through news rooms into news columns and living rooms, increasingly providing a shared national news experience, a daily common public knowledge of selected events and personalities.

As Susan R. Brooker-Gross observed after studying spatial organization of newsbrokerages, "in their centralization, the news wire services gained an increased control over the definition of news."[152] Harold A. Innis depicts the same phenomenon, adding the dimension of one-way communication stemming from centralization.

> Technological advance in communication implies a narrowing of the range from which material is distributed and a widening of the range of reception in which large numbers receive, but are unable to make any direct response. Those on the receiving end of material from a mechanized central system are precluded from participation in healthy, vigorous, and vital discussion. Instability of public opinion which follows the introduction of new inventions in communication designed to reach large numbers of people is exploited by those in control of the inventions.[153]

After twenty years the "most notable development" in 1898, according to Ida Tarbell, had been "an extraordinary unification of the nation's economic life.... The triumph of industrial consolidation knitted the country together in ever closer bonds, increasing the feeling of nationhood."[154] Alongside industrial consolidation, nationhood was also being fostered by a steady stream of newsbroker dispatches that daily reported to the nation's reading public with compelling immediacy that nation's triumphs and tragedies, problems and solutions. Rather than a mirror image of the selected events, the reports' bulletins, frequent updates, and growing reliance on the summary first paragraph fragmented and reorganized those events to suit the newsbrokers' quest for attention and the growing expectations of editors and readers for dramatic and significant news on the national scale. The "rational" news report was making rapid incursions on the consciousness of local newspaper editors and a nation filling with habitual newspaper readers.

The future of newsbroking would have looked bright from the vantage point of the late-1880s, were it not for the rigid agreements and trusts that were saving AP and UP from each other, but threatened to alienate newspaper customers if the scheme were exposed. Chapter 5 depicts the discovery of the AP-UP collusion and the investigation of it before exploring the odd mixture of newsbroker habit and reform leading to a newsbroker war in the 1890s.

Chapter 5
REACTION AND WAR

What I want the committee to be satisfied about is, that in carrying out [the United Press contract] in behalf of the Assd. Press, I have faithfully conserved Associated Press interests, and have protected our papers at every point.

William Henry Smith to Victor F. Lawson and Frederick Driscoll,
Smith Papers, Ohio Historical Society
(February 19, 1891)

If this ever comes to trial it will be shown that . . . it was only my personal popularity here that kept things from going to smash years ago. . . . A trial will develop the whole story from the inception of the change in 1882 . . . down to the fatal date Dec. 10, 1892. . . . It will be impossible for me to put a limit to the revelations, as I succeeded in doing pending the contest over the United Press agreements.

William Henry Smith to Whitelaw Reid, Smith Papers,
Indiana Historical Society
(March 14, 1893)

William Henry Smith had much on his mind in the early 1890s as he watched his own Associated Press edifice and that of its United Press corespondent slowly crumble into wreckage. No doubt dismayed that business practices deemed appropriate a decade ago had so quickly come into disfavor, Smith was attempting to convince his enemies that he meant only to protect their interests while he was seeking assistance from his friends to make a cover-up work one more time. This chapter describes the discovery and investigation of the gentlemen's agreements and stock pools between AP and UP that are outlined in the previous chapter.[1] Newspaper editors' reaction to these revelations, as this chapter points out, was a mixture of the old habits of collusion and of a new reformist zeal.

And just when some accommodation between the two newsbrokerages appeared on the horizon, warfare erupted, leading to the demise of United Press.

There are no winners in this chapter—only survivors and a few losers. Even the reformers who established a more united national Associated Press in Illinois were willing at times to seek a negotiated settlement with UP similar to Smith's accords with UP's Walter P. Phillips. So dark and disturbing are the episodes depicted in this chapter that one cannot help but be saddened by journalism's loss of responsibility and respectability between 1893 and 1897. Here was a life-and-death struggle in which contracts, memberships, news reports, and even court decisions were the weapons of a warfare not likely to benefit the public in any way.

Discovery

AP-UP stock pools were a closely guarded secret among participants, and the working arrangements for news exchange were kept as quiet as daily operations would permit.[2] Some agents, telegraphers, and local publishers, of course, knew of the news exchanges at specific locations, but most AP members were initially unaware of the agreements, a condition that would diminish as AP news stories increasingly turned up in the columns of UP competitors, sometimes in identical form. From an AP publisher's viewpoint, UP seemed to grow steadily in size and quality during the 1880s, reaching a point of equality with and similarity to AP by late in the decade. Local publishers noted the trend, at first with curiosity, then with concern, and finally with outrage as clues to the working arrangements became too obvious to ignore.

Barely three months after the AP–New England AP-UP tripartite agreement was penned, a few AP publishers privately voiced concern over rumors of AP-UP intercourse, not just in some bureaus but at the highest levels of the two agencies. In August 1887, Frank R. O'Neil of the St. Louis *Missouri Republican* wrote Joseph Pulitzer, whose *New York World* made him a NYAP partner while he still retained a WAP membership through his *St. Louis Post-Dispatch*. O'Neil said,

> I have very good reason to believe that the United Press . . . is receiving regularly a copy of the news gathered by the Associated Press, and that it uses the same in making up its budget. If

this be true, it very seriously affects the value of our Assd. Press franchises. . . .

O'Neil noted that a new daily then starting in St. Louis was to receive UP news,

> which fact gives special interest to this arrangement between Phillips and Wm. Henry Smith, whatever it may be. The Western Associated Press holds its annual meeting at Detroit on the second Wednesday of September, and as this will be our only opportunity within a year to correct whatever evil practices have grown up in the service, I want to be prepared with the facts. . . .[3]

Nothing appears on the minutes of the 1887 WAP meeting to suggest that O'Neil used this annual "opportunity" to raise his objections.

It would, however, be a Western AP annual meeting three years later where the AP-UP agreements first came under attack, and inevitably WAP would be the forum in which joint executive committee schemes would begin to unravel. Although the smaller AP auxiliaries were, in the main, grateful for and unquestioning of what the WAP and NYAP delivered as news and billed as assessments, the WAP membership operated under bylaws promising protection of AP franchises and cooperative self-government. Although the pervasiveness of the joint executive committee had undermined WAP's democratic apparatus for nearly a decade, some doggedly individualistic publishers in WAP continued to believe that WAP's annual meetings were the place for expressing grievances, controlling the agency by majority rule, and, if necessary, throwing rascals out of office.

One might suspect collusion when similar stories appear in competitors' news reports, but this was far from proof in a period when appropriating another's news was widely practiced. The more obvious and provable evidence of collusion, on the other hand, arose from WAP's uneven enforcement of Bylaw XIII, which prohibited WAP members from trafficking with non-WAP papers and news agencies. Over the years, mergers and purchases had put some WAP members in possession of newspaper properties holding UP franchises. Although most of these members were forced under Bylaw XIII to give up their new UP franchises, a few were permitted to keep the UP connection without objection from WAP's board of directors. When the *Pittsburgh Chronicle,* an AP paper, merged with the *Pittsburgh Telegraph,* a UP paper, for example, the resulting

Chronicle-Telegraph was allowed to receive the news of both AP and UP.[4] Meanwhile the *Chicago Times* was losing its WAP membership under Bylaw XIII for trafficking with non-AP news agencies,[5] and other publishers were threatened with expulsion for even attempting a link with UP. Writing Smith in 1891 after some of the evidence of collusion had begun to surface, Felix Agnus, editor of the *Baltimore American,* angrily asserted,

> it is not long ago that "The American" was making arrange-
> ments to procure additional news through the United Press As-
> sociation, when then and there you stopped me; the rivalry
> between you and the United Press Association was so great that
> you charged one of my editors with giving said Association im-
> portant news and wanted me to discharge him. Now, you make
> a business contract with that Association, and do not inform
> your patrons of such an agreement having been made. . . . I do
> most positively and earnestly enter my protest against such
> proceedings, as I consider it unfair to have stopped me from
> making arrangements with this Association, when you coolly
> do the same thing without even giving me a chance to protect
> myself.[6]

Perhaps the most awkward challenge to Bylaw XIII arose with Dana's *New York Sun,* which introduced an evening edition in March 1887.[7] Ineligible for an AP franchise, the *Evening Sun* acquired a UP franchise. What's more, the guiding spirit behind the evening edition, William M. Laffan, and the *Sun's* managing editor, Chester S. Lord, also organized the Laffan News Service to augment the new edition's news resources. The Laffan service, in turn, began delivering a news report to other newspapers, some of them WAP members. The list included by April 1890 the *Boston Herald, Phila-delphia Press, Pittsburgh Dispatch, Cincinnati Commercial Gazette, St. Louis Republic,* and *Chicago Herald.*[8] This interlocking of franchises was enough to cause the *Pittsburgh Post* to complain to the WAP board of directors in 1889. There had been enough such protests to cause the board to print the *Post's* letter in its minutes "as a sample of letters received from time to time on the. . .subject."[9]

At the next WAP annual meeting, on August 5, 1890, the *Pitts-burgh Post's* John S. Rittenour broke the issue into the open with a "lengthy memorial" about interlocking AP-UP franchises, followed by four resolutions attempting to get more of WAP's decision-making process on the record and requesting "a statement of the character of relations existing between the Western Associated Press on one side and the United Press or other news associations on the other side."[10] All of Rittenour's resolutions were tabled or referred to the board, but later in the same meeting Edgar W. Coleman of the *Milwaukee Herold* tried again, moving,

> that the Board of Directors shall report at a special meeting of the Western Associated Press, within ninety days, the relations now existing between the Western Associated Press and the United Press, and what, in their opinion, will be the ultimate outcome of these and similar arrangements to be entered into in the future by the two associations.

This resolution was adopted,[11] unlocking the door to a full investigation of the trust and arrangements.

For the next two years, factions in both the WAP and NYAP would struggle to stonewall or investigate each other. Rumors, accusations, and denials flew in all directions; the AP was tearing itself apart. H. E. Baker, of the *Detroit Advertiser and Tribune* and the only secretary WAP ever had, expressed WAP's indignation over AP-UP ties in a letter to Smith the day after the Coleman resolution was passed.

> Our members don't like the partnership that we seem to have got into [with UP]. While it may not be possible to extricate ourselves altogether...it does seem as though it were easily feasible to withdraw....Our feeding them with our news *is* disgraceful and surprising, and unless that sort of thing comes to an end, I believe great mischief will result.[12]

In mid-September at a special meeting, the WAP board heard Smith's "somewhat detailed statement" about AP-UP relations. Afterward director Victor F. Lawson of the *Chicago Daily News* asked for a special committee to consider the questions raised and to prepare a report. Lawson, Smith, and director A. J. Blethen of the *Minneapolis Tribune* were named by president I. F. Mack to form that committee.[13] Blethen, just beginning his only year on the board, was the swing vote, Smith attempting to paint AP-UP relations in a positive light and Lawson in his second year on the board challenging those relations and what he saw as WAP's aging and inept management.

Mack could not have made a worse choice than Lawson if he wanted to preserve harmony in AP, and in relations between AP and UP. At WAP meetings maverick Lawson regularly attacked the agency's secrecy and closed circle of leaders. Later in the midst of the Lawson-WAP management contest, Whitelaw Reid observed, "It is, of course, the old struggle between the outs and the ins,"[14] but in this case the "outs" wanted reform as much as power. Lawson represented the second generation of WAP editors, many of whom appreciated neither the long uphill battle of their forebears in the West nor the clubby, secretive, and now conspiratorial way those forebears continued to direct WAP.

Moreover, Lawson's demeanor was inappropriate to the delicate task of probing and recommending changes among a handful of friends and associates. "Those who did not know Lawson well," says Lawson's biographer, Robert Lloyd Tree, "thought him arrogant and irritable. Even his close associates felt uncomfortable in his presence, for he could be extremely blunt and insensitive to the feelings of others."[15] Lawson, despite his faults, could not be ignored. Not only had WAP's membership sanctioned his investigation, but he presided over the nation's second largest newspaper circulation in the early 1890s.[16]

WAP's full membership reassembled on November 19, 1890, to hear the Lawson committee report. It covered some of the reasons for establishing the joint executive committee, summarized the provisions of the 1888 working contract, and touched on the tripartite contract involving New England. Although it mentioned a trust agreement, the committee clearly had insufficient information at that point to discuss the trust knowledgeably. Finally the committee recommended that a three-man committee be appointed to confer with the NYAP and UP and recommend "a plan of reorganization of present relations." R. Smith attempted to head off further investigation by presenting a "provisional agreement" signed three weeks earlier by AP's joint executive committee and UP's officers. Not wishing to be railroaded, however, WAP members ordered R. Smith and Haldeman to withdraw their names from the new agreement and approved the Lawson recommendation to extend the investigation. The new committee consisted of Lawson, Frederick Driscoll, of the *St. Paul Pioneer Press,* and R. W. Patterson, Jr., *Chicago Tribune* general manager and Joseph Medill's son-in-law.[17] It was a loaded committee—only Lawson was a director, all were relatively young men, two represented leading papers in Chicago, where discontent with WAP's management had been growing for several years,[18] and Patterson, like Lawson, was a known antagonist of WAP's management.

INVESTIGATION

The minutes do not indicate how the committee was selected, but several months later R. Smith said that since he and Haldeman had nothing to hide or be ashamed of, they had moved that Lawson and Patterson, as the two most vocal opponents of WAP's management, be appointed to the committee.[19] Such a miscalculation reflected the unrecognized and irreconcilable gulf dividing the precepts guiding the old protectionist editors, who saw competition as a greater evil than collusion, and those motivating the younger progressive editors, who believed in reform through democratic confrontation and openness.

Lawson's correspondence indicates that a month passed after the new committee was named before he began to turn his attention to its task.[20] And even two and a half months after the committee's appointment, Lawson at the end of January 1891 wrote Driscoll, "I must confess that neither Mr. Patterson nor I have made very much progress in this business. The simple fact is that it is an exceedingly hard nut to crack."[21] Initially the view on all sides seems to have been that the committee would confine itself, as Lawson said in early January 1891, "to mark[ing] out some policy of reorganization that would suit us from our end of the line, and then attempt to work such a plan through with the New York Associated Press and the United Press."[22] President Mack later commented that he, too, conceived the committee's mission as narrowly examining WAP-NYAP relations and WAP-UP contracts and determining whether those or some other arrangements would best serve WAP's interests.[23] These early perceptions suggest that Smith, while concealing stock exchanges and dividend payments, had convinced his colleagues of all persuasions of the need, if not the desirability, of relations with AP's competitor.

But Smith and his friends knew what lurked below the surface, not far beyond the view of the committee, and this new investigation became "a matter to be very carefully handled," as R. Smith put it. Even prior to the appointment of the new, more hostile committee, R. Smith wrote Smith that

> We are now in a sort of crisis, and if our people insist upon ventilating everything in public, or which is the same thing in our general meetings, there will be a break-up that will fall most heavily upon those who are so anxious to suspect everything and meddle with all of the details.[24]

Lawson was prepared to hew to the original narrow definition of the committee's responsibility until January 1891, by which time WAP members vigorously and in large numbers in correspondence to the committee were voicing opposition to any contract with UP.[25] And as this deluge of anti-management mail poured in, Lawson finally began to pry loose some of the secrets guarded by the ruling clique. A nineteen-page memorandum from general manager Smith, purporting to explain WAP's relations with other news agencies, boasted instead of WAP's growth and achievements under Smith, but carefully avoided any mention of either UP or its stock.[26] In response, Lawson demanded that Smith send all WAP contracts to him and inquired on the basis of gossip reaching Lawson if it was true that Smith wanted to retire from the WAP service.[27] Smith called the rumor "ridiculous, and perhaps meant to be mischievous,"[28] but little more than a month later, Smith wrote Lawson, "It is my purpose to retire from the service at the close of the fiscal year."[29]

Meanwhile Lawson pestered Smith about large surpluses, unpublished financial statements, hidden funds and agreements, the reasons for links with UP, and the like. Preserving a calm exterior, Smith cheerfully replied, although carefully selecting the subjects on which he would reply. "I should like nothing better," Smith wrote Lawson and Driscoll in mid-February, "than to take you gentlemen through all of the records of the Associated Press, the accounts, the orders, the contracts, etc. They will show good executive business and exceptional care of the finances." And finally being pressed pointedly about contracts with UP, Smith wrote that "what I want the committee to be satisfied about is, that in carrying it out on behalf of the Assd. Press, I have faithfully conserved Associated Press interests, and have protected our papers at every point."[30]

Between January and June of 1891, the Lawson committee's field of focus broadened markedly as the extent of AP-UP relations gradually surfaced, as more WAP members stepped forward to oppose those relations, and as the committee realized that the root of the AP-UP relationship went deep into the eight-year-old joint executive committee. Two goals seemed increasingly important to the Lawson committee: first, that at least the current WAP members of the joint committee should step down, turning their UP stock over to the AP, and perhaps also that the joint committee plan should be abandoned in favor of some other structure; and second, that any future relations with United Press should be aboveboard and beneficial to all in the Western AP. Although Lawson's committee was expected only to formulate recommendations for WAP membership consideration based on talks with New York AP members, meetings with the Easterners were frustrating and unproductive because the seven New York partners were deeply divided on the issues Lawson's investigation was developing.

The old 1882 alignments of anti–Jay Gould members (*Times, Journal of Commerce,* and *Herald*), pro-Gould members (*Tribune, World,* and *Evening Mail and Express*), and the *Sun* as the swing vote had been altered by ownership changes and the existence since 1882 of an inner circle within the NYAP consisting of the joint executive committee. The Gould faction subsided after the joint committee was established, Gould selling the *World* to Joseph Pulitzer in April 1883, and Cyrus W. Field selling the *Evening Mail and Express* to Elliott F. Shepard in March 1888.[31] After eight years of the joint committee plan, the New York AP was divided between those members on the committee (*Tribune, Herald,* and *Sun*) and those members outside the committee (*Times, Journal of Commerce,* and *Evening Mail and Express*), with the *World* of Pulitzer, who continued to hold a WAP membership in St. Louis, taking the independent course.

Lawson quickly discovered that dealing with the NYAP was not simply a matter of counting votes, however. Since he talked of changes on the joint committee (and perhaps dissolution of the committee), assignment of UP stock by committee members to their respective APs, and possibly a fresh start in relations with UP, Lawson threatened newsbroking stability, existing contracts, and the rights of individuals to own stock and to operate under long-standing partnerships and corporations. The complex web of personalities, individual rights, and contracts binding various APs among themselves and with UP that had grown up over many years could not be dismantled without fear of lawsuits, the loss of pivotal AP members to the ranks of UP, and a general upheaval in the finely tuned apparatus that daily delivered the news to many newspapers across the country in an atmosphere largely without competition.

Complicating Lawson's work was the fact that several key New York AP members were conveniently absent from the city and thus able to avoid the debate and keep their options open. The *Tribune's* Whitelaw Reid, NYAP's most reliable joint executive committee member and Smith's and WAP's best friend in the East, had been in Paris as U.S. ambassador to France since April 1889 and was represented at AP meetings by his private secretary, Donald Nicholson, who said just enough to assert Reid's presence without revealing Reid's views. Another joint committee member, although an inactive one, the *Herald's* self-exiled James Gordon Bennett, Jr., maintained his silence in Europe, his representative in New York, G. G. Howland, expressing Bennett's momentary indifference to AP affairs. And Pulitzer, who controlled NYAP's swing vote, was touring Europe early in 1891, his representative in New York, William L. Davis, remaining uncommitted to either side although privately observing that the *New York Times* "was a feeble paper in feeble hands" and Shepard of the *Evening Mail and Express* "was a fool."[32] Shepard, George Jones of the *Times,* and David M. Stone of the *Journal of Commerce* had more or less lined up against the joint committee and its UP connection.

Even among those NYAP partners present in the city early in 1891, Lawson found division and indecision. Shepard too eagerly sought to press the investigation in order to advance his own status in the NYAP. Jones, saddled with the diminishing fortunes of a faltering newspaper, was more an aggrieved lone voice of doom and despair than a power in the NYAP. And Stone, also directing a minor newspaper property, vacillated between maintaining a parliamentary distance from the debate as befitted a NYAP president, and attacking the inner circle as a disgruntled outsider. The *Sun* and Charles A. Dana steered the most erratic and unfathomable course, much to the frustration of all concerned. The emergence of Laffan as a force at the *Sun* and his involvement in non-AP newsbrokerages, as described earlier in this chapter, made the paper's position unclear. Outside of Reid, Dana was NYAP's only other active participant in the joint committee and purchaser of UP stock, and although he was repeatedly solicited for his views because of his central role in the matter, Dana merely fluctuated between wild threats to join UP or derision of the investigation and long periods of maddening silence.[33] Smith attempted to convince Lawson in January that all NYAP members accepted the joint committee and "all get on together harmoniously,"[34] but if Lawson did not already know this to be a bluff, he realized that it was in the next few months.

Smith's goal was to hold the Lawson investigation at bay until Pulitzer returned and was persuaded to support the status quo and until the WAP's annual meeting late in the summer, where he hoped to help reelect a board that was friendly to the joint committee and the old management. The joint committee operated under a contract extending to early 1893, and if Smith could find four votes in New York and four more on WAP's board to sustain that contract, the committee's membership, perhaps even the working arrangements and stock pool with UP, could be preserved. But as he struggled to pull together a coalition in both camps, his wife's illness of several months worsened, calling Smith to her bedside, first for two months beginning in February 1891 in Winter Park, Fla., and then back in Lake Forest, Ill.[35] Beyond the reach of his inquisitors and thinking his absence was "the sole chance to thwart the machinations of the malcontents," Smith, writing Reid on May 5, portrayed his wife's illness as the excuse he needed to defuse the confrontation: "I relied on delay and its probable effects, viz: divisions among the [Lawson committee] schemers, and the influence of the 'sober second thought.' It has transpired as I predicted."[36] Six days after he wrote those words, Smith's wife died on May 11.

Matters had already progressed, however, well beyond the point where Smith's actions or absence could have any effect. In his absence Patterson had mounted a public campaign to overthrow Smith and the joint committee. Privately calling Patterson "impulsive and foolish to a remarkable degree," Smith claimed the campaign "has come very near bringing on a collision" in the NYAP that would break up that agency and its relations with the WAP.[37] Moreover, a resolution was prepared by Smith with the WAP board's approval endorsing the joint committee. Presented to the NYAP at a joint NYAP-WAP board meeting on May 13 "to meet any rumors that had been set afloat" suggesting that the WAP was backing away from its relations with the NYAP, this resolution would within a month boomerang on Smith and his friends.

The discussion at and following that May 13 meeting revealed to Lawson two significant facts: first, that preserving the joint committee meant retaining its present members as designated participants in that delicate apparatus, and second, that a demand for Dana, Reid, R. Smith, and Haldeman to relinquish their United Press stock to either UP or AP would be violently opposed by some on the committee and could lead to defections to UP and perhaps the breakup of the NYAP. Within AP's inner circle the May 13 meeting offered the comforting suggestion of victory. By firmly stating their support for existing NYAP-WAP relations and by refusing to participate in a vote on a motion by Shepard to establish a joint investigating committee as being "absurd and illegal," AP's leadership quite smugly thought they had lessened Lawson's threat considerably.[38]

The Lawson committee, however, went ahead with its work, believing that any reorganization of AP-UP relations must be preceded by abrogation of existing contracts with UP and surrender of UP stock by the two Smiths and Haldeman. Such a course was risky to NYAP-WAP relations, but Lawson was increasingly willing to formulate bold recommendations, given what he now knew to be growing support in WAP's ranks for reform within AP. On Thursday, June 4, 1891, Lawson privately confronted the two Smiths and Haldeman with his demands that they return their stock to UP and withdraw from AP's leadership. With his committee's report still in draft form, Lawson offered the three old friends a more lenient description of their collusion in the report, in exchange for their retirement from WAP's board and executive committee and from the joint executive committee. On that date Lawson received from Smith curtly and protectively worded replies to several questions posed earlier by Lawson, Smith commenting that the purchase of UP stock had been "a risk" but that "no one expressed a doubt as to their right in the premises, or as to the perfect propriety of their act."[39]

Lawson and Smith also talked that day with President Mack present, an hour-long conversation about which Smith later prepared an extensive memorandum. During the meeting Lawson threatened to seek censure of both Smiths and Haldeman if they did not return their stock to UP and withdraw from the leadership, and at the end he forced Smith to telegraph the Lawson ultimatum to R. Smith and Haldeman.[40] Richard Smith's telegraphed reply was firm and dignified.

No return of stock or resignation for me. If fight is desired, let it come and the more aggressive the better. I shall never imply even an admission that duties were not faithfully performed. . . . Let everybody stand up like men and defend their honor. This is now the vital question.[41]

Haldeman's telegram, arriving the next day, was defiant: "Let the Committee do their worst. I will fight to the bitter end. I have done right and have no apologies to make and do not propose to change the position I have occupied. Stand firm and yield nothing."[42] In a note to Lawson, written on mourning stationery, William Henry Smith said, "You will pardon me for adding a word of caution: It is possible to dismember the Associated Press. I believe you will find honorable recompense for an important service by calling a halt."[43] As subsequent events revealed, the two Smiths and Haldeman, whether out of preoccupation with management affairs or out of an arrogance spawned by eight years of association with New York's leadership, had lost touch with the membership and misjudged the sentiment of WAP's rank-and-file when the issue came to a vote, as it ultimately would.

Two days later, on June 6, at a NYAP meeting, Smith's prospects brightened considerably when efforts to replace Reid and Dana on the joint committee with Shepard and Jones were defeated, as was a scheme to incorporate the NYAP and thus undermine the joint committee's powers. A motion by Davis of the *World* to terminate the UP contract because, in Smith's words, "the contract worked to the disadvantage of A.P. and [because the NYAP] *wanted to make a new one*" was adopted, the *Times, World, Evening Mail and Express,* and *Journal of Commerce* voting for the motion, the *Tribune* voting against, and the *Sun* and *Herald* not voting. In the aftermath of the meeting Smith wrote Reid that "victory [is] perched on our banner."[44]

Perhaps so in the East, but in the West Lawson was relentless, notifying R. Smith and Haldeman on June 15 that his committee's report was complete,[45] and spending the next month securing an early hearing for his report by the WAP membership.[46] Pinning his hopes on members' revulsion at the revelations in his report about the mismanagement of the Western AP, Lawson wrote each WAP member ten days prior to the annual meeting, scheduled for August 18–19, 1891, that the agenda "is of such exceptional importance that every newspaper in the Association ought to be represented and represented by a PROPRIETOR—not by any mere employe."[47] Meanwhile committee member Patterson visited WAP members, "his object [being] to elect a board of directors who would remove" Smith as general manager at the upcoming annual meeting, according to R. Smith, who commented that this "undoubtedly is the line upon which the fight will be conducted." Patterson was also informing the members whom he visited that the Chicago AP press would act in unison at the meeting and favored the eventual reorganization of the WAP.[48] The first day of meetings was set aside for consideration of the Lawson report, and the second day was reserved for standard annual meeting business of the WAP, including the election of directors.

The nineteen-page report of the committee, supplemented by reprints of the two AP-UP trust agreements and of the report of the earlier Lawson-Blethen-Smith committee, was a thorough and convincing document, leading its reader step-by-step through the gradual buildup of working arrangements and stock pools between AP's joint executive committee and the UP. It also attacked President Mack for attempting to interfere with the committee's investigation and for making unauthorized statements about WAP intentions to members of the NYAP.[49] Several committee recommendations proposed censure for Mack and retraction of his correspondence with the NYAP. A substitute motion, stating simply that Mack's correspondence was "not the sense of this Association" was adopted 34 to 21, followed by a voice-vote reaffirmation of existing WAP-NYAP relations.[50] As for AP-UP relations, the Lawson committee recommended: (1) abrogation of the comprehensive 1888 working agreement with UP; (2) negotiation by the joint executive committee of a new contract with UP, which had to be approved by both APs before it could take effect; and (3) recovery by WAP of UP stock and dividends held by the two Smiths and Haldeman.[51] Confronted with such bold, and possibly risky, steps, WAP's membership, instead of voting on them, referred the Lawson recommendations to the board of directors, providing that any new contract with UP should be approved by WAP members.[52]

Seeking Reforms

The real showdown was, thus, postponed until the annual meeting the next day; the election of directors would determine the future of AP-UP and WAP-NYAP relations. As usual, all seven WAP seats were up for election. Over the previous seven years an average of 2.14 new directors had been placed on the board each year.[53] This, however, would be a different election in at least two respects. First, for the first time since 1867 Richard Smith and Walter N. Haldeman withdrew their names from the slate. Second, eight of the eleven nominees were not current directors, a very high percentage of new blood on the slate of candidates. It was a sign that Lawson forces had influenced the nominating process.

With fifty-six ballots being cast, those elected to the board were

Eugene H. Perdue, *Cleveland Leader*, reformer, 56 votes;

Charles W. Knapp, *St. Louis Republic*, reformer, 55 votes;

William A. Collier, *Memphis Avalanche*, reformer, 44 votes;

Michel H. de Young, *San Francisco Chronicle*, reformer, 40 votes;

Victor F. Lawson, *Chicago Daily News*, reformer, 36 votes;

Frederick Driscoll, *St. Paul Pioneer Press*, reformer, 32 votes.

The remaining nominees received the following votes:

Samuel E. Morss, *Indianapolis Sentinel*, old guard, 30 votes;

Albert J. Barr, *Pittsburgh Post*, reformer, 30 votes;

Sidney E. Haigh, *Madison* (Ind.) *Courier*, old guard, 27 votes;

Lucian Swift, Jr., *Minneapolis Journal*, old guard, 26 votes;

William Penn Nixon, *Chicago Inter Ocean*, old guard, 19 votes.

In a run-off election for the seventh board seat Barr received 32 votes, Morss 22 votes, and Haigh 2 votes.[54] (The labels "reformer" and "old guard" above are based on the roll call vote the previous day on whether WAP should support Mack's correspondence to the NYAP on retaining the joint committee in its existing form.)

Only Lawson and Barr were incumbents, and Morss was rebuffed in his bid for re-election. In all, five new directors were elected, and all seven were "reformers." Writing a friend in Philadelphia after the meeting, Lawson said, "The 'revolution' has taken place and the administration. . . has been defeated by the election of an entire new board of directors, six of whom were on our ticket and the remaining one—M. deYoung. . .—was with us in the fight. . . ."[55] The board then elected William Penn Nixon of the *Chicago Inter Ocean* as president. Although a member of the "old guard," Nixon's correspondence reveals him to have been a conciliator and a compromiser.[56]

For William Henry Smith, August 1891 was not the unmitigated disaster he might have dreaded. His article publicizing AP appeared that month in *Century* magazine, giving him an opportunity to boast that AP "enjoys the public confidence in its reliability to a degree unapproached by any other organization. [It] has been equal to every emergency."[57] As for the annual meeting confrontation, Smith called the outcome "a personal victory for me" but "the overthrow of one or two friends," noting that R. Smith and Haldeman were "only half way out of the woods."[58] Smith found in Lawson's report evidence that UP people had helped the committee gather its evidence against the joint executive committee. To Reid, Smith wrote "Mr. Walsh and Mr. Phillips supplied the committee with confidential details which shows how thoroughly they have betrayed you and others."[59] To Dana, Smith wrote, "This extraordinary performance shows how little dependence can be placed upon Mr. Walsh and his associates."[60] Although the record urges no conclusion on the matter, Smith's show of indignation may, by its persistence, betray Smith's own assistance to the committee to preserve his own standing in AP.

WAP's new board of reformers moved immediately on several fronts.[61] First, noting that the old WAP bylaws had allowed the accumulation of power in a few hands, the board gradually realized the need to wind up WAP's business and reorganize as a new corporation in Illinois. This was accomplished on December 15, 1892.[62] (This new corporation is discussed below.) Second, it attempted to abrogate the old joint executive committee agreement of nine years' standing. R. Smith and Haldeman refused to resign from the committee, feeling obliged to stand by their New York colleagues in order to protect contract obligations the committee had made on behalf of the WAP. The new WAP executive committee, however, declared their seats vacant on October 29, 1891, and elected Lawson and Driscoll as their replacements.[63]

R. Smith, while eager to leave the committee, ignored WAP's move "out of respect for Messrs. Dana and Reid,"[64] and did not formally resign until April 1892, after the old joint committee had held one last meeting in which he "discharged all obligations to the New York gentlemen."[65] Haldeman had left three months earlier when Dana had left the New York AP.[66] Finally, there is evidence that the new WAP board drew away from UP. Although the break-off in AP-

UP relations seems to have been preparatory to a fresh start at collusion between the two agencies, it affected news-gathering. A trade weekly in late 1891 reported that A. J. Stofer and H. C. Clarke would cover congressional proceedings for UP during the coming winter, "an arrangement made necessary by the severance of the contract between the United Press and Associated Press."[67]

The new WAP board moved carefully with William Henry Smith, whose ability to muster a good news report and call on the support of at least some editors could make him either a valuable ally or a fearsome adversary. Relations between the board and Smith were strained for several months after the August 1891 annual meeting.[68] The Lawson forces wanted Smith to turn over his UP stock and dividends to WAP, and Smith wanted to rid himself of association with those men whom he called "aggressive gentlemen [who] indulged in much calumny."[69] Adding to his stature after the Lawson revolution was the fact that Smith had gathered support from the Southern, New England, and New York State APs, all of which had placed "their affairs almost without restriction" in Smith's hands by mid-July 1892.[70] In fact, the Southern AP in October 1892 elected Smith its general manager, with power to execute contracts on behalf of the SAP.[71] Such support, together with the power he still wielded over the AP news report, commended Smith to WAP's reform directors as a useful associate.

Smith's UP stock, which he possessed at the request of R. Smith and Haldeman, was finally returned to UP in mid-November 1891, and was reissued to R. Smith and Haldeman one month later.[72] To resolve the matter of the UP dividends Smith had received, he offered in mid-June 1892, and the board accepted, his services in winding up WAP's business without compensation to an extent equal to the UP dividends he had received. He called it "an earnest of my interest in the organization which I have spent the best years of my life in building up."[73] On July 31, 1893, WAP ceased to exist,[74] and Smith, after talking about retirement for two years, was able finally "to get at my historical work . . . surrounded [in Lake Forest] by books and flowers, and trees, and horses, and cows, to be at last a happy man for such brief period as Providence may have in store for me."[75]

At the age of fifty-nine, with his wife "among the blessed on the shining shore, & none hav[ing] a claim upon me, I may properly follow my inclination,"[76] Smith might have had a long and productive retirement. His health, however, had always been unpredictable, and he died from pneumonia at his home on July 27, 1896. His political history of slavery[77] was nearly ready for publication when he died, and was completed and published in 1903 by his son-in-law, Charles R. Williams,[78] who also fulfilled Smith's commission to edit and publish the papers of Rutherford B. Hayes[79] and prepare a Hayes biography.[80]

A religious man, loyal to his friends and associates, Smith bore himself with dignity and efficiency through some of newsbroking's most trying years, years when business principles required ruthlessness and cunning for survival. While holding competitors at bay and holding together flimsy alliances within and between New York and the West, Smith greatly expanded the leased wire system, introduced typewriters into the service, and brought diversity and volume to the news report. Although ungratefully and ignobly fired by the NYAP on November 18, 1892,[81] he continued to work on the national scene through his old WAP and the emerging new Associated Press of Illinois to preserve the news machine he had labored to build over two decades. During his tenure in newsbroking Smith corresponded firmly, frankly, and with an even keel. Only in rare moments did he lose his steady demeanor. To a nonjournalist friend in 1887 he reported that

> I am still subject to the influences of active life, more often compelled to contend with the fierce passions of selfish men sweeping all before them like a whirlwind, than is agreeable to one whose nature is mild and peaceful. But if not altogether happy, I make a gallant fight and keep my colors always aloft.[82]

And in 1894, amid a scattering of entries in a book of memoirs, Smith wrote of himself and two old political friends: "We have much to regret, but no unworthy motives, no unmanly acts, no unpatriotic deeds to embitter the evening of life."[83]

RESTRUCTURING

WAP's new reformist-minded board had, of course, to deal with the NYAP and UP separately after the old trust and working agreements with UP and the joint executive committee with NYAP were abolished. WAP efforts to resurrect a workable joint executive committee (minus R. Smith and Haldeman) ran headlong into a disorganized and disintegrating New York AP. The absence of R. Smith and Haldeman had encouraged power-hungry representatives of the *World, Herald, Times,* and *Evening Mail and Express* in New York to withdraw support of Reid and Dana as liaisons with the West. Reid, still in Paris as U.S. ambassador early in 1892 and later that year the vice-presidential candidate on the losing Republican ticket headed by Benjamin Harrison, refused to set a definite course of action, thus allowing the *Tribune* to drift through most of 1892 as a silent NYAP partner, secure in the knowledge that it possessed a block of UP stock. Dana, unpredictable and inclined to bear grudges, took his removal from the joint executive committee as an insult and withdrew from the NYAP on January 2, 1892, moving his *New York Sun* and Laffan News Service into UP's camp.[84] A measure of Dana's fickleness can be found in his speech at Union College twenty-two months after leaving the NYAP. UP is the "most perfectly organized" newsbrokerage, Dana told the students, one "which has revolutionized and is revolutionizing the operations of the profession. [UP is a] great and wide-reaching agency."[85]

Most of 1892 was consumed with the West and UP attempting to negotiate a mutual protection, news-exchange pact while the remaining six NYAP partners bickered among themselves, unable to decide whether to form an alliance with the West or UP. Claiming that 75 percent of AP's papers wanted WAP and UP to "come to some amicable arrangement," Allan Forman, editor of *The Journalist,* observed in September, 1892, that "the enmity between the 'A.P.' and the 'U.P.' does not exist outside of New York City . . . ; it is the New York people who are causing the discord."[86] The matter was settled for NYAP late in 1892 when UP and the West suddenly agreed to a provisional territorial division, giving UP everything east of the Allegheny range and north of the Potomac River and AP the rest of the country, both agreeing to exchange news and not to raid each other's territory for subscribers.[87]

Although the pact fell apart within three months, its initial effect was to force the NYAP to disband on December 10, 1892, and join UP. In addition to the *Sun,* the *Tribune, Herald,* and *World* received UP stock. Other former NYAP papers—the *Times, Journal of Commerce,* and *Evening Mail and Express*—received UP news report franchises but no stock. The old NYAP agency, which began to take shape with the onset of telegraphy in New York City, had first revealed itself in the chartering of the *Buena Vista* in 1848, and was first formally identified as the Harbor News Association early in 1849, had at last been brought down by its own jealousies and indecisiveness, never having attained a legal status beyond partnership.

Its offices in the Western Union building, which it had occupied since early 1875, were vacated, and AP's gear was moved into the offices that UP had occupied in the new *New York World* building on Park Row since January 1, 1891.[88] Within two years, however, UP occupied "sumptuously fitted up rooms [in the Western Union building], facing on Broadway," according to Charles S. Diehl, while the AP had "unpretentious, but convenient" offices in the same building.[89]

Meanwhile, events progressed rapidly in the West. A new Associated Press, incorporated in Illinois, came into being on December 15, 1892, and Melville E. Stone, founder and former publisher of the *Chicago Daily News* and since 1888 a Chicago banker, was persuaded to become general manager of the new AP in March 1893 at $10,000 per year, receiving a permanent appointment on July 24, 1893. The new agency's news report first appeared on August 1, 1893, replacing WAP's and serving 207 newspapers in twenty-nine states over 9,806 miles of leased wire.[90] A printed circular, dated April 12, 1893, and signed by both Stone for the new AP and Smith for the old WAP, promised publishers that the "perpetual franchises of the Western Associated Press will be replaced by the 90 year membership contracts of the Associated Press."[91] The first sixty-two members[92] of the new AP were the existing WAP members, constituting the nucleus of power and privilege in the new agency. All but two of the first members (*Galveston News* and Springfield *Illinois State Journal*) automatically received local board status with which to scrutinize and pass on local applicants for AP membership. Six hundred shares at $50 each, for a total capitalization of $30,000, were issued, but in December 1893 capital stock was increased to $100,000 and the board increased from nine to eleven directors.[93] Stock was purchased by members, but held in trust by AP.

Organizers and the first board of the new AP consisted of the seven "reform" directors elected by the WAP in August 1891, plus James E. Scripps, of the *Detroit Tribune and Evening News,* and Washington Hesing, of the Chicago *Illinois Staats-Zeitung.* As AP later began to capture newspaper members in UP territory, these incursions were reflected on the board. In 1894 E. H. Butler of the *Buffalo Evening News* replaced Collier of the *Memphis Appeal-Avalanche.* Clayton McMichael of the *Philadelphia North American* and Frank B. Noyes of the *Washington* (D.C.) *Star* filled two new board seats created in 1894. Thomas G. Rapier of the *New Orleans Picayune* replaced Butler in 1895, and Stephen O'Meara of the *Bos-*

ton Journal replaced Scripps in 1896. (See table 7 in the Appendix for a complete list of AP directors and officers between 1892 and 1920 and for sources of board changes.)

The new AP divided its membership along two dimensions. A newspaper could be a stockholder and, thus, participate in board elections and votes on resolutions and bylaw amendments. A newspaper could hold no more than eight shares (a $400 investment), and most holders purchased the maximum. Votes were tallied by shares of stock. Stockholders represented only one-third of total membership between 1894 and the death of the UP in 1897, when a rapid influx of new members lowered stockholders to one-quarter of total membership. The other dimension of membership was Series A or B certificates. A Series A member sat on the local board, which voted on applications of local competitors for AP membership. Series B members received the news report but had no voice in the admission of local papers. Stockholders and Series A members were largely identical lists, although the latter was somewhat smaller, as the following analysis of AP membership in mid-May 1896 indicates.[94]

	Morning Papers		Evening Papers		Total Membership	
Stockholders & Series A	73	36.7%	43	19.2%	116	27.4%
Stockholders Only	16	8.0	6	2.7	22	5.2
Series A Only	2	1.0	4	1.8	6	1.4
Series B Only	108	54.3	171	76.3	279	66.0
Totals	199	100.0%	224	100.0%	423	100.0%

Although evening papers represented 53 percent of the total membership, only 21 or 22 percent of that group owned stock and also held Series A certificates. Nearly 45 percent of all morning papers in AP, on the other hand, owned stock and 37.7 percent of the morning papers had Series A certificates.

This new AP had inherited the privileges that WAP had accorded its leading members for years; in fact, it had converted a somewhat informal franchise right into a legal Series A status. Moreover, although the old second-class auxiliary tributaries were eliminated and their members invited to join the new AP, the dominant role historically played by WAP's leading metropolitan dailies was preserved in the new agency through stockholding, and its attendant voting rights. These inequities, in addition to being formally codified in the bylaws, were spread plainly and repeatedly across the record of the new AP's deliberations.

Meanwhile, in contrast to this formalization of privilege, openness, which had been a cornerstone of the reformers' attack upon the old WAP management, became a compulsion of the new AP leadership. Membership meetings and the regular board meetings following those annual meetings had, for years, been the only proceedings published by WAP, and these in very sketchy form. Between 1884 and 1889 published minutes of these regular meetings annually averaged only 7.83 pages in type. The 1890 WAP *Proceedings* was larger, containing twenty-five pages, but much of the increase was due to inclusion of a special membership and board meeting, the first Lawson committee report, and minutes of a joint executive committee meeting. The 1891 *Proceedings*, the first prepared under the reform board, however, contained eighty-eight pages of minutes of membership, board, and even executive committee meetings, all meticulously detailed and sprinkled with reprints of significant correspondence. A full report from the board also reappeared in the 1891 *Proceedings* after an absence of ten years. The *Annual Reports* of the new AP between 1893 and 1900 maintained this preoccupation with thorough and open record-keeping, going so far as to reprint court decisions bearing on AP operations, annually printing the bylaws, and periodically naming in separate lists all members, stockholders, members of local boards, and the assessments charged each member. The slim, fifteen-page *Proceedings* of the WAP in 1889 contrasts sharply with the 520-page *Annual Report* of the AP in 1898.

The new AP also practiced openness, interestingly, by recording in great detail its negotiations with United Press. Whereas the two Smiths and Haldeman had signed working agreements and entered stock pools with UP *secretly,* AP's reform board unashamedly pursued the same ventures with UP *openly,* several times coming close to establishing relations with UP similar to those attained by the WAP-NYAP joint executive committee. The old management had erred not in pursuing the then-acceptable business principles developed to avoid competition, but in doing so secretly and for personal advantage. A provisional AP-UP agreement[95] beginning in mid-October 1892, as noted above, established a news exchange and territorial exclusivity. As mid-February 1893 drew near, when the agencies would convert this agreement into a permanent pact, UP became hostile, however, filing a suit to recover about $30,000 from the old WAP and taking possession of WAP's account books, which were in the New York City office. Despite such provocations Lawson and his friends went to New York to sign the permanent contract, only to learn that Dana, who had become UP's president, refused to sign, without giving clear-cut reasons. To William Henry Smith, watching from the sidelines, UP's defiance arose in the old NYAP faction of the UP, and specifically in "the passions of [Dana's] malignant heart." Dana, Smith wrote to Reid, "is a child of Satan. Consider for one moment the blackness of the heart that inspired the wicked editorials in the Sun after the death of Grant and recently after the death of Hayes. Lovable? No, repellant."[96]

But AP exhibited some aggressiveness, too. The Reuters contract for the international cartel news exchange seemed destined to follow NYAP into UP. And UP's William Laffan too casually assumed that it would and could await his attention in London at the end of a long junket across Europe. Meanwhile, one of William Henry Smith's longtime assistants, Walter Neef, was in London, where he had gone in the fall of 1890 and served as AP agent until Phillips fired him in the wake of NYAP's death in late 1892.[97] Unemployed but continuing his personal contacts with British journalists, including the leadership at Reuters, Neef was commissioned by Lawson to seek a separate contract between the new AP and Reuters after UP balked at signing a permanent agreement with the AP in mid-February 1893. Lawson told Neef "to make instant and vigorous action for the protection of the Western Papers."[98] Neef replied that the Reuters people had been surprised by not hearing a word from the WAP or its AP successor in the three months since the breakup of the NYAP.[99] Such news prompted Stone to leave for London on March 6 to execute a contract with Reuters. Arriving there on March 17, Stone found that Neef had already worked out a contract with the agency. Stone affixed his signature to the document on March 20 and returned to the United States. The contract continued the news exchange with the world cartel in the name of the new AP.[100] Reuters, it turned out, had been persuaded to abandon negotiations with UP and sign with the new AP on the advice of its bureau manager in New York City.[101]

While William Henry Smith may have marked his release of Walter P. Phillips in 1882 as a chief blunder of his career, Phillips may have felt the same way about releasing Neef in London ten years later. The Reuters contract was impressive leverage for the new AP and left Phillips lamely to rationalize that

> Mr. Laffan peremptorily refused to have anything to do with
> Reuter, as we did not need him. We were unwilling . . . to mort-
> gage our future for $200,000. . . . That contract. . . binds the As-
> sociated Press, and it would bind us if we assumed it, not to sell
> news abroad during the life of the contract. We are gathering
> news in Europe for use in America and we purpose selling it
> there, together with an American and South American ser-
> vice.[102]

Strong words, but in fact in the view of many American newspaper
publishers UP had been outmaneuvered, and even though AP was
bound by its new contract not to sell news in Europe and to receive
most of its foreign news from the cartel, capturing Reuters spoke
loudly to U.S. journalists of the new AP's spunk and stability.

NEWSBROKER WAR

A provisional truce between AP and UP remained in effect while
the two agencies pursued negotiations through several rounds of
proposals and counter-proposals during the summer of 1893, but
late in August when Haldeman informed AP that his *Louisville
Courier-Journal* was joining UP,[103] AP declared this a violation of
the truce, and prepared for war, giving a four-man committee one
final chance at making peace. Significantly no one on this committee was an AP director. Only one was in AP's reform faction, David
M. Houser of the *St. Louis Globe-Democrat,* while the other three
were in the old guard: I. F. Mack of the *Sandusky* (Ohio) *Register,*
Richard Smith of the *Cincinnati Commercial Gazette,* and W. A.
Bunker of the *Kansas City Journal.* The committee was met with a
UP proposal offering UP franchises to all AP papers; UP would not
talk of news exchanges.[104]

AP's stockholders on October 4, 1893, declared war on UP, vowing to establish a "national, mutual news-gathering association for
the benefit of its members and the public it serves" by admitting
members to AP from all regions of the country provided "this shall
not impair the existing rights of members."[105] Lawson and Stone
went east that fall, seeking the support of former Midwestern journalists who were running Eastern papers. Several New York papers,
including the *World,* abandoned UP, as did some in Upstate New
York and New England, six Philadelphia papers, three in Baltimore,
and two in Washington, D.C.[106] Stone sent his assistant general
manager, Charles S. Diehl, east to take charge of AP's Eastern,

Southern, and foreign service. Diehl was also expected to recruit members for AP, and the account in his autobiography of his many trips up and down the coast, convincing some editors to abandon UP and meeting strong resistance from others, reveals some of the stress and undercurrent of this developing agency war.[107]

Edwin M. Hood, head of the reporting staff on Capitol Hill, watched and pondered these developments with more than passing interest, making occasional comments in his diary. On January 2, 1893, he wrote,

> The Associated Press—that Rock of Gibraltar as we were wont to call it—yielded up the ghost and died an unnatural death Dec. 10, 1892. Undoubtedly, it was brought about mainly by W. P. Phillips who thus stands revenged for his treatment ten years ago. All of the assets were absorbed by the United Press— myself among them.

On January 1, 1894, Hood recorded,

> West. Press, under name of "Associated Press" broke away from United Press last summer and are making bitter war on us. C. A. Boynton, Washn. agent & Merrilat with them as Day Manager. Could have gone with them but I decided to hold on. Possible I may regret this later on as they are making great inroads on our papers.

Finally, on January 6, 1895, he noted, "Feb. 12, '94, left the United Press and went with the Associated Press...taking the uptown depts. and giving up Capitol work."[108]

Beginning with sixty-two members on March 1, 1893, AP's growth was indeed phenomenal, much of it at UP's expense. AP membership was 207 on August 1, 1893; 381 on December 31, 1894; and 396 on February 1, 1895.[109] The net increases were at a rate of one paper added every 1.06 days up to August 1, 1893, one paper added every three days during 1894, and one paper added every two days in January 1895. Table 1 in the Appendix, however, reveals that by 1895, although AP had surpassed UP, together the agencies served only 37 percent of the nation's dailies. UP still dominated New England and the Middle Atlantic and South Atlantic regions, while AP held the edge in other regions. AP in 1895 had members in all but two states or territories; UP had subscribers in all but fourteen. Significantly, however, both newsbrokerages had a presence in each region, making this truly a news war on a national scale.

By February 1895 AP's board reported that the war with UP had cost AP $209,415 to date, the agency running monthly deficits of about $70,000.[110] UP showed monthly deficits averaging $20,221 between September 1893 and February 1894[111] and $16,618 from February to July 1894.[112] United Press, said AP, had repeatedly made "informal overtures...looking to a termination of the present contest," all of which were rebuffed as being unfair to Eastern AP papers. Moreover, the board invoked a bylaw prohibition on members' trafficking with opposition news organizations, and added the *New York Herald, Tribune, Sun,* and *News* to its list of opposition or "antagonistic" news organizations.[113]

Added to the war's continuing financial burden, the spring of 1895 brought new stresses for UP. An unexpected increase in telegraph tolls west of the Rocky Mountains, followed by assumption of the full expenses of the Central News Agency of London (UP's source of European news) after Central was abandoned by its London newspaper clients, were the "bad half hour with fate," as one trade weekly put it. UP was forced to seek new negotiations with AP in May. Eight days of conferences over a UP proposal that would have subordinated UP to the Associated Press in a co-existence pact yielded no settlement. The published record of the meetings reveals both the sincerity and the futility of the effort for both sides.[114] Increasing costs, unmatched by sufficient growth in membership, however, made extrication from these hostilities an urgent goal for United Press. Only accommodation with AP could have eased UP's financial distress, the latter unable to declare bankruptcy as long as contracts with leading Eastern and Southern newspapers had to be honored. In AP's camp, meanwhile, continuing heavy assessments on members and the hesitancy of Eastern publishers to abandon UP drew AP men to the bargaining table, where they met with increasingly enticing UP proposals.

But, as *Fourth Estate* noted, "there is no possibility of a union" because AP "is both legally and in honor bound to protect its franchises absolutely, and even if its directors were so inclined...it would be impossible to interfere with existing relations." In actuality, AP's board was inclined to approve a pact with UP growing out of the May 1985 meetings until their lawyers advised them that such approval would be contrary to other AP obligations.[115] United Press responded to this latest breakdown in negotiations with several leaflets and pamphlets attacking AP,[116] and AP replied with an open letter to the nation's newspaper editors in mid-July 1895.[117]

Meanwhile, the AP board boasted that monthly deficits had been brought down to about $4,000,[118] and lamented that AP attempts to recruit new members had in a few instances run headlong into existing AP members' protests against admitting local competitors, leading the board to say, "it can only be a question of time when [invoking the protest right] must be seriously dealt with as the only remaining obstacle of consequence in the way of a settlement of the contest with The United Press."[119] Vestiges of this right of protest would impair AP's growth until 1945, when a U.S. Supreme Court decision held it to be a violation of antitrust laws in a case arising from the *Chicago Tribune*'s protest of the admission to AP of Marshall Field III and his new *Chicago Sun*.[120]

Early in the contest Whitelaw Reid observed, "Everything would now seem to depend on the financial strength and skill in management shown by the two competitors."[121] One interested observer, E. W. Scripps, assessed the war in similar terms, commenting that in 1895

> the United Press, under Walter Phillips, had arrived at its zenith. It included in its membership. . .the leading New York City papers at that time. . . .Its principal financial backer and controlling spirit was John P. Walsh. . . .It included all of the Scripps papers at that time, as clients, or members or subscribers.
>
> John P. Walsh was one of the Napoleons of finance who ended his days in the State Prison.
>
> Phillips was a brilliant and enterprising genius in the way of a purveyor of news. He had no capacities as an executive, and, because of Walsh's power over the concern, he was doing things that no manager of a press association should do. . . .
>
> The management of the United Press threatened even the existence of a free press in this country.[122]

By mid-1896 it was clear that UP's management was stretched to the breaking point by a shrinking clientele, having to make financial concessions to its small clients and drawing more substantially on its large New York papers. Figures for 1896 in table 4 of the Appendix suggest UP's dire condition. Totaling only 70 percent of AP's costs, UP's expenses went for a less stable and smaller news-gathering system. AP commanded a much larger leased wire system and a larger in-house news-gathering staff. UP was still strapped with heavier per-word tolls to move its report, and a less efficient and more expensive system than AP's leased network. Finally, UP paid nearly 16 percent of its expenses to outside sources for news. Much of this payment went monthly to remnants of the New England, Southern, and New York State APs for news delivered by them to UP's headquarters. Phillips in mid-July 1896 had reintroduced the old auxiliary agency system, which had been the backbone of AP's operation until 1892, to cut costs in UP, Phillips renaming UP the "United Associated Presses."[123]

As 1896 dragged on, UP management drew increasingly on the cash reserves of UP's three leading New York City stockholders, the *Sun, Herald,* and *Tribune.* While AP's members shouldered the lighter burden of a guaranty fund spread proportionally among many papers, members of UP's New York City contingent each paid monthly UP assessments ranging from $4,000 to $5,000 during the first half of 1896,[124] leading to speculation that these papers might eventually have to abandon UP to protect their profits. In late July of 1896, Reid was privately quoted as saying that he was "tired [of] throwing good money after bad without prospect [of] success under present conditions." He went on to suggest changing UP's management. If Dana refused to replace UP's top men, Reid reportedly said, the *Tribune* would seek an AP membership. Bennett agreed with Reid.[125]

Dana, however, would not hear of management changes, and this led to secret talks between AP and the *Herald, Tribune,* and *Times.* Pivotal to these talks were the sentiments of Joseph Pulitzer, whose *World,* it will be recalled, had jumped to the AP in the fall of 1893. Pulitzer welcomed the *Tribune* and *Herald* into AP, but not the *Times,* which at that time was in receivership and about to pass into Adolph S. Ochs's hands.[126] Bennett wished all three and the *Sun,* if it desired, to enter AP on an equal footing,[127] but Pulitzer prevailed, permitting the *Times* to receive a Series B certificate.[128] The protracted secret talks seemed on the verge of producing the desired defection to AP in February 1897,[129] when Dana got wind of them and blew them out of the water with a published condemnation of the proceedings. "Our associates in the conduct of the United Press," roared the *Sun,*

> having entered upon negotiations for the surrender of the United Press to the Chicago Associated Press, without even asking for our consent, it becomes proper that we should now give public notice to whom it may concern [that] *The Sun* has no part in these negotiations, but firmly rejects them, believing them to be conceived in bad faith, and conducted in folly. Fur-

thermore, *The Sun* makes known that thirty days from the date hereof, it will cease to be a member of the United Press.

The Sun will also continue to collect the news for itself. . . .[130]

After four years of conflict and fruitless negotiation, the newsbroker war ended abruptly, precipitated not by a New York agreement or by Dana at the *Sun,* but by the decision of one paper, the *Boston Herald,* to switch to AP. The *Herald,* plus Boston's *Advertiser* and *Record,* represented the linchpin of the New England Associated Press, still intact but now allied exclusively with UP. Beating off an attempt by the NEAP to enjoin the paper from moving to AP, the *Herald* began receiving AP news reports on March 23, 1897. Like the toppling of the first of a row of dominoes, the *Herald's* move to AP set off a chain reaction for AP in this UP stronghold. Maine's newspapers immediately came into AP as a body, and the rest of NEAP's membership was admitted to AP in short order.

Meanwhile, the bloodletting in New England served as a signal for the *New York Herald, Tribune,* and *Times* to jump to AP, leaving only the *Sun* and William Randolph Hearst's *Journal* as UP's strongholds in New York City. Indeed, by May 7 AP's membership rolls listed eighteen New York City papers, five of them foreign-language journals and two being the *World's* morning and evening editions. Included in the list were six of the seven old New York AP partners, with the *Sun* the only holdout. In the face of such an exodus, UP president Dana filed for bankruptcy on March 29, 1897. The following day the New York State AP dissolved its corporate existence at an emergency meeting, thus permitting its members to abandon their UP contracts and seek AP's news service.[131]

On one day alone (April 1, 1897), AP's board received applications from nineteen UP papers scattered all over the country,[132] and late that day the board received a telegram from Patrick Walsh, general manager of the Southern AP, asking on what terms the SAP's thirty members, then meeting in Augusta, Ga., could be admitted to AP.[133] On April 3 the *New York Herald, Tribune,* and *Times* among other papers were formally admitted to AP membership.[134] On April 8, 1897, UP discontinued its news service,[135] and the AP, Diehl reports, bought UP's "fine rugs and furniture, and took over its offices facing on Broadway."[136] Dana's *Sun* chose to stay outside the AP, turning to its own Laffan News Service rather than join the enemy. It was Dana's last spiteful act in the newsbroking field; six months later, on October 17, he died, the last of New York's leading journalists who had attended the birth of the New York Associated Press partnership nearly half a century earlier.

Table 1 in the Appendix shows that one month after UP's death, AP served nearly 30 percent of the nation's dailies, an increase of 60.9 percent over its total membership two years earlier. AP's biggest gains, as might be expected, were in the three Atlantic seaboard regions, which had been UP strongholds. AP's increases in other regions were far more modest; in fact, the number actually declined by a few papers in the West South Central and Pacific regions. About the time UP was closing its doors and AP was gathering in the spoils of victory, *Cosmopolitan* magazine was publishing, no doubt to its chagrin, an article in which Thomas B. Connery, who had been managing editor of the *New York Herald* from 1870 to 1885, carefully depicted both AP and UP as strong and formidable competitors.[137]

Silencing UP was no simple business victory in the view of the AP men who engineered it. Victor F. Lawson for many years kept on his desk a framed copy of the March 31, 1897, notice from UP's assignee announcing that the agency would discontinue its news report on April 8.[138] To Lawson this had been a fight ''for the preservation of the independence of the American Press,'' wrote his biographer, Charles H. Dennis, a fight for ''principle.''[139] John R. Wilson of the *Chicago Journal* wrote during the fight of the ''maintenance of the liberty of the American press from selfish designs of a New York coterie of publishers'' and of ''loyalty to the cooperative principle of the Associated Press.''[140] And general manager Stone offered the following vision of AP's goal:

> A national cooperative news-gathering organization, owned by the newspapers and by them alone, selling no news, making no profits, paying no dividends, simply the agent and servant of the newspapers, was the thing. Those participating should be journalists of every conceivable partisan, religious, economic, and social affiliation, but all equally zealous that in the business of news gathering for their supply there should be strict accuracy, impartiality, and integrity. That was the dream we dreamed.[141]

When 150 of the total of 171[142] AP stockholders met for their annual meeting in the Recital Hall of Chicago's Auditorium Hotel on

May 19, 1897, they well knew "the pleasure and the satisfaction of this hour," as Lawson observed in opening the proceedings. "Since the last meeting," he continued, "the principle of self-ownership, self-administration, in that thing which lies at the basis of the news-paper properties of this country, has achieved an expression that has never before obtained in the history of the press...."[143] The stockholders, then proceeding for the rest of the day to exercise their "principles," filled thirty-five pages of type with resolutions directing the board on this and that matter, considering several amendments to AP's bylaws, and filling one-third of the seats on the board.[144]

That evening over a dinner of fillet of black bass, spring lamb, roast Philadelphia squab, and an assortment of drinks and other delicacies, with Altamaro's Mandolin Orchestra and the Roney Quartet of Boy Singers providing background music, the editors and publishers of the victorious AP at last permitted themselves a convivial celebration after four anxious years of bitter conflict. Directors received silver medals, Lawson received a silver service, Stone a silver loving cup, and Diehl a gold watch. During four hours of wit and fellowship,[145] "a night of brilliant speeches and repartee," according to Diehl,[146] some looked to the past and others to the future. St. Clair McKelway of the *Brooklyn Daily Eagle* observed that "to the old guard which neither died nor surrendered, belongs the past." The old guard, he continued, "proposes to put its stamp of personal esteem and affection in this presence on the exemplars of past service, to be an inspiration and an incentive for all the future."[147] About the future, Charles H. Taylor of the *Boston Globe* cautioned,

> We have not only the strongest news association that has ever been known in this country, but the strongest ever known in the world.... You want to remember that when you are on top of the hill all roads lead down. You want to remember that the more business you get the more polite you want to be. We are together, and this is an Association that can last for ninety years with good management.[148]

As this book goes to press, the Associated Press has just passed the ninety years Taylor predicted for AP if it had "good management."

DISCUSSION

The first four chapters of this book constantly portray newsbroking affiliation as protection for the newspaper publisher from local competition and an inadequate news report. Whether inside Associated Press or among the "outside press" the cry of the leadership was: affiliate, for there is safety in numbers and protection in the local franchise. So well did the leaders of AP and UP convince their clients of these principles, that when news-exchange agreements and stock pools between AP and UP were revealed, those local publishers responded with stern, unforgiving self-interest, as this chapter describes. From the local perspective, the trust was discovered and disassembled none too soon: trusts had a habit of evolving into full-fledged monopolies, which disenfranchised local businesses. Second-generation reformist publishers, primarily from the Midwest, objecting to the secrecy, personal gain, and tilt of control once again toward New York City implicit in the trust, reacted with a reorganization emphasizing starkly public proceedings, partially democratic procedures (at least for Series A papers and stockholders), and representation of all regions of the nation on the board of directors.

The ensuing battle and victory over UP eliminated after a quarter of a century or more all vestiges of regional auxiliaries and brought the AP under a single national board and management. Paradoxically, this national unity was accompanied by a stronger emphasis on local publisher rights and protections than had existed under the joint executive committee. Stockholding, Series A memberships, open and democratic deliberations, and an enlarged board expressly representing all regions of the nation swung the political balance toward the local newspaper publisher, at least for the time being. Only a strong and progressive management, a growing significance of the news report, or the nudge of new newsbroking competition could resurrect AP's equality with its members. As the next two chapters indicate, all three factors were in evidence after 1897, pushing not only AP but its new competitors past equilibrium with the newspaper press to a position of institutional status, independent of the newspaper press.

In one area, however, an AP policy that had grown up over the years was codified as a bylaw provision in 1893 prohibiting members from receiving the reports of AP's competitors. Back in 1884, William Henry Smith had told a Senate committee that there were "certain rules governing the Associated Press which all papers are required to observe." The "value of the news to its owners," Smith continued, consists in the control of it, and in the safeguards which may be thrown around it. If members of the Associated Press were permitted to have dealings with a rival association there would be no security for the news of the Associated Press. . . . [149]

Membership in AP's club precluded reception of others' news reports, even though those others had no qualms about their subscribers receiving AP news. It was one of the few areas in 1897 of AP's dominance over its newspaper members.

Aside from the obvious hypocracy in this statement of a man who, as he spoke these words, was having "dealings with a rival association," Smith could not have foreseen such conditions in the next century as strong new newsbrokerages that offered publishers an alternative to AP's lackluster news report and as powerful new newspaper chains that made extreme demands on AP's protectionist structure. These conditions and clashes form the narrative of the next two chapters, which depict newsbroking's emergence as a social institution.

Chapter 6
LITIGATION AND RELOCATION

It was quite true that control of the press was wrested from governments at the beginning of our Republic. The first amendment . . . forbade any attempt in the United States to stop free speech or a free press. . . . Government might not enchain the press, but private monopoly might. . . . And this business of news gathering and purveying had fallen into private and mercenary hands. Its control by three men was quite as menacing as that of the governmental autocrats of the ages agone. There could be no really free press in these circumstances. A press to be free must be one which should gather the news for itself. . . .

[The Illinois Supreme Court in 1900] held that . . . the Associated Press was so affected with a public duty that it must serve its news to any applicant. A compliance with this extraordinary judgment meant a destruction of the fundamental right of the members to unite for the collection . . . of the news for their own exclusive use.

Melville E. Stone, **Fifty Years a Journalist**
(1921)

In these two paragraphs—twenty pages apart in his autobiography[1]—the general manager of the Associated Press from 1893 to 1921 implies that while newsbroking by profit-making businesses thwarts press freedom, newsbroking the AP way ensures press freedom, albeit only for those newspapers lucky enough to be AP members. This myopic vision of AP as the defender and preserver of America's freedom of the press had its roots in AP's painful and prolonged confrontation with the first United Press. The world of journalism was increasingly threatening for AP members, those established and respected newspapers, after the Civil War. New competitors, both national newsbrokers and local newspapers, persistently appeared, and the public's tastes in journalism were changing. In this hostile setting freedom and survival became entwined for the publishers of these older journals, and their AP memberships grew to be an important protection of their right as well as their property.

In the post–Civil War period, however, no threat to an AP paper's right to publish was greater than that posed by the first United Press. Aggressive and effective, UP held out the olive branch of alliance with one hand while holding the sword of competition with the other. Chapters 4 and 5 trace the growth after 1882 of an AP-UP trust born of distrust and fear, and the rise after 1892 of an AP-UP war with national supremacy as the prize. But the death of the first UP in 1897 failed to bring prosperity and security to AP. With AP's membership representing only 30 percent of the nation's daily papers one month after UP's bankruptcy (see table 1 in the Appendix), there was ample opportunity for competing newsbrokerages and supplemental wires to find customers. And with AP bylaws that protected existing members by severely limiting new memberships, AP's growth was stunted and many rejected applicants were left frustrated and angry.

This chapter picks up the story of AP's travail after UP's death in 1897. It is a story of leadership changes, a new wave of competition, internal strife over membership policies, and eventually a court decision that sent Associated Press scurrying for protection in New York state. And through it all, AP's officers strove to preserve, as Stone called it, "the fundamental right of the members."

PERSONNEL CHANGES

Much of the post-1897 history of newsbroking in the United States is told in reasonable detail in a variety of sources,[2] leaving this chapter and the next free to summarize it only briefly, at least through 1920. Beyond the obvious AP-UP war that led to the death of the latter in 1897, the most striking feature of the watershed 1890s was the total turnover in editorial supervision and top management of the newsbrokerages.

On the publishers' side, of the four active members of the joint executive committee—Richard Smith, Walter N. Haldeman, Whitelaw Reid, and Charles A. Dana—only Reid did not begin to slip out of sight after 1893. Smith, seventy years old in 1893, had one last AP fling, it will be recalled, in late summer 1893, when along with others of the old guard, he attempted to head off open AP-UP warfare. After that, one loses track of him, except to note that his *Commercial Gazette* in Cincinnati was merged with the *Tribune*, forming the

Commercial Tribune, in 1896.[3] Haldeman, seventy-two years of age in 1893 when his *Louisville Courier-Journal* bolted to the UP and broke the AP-UP truce, was back in the AP membership by February 1, 1895, and was listed as a member of the new AP of New York when it organized in 1900. He died in 1902.[4]

Dana, as president of the faltering United Press, gradually diminished in visibility until both that agency and he died in 1897. William M. Laffan, who guided the *New York Sun* and the Laffan News Service until his own death in 1909, found himself in the backwaters of supplemental news service. Reid remained active in the New York City local board of AP and was an AP director from 1900 to 1905. Otherwise, the power conferred upon seven New York City publishers or papers for fifty years because of their pivotal New York Associated Press partnership came to an end in the 1890s.

The new AP, first in Illinois and then as a New York corporation after 1900, brought a different group of New York people to the forefront in the organization. S. S. Carvalho and John Norris represented the *New York World* on the board from 1894 to 1900 and were followed by Edward P. Call of the *New York Evening Post*, formerly a non-NYAP partner. Among the six incorporators in 1900 of the AP in New York, the two from New York City were Adolph S. Ochs of the *New York Times*, the old NYAP's new kid on the block, and St. Clair McKelway of the *Brooklyn Daily Eagle*, formerly a non-NYAP partner. On the first board of the AP of New York was Don Seitz of the *New York World*; Reid, *New York Tribune*; and Herman Ridder, *New York Staats-Zeitung*. Seitz and the *World* stayed only one year, replaced by Clark Howell of the *Atlanta Constitution*. Reid was replaced after five years by Ochs of the *Times*. After sixteen years on the board, Ridder, formerly affiliated with NYAP without being a partner, was replaced by Oswald Garrison Villard of the *New York Evening Post*.

Never after 1893 would the AP board include representatives of New York's *Sun*, *Herald* (or the later *Herald Tribune*), *Journal of Commerce*, or *Evening Mail and Express*. The *Sun* and *Herald* retained a visibility in newsbroking after 1893 only on the board of the sinking United Press, and after 1897 the *Sun* survived as a newsbroking force by running the independent Laffan News Service until 1916. Other rising publishers in newsbroking in the 1890s or soon after were E. W. Scripps, only a moderately powerful client of the old UP, and William Randolph Hearst, an insignificant AP member until 1900.

In the Midwest, as we saw in chapter 5, five of the seven directors of the old Western Associated Press retired or were turned out in 1891, and all on the new board that year were classed as "reformers." These seven, plus two other reformers, became the first board of the new Associated Press of Illinois in 1892. In the next eight years the board was expanded and some directorships changed frequently to reflect and reward AP's expanding membership during its war with UP.

On the management side, William Henry Smith retired from AP in 1893 and died three years later. Walter P. Phillips went down with UP in 1897, and after a brief employment with the Scripps-McRae News Association, turned his attention to the Columbia Graphophone Company and the American Red Cross. (Before he died in 1920, Phillips, like Daniel H. Craig before him, had a brief fling at promoting a high-speed automatic telegraphic device.)[0] The managers who came to the fore in their stead—Melville E. Stone, Robert F. Paine, William Waller Hawkins, Hamilton B. Clark, and Roy W. Howard, among others—although not newcomers to journalism, had little or no experience in newsbroking before taking leading roles in its development, as we shall see.

It was an entirely different story for the lieutenants, bureau chiefs, reporters, and operators, who for the most part survived the shakeup in AP and the subsequent AP-UP battle. Some advanced rapidly as the result of the unsettled times, for example Charles S. Diehl, as we shall see. A few others lost ground, for example Richard Smith, Jr., who from about 1891 to the end of 1894 was chief of AP's New York City bureau. After 1894 he dropped from sight in AP, perhaps a victim of the friends he had kept. He had secured his AP job and the post in New York City from William Henry Smith, and his father was Richard Smith of Cincinnati, whom the AP reformers had forced out of power in the Western AP for accepting UP stock while a member of the joint executive committee. It should be no surprise that sometime after the younger Richard Smith left AP, he became managing editor of the *Indianapolis News*, which was owned by Delavan Smith, William Henry Smith's son.[1]

In most cases, however, AP staffers with talent and experience held on to their jobs during the transitions from Smith to Stone and from an Illinois to a New York corporation. Charles A. Boynton, for many years Smith's eyes and ears in New York City, became chief of AP's bureau in Washington in 1892, remaining in that post until

1908.[7] Walter Neef, secretary and assistant to Smith since the 1870s, was AP's London agent from 1890 to 1892, when he was fired by United Press, the new proprietor of the New York AP's news-gathering apparatus. Neef regained his London position in 1893 under the new AP of Illinois and continued in that post until his death in 1905.[8] Addison C. Thomas, variously a reporter, night manager, agent, and superintendent in AP's Chicago bureau since 1880, remained as chief in Chicago at least until mid-1904.[9]

The two rising newsbroker stars in the 1890s were both Chicago products—Charles Sanford Diehl and Melville E. Stone. Born in 1854 and at the age of fourteen setting type at the *Wenona* (Ill.) *Index*, Diehl spent some time setting type in Ottawa, Ill., before arriving in Chicago in 1871. After the great fire that year, Diehl became a reporter for the *Chicago Times*, covering a wide variety of stories, including portions of the Indian Wars.[10] In 1883 Walter Neef invited Diehl to join AP's Chicago staff as day editor, and in May 1887 Diehl ventured to San Francisco to open AP's first West Coast bureau. He was summoned back to Chicago in October 1893 to become Stone's assistant general manager.[11]

Stone was born a few miles north of Bloomington, Ill., on August 22, 1848, one of six sons of a Methodist Episcopal minister. After stints on the *Chicago Republican*–turned–*Inter Ocean* in 1868–73 as reporter, editor, and city editor and on the *Chicago Mail*–turned–*Post and Mail* in 1873–75 as editor and Washington correspondent, Stone brought out the first issue of the *Chicago Daily News* on Christmas Day, 1875, beginning regular publication on January 1, 1876.[12] Nine months later Victor F. Lawson became the new paper's publisher and business manager,[13] and Stone continued as editor. In May 1888, the partners amicably separated, Lawson paying $100,000 for Stone's share of the then-thriving newspaper and Stone promising to stay out of Chicago journalism for ten years.[14] After nearly two years of travel abroad Stone returned to Chicago to become vice-president of the Globe National Bank, treasurer of the Chicago Drainage Canal, president of the Citizens' Association and the Civil Service Reform League, and vice-president of the Union League Club.[15]

Early in 1893, while Lawson kept discreetly out of sight, the other two members of AP's executive committee, Frederick Driscoll and Charles W. Knapp, approached Stone to succeed William Henry Smith as AP's general manager. Stone later commented that AP's outlook was certainly not inviting. Against them was arrayed the wealth of the entire Eastern journalistic field and they had apparently been cut off from all relations with the foreign news agencies. . . .

On the other hand, the business of banking had never greatly appealed to me, although I had been undeniably successful in the enterprise. I had a secret longing to return to the printers' craft.[16]

For "something like five years" Stone continued his banking obligations while serving as AP's general manager.[17]

NEW SUPPLEMENTAL WIRES

The six years of continuous turmoil and realignment in newsbroking—extending from the time of AP's internal revolution and reorganization as an Illinois corporation, and including the hotly contested battle between AP and UP that led to UP's death in April 1897—had focused national attention on news-gathering and suggested opportunity to entrepreneurs standing on the edge of the battlefield. Something called the Union Press Exchange, with William H. England as president and with addresses in New York City and Chicago, offered a 25,000-word news report in 1892 sent out over leased wires.[18] There is no record of how long UPE survived. The American Press Association, a feature syndicate dating from 1882 (and not to be confused with the APA successor to Hasson's News Association described in chapter 2), had relied for more than ten years on mail delivery of its material. Although the APA syndicate had been a customer of AP for current news, the APA-AP contract had forbidden the APA from retransmitting APA copy via telegraph. On March 15, 1893, only weeks after AP's joint executive committee disbanded, the APA syndicate announced formation of its own "Telegraphic News service, having a system of leased wires from Boston through New York, Philadelphia and Washington to the more important Western cities."[19] AP's new Washington bureau chief, Charles A. Boynton, wrote William Henry Smith the day of the above announcement, calling this APA move "the new opposition organization." Reporting that S. J. Flickenger had left the *Ohio State Journal* in Columbus to become general manager of the new operation, Boynton said the enterprise had started its service on March 14, 1893, had outlets in seventeen cities, and expected to reach San Francisco and Dallas with leased wires within a week.[20]

A post–World War I supplementary or alternative service was the Federated Press, created in November 1919 by thirty-two editors attending the Labor Party convention in Chicago. Asserting that they were "unable to obtain unbiased news service from the existing press associations," they formed Federated as a cooperative membership service "to furnish straight, uncolored news of all sorts." The managing editor was E. J. Costello, who previously had spent seven years on AP's staff, and the general news manager was Louis P. Lochner, who in 1921 joined AP's Berlin news staff, remaining there until Germany declared war on the United States twenty years later. Within a year, Federated served "one hundred-odd" dailies and weeklies, including many with Socialist, Farmer-Labor, and Non-Partisan League leanings. Among its early domestic and foreign staffers were William Hard, Scott Nearing, Paul Hanna, Lawrence Todd, Carl Sandburg, Anna Louise Strong, Frederick C. Howe, George Lansbury, E. D. Morel, W. N. Ewer, H. N. Brailsford, M. Phillips Price, Sanford Griffith, and Frederic Kuh.[24] Federated was an early version of numerous political, ethnic, and alternative news services that have appeared in the twentieth century.

Another news brokerage founded in 1919 catered to the black press. Still excluded for the most part from mainstream American journalism, published in the relative isolation and obscurity of local religious, fraternal, or community settings, and facing a shaky financial base and high illiteracy in the black community, black newspapers assembled themselves and their news-gathering machinery more slowly than did the white press. I. Garland Penn notes that there were ten black papers in 1870, thirty-one in 1880, and 154 in 1890,[25] most of them weeklies and published on a shoestring. In March 1884, Charles Carroll Stewart, Washington correspondent for the *Baltimore Vindicator*, organized a national news bureau including all the representatives of the black press in Washington.[26] On April 23, 1890, an association of Washington correspondents of the black press, the Associated Correspondents of Race Newspapers, was formed to create "a more perfect union of the correspondents at the national capital," they said, "and to promote in every legitimate way the best interests of our race through the medium of the press."[27] Forty correspondents, reporting for ten newspapers, were listed on the association's rolls in the first few years. Officers during the first year were president Edward Loften Thornton, *New York Age*; first vice-president John E. Bruce, *Cleveland Gazette*; second vice-president C. Carroll Stewart, *Indianapolis World*; recording secretary Charles A. Johnson, *Chicago Appeal*; corresponding secretary Benjamin C. Whiting, *Indianapolis Freeman*; treasurer R. J. Raymond, *Chicago Advance*; and manager C. E. Lane, *Knoxville Negro World*.[28]

Frederick G. Detweiler in 1921 identifies six news associations functioning in black journalism—the Reciprocal News Service of the National Negro Press Association in Nashville, the Capital News Service in Washington, the Negro Press Syndicate in Washington, the NAACP and Exchange News Service of New York and Boston, the press services of Tuskegee Institute and Hampton Institute, and the Associated Negro Press of Chicago.[29] The last-named agency more closely resembled the Associated Press than did the others. Founded in 1919 by Claude A. Barnett, advertising director of the thriving, fourteen-year-old *Chicago Defender*, the Associated Negro Press in the beginning described its purpose as placing

> within the reach of our newspapers and other journals the expert results of an efficient newsgathering organization that "scours" the world for race news and thereby makes it possible for our publications to present to their readers an authoritative and uniform accounting of matters of genuine interest from every corner of the globe.[30]

Listing eighty-eight newspaper members after one year,[31] the ANP mailed its news to its predominantly weekly members, and encouraged members to supply news from their communities for the use of all ANP papers. Nahum Daniel Brascher was ANP's first editor-in-chief.[32] The agency lasted until 1964; Barnett died in 1967.[33]

MEMBERSHIP HEADACHES

While black journalists carved out a harmonious, if isolated and modest, niche for themselves in news-gathering, white newsbrokers seemed unable to bring peace and harmony to their affairs. Melville E. Stone took the old UP's death as the occasion to write proudly and optimistically for public consumption of AP's success and centrality to American newspapering. He asserted that

> The phenomenal progress and the success of the American newspaper can, in a large measure, be attributed to the methods of . . . news-gathering agencies, foremost among which is the "Associated Press." Its close identification with American newspaperdom for the past decade or more, and its history, are in a large measure the history of journalism in America.[34]

But whereas Stone contended that membership in the AP was a prerequisite for the "complete newspaper," AP's bylaws, board of directors, and members' protests conspired to deny AP memberships to some legitimate and worthy newspapers.

At first and on the surface, AP's membership admission apparatus worked smoothly in the wake of the old UP's death. During the first six weeks after UP collapsed, according to AP's board, all went well. "News contracts were written with every newspaper the Board had authority under the By-laws to admit to membership," the board reported, observing with some self-satisfaction that

> It is most gratifying to your Board to know that although the application of [a] manifestly wise policy has necessarily run counter to the personal feelings, and possibly present interest, of not a few of the members, it has been, as a rule, cheerfully concurred in by the stockholders. . . . [35]

Gaining stockholder support, however, could not save the board from the wrath of the broader membership, some sectors of which were adversely affected by the board's admission policy, and of some outside papers that felt entitled to an AP membership.

With the passage of a year, AP's board conceded that the rush of applications following UP's death had presented "many difficult problems." Although claiming to deal with the "members of the failed concern in a spirit of the broadest liberality," qualified only by a regard for the "manifest obligations to those who had been loyal, generous, and long-suffering members"[36] of AP, the board was forced to admit in May 1898 that

> Not a little litigation has resulted from the effort of your Board to place The Associated Press upon a broad basis of permanent efficiency. It is peculiarly gratifying to be able to report that in every case that has thus far gone to a hearing, the courts have sustained the contentions of our counsel.[37]

Fearful that some of the new legal concepts, such as public interest, antitrust, and restraint of trade as legitimized by the Sherman Act of 1890 and several new state laws, might trip up AP's efforts to control its own membership, Stone and the board gave no ground, dispatching attorneys into courtrooms in many regions of the country and wherever members and non-members challenged AP's by-law authority to admit or reject membership applications and to restrict members' affiliations with other newsbrokerages. Even before UP declared bankruptcy, the *Minneapolis Tribune* had sought in federal court to enjoin AP's board from admitting the *Minneapolis Times* over the *Tribune*'s protest. Buttressed by a grandfather policy opening AP to all papers that were members of either AP or UP on October 15, 1892, AP was able to get the injunction rejected in November 1896, a decision upheld by the U.S. Circuit Court of Appeals the following fall.[38]

In a similar action the *Columbus* (Ohio) *Press-Post*, a former UP paper, applied for AP membership on April 1, 1897, and, under the grandfather policy, was admitted. The *Ohio State Journal*, holder of a Columbus morning AP franchise, sought to enjoin AP from serving the *Press-Post*'s morning edition, and the injunction having once been denied by the courts, the matter was dropped when the *Press-Post* ceased to publish its morning edition.[39] The *St. Louis Star* used a different approach when in September 1897 it petitioned for a writ of mandamus to compel the AP to supply its news upon the same contract terms granted other newspapers in St. Louis, specifically the *Post-Dispatch*. The *Star* argued that mandamus action was appropriate because AP was a quasi public utility affected with a public interest. A writ was at first issued by the Missouri Supreme Court, but after a full hearing the writ was denied, the court observing that AP's business

> is one of mere personal service, an occupation. Unless there is "property" to be "affected with a public interest," there is no basis laid for the fact or the charge of monopoly....
>
> Nor is there any more property in "news," to wit, "information," "intelligence," "knowledge," than there is in the "viewless wind," until the "guinea stamp" of a copyright is impressed upon its extended similitude, thus giving one of the elements of property, to wit, governmental protection for a limited time.[40]

Stymied for the moment by a court system still shy about encroaching on contracts and business autonomy with some newfangled notions of monopoly and public interest, publishers adversely affected by AP's bylaws and policies turned to state legislatures for relief from the wire's exclusionary and selective tactics. By 1897 Nebraska had mandated that

> Every telegraph company and every press association engaged in the transmission, collection, distribution, or publication of dispatches shall afford the same and equal facilities to all publishers of newspapers, and furnish the dispatches collected by

them for publication in any given locality to all newspapers
there published on the same conditions as to payment and delivery.

Violators were guilty of a misdemeanor and could be fined from
$100 to $1,000 and held liable for damages to the newspaper as the
result of such "discrimination."[41] Over the veto of the governor,
Kentucky's general assembly passed the following on February 24,
1898:

> That all foreign corporations formed for the purpose or engaged
> in the business of buying, gathering, or accumulating informa-
> tion or news...shall...at all times, vend, supply, distribute,
> and publish the news and information...to any and all persons,
> firms and corporations organized under the laws of this State
> ...when such person, firm, or corporation desires to buy or be
> supplied with such news and information....[42]

The law and adverse court decisions, some of which we will examine later, played a significant role in shaping newsbroking and especially in rewriting AP's bylaws, but nothing had a greater impact
on national news-gathering than AP's shortsighted handling of
E. W. Scripps's newspapers. AP's exclusive contracts with members,
which Scripps abhorred, and the AP board's judgment that Scripps
posed no threat to the Associated Press combined to force Scripps
to walk a separate road and develop a news-gathering agency that
by World War I was a serious challenger to AP.

Still in the early stages of fashioning what Alfred McClung Lee
calls the "first of the great modern newspaper chains," Edward
Wyllis Scripps in 1897 directly controlled the *Cleveland Press, Cincinnati Post*, Covington *Kentucky Post, St. Louis Chronicle*, and
Kansas City World (collectively called the Scripps-McRae League),
had large minority holdings in the *Detroit Tribune and Evening
News*, and was in the process of launching a Pacific Coast newspaper group.[43] Scripps recalled how before the old UP's death its
manager, Walter P. Phillips, "made my acquaintance and began to
cultivate me....He gave me every favor he could." The "backbone" of UP's Midwestern evening service, Scripps's handful of papers soon received preferred treatment, UP granting protest rights
for a field of from 100 to 150 miles in radius around his papers, delivering its report for about $20 per week to his papers, and allowing
his papers to use UP's leased lines to move internal Scripps copy,
amounting to a weekly subsidy to the Scripps group of from $40 to

$50. Scripps later commented that "Of course, I soon enough recognized that we were all grafting the United Press out of existence."[44]

When war developed between AP and UP, Scripps briefly fancied himself as the power broker, the single figure holding the balance of power between the two agencies. The "crash" of UP and the rapid defection of its New York papers to the AP, he later said, meant that in "an instant I found myself a very insignificant factor."[45] Brother James Scripps, who had supported the AP reformers and held an AP membership for his *Detroit News*, and E. W.'s partner Milton McRae, who had established warm relations with AP's hierarchy, both thought Scripps had blundered by riding UP to its grave and were eager to see his papers added to AP's membership. Scripps sent McRae as an emissary to the AP camp, later explaining that when McRae was scared, he "always shows that he is scared" and that "I wanted those [AP] fellows to feel that I was scared. I wanted them to be arrogant and sassy." The AP officials told McRae just what he wanted to hear, and he reported to Scripps that, in Scripps's words, "if we would be good and humble and submit our request at the next meeting of the directors of the Associated Press, we might be voted in, and probably would be."[46]

Scripps had no idea of joining AP. Privately he objected to AP's use of exclusive contracts that protected members from competitors. AP's "plan was to establish a monopoly pure and simple," Scripps said.[47] Although exclusive contracts would protect his existing papers, "I was just at that time feeling very cocky," Scripps later wrote. "I considered myself a sort of man-of-destiny. I had ambitious plans of planting a score or more of new papers," and, if he acquiesced in AP's plan, "we would never be able to start another new newspaper."[48] This Scripps had to impress upon McRae if the latter was to overcome his initial joy over finding a seemingly safe haven for Scripps-McRae papers in the AP.

Scripps and his entourage—George Scripps, McRae, and Robert F. Paine—moved into a suite in Chicago's Auditorium Hotel in May 1897. The famed Auditorium had been the site of AP's jubilant stockholders' meeting and banquet celebrating the death of United Press, and, in the days following that celebration, AP's board of directors was processing the flood of membership applications, rewarding traitors to UP and powerful publishers and permitting AP members to deny membership (through the protest right) to insignificant or lesser lights in newspaperdom. It was during the second day of the board's tribunal, May 21, that McRae was permitted to present his applications for four of the five Scripps-McRae papers (he excluded the Covington *Kentucky Post*), advising the board, under orders from Scripps, that "unless all can be admitted, I should want to withdraw the applications of all." His applications were accompanied by notarized statements that the *Cleveland Press, Cincinnati Post,* and *St. Louis Chronicle* were entitled to AP memberships under AP's grandfather policy because the papers were receiving UP news reports on October 15, 1892.[49] The applications drew unanimous opposition from local AP boards for Scripps-McRae admission as Series A members. Cleveland's local board consented to a Series B membership for the *Press*; the Cincinnati board objected to admission of the *Post*; the St. Louis papers were split on admitting the *Chronicle*; and in Kansas City the *Star,* after objecting, changed its mind and said it would permit a Series B contract for the *World* for one year.[50]

The matter was postponed until the following morning, when the directors announced they were ready to write ninety-year contracts for the *Post, Press,* and *Chronicle* with the issuance of two shares of AP stock to each paper, and to write a one-year contract for the *Kansas City World*. At that moment, however, strong exception to the action was unexpectedly voiced by the Pulitzer Publishing Company on behalf of its *St. Louis Post-Dispatch*.[51] That afternoon, a motion to defer action on the application until the Pulitzer people could be heard failed, leaving the board able to grant service to the *Post, Press,* and *World* but denying service to the *St. Louis Chronicle* in light of Pulitzer's protest. True to his promise, McRae withdrew the applications of all Scripps-McRae papers,[52] returning to Scripps with the news that, as Scripps later wrote, "no other place was open for us but that of humble clients."[53] Scripps describes his next move—the creation of his own newsbrokerage—as follows:

> I had prepared my scheme, and even the form of the telegraph announcement to be sent out to all the [old] U.P. clients. We were going into the associated press business, and solicited patronage. Immediately after the rejection [by AP] of our offer we put on the wires this announcement.[54]
>
> The proposal was that the firm of Scripps-McRae was going to start a press association and finance it, and that we would on the instant or application, serve all would-be clients with the evening reports.[55]
>
> We had a news association organization built up under the old arrangement with Phillips. It was called the Adscititious Re-

port and managed by Paine. We had the nucleus of an organization: We named this the Scripps-McRae Press Association.

On the Pacific Coast the United Press had never done any
business, and as I had several papers there, I had organized a little service for my own Pacific Coast papers and had some clients. It was called the Scripps-Blades Service.[56]

Scripps-Blades was shortly renamed Scripps News Association. Its
business manager was Hamilton B. Clark and the news manager was
Max Balthazar.[57] Robert F. Paine remained in charge of the rechris-
tened Scripps-McRae Press Association, with the title of general
manager.[58] The old UP's Walter P. Phillips was employed by Paine as
head of the agency's Eastern office "for a time . . . so that we could
have the benefit of his practical experience and of his services in soliciting clients," Scripps later wrote. "The Phillips arrangement was
soon concluded."[59]

Within "a few hours" after releasing his invitation for papers to
join his press associations, Scripps learned for the first time that
something called the Publishers' Press Association had just been organized in the East, "backed by some wealthy men" with Jacob B.
Shale as its president and manager. "This information staggered
me," Scripps later recalled. "It meant that I would have all the cost
of collecting and sending out a full service with perhaps half or less
than half the revenue that I had calculated on."[60] Scripps continued,

> A few days later I went to New York and met the heads of the
> rival press association. . . . I met [Shale] and his board of direc-
> tors, and, at the conference held in the Astor House, we agreed
> upon a compromise, namely, a division of the field. The Pub-
> lishers' [Press] Association was to serve all of the clients in the
> states bordering on the Atlantic Ocean, while my association
> was to serve the papers of the rest of the country. Numerically,
> the clients of the Publishers' Press Association greatly outnum-
> bered my own, but, with few exceptions, all of the strong pa-
> pers in the Atlantic States had joined the Associated Press . . . ,
> so that none of the clients of the Publishers' Association could
> afford to pay more than a very small assessment.[61]

The compromise provided for an exchange of news dispatches, with
PPA responsible for Eastern and cabled European news and the
Scripps agencies covering the rest of the country. "It required only
a few weeks," Scripps recalled, "to teach the Publishers' Press that
they could not pay cable tolls." After two years of cooperating with

the *New York Sun*'s Laffan News Service for foreign news coverage, Scripps and PPA cut loose from Laffan early in 1899 and began to rely on their own (primarily Scripps-McRae's) correspondents for foreign news. [62]

The PPA (also occasionally referred to in the trade press as the News Publishers' Press Association), which was incorporated in New York State on March 17, 1898,[63] grew out of a series of meetings nearly a year earlier of publishers being excluded from AP membership as the old United Press lay on its deathbed. PPA's first officers were president Thomas J. Keenen, Jr., *Pittsburgh Press*; vice-president Luther P. Stephens, *Columbus* (Ohio) *Post*; secretary Shale, *McKeesport* (Pa.) *News*; treasurer William L. Brown, *New York News*; and general manager W. F. Bassett. Within one month Bassett resigned and was replaced by J. L. Ward as general manager. PPA's news service started April 9, 1897, the day after UP's news report was suspended. It was a service for evening papers only, and it employed at the start a leased wire running from New York City through Pittsburgh, Cleveland, and Chicago to Milwaukee. On its first day of operation it served twenty-two papers, including Hearst's *New York Evening Journal*. By June 8, 1897, when Scripps-McRae and PPA actually signed their agreement to cooperate, PPA's officers were Shale as president, Andrew McLean of the *Brooklyn Citizen* as vice-president, Keenen as secretary, and Stephens as treasurer, and it leased wire ran from Washington, D.C., to New York City and west to Denver. [64]

THE *INTER OCEAN* CASE

Confronted with even the modest beginnings of a Scripps-McRae-based newsbrokerage, AP's board on September 23, 1897, only four months after McRae had withdrawn his membership applications, declared the Scripps-McRae Press Association and the five papers in Scripps's Midwestern chain "antagonistic" to the AP, meaning that AP members were prohibited from having news relations with any of them. [65] The Scripps organization thus joined Laffan's News Service as antagonists of the AP organization. Formally AP's bylaws seemed not to preclude AP papers from taking the service of other newsbrokers along with AP's. The bylaws said,

> Nothing in this or other by-laws shall be taken to prohibit any member from purchasing news from any person or organi-

zation which has not been formally declared . . . to be antagonistic or in opposition to The Associated Press.[66]

The rub was, however, that any news organization even remotely resembling opposition was declared antagonistic by AP, and a member found trafficking with an antagonistic agency was subject to punishment ranging from a $1,000 fine to suspension from AP membership by a two-thirds vote of the board.[67]

Earlier AP's officials had rejoiced when the New York Court of Appeals in January 1893 upheld a similar bylaw provision of the old New York State AP. George E. Matthews, publisher of the *Buffalo Express* and an AP member, gained a preliminary injunction staying NYSAP's attempt to suspend Matthews's membership because he received UP news. In a second hearing the injunction was withdrawn and Matthews appealed. Writing for the Court of Appeals, Rufus W. Peckham affirmed the lifting of the injunction, observing that

> It seems to me this by-law is a natural and reasonable restraint upon the members of the association, appropriately regulating their conduct as members thereof, with respect to the business which the association was specially organized and incorporated to transact. Its success must greatly depend upon the number of its members and that in its turn must depend upon the efficiency, reliability, and promptness with which it collects and distributes its news.[68]

The notion that the right, indeed the primacy, of contracts should be immune from government intervention, suggested by Peckham above, was growing in America alongside its opposite—that some businesses were affected with a public interest and thus susceptible to regulation and that some labor-management relations could be controlled by states.

Peckham would take a seat on the U.S. Supreme Court in 1895, where, with other justices of his persuasion, he exemplified, as Benjamin F. Wright says, "that brand of *laissez faire* ideology which the judiciary grafted on to the due process stem after 1890."[69] Peckham is perhaps best remembered as the author of the Court's opinion in the *Lochner* case,[70] which Robert G. McCloskey describes as "one of those moments in the Court's twentieth-century history when the judges temporarily embraced the illusion that the regulatory movement could be halted, rather than merely delayed, by judicial pronouncement."[71]

Euphorically the Associated Press could bask in the light of Peckham's pro-business views in 1893, especially as they upheld AP's antagonism mechanism. But closer to home and seven years later storm clouds gathered and obscured the light; a case similar to *Matthews* arose in Chicago with far-reaching consequences for AP.

The *Chicago Inter Ocean* had been in the AP at least since December 1866,[72] when the paper was called the *Republican* and the news agency was called the Western AP. With the exception of 1891–94 the paper was controlled by William Penn Nixon from 1875 to 1897.[73] Nixon was on AP's board and executive committee from 1880 to 1883, and was president of the WAP and AP during the 1891–94 period of transition caused by the Lawson revolution described in chapter 5. (See tables 6 and 7 in the Appendix for AP officials and sources.) The *Inter Ocean*, however, changed its mission when in July 1897 Charles T. Yerkes purchased a majority of its stock.[74] Yerkes was prospering in Chicago by purchasing street and elevated rail companies, making a few improvements in them, and then selling them at inflated prices. To protect his holdings, he sought "eternal monopoly" laws from the Illinois General Assembly and the Chicago City Council, paving the way for his laws with generous bribes. When Chicago mayor Carter Harrison II attempted to block Yerkes's ordinances, Yerkes bought the *Inter Ocean* and imported George W. Hinman from the *New York Sun* as editor-in-chief to fight Harrison. Nixon, at age sixty-four, was retained as publisher but was a figurehead in the paper, his attention diverted by political activities and an appointment as collector of the port of Chicago in 1897.[75] Through Hinman the *Inter Ocean* added the Laffan News Service to its AP news report.

Because the Laffan service had been declared "antagonistic" to the AP back in 1893, the *Inter Ocean* was summoned to appear before AP's board on January 20, 1898, to face charges of trafficking with an antagonistic agency.[76] The day before the scheduled appearance, however, the paper petitioned the Cook County Circuit Court for an injunction to restrain AP from punishing or expelling the paper for receiving Laffan's news. The Circuit Court refused the injunction, but expressed the view that AP's contracts and bylaws might be in restraint of trade. The Illinois Appellate Court on June 28, 1899, affirmed the refusal of an injunction, and the *Inter Ocean* appealed to the Illinois Supreme Court.

On February 19, 1900, the state's high court stunned the Associated Press by not only reversing the lower courts on the injunction question, but also declaring AP to be a public utility, affected with the public interest. Relying on the *Munn* decision of the U.S. Supreme Court in 1877,[77] the Illinois court reached for a minor phrase in AP's charter (that said one of the agency's objects was "to purchase, erect, lease, operate, and sell telegraph and telephone lines"[78]) to hold that AP was not immune to government supervision. Although AP had leased and operated lines in the delivery of its news service, it had not engaged in telegraph or telephone service for public consumption. The Illinois court, however, took the position that the Associated Press

> voluntarily sought corporate existence to engage in an enterprise which invested it with, among others, the power of eminent domain. It was organized, among other things, to purchase, erect, lease, operate, and sell telegraph and telephone lines—a business which is essentially public in its nature and renders a corporation so engaged amenable to public control.[79]

Not only did the telegraph reference in the charter point to public interest, but in the court's view, AP's business of disseminating news was equally affected with public interest, the court observing that

> The Associated Press, from the time of its organization and establishment in business, sold its news reports to various newspapers who became members, and the publication of that news became of vast importance to the public, so that public interest is attached to the dissemination of that news. The manner in which that corporation has used its franchise has charged its business with a public interest.[80]

The contract binding the *Inter Ocean* to AP and the latter's bylaw prohibition on trafficking with "antagonistic" newsbrokerages, the court found to be in restraint of trade. Bylaws, said the court,

> must be reasonable and for a corporate purpose, and always within charter limits. They must always be strictly subordinate to the constitution and the general law of the land. They must not infringe the policy of the State nor be hostile to public welfare. [The antagonism] by-law tends to restrict competition because it prevents its members from purchasing news from any other source than from itself.... Its tendency, therefore, is to create a monopoly in its own favor...and such provision is illegal and void.[81]

In the wake of the *Inter Ocean* decision, AP unsuccessfully sought a rehearing before the state's high court and rescinded its various past antagonism declarations.[82] Meanwhile the trade weekly *Newspaperdom* editorially summed up the industry's various responses to the Illinois decision.

> In one class are the present members of and subscribers to the Associated Press, who are naturally anxious to conserve the value of that big item in their annual inventory—the telegraphic news franchise; in the other are the present outsiders, who are curious to know what bearing the new order of things is to have upon their relations with a competitive organization, or who are wondering what their chances are to be to secure the service of the preeminent association.[83]

Stockholders of the Publishers' Press Association, coincidentally holding their annual meeting the day after the Illinois Supreme Court announced its *Inter Ocean* opinion, generally believed the decision would greatly increase PPA's membership rolls.[84]

AP president Victor F. Lawson immediately assured AP members that the board was looking into bylaw changes necessary to bring the AP into "harmony with the law."[85] Despite early optimism, the full extent of the damage wrought by the court's decision on AP was not measurable until May 7, 1900, when the Circuit Court entered its final decree, nullifying AP's membership contracts and the bylaws holding members punishable for trafficking with competing news organizations.[86] Nine days later 164 AP stockholders (88.6 percent of all stockholders, representing 90.6 percent of AP stock[87]) gathered in Chicago and heard their board report that

> The scheme of organization... adopted in 1892 was believed at that time to be not only a lawful one, but one which [would] call for the best energies of the management, bring into membership strong, healthful newspapers, and put under close check all of the agencies employed for the collection and distribution of information....
>
> Unfortunately, it transpires that there were serious defects in the plan.... There was no law in existence in Illinois or elsewhere, in 1892, which, so far as we were advised, was precisely adapted to our needs. Under the circumstances, an incorporation was effected under the general laws of Illinois, and an earnest effort was made to bring the Association in harmony with its provisions.

> A Chicago member who had shared in the work of organizing
> the corporation seized upon the defects, and a prolonged litiga-
> tion followed, resulting finally in a decision by the Supreme
> Court of Illinois that the business of The Associated Press has
> become...impressed with a public interest....[Y]our Board
> has no alternative but to recommend to you the adoption of
> such amendments to your by-laws and contracts as will bring
> the corporation and its methods into conformity with the
> law....[88]

The revamping of bylaws required to meet the court's specifica-
tions was extensive, a bitter pill for many of the stockholders to
swallow. Edgar W. Coleman of the *Milwaukee Herold*, the same publisher whose motion at an annual meeting of the Western AP nearly
ten years earlier had launched the Lawson investigation of the old
AP management, rose during the meeting and sounded the battle
cry for many of his colleagues. "I do not believe there is any court of
law in the world," Coleman asserted,

> that can force me to surrender my rights and my property, sim-
> ply because a Board of Directors recommend that I shall do so. I
> am here to protect my interests, and I have a right to vote as to
> whether my interests shall be protected or not.[89]

Whereupon a motion to reject the board's recommended bylaw
amendments passed 135 to 2 with 27 abstentions.[90] The sense of the
group was summed up by Charles H. Taylor of the *Boston Globe*. "I
do not care to linger in Illinois any longer than I must. I would like
to find out," he continued, "if we can not preserve the old lines
somewhere else, and do our co-operative business in the old way."[91]
It is unclear from the record whether these stockholders knew of
plans in the offing to transplant AP to the protection of New York
state statutes.

In a *New York Tribune* interview after the May stockholders
meeting, Stone, who had resigned as AP's general manager in the
wake of stockholders' unwillingness to amend their bylaws, first explained that he felt that it was his "duty as a good citizen to put myself in obedience to the court decisions of the state." He then hinted
at the future, saying that

> Some of the members of the [AP] will organize another associa-
> tion, more in harmony with their views, and, as suggested by
> some of them, they would like to have me with them in the new
> organization. Where it will be organized, by whom it will be

formed, or what will be its characteristics, is for the future to determine.... How many of the officers, employees and members of the present Associated Press will cast their fortunes with the new organization is a question. There may be some competition between the associations, and they may prove to be rivals.[92]

From the outside the *New York Sun* chided the AP, "an unprincipled and unscrupulous combination," for bringing about its own "collapse" by attempting to defeat the *Sun* and its Laffan news agency. The paper reported that circulars were advertising the rejuvenation of the old New York State AP and of the Southern AP to take over the AP business.[93]

SHELTER IN NEW YORK STATE

But the *Sun* had, perhaps intentionally, missed the real story. The same day the *Sun* published its view of AP's affairs, Stone sent out announcements to AP's members that a new corporation was forming in New York state "to carry out the purposes for which the Illinois Association was originally incorporated." Using a new letterhead, showing a New York address and listing AP's directors as Stephen O'Meara, *Boston Journal*; treasurer Adolph S. Ochs, *New York Times*; St. Clair McKelway, *Brooklyn Daily Eagle*; William L. McLean, *Philadelphia Bulletin*; president Frank B. Noyes, *Washington* (D.C.) *Star*; and secretary A. H. Belo, *Galveston News*, Stone enclosed application papers, assuring his addressee that the purpose "of this whole operation is to protect our friends in their rights."[94] The "directors" on Stone's letterhead were, in fact, the six incorporators who brought the New York version of the Associated Press into being on May 23, 1900. This new AP was organized under a New York State Membership Corporations law passed May 8, 1895, and gave as its purpose for incorporating the following statement:

> to gather, obtain, and procure... information and intelligence, telegraphic and otherwise, for the use and benefit of its members and to furnish and supply the same to its members for publication in the newspapers owned or represented by them.... [95]

To avoid a repetition of the adverse court decision in the *Inter Ocean* case, friendly New York legislators on April 19, 1901, amended the state's membership law to recognize membership corporations organized for the purpose of gathering, obtaining and procuring information and intelligence, telegraphic or otherwise, for the use and benefit of its members, and to furnish and supply the same to its members for publication in newspapers owned or represented by them. . . . [96]

The amendment's language was obviously lifted from AP's articles of incorporation.

Under New York law the new AP was obliged to make all former recipients of the news report "members" with one vote each, and memberships were to be in the names of individuals and not corporations. Although stockholding was prohibited by the New York law, AP preserved its members' stock and added voting rights through the issuance of $25 bonds. No member could own more than forty bonds, but each bond purchased gave a member one additional vote in directors' elections. All newspapers entitled to AP's report as of May 21, 1900, could gain membership in the new corporation, and the protest rights that some of the old Illinois corporation members had were to be preserved. Though members were still required to furnish their local news exclusively to AP, gone were the declarations of antagonism and the prohibition on taking news from other agencies, replaced by strong admonitions to protect the news report from outsiders.[97]

The crippled Illinois corporation was left in the hands of caretakers. Stone and Lawson resigned their Illinois positions at a board meeting the day after the stockholders refused to amend their Illinois bylaws. Charles S. Diehl replaced Stone in Illinois, and Charles W. Knapp succeeded Lawson as president.[98] During the stockholders meeting all four vacant directorships were filled by new faces—George Thompson, *St. Paul Dispatch*; E. P. Call, *New York Evening Post*; Charles H. Grasty, *Baltimore News*; and Edward Rosewater, *Omaha Bee*. Two of these seats had been vacated by the resignations of Frederick Driscoll, *St. Paul Pioneer Press*, and John Norris, *New York World*. The other two opened when their occupants, McLean and Noyes, declined to run for reelection.[99] Noyes and McLean, it will be recalled, had moved on to become incorporators of the New York AP.

The continuity between the later Illinois boards and the early New York boards shows how closely intertwined the two organizations were. Six of the nine Illinois directors during 1899–1900 were on the first (1900–1901) New York board,[100] which under the new bylaws had fifteen directors. A seventh Illinois AP director, Clark Howell, *Atlanta Constitution*, turned up on New York's 1901–2 board. In addition, two of the new Illinois directors elected in 1900—Thompson and Grasty—also sat on the first New York board. Thus, by 1901–2 nine of fifteen New York directors had been on the Illinois board at some point during 1899 and 1900. A tenth New York director, O'Meara, had been on the Illinois board between 1896 and 1899. Noyes, who had been on the Illinois board from 1894 to 1900, was elected president of the New York agency.[101]

During the summer of 1900 AP editors expressed no little anxiety over whether their rights would be protected in the transfer to New York. The New York City members discussed AP affairs repeatedly in a series of meetings in June and July and agreed on September 8 only to allow their individual members to join the New York corporation if they wished.[102] The New Yorkers' indecisiveness sprang from a preoccupation with seeking ways of negotiating with the *Inter Ocean* and with preserving rights of refunding guaranty funds held by the Illinois corporation. If the New Yorkers were uncertain, many AP editors around the country were downright fearful. One correspondent wrote Whitelaw Reid in June, "There are grave doubts as to whether Stone can carry through his new organization."[103] The trade weekly *Fourth Estate* reported on June 16 that

> All the week country publishers have been flocking to New York to find out just where they are at. . . . The rumors and dispatches printed concerning the new organization have had a disquieting effect on the members, who naturally want to get their information concerning the situation at first hands.
>
> A number of them said they had no objection to joining the new association if the other members of the Associated Press did the same thing, and the franchises and business of the old concern were to be taken over.[104]

One such "country publisher" was C. S. Burch of the *Grand Rapids* (Mich.) *Evening Press*, who wrote a colleague in Detroit on June 19 about his recent trip through the East. Burch reported that he had

> endeavored to find out all I could as to the attitude of the old members toward the new association. . . . There seemed to be a general feeling among the newspaper men that I talked with that unless all, or a very large majority of the members of the old Associated Press, were willing to transfer their allegiance to

> the new association...the change of base should be brought
> about in some other way....[T]he feeling of uncertainty on the
> part of a good many members of the old Associated Press
> seemed to throw things into the air temporarily....[105]

From the West Coast came a circular from V. S. McClatchy of the
Sacramento Bee questioning the proposed New York bylaws, which,
in his view, gave "absolute power in all matters" to the directors,
who would "not be responsible in any way to membership for an
abuse thereof."[106]

Such sniping and hesitation could hardly have been glad tidings
for Stone, who struggled through the summer to cope with inqui-
ries, requests, and the transfer of more than six hundred newspapers' rights and privileges from Illinois to New York. Writing Don
C. Seitz of the *New York World* in mid-June, Stone commented that

> There is an endless amount of detail in this business and I am
> working at it as rapidly as possible. A great deal of it is detail
> which I cannot surrender to a subordinate, and even the work
> of subordinates I have to inspect very carefully before I send it
> out.[107]

By September, matters were reaching crisis proportions on both
fronts. The Illinois corporation still had not adjusted its bylaws to
conform to the court's final decree; the New York corporation,
while reasonably ready to take up AP's business, found members of
the Illinois AP reticent to sign on with it; and although the New
York City AP association had cleared the way for its individual papers to sign up with New York, none had.

The logjam began to break up when fifteen stockholders of the
AP of Illinois requested a special stockholders meeting for Chicago
on September 12, officially to try once more to settle the corporation's obligations to the state,[108] but unofficially to determine the
future course of the AP. The publishers' interest may be measured
by the fact that this second stockholders meeting in four months
drew, in person or by proxy, 87.4 percent of the 183 stockholders,
representing 88.8 percent of the 1,144 shares of AP stock.[109] President Knapp explained that stockholders' unwillingness to change
the bylaws in conformity with the *Inter Ocean* decision had left the
corporation and its officers in the quandary of continuing to do
business under contracts and bylaws that had been held to be illegal, steadily increasing the possibility of threatening damage suits.
Knapp's appeal for the stockholders to amend their bylaws was but-

tressed by strong words from AP's attorney, John P. Wilson: "it is a serious question whether some action should not be taken by The Associated Press to relieve itself from the perils of the present situation." Advising the board that it was not feasible "to do business for [an extended] length of time in violation of the law," Wilson asked,

> would it not be wise to give the stockholders another opportunity . . . to authorize the officers and stockholders to conduct the business of the corporation in conformity with the decision of the Supreme Court in the *Inter Ocean* case.[110]

Again the stockholders would not radically alter their bylaws, instead unanimously agreeing to eliminate only those provisions requiring them to deposit their stock with the treasurer and to surrender ownership of their stock when they withdrew from membership.[111] Noyes, one of the six incorporators of the new New York agency, then rose to move that because

> it is impracticable to conduct an association on the basis indicated by the court . . . therefore be it
> *Resolved*, That the directors of The Associated Press be directed to take the necessary steps to wind up the service and affairs of the association, having always in view that ample time be first given all members to arrange for other news facilities.[112]

Attorney Wilson said he thought no court would compel the AP to continue to live and to transact business, and Noyes's motion carried unanimously.[113] The stockholders' final act was to authorize the board

> to make such arrangements as they may deem advisable and legal, with such other news association as . . . it is deemed wise to have relations with, for the use of the property of this company in the carrying out of its business.[114]

The most significant event of the meeting, however, does not appear in the minutes, but rather occurred during a recess, when thirteen stockholders, representing all regions of the country, were named as a committee to "examine the charter and by-laws of THE ASSOCIATED PRESS of New York and to report as to the advisability of joining that association."[115] One week later, after meeting with New York incorporators, the committee advised AP's membership via the AP wires that it had proposed several amendments to the new bylaws that would "safeguard the rights of members more effectively." The committee said, "it is advisable for members to join [the New York] association" and to "do so at once." Noyes, president of the New York corporation, accompanied the committee's report with notification that the new AP would begin delivering a news report at midnight on September 30, barely ten days away.[116] The day after the committee released its report, the New York City papers applied "unitedly" to Stone for membership in the new AP of New York. In all, eighteen papers in the city were eligible for AP membership. Of the original seven members of the New York AP partnership of the 1850s, only the *New York Sun* was not eligible to join.[117]

The first annual meeting of the new corporation convened on November 21, 1900, fifteen directors were elected, and Frank B. Noyes was chosen president of the new AP, a post he filled until 1938.[118] Beyond eight Sunday-only papers, 604 dailies were members on September 29, 283 (or 46.9 percent) of which were morning papers and thirty-one of which were foreign-language dailies. (According to figures in table 1 of the Appendix, of 622 dailies in the Illinois corporation in September 1900, eighteen were lost in the transfer from Illinois to New York.) The protest right was extended to 274 dailies, including 56.9 percent of the morning papers and 35.2 percent of the evening papers. The largest group had protest rights effective within a radius of sixty miles (102 papers or 37.2 percent of the papers with protest rights), and the next largest group had protest rights effective only within their cities of publication (69 papers, or 25.2 percent of the papers with protest rights). The sixty-mile and city-of-publication areas were also the largest and smallest protest areas, except for a 150-mile radius given the *Spokane Spokesman Review*.[119]

Although the AP was then considered primarily a news service for morning papers, evening papers constituted the majority of its members, rising from 53.1 percent of membership on September 29, 1900, to above 60 percent within a few years.[120] Alfred McClung Lee notes that nationally evening papers comprised roughly 70 percent of the total dailies during this period.[121] Thus, AP's membership was somewhat skewed to the morning field, in comparison with the national picture. But one begins to grasp AP's morning emphasis by examining expenses and revenues for its morning and evening service. In 1905 Stone showed that three-fourths of the morning AP members and only half of the evening papers received the full leased wire news service, the remainder taking an abbreviated "pony" report. Here was one reason for putting effort into the longer leased wire report—the largest single group of members was the morning leased wire papers, representing one-third of the total membership. Additionally the morning papers, both leased wire and pony, generated 56.7 percent of AP's revenue, and, although accounting for 59.4 percent of AP's operating expense, they contributed 53 percent of AP's after-expense surplus.[122]

DISCUSSION

Seen from an Associated Press vantage point, the last third of the nineteenth century was a grueling steeplechase, an endless course of difficult hurdles and dangerous hazards blocking AP's path to the finish line and the utopia of security and longevity. Not since Daniel H. Craig's stunning conquest of Abbot & Winans in the 1850s had any branch of the AP system known the splendid singularity of non-competition for a significant period of time. In those simpler ante-bellum days Craig could realistically want to be the only newsbroker for all the nation's newspapers, the monopolist of news-gathering. And for a few years he succeeded in being just that. But after the Civil War AP had to be content merely to contribute in any way it could to the continued prosperity of those newspapers with which it had long-standing and binding ties.

William Henry Smith was certainly proud of his 1880s AP news report and the technical innovations that speeded that report to his members, and he might even have agreed with the notion that rival newsbrokers would help keep his news report more complete and accurate (although we do not have Smith on record as actually saying that). But foremost in Smith's mind—and that of his successor, Melville E. Stone—was the protection of the rights and privileges of membership for the minority of the nation's papers belonging to AP. Such protection included offering the best news report to members and keeping that news report out of the hands of members' local competitors.

A parade of competing newsbrokerages coupled with an explosion of new newspapers between 1865 and 1900 kept AP's officers constantly on the battlefield defending members' rights by warring with telegraph companies, competitors, and even the officers of other APs. And to complicate matters, in the last decade of the nineteenth century the AP dream of protectionism and selectivity on a national scale encountered rising antitrust and regulatory fervor across the land, powerful new financial forces arising from fledgling newspaper chains outside of AP, and the growing realization that AP could not remain competitive, let alone superior, without admitting more new newspapers than some existing members could tolerate. Stone and AP's board of directors struggled to design and apply an admissions policy that would swell AP's membership slowly enough to avoid angering conservative members and yet fast enough to keep the courts from dictating AP's affairs.

In the end the turning point occurred in AP's own backyard, Chicago, and had nothing to do with membership applications and protest rights. Rather, the incident arose from AP's paranoid preoccupation with keeping its news report out of non-AP news rooms by forbidding AP members from receiving news reports from agencies that AP called "antagonistic." Although members were not to divide their loyalty between AP and another newsbroker, the *Chicago Inter Ocean* did precisely that, setting up a legal challenge to AP's rule. The Illinois Supreme Court said not only that the paper could take its news from whomever it liked, but that the AP was a public utility and, therefore, was obliged to serve all who applied. AP moved itself and its more-than-600 memberships to New York.

This late-nineteenth century odyssey of confrontation, conciliation, and conflict had steeled AP to its seemingly endless task of keeping the outsiders out and creating through bylaws, reporting, and assessments an ironclad fortress for its members. As the challenges from outside changed, but refused to subside, AP's hierarchy spoke increasingly of its crusade to preserve press freedom, at least for itself and its members. Conveniently ignoring the fact that its own newspaper members were profit-making private property, AP began to describe private competitors as "mercenaries" and to assert that its nonprofit, cooperative structure better fulfilled the First Amendment mandate for a free press. Stone's words quoted at the start of this chapter clearly assert a "fundamental right" of AP members that was superior to the law and to the rights of the press as a whole. The press was free only if AP could serve it, and AP would serve only that portion of the press that was qualified for membership. Press freedom and AP operations were synonymous, and any threat to AP, whether from journalism or government, was a threat to press freedom.

Not until 1945 was this dogma finally silenced, when the U.S. Supreme Court examined AP bylaws that made acceptance to membership extremely difficult if existing members opposed the applicant. Finding that this selectivity violated antitrust laws, Justice Hugo L. Black, writing for the court's majority, went on to say that such selectivity was also a restraint of press freedom. "Surely a command that the government itself shall not impede the free flow of ideas," observed Black,

> does not afford non-governmental combinations a refuge if they impose restraints upon that constitutionally guaranteed freedom. Freedom to publish means freedom for all and not for some. . . . Freedom of the press from government interference under the First Amendment does not sanction repression of that freedom by private interests. [123]

Chapter 7
THE MATURE INSTITUTION

Is it not time for the Associated Press, which has incorporated itself as a
membership corporation for news gathering purposes, and therefore beyond the laws controlling money-making corporations, to establish higher
standards of conduct in the use of news? It punishes now for premature
publication, and can expel for demonstrated wilful violation of its by-laws
or corruption. Then why not for corruption of the news or for conduct generally prejudicial of public welfare?

*Oswald Garrison Villard, "Some Weaknesses of Modern
Journalism"*
(May 1914)

Operating his independent news agency during the Civil War, within
twenty years of the origins of newsbroking, Henry Villard would
have found his son's words above very strange indeed. Subject to
the constant, and at times demanding, fickleness of client newspaper editors, the occasional forays of greedy telegraph proprietors
into the news business, and the unsettled techniques of a maturing
news-gathering system, the elder Villard knew well the subservience of newsbroking to its journalistic and telegraphic masters, a relationship that taxed and confounded many a sturdy
nineteenth-century news agent. But half a century later, when the
younger Villard proposed to a University of Kansas audience[1] that
the Associated Press had the visibility and power to be a force for
better news coverage among the nation's newspapers, one cannot
help but believe that newsbroking had grown substantially by 1914.
The AP of the younger Villard's day was distinct from its membership, greater than their sum, perhaps even an influence in journalistic matters on the national scene. AP's general manager Melville E.
Stone commented during AP's annual banquet in 1897 that "the
masters of the stockholders are the directors, and the master of the
directors is the General Manager."[2] Stone's remark was intended as

humor, but by 1921 AP's operations could easily be viewed as conforming to Stone's comment.

In Volume 1 of this research, newsbroking is described as having emerged along the pre-existing interface between the institutions of newspaper journalism and transportation-communication. Permanent newsbroking was prompted by the appearance in the latter of telegraphy. For newsbroking to attain the status of social institution,[3] it, like any structured pattern of human behavior, had to achieve a reasonable independence from adjacent or host institutions. In this volume we have watched as newsbroking's rapid expansion of leased wire networks finally brought essential technology under newsbrokers' control, concurrently diminishing the threat that newsbroking would arise within telegraphy and telephony.

But this volume has also restated numerous times newsbroking's continued subservience to newspaper journalism and to local editors' protectionist tendencies, regional jealousies, and desires for a voice in newsbroking operations. The structural break with newspaper journalism was largely accomplished between 1897 and 1920, as the result of three developments: (1) new competitors for AP arose and survived, stimulating broad and rapid expansion of all newsbroking operations; (2) the new competitors were privately owned and operated on commercial principles, forcing AP out of its protectionist cocoon and into the marketplace in search of news and members; and (3) a series of international crises between 1897 and 1920 enhanced newsbroking's value to editors, supplementing or supplanting newspapers' reliance on special correspondents.

Chapter 6 describes the beginnings of this final metamorphosis into a social institution by emphasizing the changing of the guard, the continuing appearance of new newsbrokerages, and the revising, with government's help, of AP's membership policies. This chapter continues that description by concentrating on the emergence of a second United Press and of Hearst's various news services and on the emergence of newsbroking as a national institution during and after World War I.

THE SECOND UNITED PRESS

E. W. Scripps's two regional news agencies and their Publishers' Press Association ally in the East (see chapter 6 for their origins) had grown in their first year to 150 clients.[4] Ten years later when

United Press Associations emerged from this triumvirate, it was serving 369 newspapers.[5] Although UP's historian would later call Scripps's pre–United Press arrangement "a poor excuse for a news agency,"[6] its growth was phenomenal compared to AP's. Between the death of the old UP and 1907, AP grew from 637 to 800 members,[7] a rate of 25.6 percent, but the Scripps agencies during the same period experienced a growth rate of 146 percent. All was not well, however, with the Scripps alliance, especially in relations between the Publishers' Press Association and the Scripps organization. PPA was finding the going rough, especially competing with AP.

The AP ban on its members taking other news services, it will be recalled, had ended when AP reorganized in New York state, but AP's new bylaws, to protect the "inviolability of [the AP] news service," asserted that

> When the Board of Directors shall decide . . . that the purchase or receipt of news from any other person, firm, corporation or association . . . by a member . . . establishes a condition that will be likely to permit [AP's] news . . . to be disclosed to unauthorized persons, such members shall immediately discontinue purchasing or receiving such news. . . . The decision of the Board of Directors as to the establishment of such condition shall be final, and the fact shall not thereafter be open to question by a member.[8]

Theft of a competitor's news was a serious threat as long as news reports reached many newspapers over leased telegraph loops running into news rooms and were transcribed on typewriters by telegraph operators employed by the newsbrokerage. While this new AP bylaw addressed the theft issue, it had the same effect in many cases of prohibiting AP members from receiving other news reports.[9] The *Albany* (N.Y.) *Times-Union* and *Rochester* (N.Y.) *Post-Express*, both AP members, were receiving PPA news reports in their offices when AP's board declared that the presence of PPA operators threatened AP's news report. The *Post-Express* cancelled its PPA contract, and the *Times-Union* removed PPA's operator and wire, relying subsequently on a messenger service to bring the report from elsewhere in the city. PPA, in August 1903, petitioned the New York attorney general to restrain AP from enforcing this bylaw, but on January 7, 1904, the attorney general, citing *Matthews v. New York State AP*, denied the petition, saying the bylaw "was entirely within the power of the defendant to establish," neither "creating a monopoly [n]or in restraint of trade."[10]

To Scripps, who was in the newsbroking business primarily to protect his own newspapers and was willing to absorb the expense in the process, such a decision was insignificant except as it might affect those Scripps papers also taking AP.[11] But to PPA the decision meant clients and revenue. Scripps had heard rumors that his PPA ally had built up large debts, and worse, as Scripps later related, that

> corrupt influences were doing their work on the Publishers Press, so that important news from Washington and New York and other places which could have its effect upon the stock market was being colored or suppressed. Even false reports came over the wire.[12]

With his contract with PPA about to expire, Scripps determined either to buy PPA or enter the Eastern field in competition with PPA. Milton McRae remembers the negotiations for purchase of PPA as occurring in 1904,[13] but UP's official literature places the purchase in 1906.[14]

The idea of buying PPA came from John Vandercook, who was in his early thirties and had already been on the staff of the *Cleveland Press*. He had also served as Scripps-McRae News Association's New York City agent, European news agent for Scripps-McRae, and editor-in-chief of the *Cincinnati Post*. From his days in New York City, Vandercook knew PPA's weaknesses, and Scripps sent him to negotiate the takeover. Although Vandercook turned down a PPA offer to sell for $300,000 plus assumption of PPA's large indebtedness, Scripps "recognized that Vandercook was a too anxious would-be purchaser to make a good bargain, . . . willing that I should pay any sum of money to get" PPA, Scripps later wrote. So Scripps next sent McRae, accompanied by Vandercook, who engaged a suite at the Waldorf where they met Shale and T. J. Keenen of PPA and, after a forty-hour negotiating session, agreed at three in the morning to buy PPA for $150,000, free of all indebtedness.[15] Scripps later commented that "in this transaction Mr. McRae performed such a service to me and all those interested in the Scripps papers and United Press [as] to offset a multitude of errors committed in other fields."[16]

United Press Associations was Scripps's next step, incorporated in New York state on June 21, 1907, and publicly announced in the

Cleveland Press on July 15. The incorporators were Hamilton B. Clark, Roy W. Howard, and Jacob C. Harper. Stock in the privately owned UP was divided as follows: Scripps, 51 percent; Clark, who became the new UP's first chairman of the board and business manager, 20 percent; Vandercook, who was elected the first president and news manager, 20 percent; and Max Balthazar, who was in charge of the West Coast operation, 9 percent.[17] Harper was a Scripps attorney, and Howard was a young rocket soaring up through the Scripps organization.

One of the many Midwestern journalists who invaded the East early in the century to occupy leading media jobs—Stone, Diehl, and Kent Cooper over at AP being other examples of this migration—Roy Howard, who was born in 1883, landed his first newspaper job fresh out of high school as a reporter on the *Indianapolis News*. It was followed by brief news jobs with the *Indianapolis Star* and the *St. Louis Post-Dispatch*. In 1906 Howard entered the Scripps world as a correspondent in New York City for the Scripps-McRae News Association and was named general news manager of PPA after Scripps bought that agency. Howard retained the same position in UP for New York City when UP was formed the following year. In January 1908, Clark directed Howard in the East and Balthazar in the West to exchange positions temporarily to get a feel for each other's operation. Thus Howard was in San Francisco in April 1908, when he was ordered back to New York to become, at the age of twenty-five, UP's general news manager, replacing Vandercook, who had died after emergency surgery while in Chicago breaking in a new bureau chief.[18]

Selecting Vandercook's successor was the job of Scripps, who had only recently met Howard and was looking elsewhere for a replacement until associates urged Scripps to appoint Howard. "My fancy was tickled with the idea," Scripps wrote years later. "My propensity for experiment demonstrated itself again. I recall that I was much amused, and that I told my wife what I had done. However, Howard made good." Scripps, who enjoyed writing about his lieutenants, had a perfect subject in Howard, as the following description from the boss's pen reveals:

> He was a striking individual, very small of stature, with a large head and speaking countenance, and eyes that appeared to be windows for a rather unusual intellect. His manner was forceful, and the reverse from modest. Gall was written all over his

217

face. It was in every tone and every word he voiced. There was ambition, self-respect and forcefulness oozing out of every pore of his body. . . . Howard's self-respect and self-confidence, right from the start, were so great as to make it impossible for them to increase. Doubtless to himself his present situation in life, his successes and his prosperity, all seem perfectly natural, and no more and no less than he expected, if he ever wasted his time in forecasting. Of which, I have very much doubt.[19]

The loose and populous United Press hierarchy of multiple titles and functions, a hierarchy that seems in the early years to traffic in talent with the parent Scripps-McRae newspaper organization at a high rate, has baffled even the company's publicists and historian, who cannot agree on Howard's eventual path to UP's presidency. All agree, however, that after 1912, when Howard became president, UP's steady growth as a news report, as an international news-gathering agency, and as a list of clients is attributable to Howard's energy and skill. Perhaps Howard's drive to build UP is best summed up in the following recollection of another colorful UP president of later years, Hugh Baillie, who as a beginning reporter in UP's West Coast bureaus watched Howard in action:

Howard would come tearing into the UP bureau, and would rip through the "exchanges"— the copies of the client newspapers that came into the office every day. Here he would hunt for UP credits, counting up how many of them there were and how prominently they appeared, meanwhile pronouncing loudly his dictum that "the news report is no good unless it gets printed." Then he would get on the wire and make the fur fly in other bureaus all over the world. Years later, when I was president of the United Press, I did much the same sort of thing myself.[20]

Poet Stephen Vincent Benet once sketched Howard as follows:

Sartorially magnificent, small and spruce, bursting with energy, he dashed about the country organizing UP service, selling it to hypnotized publishers, exhorting laggard correspondents to mighty feats of newsgathering, rushing coatless to excel them at their own jobs.[21]

SERIOUS COMPETITION

It is generally agreed that Howard and World War I were the best things that could have happened to the fledgling United Press. Howard "traveled, organizing bureaus, hiring, transferring and firing," says biographer Forrest Davis. He sold the service to newspapers and to his own employees, "a job where he showed his indisputable talent for promotion and salesmanship." In short, Howard "made United Press important, and importance was what the service needed," says Davis.[22] Compared to the formidable AP, tiny UP hardly qualified as a competitor in the early years, presenting the ludicrous picture of a handful of overworked, underpaid, raucous kids[23] bouncing like pingpong balls from bureau to bureau, daring to write short, punchy lead paragraphs and to inject some color into their "stories." Surely the established press preferred AP's gentlemanly reporters, who with measured determination produced traditionally overwritten and strained "dispatches." Jack Alexander in a biography of UP's Hugh Baillie many years later described UP's as "the belligerent attitude of an intoxicated field mouse squaring off against an elephant."[24]

When Howard took control of United Press in 1912,[25] it was strictly an evening service of from 10,000 to 12,000 words per day, six days a week, with a "double trick" on Saturdays for clients' Sunday morning papers. Its bureaus opened at 8 in the morning and closed at 5 in the afternoon; its headquarters had been on the third floor of the *New York World*'s building since 1909, possibly the same rooms Walter P. Phillips' old UP had occupied between 1891 and 1893. (This occupancy of space in the building of an AP member, of course, caused the AP board, concerned as always about the inviolability of AP's report, to request *World* representatives to explain its position. The *World*'s Don C. Seitz curtly replied, "I have said all I care to say—to the Board of Directors," suggesting that AP should mind its own business. UP headquarters stayed in the World Building until 1931, when they moved into the *New York Daily News*'s new building.)[26] Four leased wires radiated from New York headquarters, extending to clients and bureaus in New York state, New York City, Washington, D.C., and Chicago–Denver–San Francisco. Until 1908 the western leased wire stopped at St. Louis and 2,000 words daily were telegraphed by commercial lines at commercial rates to San Francisco, where they were expanded to form a 4,000-word-per-day West Coast report. The leased line was finally extended to the Pacific in 1910, the same year that a spunky young Indianapolis UP staffer, Kent Cooper, jumped ship for a position with Associated Press.

Four years earlier Cooper had devised a system for delivering an abbreviated news report for small daily papers by use of telephone dictation, replacing telegram delivery to such papers. The system, dubbed the "pony" service, delivered a 1,000-to-1,200-word report daily to ten papers simultaneously within fifteen minutes. UP "rewarded" him by sending him into the countryside to sell the pony service to small papers, a task that became a chore and sent Cooper in search of a better job.[27] Cooper signed on with AP in 1910, and fifteen years later began a twenty-three-year tenure as AP's general manager. His reasons for migrating from UP to AP are instructive about the two agencies' personalities at the time.

> I thought I might go further with [AP] than I could at the United Press where there were several competent young men with high ambitions, including Roy Howard, then only twenty-seven years old. Some of them, like Howard, had even met Scripps, the owner. They had gotten personal inspiration and assurances from him. I had been there seven years and had not met him.
>
> Moreover, in my travels for the UP, I had observed The Associated Press at work. Its men were elderly. I had seen few young AP men anywhere. At the UP I was in competition for advancement with men who were my own age or younger. Even Clark, [UP's] president, was young enough to be Melville Stone's son. I thought I might have less rivalry at The AP.[28]

Calling UP "brashly and naively Midwestern" in its early years,[29] UP historian Joe Alex Morris depicts Howard's strategy as avoiding head-on competition with AP. Howard told his chiefs and reporters to find and deliver what telegraph editors found missing in AP's reports, rather than trying to imitate AP. "Study the way [Joseph] Pulitzer and Hearst humanize the news in their papers," Morris quotes Howard as saying. "Get interviews with people in the news. People are usually more interesting than the things they are doing. Dramatize them." Howard told his people that dullness and routine were not synonymous with objectivity; news stories could be both unbiased and readable. But for an exclusively afternoon clientele, which received short shrift from AP, Howard demanded, in addition to colorful and readable copy, as much hard news and as many scoops as his small staff could handle.[30] Illustrating UP's drive for readable but breaking news, William G. Shepherd, one of UP's World War I correspondents, tells how, in an effort to circumvent Austrian censorship, he had described an Austrian retreat in "thirty paragraphs of the sheerest slang, covering the retreat like a star baseball writer covering a world's series game." He guessed that the censor did not understand one-third of the story, but, refusing to admit that he didn't, the censor passed it along for transmission. Shepherd expected UP headquarters to "decode, or deslang," the story, but it didn't, sending the original to clients, some of whom wrote UP asking for "some more of that snappy stuff."[31]

Howard finally inaugurated a morning service in June 1919, serving a grand total of eight morning papers. (The list of morning papers serviced by UP was still only 125 in 1932.) Since the morning report of hard news was AP's strength, Howard's morning report specialized in "features, exclusive interviews, and lively sports stories," according to Morris. Primarily a feature service in the beginning, Howard christened the morning service United News, to distinguish it from the afternoon news-and-feature United Press service.[32]

World War I was UP's opportunity to gain a foothold in newsbroking. It is axiomatic in journalism that war prods editors to increase their news sources. While AP's membership began shooting upward as the war approached, surpassing one thousand by mid-1917, UP's growth was equally impressive before and during the war. Morris offers these figures: 392 in 1909, 491 in 1912, 595 in September 1914, 625 in 1915, and 745 in 1919.[33] In two respects UP had an advantage over AP in World War I. First, by retaining its contract with Reuters News Company for the world cartel's news, AP was limited in the expansion of its own foreign staff. As hostilities tore up the cartel— Wolff in Germany being eliminated and Havas in France being severely restricted—AP had to play catchup with its own staff late in the war to plug holes in the cartel's news coverage.

Howard had a chance in 1912 to replace AP as Reuters's North American partner, but he turned down the offer.[34] Free of the cartel limitations, UP was better prepared from the start to cover the war, and scored some notable beats early in the proceedings. Operating outside the cartel also gave UP one of its biggest breaks—entry into South America. The South American venture began several blocks away in AP's headquarters when *La Nación* of Buenos Aires wired AP on September 8, 1914, requesting the wire's direct service as an alternative to Havas, which was forced upon the South American newspapers by the territorial terms of the world cartel. With many German immigrants as readers, *La Nación* had tried in vain to get German government communiques from Havas, which was not interested in handling what it felt was enemy propaganda. The cartel prohibited AP's distribution of news outside of North America, and, although Cooper lobbied hard at AP to start the service and AP's board held extensive discussions on the subject, Stone's view prevailed: AP should not tamper with the cartel contract that twenty years earlier had helped the young, reorganized AP attract members when competition with the old UP was at a critical point. Not hearing from AP, *La Nación* turned to UP, which signed a ten-year contract with the paper in the summer of 1916.

Prospects for Western Hemisphere expansion by AP, however, did not end with UP's victory by default in Buenos Aires. Stone was approached in 1917 by the U.S. State Department, which proposed that a number of leading South American editors be added to AP's list of correspondents, with the State Department promising to pay their salaries as an effort to improve U.S.–Latin American relations. The department was also interested in creating similar arrangements in China and Japan. AP dismissed the proposal because it involved a government subsidy. The following year, however, *La Nación*, dissatisfied with UP service, again sought an AP report, and this time the board secured concessions in its contract with Reuters and sent Cooper to South America to organize a service there. When he arrived, Cooper found Howard dashing around the continent patching together a string of UP clients. Having lost the prestigious *La Nación*, Howard succeeded in signing up its equally wealthy Buenos Aires competitor, *La Prensa*, which netted UP substantial revenue over the years. Although both AP and UP moved into South America at about the same time, *La Prensa*'s power gave UP the edge there for many years.[35]

UP's other advantage over AP during World War I stemmed from its exclusively afternoon news service. Morning dailies traditionally had the edge on domestic news; they were able to summarize and put in perspective the major news of the previous day, especially Washington, D.C., affairs, and sports events in Western time zones, completed too late for afternoon papers' deadlines. With a five-hour time difference between London and New York, the bulk of the war news, which was filed late in the day (European time), arrived in the United States between 10 A.M. and 2 P.M. It was perfectly timed for an afternoon newsbrokerage and its afternoon clients, leaving the morning papers and AP to scrape around for additional details and new angles for stories that otherwise largely repeated what the afternoon papers had already reported.[36] UP poured some of its best reporters into the battlefield and its European bureaus to exploit this time differential.

Emerging from World War I, UP was moving rapidly on several fronts to close its numerical gap with AP. Already a fixture in South America, and beginning a morning service in 1919, UP inaugurated a service to Europe in 1921; it established a news exchange with the new British United Press, financed and run by Canadian interests, in 1922; and it began service to Tokyo in 1924. AP did not break its ties with the world cartel until 1934, when general manager Cooper finally realized his dream of becoming an independent news-gatherer and distributor on the world stage. E. W. Scripps stepped out of semi-retirement in 1920 long enough to oversee the reorganization of his various newspaper holdings, calling on Howard to become general business manager of the Scripps-McRae newspaper chain, which by 1922 bore the name Scripps-Howard. Howard's resignation from UP in June 1920 brought a colleague of fourteen years' UP service, William W. Hawkins, to the presidency. A Missouri native and a staffer since the Publishers' Press Association days in 1906, with stops at UP bureaus in New York City, Albany (N.Y.), San Francisco, and Washington, D.C., Hawkins was president until 1923, when he followed Howard into the newspaper chain.[37] Hawkins, in turn, was followed by Karl A. Bickel, who yielded the presidency to Hugh Baillie in 1935.

Seventy years old when World War I ended and having spent a quarter of a century directing AP operations, Melville E. Stone recognized that, as he put it, "in obedience to the natural law I would soon have to drop out of the activities of my vocation."[38] Efficient and although set in his ways able to produce a comprehensive report that generally satisfied the more than one thousand AP members, Stone enjoyed the status of an elder statesman in American journalism who had twice—in 1893 and in 1900—helped rescue the Associated Press from oblivion.

As World War I ground on toward its conclusion, which was still half a year away, AP honored its general manager at a membership luncheon in the spring of 1918. Fifteen hundred copies of a handsome commemorative volume were printed at the request of the board. Profusely and richly illustrated and containing tributes cast in glowing terms from Victor F. Lawson, Frank B. Noyes, and AP attorney Frederic B. Jennings and reprints of articles and speeches by Stone over the years, the book noted that

> through the most momentous epoch of the history of the world, [Stone] has labored unceasingly in the leadership and upbuild-

223

ing of the great co-operative organization of American newspapers which has won a high reputation for efficiency, fair
dealing and accuracy in reporting the activities of men and of
nations in peace and war.[39]

Stone's personal copy had twenty-five $1,000 Liberty Bonds tucked
among its pages.[40] With the title *"M.E.S.", His Book: A Tribute and
a Souvenir of the Twenty-five Years, 1893-1918, of the Service of
Melville E. Stone as General Manager of the Associated Press*, the
volume, surely in the minds of some at AP, was intended to suggest
to Stone that it was time to step down.

While his administration had drawn increasing criticism from
outside AP for its stodginess and establishmentarianism, an internal
AP study committee had tactfully observed in 1908 that among AP
employees "there is a lack of responsiveness to suggestions and a
disposition to adhere too rigidly to the limitations and restrictions
that have become tradition in The Associated Press." In another
place the committee suggested that the "problem presented by the
superannuation of faithful employees of the Association is one that
demands consideration and solution."[41] In 1910 the office environ-
ment that suited Stone presented an alarming picture to thirty-
year-old Kent Cooper, who, in search of a job at AP, was about to
meet Stone for the first time. "The furnishings of the executive office" at AP, Cooper later wrote,

> remained just as they were when first installed there in the old
> Jay Gould Western Union days. Perhaps they could be described
> as mid-Victorian. There was a red carpeted room about forty
> feet square which was used by the Board of Directors for its
> meetings. Mr. Stone's desk was in one corner of it....
>
> Mr. Stone's old secretary, Philip H. Kerby, Mike Moran and
> Colonel Austin G. Durrie, eighty-eight-year-old brother-in-law
> of James W. Simonton...were in [an] anteroom, which was
> nothing more than a cubicle outside of Mr. Stone's office. Ex-
> cept for young Moran...the place was not even pleasantly
> antique—it reeked with old age.[42]

Stone finally retired in 1921, replaced by a hand-picked successor, Frederick Roy Martin, Stone filling the post of counselor, which
was created just for him.[43] Stone died in 1929.[44]

Cooper became general manager in 1925 and began rebuilding
AP as a more modern news agency. Two years after Cooper took
over, Silas Bent, writing in the *Independent*, observed that "the dis-

quieting truth is that the AP has succumbed to what I may call United Pressure. It has bobbed its hair and got out its lipstick in order to keep up with a flapper."[45] Nearly two decades later the changes wrought by Cooper were still the subject of comment and criticism. One former AP director, Oswald Garrison Villard, commented in 1944 that some of AP's activities under Cooper "must have made Melville Stone turn in his grave." AP, Villard observed,

> has followed the general trend of the American press in the direction of amusement and entertainment features, including many light and "spicy" items of dubious value, intended to offset the criticism that the Associated Press dispatches are always heavy and deadly factual.[46]

AP and UP grew more similar after 1920, with AP adding bylines, livelier writing, and more features to its service and UP becoming more "respectable" with age, size, and a morning news report. AP and UP were, in fact, similar enough after World War II that International News Service sought clients with a promotional approach that AP and INS or UP and INS were all the daily newspaper needed, AP or UP for the spot news and INS for supplemental news and commentary, which general manager Seymour Berkson was then emphasizing at INS.[47] Some telegraph editors in more recent times admit to being unable to tell AP and UP or UPI apart day-to-day and must resort to time-honored clichés—AP is more accurate, UP is faster and better written—in discussing the agencies' merits. One recent examination of the news reports of AP and UPI found no significant difference in the accuracy of the two agencies.[48] But in one area the two agencies have never agreed—their system of organization. AP adores its cooperative membership structure; UP was always more comfortable as a commercial, profit-making seller of news.

AP president Frank B. Noyes, writing in 1913, the twentieth anniversary of the modern AP's founding, asserted that AP was the servant of its membership, handling for all the news that each member was obliged to supply from his local community and supplementing that report with dispatches from major news centers. Without the need to make a profit, AP concentrated on economical delivery free of corporate bias. Insisting that "a powerful, privately owned and controlled news-gathering agency is a menace to the press and people," Noyes set AP in opposition to

> news-gathering concerns with private or limited ownership
> which dealt at arm's length with newspapers to which they sold
> news at such profit as might be secured, and over which the pa-
> pers who bought from them had no more control than over the
> paper-mill supplying them with print paper.[49]

UP president Karl A. Bickel, in 1927 observing the twentieth anniversary of UP's founding, expressed UP's side of this ongoing debate, asserting UP to be "militantly and aggressively a business
institution." Noting that like the goal of "every great and enduring
privately owned American newspaper, to render a service and to
make a profit," United Press "was organized upon the same firm
and sound business principles that have made the great business institutions of the United States the marvel of the world for efficiency
[and] stability." To gain a "real guarantee of complete impartiality
and genuine permanence in service," Bickel continued, "concentrated business control, under normal business conditions is essential." Turning his attention to AP, Bickel commented that

> there is no more reason to believe that a socialistic experiment
> in the press association field is the one and only method of at-
> taining efficiency—experience having demonstrated to the
> contrary—than there is to believe that such an economic adven-
> ture is essential to make newspapers sound and prosperous.[50]

INTERNATIONAL NEWS SERVICE

Still to be introduced is William Randolph Hearst's legendary International News Service. A service, which at times shared its management with the Hearst feature syndicate, which made no attempt to
cover the news as comprehensively as UP and AP, and liberally
sprinkled its news report with features and the work of specialty
and guest writers, INS straddled the fence between newsbroker, as
it is defined in this study, and feature syndicate.

Hearst had been a relatively inconsequential member of Associated Press until 1900. In 1893 Hearst's only paper, the *San Francisco
Examiner,* applied for AP membership during the same March meeting in which Stone was first discussed as a possible general manager
for the reorganizing AP.[51] Action was deferred until the following
February, when the *Examiner,* along with sixteen other California
dailies, was admitted, Hearst and each of his San Francisco competitors (*Chronicle, Call, Bulletin,* and *Post*) getting Series A con-

tracts.[52] When he acquired the *New York Journal* in September 1895 for $180,000,[53] Hearst, who was blocked from AP membership by the franchise there of Joseph Pulitzer's *New York World*, secured the UP news report (that is the old UP) for the *Journal*. A year later, when Hearst introduced his *New York Evening Journal*, he received an evening UP franchise for his new paper, and to the surprise of some, at the same time moved his *San Francisco Examiner* out of AP and into UP.[54]

During negotiations early in 1897 pointing toward the eventual admission of New York City's UP contingent (*Tribune, Herald, Times,* and *Sun*), Pulitzer would not consider granting Hearst's *Journal* an AP membership under any conditions. Thus, when the old UP filed bankruptcy papers on March 29, 1897, the *Tribune, Herald,* and *Times* jumped to the AP, the *Sun* stayed behind, determined to rely on its own Laffan News Service, and the *Journal* appeared to be left out in the cold. Only days before the UP news report was suspended, on April 8, Hearst acquired the *New York Advertiser,* the morning sister paper of the *Commercial Advertiser,* both papers holders of AP memberships. It was reported that he spent from $225,000 to $260,000 for this modest newspaper property for its AP report.[55] To preserve the *Advertiser*'s AP membership, Hearst's New York paper was officially renamed the *New York Journal and Advertiser.*[56] The *San Francisco Examiner*'s AP membership was restored soon after UP's collapse.

When AP moved to New York state in 1900, Hearst's *San Francisco Examiner* and *New York Journal and Advertiser* retained their memberships and both were granted protest rights.[57] Hearst, however, wanted more from AP—membership for his new *Chicago American* and the evening edition of the *New York Journal*—and when in December 1900 AP balked under protests from members in both cities, Hearst petitioned the Illinois Supreme Court for a writ of mandamus, seeking to compel both the old Illinois AP and the new one in New York to adhere to that court's earlier *Inter Ocean* decision. The case went up and down the Illinois court system for nearly seven years, being appealed and remanded numerous times, with each denial of a petition bringing another blizzard of Hearst petitions.[58] Although AP's board reported with satisfaction in September 1901 that this Hearst litigation was the only case still pending in the aftermath of the *Inter Ocean* decision and AP's move to New York, the board exasperatedly observed three years later that the case dragged on at a cost of nearly $21,000 to the AP in legal fees.[59] Not until July 9, 1907, did the Cook County Circuit Court finally sustain the AP and dismiss Hearst's case.[60] As the AP board saw it, Hearst was "strenuously endeavoring to break down for his own benefit all rights of exclusion from membership in the Association."[61]

AP's officials and Hearst reversed roles in 1924, when Hearst exercised his protest right to block admission of Paul Patterson's *Baltimore Evening Sun* and Frank E. Gannett's *Rochester* (N.Y.) *Times-Union*. Kent Cooper does not deny the truth of Hearst's assertion that AP's board favored admission of the applicants.[62] Under the bylaws, the applicants could seek a four-fifths vote of the full membership to override Hearst's protest. In the 1924 annual meeting, both applicants fell short of the needed 80 percent, Patterson receiving 62.7 percent and Gannett, 59.5 percent.[63] The board members, who voted as individuals for the applicants, according to Cooper, "were generous in defeat."[64] Cooper was understanding of Hearst's member-competitor relationship with AP, recounting in his autobiography the following Hearst comments in a 1921 conversation:

> "I have never understood, Mr. Cooper, why apparently I have to be the only member who has to deal at law with The Associated Press, of which I am a member. . . . The AP to me is a most important institution. . . . I have always trusted the accuracy of The Associated Press news report. I wish I had the service for the several papers in our organization that do not have it. If they could get it, I would have no reason to operate the International News Service. You might tell that to the Board for me."
>
> "Tell them," he said, "that I have no personal ill feeling but that I am always going to insist upon my rights; that they cannot object that we have to operate a news service competitive with The Associated Press since we have newspapers that cannot get The AP. The trouble is that feeling a loyalty to The Associated Press and having newspapers in its membership, I am in competition with myself by having to operate another press association. Tell them I am not any happier about that than they are."[65]

Calling him "the biggest financial underwriter The Associated Press has ever had," Cooper explained that Hearst "once owned more newspapers which were represented by membership in The Associated Press than any other individual" and paid over sixty years ''many millions of dollars in weekly assessments'' for his papers to receive AP news.[66]

Early signs of Hearst's newsbroking competition with his own AP membership appeared in 1903, when AP took official notice of a leased wire running between the *San Francisco Examiner* and the *New York American* (formerly the *Journal*) through the office of the non-AP *Chicago American*.[67] Under AP's bylaws, it will be recalled, Hearst could have been expelled for threatening the ''inviolability'' of the AP news report, but AP apparently found it advantageous to negotiate the removal of non-AP wires and operators from AP papers' newsrooms, rather than test this bylaw provision by rigid application. In early 1910 AP could report that ten of its member papers (only one of which was Hearst's, the *San Francisco Examiner*) had ''voluntarily ordered the wires and operators [of other newsbrokerages] removed to other buildings. . . .''[68]

It is impossible to follow the early and numerous changes in name, report, and service field of Hearst's newsbrokerages. An ''inveterate dealer of solitaire,'' writes Moses Koenigsberg, Hearst by

> reshuffling. . .the cards at solitaire before the deck was exhausted betrayed the same impatience with which Hearst repeatedly shifted a policy of business operation sometimes before the current method had been fully installed. His handling of his syndicates and news services had typified the practice. Consolidation and segregation shifted back and forth over the years.[69]

As close as one can come to tracing INS's lineage with the few available sources,[70] the New York–Chicago–San Francisco leased wire which AP objected to in 1903 evolved into Hearst News Service, a service for Hearst's own papers. In May 1909, American News Service was organized to sell Hearst's own wire report to outside morning papers. Curtis J. Mar was ANS's first president and general manager, followed the same year by Richard A. Farrelly. In August 1909, the service was expanded to include foreign news. To reflect this widened news field, ANS was renamed International News Service in January 1910; it was still a seven-day-a-week morning service. At the same time, Hearst inaugurated the National News Association to provide a six-day-a-week report for evening papers. At this same time Hearst's feature syndicate was included in the reports of the new INS and NNA services.

One year later, however, the features were again separated and NNA was dissolved into INS, which would be responsible for delivering news reports to both morning and evening papers. In 1916 Barry Faris was named editor of INS, a position he held until INS and United Press were merged in May 1958; and Fred J. Wilson replaced Farrelly as president and general manager. INS became a service to evening papers in 1918, while a new Universal Service delivered the morning news report. In 1928 Universal became principally a supplemental and news-feature morning service, INS emphasizing news in its evening report. Universal finally disappeared in a merger with INS in 1937, the latter left to handle both morning and evening reports. In 1923 a news service through INS was introduced for European papers. Virtually the only available client totals for these various Hearst combinations show 400 in 1918, 600 in 1930, 900 in 1936, 1,075 in late 1946, and about 3,000 when it was merged with UP in 1958.

Koenigsberg became president and general manager of the INS-Universal combination in 1919. He later observed that when he arrived, INS "was one of the sickest cats that ever clung to the door-posts of metropolitan journalism." In the previous few years, INS had been denied French and British cable facilities during World War I, tainted by charges of carrying propaganda, and cited by a federal district court for bribing AP employees to hand over AP news to INS. With a nearly $400,000 deficit for the year ending in mid-1919, INS had sunk to a "desperate plight." Koenigsberg says,

> The lowliness of its estate was indicated by the distrust it excited among those who should have been most anxious for its welfare. Editors of Hearst papers, compelled to rely on it exclusively for general news, used its dispatches with proverbial fear and trembling. It became a by-word in the organization. It was called "reliably unreliable."[71]

Through the devoted efforts of Koenigsberg and his successors (Frank Mason in 1928, Joseph V. Connolly in 1931, and Seymour Berkson in 1945), INS largely reversed its image although never totally losing its flair for gee whiz features and splashy byliners. Koenigsberg started the rebuilding process, incidentally, by adding "But First Get It Right" to INS's tattered old motto: "Get It First."[72]

Tracking the relative strength of AP, UP, and INS after the turn of the century is a difficult task. Figures were occasionally reported by newsbrokerages, somewhat more frequently and faithfully by AP than by UP and INS,[73] and a few researchers have undertaken tabulations of wire service affiliations from more recent newspaper annuals. But too often cross-agency figures are not comparable, and many figures simply have not been published. One fact, however, is clear: this glut of three national newsbrokerages emerging in the first decade of the twentieth century occurred as the newspaper industry approached its all-time peak of operating dailies. According to N. W. Ayer figures, a total of 909 dailies in 1880 grew by 82.8 percent to a total of 1,662 in 1890, by 31.8 percent to a total of 2,190 in 1900, and by 11.1 percent to a total of 2,433 in 1910. After 1910, total dailies fluctuated until, according to Ayer, daily newspapers reached their apex of 2,461 in 1916 and began their gradual slide to stable post-1950 levels.[74] In spite of AP's traditional protectionism, it threw open its doors to old UP papers in 1897, raising its membership to nearly 30 percent of all U.S. dailies, but still in 1900 its 604 members were only about 28 percent of the nation's total dailies. Relaxation of the protest right, a response to vigorous competition from UP and INS, and the approach of World War I with its newsworthy precursors on the global stage, however, gradually forced AP's membership upward, reaching 30 percent of total dailies in 1905, 35 percent in 1912, and 43 percent in mid-1917.[75] More recent trends are traced in the following figures:[76]

	1934	1948	1960	1970	1976
I. Percent of Total U.S. Dailies Served by:					
AP	60.5%	67.8%	67.6%	66.9%	67.3%
UP (or UPI)	44.1	50.8	52.3	48.9	46.9
INS	13.4	19.3	–	–	–
II. Percent of Total U.S. Dailies Served by:					
One Newsbroker	69.3%	66.0%	70.2%	71.1%	75.1%
Two Newsbrokers	17.3	20.5	24.8	22.4	19.5
Three Newsbrokers	4.7	10.3	–	–	–
No Newsbroker	8.7	3.2	5.0	6.5	5.4

AP's dominance is evident, as is the diminution in classes of dailies operating without newsbroker service and with more than one newsbroker.

MATURE NEWSBROKING

The contention of this research is that by the end of World War I newsbroking had separated itself from its parent institutions of newspaper journalism and telegraphy and was fulfilling unique and identifiable functions with demonstrable impact on society—that, in other words, newsbroking had become a social institution. Its separateness, of course, would not foreclose relations with newspapers and telegraphy. Indeed, its institutionalism relied on continuous multilayered relations with those it sought out and served, but such relationships were by 1920 those of equals, the power of the news report and successive technological innovations having attained equilibrium with the power of membership or ownership and financial support.

One may find fascinating the differences among the three agencies operating in 1920—Hearst's entanglements with AP's hierarchy, AP's efforts to keep enemy operators and wires out of its members' newsrooms, and UP's resolute reliance on American business principles, vis-à-vis the "socialistic experiment" over at AP. Without doubt each agency had its own personality by the end of World War I.

At Stone's and Martin's AP, "Olympian in its austerity," slang, for example, was taboo, says former staffer Carter Brooke Jones. "Two-bagger" was barely acceptable as an alternative for a two-base hit in a baseball story, but a "double-sacker" was out of the question. Jones says that "the worst thing that AP ever did. . . was to refer to a certain character as 'John Johnson, pugilist.' His name wasn't John—it was Arthur—but he fought under the name of Jack Johnson."[77] From the other viewpoint, however, the "greatest ambition of my journalistic career was realized," says Salvatore Cortesi, when Stone asked him to head AP's Rome bureau. Stone, Cortesi comments,

> had the rare quality of being at the same time the friend and the chief of his collaborators, so that anyone who worked under him was spurred not only by the desire to do his duty, but also by the wish to show his true affection for Mr. Stone.[78]

Until Martin's departure in 1925, AP was a mausoleum to the younger reporters and the last temple of dignified journalism to their elders.

At United Press in the late 1910s and 1920s when Hugh Baillie roared into New York City, headquarters was not run "in a quiet, decorous way" in anticipation of "the earnest inspection of a visiting study group." Baillie recalls that

> you might find the president screaming at the general news manager to get that lead out or he will get a new boy. You might

hear the news manager saying to an editor who'd had the te-
merity to talk back in front of the staff, "What's the matter
with you? Your face is as red as a spanked baby's ass! You are
pissing on the story of the day!" Nobody was embarrassed
about yelling "FLASH!" at the top of his voice when big news
came in: that was our business.[79]

It is impossible to characterize Hearst's agencies prior to 1920 except as disorganized and demoralized, constantly being shuffled
and buffeted by the storms of criticism and retaliation attracted by
Hearst and his methods. Barely six years old, INS had lost its cable
links to a Europe about to erupt in war. A *Harper's Weekly* article in
October 1915 revealed that INS's string of "name" European correspondents did not exist. The foreign staff was "simply a common,
ordinary, contemptible Hearst fake." The fact that the article went
unanswered hit Hearst's news rooms like a bomb. "Morale in the
news room," says George Murray, "hit rock bottom and stayed there
for years."[80] Another grenade was tossed into the Hearst camp
when the U.S. Supreme Court on December 23, 1918, held that
INS's appropriation of AP news dispatches for use without attribu-
tion on its own wire was unfair competition. Lifting competitors'
bulletins from first editions of newspapers had long been practiced
in newsbroking, although the better class of "borrowers" rewrote
the appropriated dispatches. In 1918, however, INS ran headlong
into Stone's long-standing personal crusade to establish a property
right in news.[81] In later years, with fakery and stealing behind it,
INS could comfortably advertise a string of real "name reporters"
writing their own brand of snappy, breathless copy. A promotional
book issued in the 1950s called INS staffers "the most vital people
in modern journalism," claiming that since its birth "INS has specialized in developing and attracting the best and most talented
writing reporters in the news service field."[82]

Clearly a young pistol-packing police reporter like Baillie seemed
destined to wind up at UP, and in a hurry to become its president; a
patient Edwin M. Hood, working his way from apprentice telegrapher to self-made and steady man at the State Department was obviously an AP man; and when things finally settled down in the
Hearst camp the likes of Arthur "Bugs" Baer, Damon Runyon,
Jimmy Kilgallen, and Bob Considine belonged at INS. Much might
even be made of the symbolism in AP's sedate house organ's being
called the *Service Bulletin* and UP's "lively, combative, and often
boastful" sheet's being dubbed *The Hellbox*.[83]

On second glance, however, this trio of quite different agencies set the style of newsbroking in the United States from an early date in the twentieth century. Their styles may have differed (and it can be argued that INS was always more a supplemental wire than a hard news wire), but their purpose was to be first and factual in reporting major news events and to be dependable and printable in the routine matter each felt was important. Their competitive quest for first word of a Pope's[84] or a President's death, a murder trial verdict, or an armistice signing elevated the "scoop" to a national prominence and impact. Sitting on live wires, hair-trigger newsbroking staffs made a cultural artifact of the "bulletin," an instantaneous "fix" to the growing legions of news junkies, introduced to their habit by newsbroking's preoccupation with verdicts and executions, floods and earthquakes, declarations of war and peace, railroad accidents and ship sinkings.

James Gordon Bennett's *New York Herald* in the 1840s could cause a local sensation among the newspaper-reading gentry with a description of his messenger's high-speed dash from Boston with a Cunard steamer's news, but United Press on November 7, 1918, sent the entire nation into the streets to celebrate an armistice that would not be signed for another four days.[85] The real significance of the famous false armistice story is not that UP's Roy W. Howard and the U.S. Navy's Henry B. Wilson were taken in by a fake dispatch, nor that UP was unreliable—the newsbrokerages have made a twentieth-century ritual of ending wars early,[86] but rather that the nation's newspaper readers, reading extra editions in this case, were willing to trust their emotions to a few lines of newsbroker bulletin—and do it all over again four days later when the real armistice was reported by the same wires. Youthful broadcasting in the 1920s, relying on both the newsbrokerages and its own developing news departments, hastened each "flash" of sensation to a nation of news addicts increasingly conditioned to expect the unforeseeable and the horrible.

After the turn of the century, the wires widened their competition for scoops to the international arena. The Spanish-American War[87] set in motion a general enlargement of foreign news staffs, even at AP, which was still limited by its contract with the world news cartel. General Manager Stone called AP's coverage of that war the agency's "first notable success,"[88] prompting AP to enlarge its bureaus in London, Paris, and Berlin, to set up new offices in Russia, Austria, Italy, and the Orient, and to tackle coverage of the insurrection in the Philippines and the Boxer Rebellion in China.[89] There followed a parade of foreign skirmishes and disasters, which AP, and increasingly UP and the Hearst agencies, covered. Year by year AP's board proudly listed its correspondents' foreign exploits in its annual report. In 1902 it noted an "imbroglio" in Venezuela, the assassination of the Serbian king and queen and "disturbed districts" in Turkey; in 1904, the death of Henry J. Middleton, AP war correspondent in the Far East; in 1905, the Russo-Japanese war and "Russian disorder"; in 1906, the Russo-Japanese war again, "disturbances" in Russia, and "the notable eruption" of Mount Vesuvius and so on.[90]

Stone was often dispatched to Europe to confer with heads of state about better transmission facilities, better relations with government officials and a lessening of censorship. He cherished these contacts, as his autobiography indicates, but they were a source of discomfort for some discerning AP members. Oswald Garrison Villard, who chaired an internal AP investigating committee in 1911, says the committee found Stone "erred in accepting decorations from foreign governments and being too friendly with people in the seats of the mighty, both in politics and in business."[91] Stone, however, was effective in opening up avenues for AP's news dispatches. The board in 1902 summarized the international news revolution in the making as follows:

> Your Board. . .calls attention to the progress made in the business of collecting and distributing the news of the world. Interest in foreign news has steadily increased until it is the plain duty of the Association to cover an event in Europe or Asia with the same care for detail and accuracy and promptness as if [it] was an occurrence within the limits of our own country.[92]

Back on the domestic front, national presidential nominating conventions and elections, which traditionally had plagued management with their expense and charges of unfair coverage, were subsiding to a routine quadrennial challenge to reporter endurance and operator agility. Such significant, if obvious, news events were settling more or less comfortably into the pulse of newsbroker operations, which after 1900 were gradually encroaching on political correspondents' traditional turf—the political interview, the reaction story, Congressional committee hearings, and intimacy with the executive branch. While carefully preserving their objectivity and avoiding obvious partisanship and interpretation, the wires broadened and deepened their daily governmental coverage. And as the presidency acquired new significance in a government increasingly preoccupied with imperialism and the deteriorating international order, the wires were the obvious pipeline between the White House and the reading public. When he stepped into the presidency late in 1901 after the death of William McKinley, Theodore Roosevelt as one of his first acts summoned the three newsbrokerages' Washington bureau chiefs—Charles A. Boynton for AP, Ed L. Keen for the Scripps–Publishers' Press Association alliance, and David S. Barry for the *New York Sun*'s news service—to announce his accessibility to them and to insist on discretion in handling White House news.[93] This meeting and Roosevelt's later establishment of a press room in the White House[94] reasserted a presidential recognition of newsbroking's indispensability to national leaders, which had been first acknowledged by Abraham Lincoln.

Outside of Washington, AP, to keep up with UP and Hearst, had to strengthen its domestic staff. The board told AP members in mid-1910 that

> The working force has been augmented by highly trained newspapermen of broad experience in all departments of news-gathering and news-handling. . . . The Associated Press is now called upon to [handle important domestic news events] largely through its own staff correspondents. Much of this news in former years was received through the special reports of members in their respective home fields. The demand, however, of the membership for a comprehensive and more rapid handling of important news occurrences has made it necessary for the management to send staff men to report many of these happenings.[95]

The cooperative plan of sharing news was increasingly inadequate in the face of steadily growing membership demand and competitive enterprise.

At the receiving end, that national readership which shared the exhilaration of a news "flash" was also being treated to glimpses of more and more diverse events at home and abroad. The agencies' rush to beat each other threw the news spotlight in rapid succession on such outposts as Pretoria, Peking, and Panama, such newsmakers as Carry Nation, Orville and Wilbur Wright, and Harry K. Thaw, and such disasters as the Galveston hurricane, the San Francisco earthquake, and the Chelsea, Mass., fire. Paradoxically, although news horizons widened, events were increasingly treated as one- or

two-day sensations and denied thoughtful reflective followup comment, giving the reader a rising sense that disaster or war could
spring up momentarily anywhere and die away just as quickly.
Moreover, as the newsbrokers strove to stay abreast of each other,
counting the minutes between each other's first bulletins on a given
news event, speed and agility replaced accuracy and completeness
as prime ingredients of the public's first brush with a news event.
Some of American journalism's uniquely twentieth-century
qualities—standardization, brevity, fragmentation—were setting in.

The growing pervasiveness and marketability of newsbrokers' reports, coupled with local editors' traditional unwillingness to apply
editing pencils or scissors to wire copy (dating from the 1840's),
amassed a reading audience of national size that, in effect, the
newsbrokers' managers and staff wrote for daily and directly. Villard in 1944 described the malady of standardization in its advanced
stages as follows:

> When one travels through the country on a fast train and buys
> successively the newspapers of larger cities, one is struck by
> their similarity. One finds the same comics, the same special
> features in almost all, the same Sunday magazine and financial
> section, and precisely the same Associated Press or United
> Press news.[96]

There was, additionally, a standardization of news reality. What
the newsbrokerages chose to cover with their growing staffs and
rangier networks of leased wires—and what they saw their competitors covering and therefore had to emulate—became the "news" of
the day. Geographically, news expanded from happenings in the obvious nineteenth-century metropolises and capitals or coverage areas of member newspapers to potentially every hamlet, highway,
and home here and abroad. Temporally, news that was measured in
months with sailing ships, in weeks with steamers, and in hours
with the limited capacity of the early transatlantic cables, became
measured in minutes, and its speed of delivery, in turn, measured
newsbrokers' success. Public affairs from Supreme Court decisions
to a deadlocked Congress, from labor unrest to international tension, were reduced to hurried, short, fragmentary accounts, formularized in their structure and mundane in their language. The
demands of a "deadline every minute," to borrow the title of UP's
1957 house history, left the correspondent no time to digest his subject, to seek added perspectives and background, to consult his con-

science and intellect. National and international events had a life span of the twelve-hour morning or afternoon cycle on the leased wire, after which they were discarded unless a new angle, an overnight lead, or a reaction piece could be found to keep them alive.

In the area of foreign affairs, the *New York Evening Post*'s Rollo Ogden, writing in the *Atlantic* in 1900, asserted that the art of foreign correspondence, once rich, perceptive, and instructive, had been lost with the rapid increase of cabled foreign news. First, Ogden embraced James Russell Lowell's condemnation of telegraphed domestic news of a half-century earlier. Ogden quotes Lowell as saying that

> Great events are perhaps not more common than they used to be, but a vastly greater number of trivial incidents are now recorded.... The telegraph strips history of everything down to the bare fact, but it does not observe the true proportions of things.... In brevity and cynicism it is... as impartial a leveler as death.... [T]his shorthand diarist confounds all distinctions of great and little, and roils the memory with minute particles of what is oddly enough called intelligence.

Then Ogden asserted that cabling has done much the same thing to foreign news. "Sensational affairs usually burst on us unannounced," Ogden said. "Their obscure but unmistakable beginnings had not been observed by the press agents" who skimmed the foreign papers for their daily dispatches. He added, "So the crisis is upon us before we know it, and the floods of hysterical cablegrams suddenly overcome us, though *not* to our special wonder, so used have we become to this jerky, staccato way of serving up foreign news."[97]

The ascent of the rapid-fire news report, diminishing major events and inflating trivia—all to the same beat of thirty words per minute on the Morse circuits, and later sixty words per minute on the Teletypes—deadened the highs, exaggerated the lows, making all stories marketable commodities, susceptible of being repackaged with new leads or new trivia late in the cycle to entice the local editor to give the item better play in his newspaper. Walter Lippmann, discussing the new news-defining process, wrote in 1922,

> before a series of events become news they have usually to make themselves noticeable in some more or less overt act. Generally too, in a crudely overt act.... [T]he news is not a mir-

ror of social conditions, but the report of an aspect that has obtruded itself.[98]

And the "pictures in our heads" created by such disjointed, unexplained fragments of human behavior insist upon being called "reality" by their purveyors and consumers.

If the real reality was getting harder for the public to discern, those national news agencies whose news reality obscured the real thing were becoming more obvious to the public. A measure of the growing impact of an institution in society is the amount of attention devoted to it by the popular journals, both in the form of attack and self-defense. From 1900 to 1920, AP, UP, and Hearst's various agencies were discussed with increasing frequency in public print. Infrequently for a while after the Civil War, popular journals had carried articles by staffers and free-lancers about AP, generally approving in tone and explaining what AP was and how it operated.[99] The practice was revived after a ten-year hiatus with William Henry Smith's article in *Century* magazine[100] in 1891 and Stone's "Newspapers in the United States, Their Functions, Interior Economy, and Management," reprinted in the trade publication *Newspaperdom* after appearing in *Self Culture* in 1897.[101] AP staffer Charles Edward Kloeber, Jr., contributed "The Press Association" to a series on the American newspaper in *Bookman* during 1904.[102] Although it mentioned competitors, the article focused on AP and was profusely illustrated with scenes of AP's headquarters. Stone returned the next year with a major five-part series in *Century* magazine entitled "The Associated Press by its Manager Melville E. Stone." The installments were entitled "Its General Foreign Service," "The Removal of the Russian Censorship on Foreign News," "News-Gathering as a Business," "The Method of Operation," and "Its Work in War."[103]

Rollo Ogden, as noted above, took a swing at cabled foreign news from the pages of *Atlantic* in September 1900, but the critical discussion of newsbroking remained primarily in liberal or opinion journals until the 1910s. There was an exchange of letters in 1906 in *The Nation* between Dr. E. Schrader of Spokane, Wash., and Stone about alleged anti-German "lies" in AP's foreign dispatches.[104] The *Independent* later that same year detected "faked cable news" that the undiscerning reader might mistake for AP's work if the agency did not insist that editors identify their cables properly.[105] William Kittle examined the AP among other agencies in *Arena* in 1909, strongly intimating AP's power over public opinion.[106] There was some discussion in *Outlook* of AP's role in a "fake" interview with a cabinet member,[107] and a couple of jabs at AP from the Socialist perspective of Max Sherover in a pamphlet issued between 1914 and 1916. Sherover observed that

> In the struggles between the masses and those who oppress and exploit them the Associated Press can be relied upon to line up on the side of the oppressors and the exploiters. . . . The subservience of the Associated Press to the Interests, to Entrenched Privilege, has been glaringly evidenced of late in several titanic conflicts between capital and labor.[108]

The public through the general circulation magazines was invited to examine AP critically for the first time beginning in 1914 when the *New York Sun*, still outside the AP and running its own news service, complained to the U.S attorney general that AP's membership bylaws and contract with Reuters created a news monopoly in violation of the Sherman Antitrust Act. Attorney General T. W. Gregory's opinion on the *Sun*'s petition, delivered thirteen months later, generally absolved AP of antitrust violations, recommending only the elimination of inviolability-of-the-news-report bylaw provisions noted frequently earlier in this chapter.[109] The *Sun*'s complaint and the attorney general's response thrust AP into the spotlight. "The Associated Press as a Trust" appeared in the *Literary Digest*,[110] and "The Associated Press under Fire" was printed in *Outlook*[111] within a month after the *Sun* filed its petition.

Three months later *Outlook* devoted six pages to a criticism of the AP by Gregory Mason and a defense by George Kennan, both prompted by the *Sun* petition.[112] *Outlook* editorially supported the *Sun*'s action a month and a half later.[113] In March 1914, Will Irwin asked, "What's wrong with the Associated Press?" in *Harper's Weekly*.[114] Citing not only the *Sun*'s legal claims but also a pending libel suit by AP against the radical *Masses* and a current fight between AP and Hearst over the latter's use of AP news in his Oakland edition, Irwin said that AP was "Tory" in bias and that "the real quarrel of the American people with the Associated Press" was that it "stands at the gate of journalism, barring the new man," the young journalist and editor. A month later Irwin, again in *Harper's Weekly*, discussed UP,[115] but while praising UP as being "our most powerful liberal and radical force" in its encouragement of young journalists, he also took the opportunity to reassert that AP was "our most powerful force of journalistic reaction."

Colliers editorially joined the fracas on June 6, 1914,[116] concluding that Irwin "is clearly in tune with the times" and that "it is only a matter of time when the Associated Press will have to conform to the current beliefs about monopoly." A month later Stone's lengthy defense appeared in *Collier's*,[117] stating that AP "enjoys no exceptional right of any sort" and strove for "a truthful, unbiased report of the world's happenings." While it might be argued that Irwin, trying to scrape together a living as a free-lancer, was here employing muckraking techniques that by 1914 had nearly lost their fashion in the popular journals,[118] his caustic comments about AP were part of a growing chorus of fashionable anti–Associated Press comment in the magazine press.

Meanwhile "an observer" in the *Atlantic* took up "The Problem of the Associated Press"[119] by asking if newsbroking was essentially monopolistic, and if so, whether AP's structure was the most desirable organization for that purpose. The writer concluded that newsbroking was a monopoly, especially as practiced by AP and that it "should...be treated like a public-utility corporation" without destroying AP's service to the public. Stone's reply appeared in pamphlet form, the *Atlantic* seemingly disinclined to grant him space for his rebuttal in its columns.[120]

The approach of war ended the debate temporarily, but between the wars sporadic comment and criticism appeared, especially in books.[121] The pages of popular journals became almost exclusively the domain of positive articles by or about newsbroking officials or of carefully objective introductions to one or another of the newsbrokerages. A story in a 1924 AP *Service Bulletin*, under the headline "Public Interested in Associated Press," told of staffers speaking to various local and national meetings about AP's work.[122] Clearly by the start of World War I, AP, UP, and Hearst agencies variously drew praise and criticism in the popular journals. A reading public, made more alert to its sources of foreign and war news by a continuous parade of international conflicts beginning with the Spanish-American War in 1898 and increasingly accompanied by government's maturing practice of nationalistic propaganda, was affixing greater significance to newsbrokerages' logos.

Perhaps not yet household words, the names of national news agencies were at least no longer mysteries to the public and were understood increasingly by politicians, some businessmen, and a smattering of publicists. In addition to a steady production of bulletins, specials, and scoops, the agencies' identities were emerging beyond the news business. AP's Edwin Hood became known as a participant in the State Department's handling of the famous Zimmermann note in 1917,[123] and AP's bylaws were scrutinized in 1914 by the U.S. attorney general. UP's Roy Howard triggered a premature national celebration over the end of World War I. Hearst's news services were found by the Supreme Court in 1918 to be appropriating AP dispatches, were exposed as fabricating foreign news stories signed by nonexistent correspondents, and were denied use of British cable facilities during the war. Twentieth-century newsbroking, fueled by hot competition and the revenue of powerful editors and newspaper chains, had become both source and subject of the nation's news as the Roarin' Twenties began.

Discussion

Early in the Civil War when the South still believed its cause was winnable, progressive Southern editors launched the Press Association of the Confederacy on the radical principles that member newspapers should cooperate in gathering the agency's news and participate in making and upholding the agency's policies. These same principles later guided formation of the Western Associated Press, which as a reaction to the New York AP's fifteen years of domination was governed by bylaws and membership-elected directors in the pursuit of cooperative news-gathering. Two decades later, aggressive editors and journalists forged the first United Press, a private business enterprise free of bylaw straitjackets, membership self-government, and long-term obligations to telegraph allies. UP's free-wheeling competition drew AP's leadership into entangling cartels and stock pools, which although consistent with 1880s business practices, sent AP's habitually self-interested members scurrying to resurrect their odd mixture of cooperation and democracy in 1893.

During AP's half-century existence up to 1900, its members conservatively regarded the agency as protection from local competition and participated vigorously either through local partnerships or regional cooperatives to limit membership to established or prosperous journals. Only a handful of AP leaders—notably William Henry Smith, Richard Smith, Walter N. Haldeman, Whitelaw Reid, and Charles A. Dana—understood the desirability of expansion and unity to combat the new national competition of privately owned agencies.

As the twentieth century dawned, AP still espoused, but with increasing difficulty, the contradictory principles of local protectionism and national expansion. WAP's fifty members in 1867 had grown to only sixty-two at the founding of the new AP in Illinois in 1893, but between 1893 and 1900 AP membership increased tenfold, although without eliminating the privilege of some members to exercise a protest right and to own AP stock, later converted to bonds. In terms of the central thesis of this research, members' continued impact on AP's independent ability to set policies on expansion of membership and news-gathering and on the nature of the news report signaled the newsbrokerage's subordination to the newspaper institution, and as chapters 6 and 7 indicate, the diminishing of membership impact stemmed principally from the threat of outside competition. Although Scripps's new United Press and Hearst's agencies were subsidized by the nation's two largest and most powerful newspaper owners and the agencies' personnel flowed freely between newsbrokerage and parent newspaper chain, both AP competitors were private businesses, free to sign any client, capable of establishing independent domestic and international news-gathering staffs, able to charge competitive rates for their services, and always free to be suspended if their services did not provide satisfactory revenue. Although subsidiaries of newspaper companies, UP and INS stood apart from the newspaper institution, signing contracts with "subscribers" or "clients" rather than entwining themselves in bylaw obligations and privileges with "members" as did AP.

Hearst and Scripps newsbroking, then, led the way to independent institutional status for newsbroking, while AP in 1920 stood on the brink of a gradual disengagement from its members' preoccupation with protection and power within AP. By the late 1920s, bondholding, originally a privilege of a minority, was extended to all members, and by 1935 more than half of AP's members held bonds.[124] Meanwhile all members were formally granted the protest right in 1928, but by then most in AP believed that exercising the protest right diminished AP's strength. Kent Cooper notes that by 1925 AP's membership would have dropped below its 1917 level, through consolidations and suspensions, if AP had not secured waivers of protest rights affecting "vast exclusive areas." At the same time, UP's unrestricted subscriber policy would have increased its list by 50 percent, Cooper says, if AP had not been available to many new papers through the waiver of protest by old members.[125]

The first ten years of Cooper's general managership, beginning in 1925, marked the demise of AP's subservience to membership power. Seeing that the loyalty of older members of AP rested on the protest right, which he said he felt would eventually be declared in restraint of trade, Cooper instituted "improvements and innovations" in AP's service to hold the loyalty of old members while meeting the innovative competition of UP and INS.[126] He gathered control over AP's system and centralized it in New York City, he expanded and diversified the news report, he undermined publishers' power via the board by creating the AP Managing Editors Association as a street-level line of communication into AP, he broke up AP's reliance on Reuters and the world news cartel, and he presided over AP's belated introduction of service to broadcasters. In another place the author attempted to trace through manifest policies, practices, and publications the drift of AP's power center from membership to general manager (occurring between 1908 and 1937) and from the general manager to administrative heads (occurring between 1937 and the mid-1960s).[127] Another measure of AP's independence from the newspaper industry was more recently revealed when AP board chairman Frank Batten told AP's annual meeting that in 1982 newspaper revenue for the first time in history accounted for less than 50 percent of AP's budget.[128]

The complexity and gradualness of AP's disengagement from subservience to its membership should not obscure the fact that its two competitors were relatively free from such pressures at their inception and carried their brand of enterprise to AP's doorstep by World War I, forcing the latter to play a game of catchup if it wanted to survive in a twentieth-century world of institutional newsbroking. Competition-bred expansion of AP's membership and newsgathering facilities, diversification and acceleration of AP's news report, a growing similarity among the newsbrokers' news reports (especially between AP's and UP's), and the impact newsbroker reporting was having on the public's perception of the world were the obvious manifestations of newsbroking's emergence as a separate institution around 1920. In the sequel the merger of UP and INS on May 24, 1958,[129] and Scripps-Howard's sale of the resulting United Press International on June 2, 1982, to a consortium called Media News Corporation[130] in no way signaled a decline in newsbroking's institutional status. On the contrary, these changes reveal the developing financial stress within the two aging parent newspaper chains, while the need for newsbroking in this nation has continued, and—at least for the moment—continues competitively.

Finally, chapter 4 traces the growth of newsbrokers' technological independence in the 1880s and 1890s through the use of leased wires, in-house operators, and typewriters for collecting and distributing the news. This independence from telegraph companies increased after the turn of the century in a steady stream of innovations geared to newsbroking's needs. After 1915, Teletype machines gradually appeared along the leased lines, replacing the receiving operators and the need to translate the Phillips code, sent by Morse code, into plain English. Radiotelegraphy supplemented and gradually replaced cable telegraphy in international newsgathering. The portable Telex machine put correspondents, especially in remote areas, in touch with home bureaus via telephone or telegraph lines. By the 1950s, Teletypesetter delivered printed or punched-tape versions of news stories, justified and hyphenated, to fit the standard newspaper column width. In the late 1970s, satellite transmission of the news report began to replace wired delivery systems to newsrooms. Wirephoto, Soundphoto, and Telephoto were the three agencies' versions, beginning in 1935 and 1936, of wired delivery via electronic impulses of news photos. Within twenty years, facsimile delivered newsbroker photos to newspapers, and after another twenty years newsbroking had entered the laserphoto area.

Such technological innovations enhanced the delivery potential of newsbroker news in all its dimensions to a growing list of subscribers, the agencies taking the lead in the news business's drive for news-gathering inventiveness. Indeed, newsbroking's technological leadership was most obvious in 1971–72, when introduction of AP and UPI terminal-computer news-processing systems triggered a strikingly rapid takeover of terminals, computers, coldtype composition, and offset printing in newspaper offices throughout the nation. Meanwhile, AP and UPI pressed ahead with their new terminal-computer-satellite systems into the outer reaches of the communication revolution of the 1980s, packaging one-way teletext news services for distribution over cable systems and experimenting with two-way videotext services by which computer or cable users can roam the wires' computerized database seeking desired news stories.

And while these new newsbroker services threaten to leapfrog the parent newspaper institution and broadcast subscribers' news products into the consumer's home or office, newsbrokers ironically have faced an old threat of their own—the takeover of news services by suppliers of technology. In the nineteenth century, AP periodically feared Western Union encroachment on the news business; in the late twentieth century AP was having to fight off American Telephone and Telegraph's efforts to dominate national news distribution.[131] As this research is being completed, that trio of institutional forces with which these two volumes of newsbroker research are concerned—newspaper journalism, technological systems, and newsbroking—is entering still another period of realignment. And like those that have preceded it, this one could establish any of the three as dominant in general intercity news systems.

APPENDIX

Table 1. Newsbroker Subscribers: Selected Years, 1880-1918
(Total Subscribers and Percent of Total Newspapers)

	AP in 1880[a]		AP in 1883[b]		UP in 1884[c]		AP in 1895[d]		UP in 1895[e]		AP in 1897[f]		AP in 1900[g]		AP in 1918[h]	
	No.	%	No.	%	No.	%	No.	%	No.	%	No.	%	No.	%	No.	%
U.S. Total	355	36.6	425	38.0	166	13.9	396	19.9	338	17.0	637	29.8	622	28.4	1027	42.2
Northeast	39	42.9	41	43.2	23	21.3	28	16.3	70	40.7	101	54.9	102	54.3	93	53.8
Maine	8	66.7	8	80.0	1	7.7	5	27.8	10	55.6	13	68.4	11	68.8	11	91.7
New Hampshire	3	30.0	1	9.1	0	0.0	2	14.3	5	35.7	7	43.8	7	43.8	9	69.2
Vermont	3	60.0	6	100.0	0	0.0	1	20.0	3	60.0	4	100.0	7	70.0	10	100.0
Massachusetts	14	35.9	14	33.3	8	17.4	14	18.4	31	40.8	35	44.9	38	45.2	33	38.4
Rhode Island	2	25.0	3	42.9	2	28.6	4	26.7	5	33.3	9	52.9	10	58.8	9	81.8
Connecticut	9	52.9	9	42.9	12	44.4	2	4.5	16	36.4	33	66.0	29	64.4	21	51.2
Middle Atlantic	77	32.1	95	34.1	55	18.7	55	12.8	141	32.7	151	34.3	125	28.2	135	29.7
New York	45	39.1	48	34.5	30	21.4	33	18.0	76	41.5	85	45.9	70	35.9	72	34.3
New Jersey	0	0.0	4	14.8	4	12.9	0	0.0	14	25.0	9	17.3	5	9.8	10	25.0
Pennsylvania	32	32.7	43	38.1	21	17.1	22	11.5	51	26.6	57	28.1	50	25.4	53	26.0
East North Central	63	28.1	83	30.6	49	16.5	104	19.2	43	7.9	139	22.5	138	21.7	185	30.8
Ohio	20	35.7	23	35.9	13	18.3	30	18.9	17	10.7	42	25.9	43	25.9	48	28.1
Indiana	13	32.5	13	23.2	7	10.3	15	11.9	5	4.0	20	13.5	20	13.1	31	22.5
Illinois	16	21.6	22	25.9	7	7.9	29	20.1	11	7.6	40	23.4	39	21.1	50	30.3
Michigan	11	33.3	15	36.6	9	22.0	16	26.2	4	6.6	18	24.3	19	26.4	35	50.0
Wisconsin	3	14.3	10	40.0	13	46.4	14	26.9	6	11.5	19	29.7	17	28.3	21	36.8
West North Central	48	37.8	69	43.4	23	13.6	65	22.0	22	7.4	75	24.9	78	26.4	143	45.8
Minnesota	0	0.0	8	40.0	3	16.7	11	27.5	3	7.5	12	36.4	13	36.1	17	37.0
Iowa	17	56.7	22	53.7	10	25.0	20	30.3	9	13.6	28	40.6	32	47.1	32	60.4
Missouri	16	37.2	14	31.8	4	7.8	15	18.3	7	8.5	14	15.9	13	15.5	23	28.4
North Dakota	1	11.1	11	50.0	4	18.2	2	22.2	0	0.0	2	22.2	2	25.0	11	100.0
South Dakota							2	9.5	0	0.0	2	9.1	2	11.1	15	78.9
Nebraska	4	26.7	4	30.8	2	11.8	3	8.6	3	8.6	6	20.7	5	17.2	11	35.5
Kansas	10	50.0	10	52.6	0	0.0	12	27.9	0	0.0	11	21.6	11	21.2	34	47.9
South Atlantic	40	48.2	36	39.6	13	16.3	21	15.0	33	23.6	51	32.5	47	29.7	136	67.3
Delaware	2	40.0	2	40.0	2	50.0	1	20.0	1	20.0	1	20.0	1	16.7	2	66.7
Maryland	5	33.3	4	30.8	2	14.3	4	25.0	4	25.0	6	40.0	6	35.3	8	47.1
Dist. of Columbia	4	80.0	3	50.0	2	40.0	2	40.0	3	60.0	2	66.7	2	66.7	2	28.6
Virginia	11	55.0	10	50.0	4	22.2	5	14.3	10	28.6	12	36.4	10	29.4	19	54.3
West Virginia	1	50.0	2	25.0	2	40.0	3	25.0	2	16.7	8	44.4	9	45.0	19	57.6
North Carolina	5	38.5	5	41.7	0	0.0	1	4.8	4	19.0	6	28.6	5	18.5	24	75.0
South Carolina	3	75.0	2	40.0	0	0.0	1	14.3	2	28.6	3	30.0	4	36.4	13	92.9
Georgia	6	37.5	6	31.6	1	6.7	3	12.0	5	20.0	10	83.3	9	36.0	22	78.6
Florida	3	100.0	2	66.7	0	0.0	1	7.1	2	14.3	3	13.6	1	6.7	27	81.8
East South Central	19	55.9	18	60.0	3	8.6	21	28.0	7	9.3	29	39.2	26	33.8	54	62.1
Kentucky	4	36.4	3	25.0	2	15.4	8	30.8	0	0.0	10	38.5	8	29.6	21	75.0
Tennessee	7	58.3	8	80.0	1	9.1	8	40.0	2	10.0	11	57.9	9	64.3	11	61.1
Alabama	3	50.0	4	66.7	0	0.0	1	5.3	4	21.1	4	21.1	6	31.6	11	45.8
Mississippi	5	100.0	3	100.0	0	0.0	4	40.0	1	10.0	4	40.0	3	17.6	11	64.7
West South Central	22	44.9	17	36.2	0	0.0	31	27.9	3	2.7	20	16.5	28	19.0	101	46.1
Arkansas	3	50.0	2	22.2	0	0.0	5	27.7	0	0.0	2	8.7	2	7.7	13	39.4
Louisiana	6	46.2	5	50.0	0	0.0	3	21.4	2	14.3	6	33.3	8	30.8	9	47.4
Oklahoma	-	-	-	-	-	-	0	0.0	0	0.0	0	0.0	1	5.6	22	36.7
Texas	13	43.3	10	35.7	0	0.0	23	39.0	1	1.7	12	18.2	17	22.1	57	53.3
Mountain	27	50.0	41	55.4	0	0.0	33	37.5	5	5.7	36	40.0	38	41.3	82	67.2
Montana	2	50.0	5	55.6	0	0.0	6	54.5	0	0.0	7	53.8	9	90.0	17	89.5
Idaho	-	-	-	-	0	0.0	1	33.3	0	0.0	2	50.0	2	33.3	7	70.0
Wyoming	3	100.0	2	66.7	0	0.0	2	40.0	0	0.0	1	20.0	1	25.0	5	71.4
Colorado	11	57.9	12	50.0	0	0.0	9	23.7	5	13.2	12	30.8	13	30.2	20	48.8
New Mexico	1	33.3	5	100.0	0	0.0	3	60.0	0	0.0	4	80.0	4	100.0	5	71.4

Arizona	0	0.0	5	55.6	0	0.0	5	62.5	0	0.0	4	44.4	4	36.4	15	75.0
Utah	5	100.0	6	100.0	0	0.0	4	44.4	0	0.0	3	42.9	4	66.7	7	87.5
Nevada	5	35.7	6	42.9	0	0.0	3	33.3	0	0.0	3	37.5	1	12.5	6	60.0
Pacific	20	29.0	25	34.2	0	0.0	38	28.6	14	10.5	35	28.5	38	25.0	98	37.5
Washington	0	0.0	3	37.5	0	0.0	7	35.0	1	5.0	7	43.8	10	71.4	23	57.5
Oregon	1	14.3	3	37.5	0	0.0	7	43.8	0	0.0	5	25.0	6	35.3	14	42.4
California	19	32.8	19	33.3	0	0.0	24	24.7	13	13.4	23	20.4	22	19.6	50	29.9
Alaska	–	–	–	–	–	–	–	–	–	–	–	–	0	0.0	7	58.3
Hawaii	–	–	–	–	–	–	–	–	–	–	–	–	2	33.3	4	44.4
Canada											44	42.7	62	52.1	–	–

a. Total newspapers and AP membership for 1880 are both from S. N. D. North, *History and Present Condition of the Newspaper and Periodical Press of the United States with a Catalogue of the Publications of the Census Year* (Washington, D.C.: Government Printing Office, 1884), pp. 107, 170.

b. AP membership is from [New York and Western] Associated Press, *(Private Circular), The Associated Press* (n.p., [1883]), pp. 3–8. Percentages are based on total newspapers in that year and in that region or state from N.W. Ayer & Son, *American Newspaper Annual* (1883), p.6.

c. UP totals are from United Press (1882-97), *The United Press* (New York: Evening Post, 1884), pp. 26–30. Percentages are based on total newspapers from N.W. Ayer & Son, *American Newspaper Annual* (1884), p.6.

d. AP membership is for February 1, 1895, from Associated Press, *Annual Report* (1895), pp. 279-83. Percentages are based on total newspapers from N.W. Ayer & Son, *American Newspaper Annual* (1895), p. 8.

e. UP totals are for July 15, 1895, from [United Press (1882-97)], *Facts vs. Lies, with an Incidental Forecast as to the Outcome of the Contest between the Press Associations* (New York: Evening Post, [1895]), facing p. 44. (The same printed list, dated July 8, 1895, is in the Whitelaw Reid Papers, Library of Congress, Washington, D.C.) Percentages are based on total newspapers from N.W. Ayer & Son, *American Newspaper Annual* (1895), p. 8.

f. AP membership is for May 7, 1897, from Associated Press, *Annual Report* (1897), pp. 128-34. Percentages are based on total newspapers from N. W. Ayer & Son, *American Newspaper Annual* (1897), p. 8.

g. AP membership is for September, 1900, from Associated Press, *Annual Report* (1900), pp. 313-20. Percentages are based on total newspapers from N. W. Ayer & Son, *American Newspaper Annual* (1900), p. 8.

h. AP membership is for March 15, 1918, from [Associated Press], *"M.E.S.", His Book* . . .(New York: Harper, 1918), pp. 312-35. Percentages are based on total newspapers from N.W. Ayer & Son, *American Newspaper Annual* (1918), p. 10.

Table 2. Finances of Selected Associated Press Organizations, 1871-73, 1875, 1881-84

I. New York, Western, and Northwestern APs, 1871-73, 1875

	1871		1872		1875	
NYAP Revenue:						
New York City & Brooklyn Papers	$182,471	35.7%	$144,921	31.5%	$131,312.99	31.9%
WAP & California AP	48,605	9.5	44,936	9.8	45,340.79	11.0
Southern AP & Washington, D.C.	106,778	20.9	106,763	23.2	86,860.13	21.1
Philadelphia & Baltimore APs	54,652	10.7	53,749	11.7	51,135.08	12.4
New England AP	36,444	7.1	36,703	8.0	34,057.99	8.3
New York State AP	11,700	2.3	12,150	2.6	15,600.00	3.8

Commercial Bureau	39,257	7.7	25,000	5.4	24,000.00	5.8
Canada & Misc.	30,923	6.1	36,072	7.8	23,526.85	5.7
TOTALS	$510,830	100.0%	$460,294	100.0%	$411,833.83	100.0%

NYAP Expenses:

Telegraph Tolls	$227,640	44.6%	$234,273	50.9%	$165,244.84c	40.1%
Atlantic Cable tolls	104,189	20.4	92.141	20.0	87,156.63	21.2
Reuters Contract	12,100	2.4	13,560	2.9	13,459.31	3.3
Other European Expenses	24,636	4.8	13,199	2.9	26,099.09	6.3
General Office & Salaries	142,211	27.8	107,121	23.3	119,873.96d	29.1
TOTALS	$510,776	100.0%	$460,294	100.0%	$411,833.83	100.0%

WAP Revenue:	1871-1872a		1872-1873a	
Membership Assessments	$180,019	95.8%	$183,920	98.2%
Northwestern AP & Others	3,390	1.8	3,392	1.8
Misc.	4,533	2.4	–	–
TOTALS	$187,942	100.0%	$187,312	100.0%

WAP Expenses:				
Telegraph Tolls	$103,090	58.6%	$107,677	59.6%
New York AP	43,500	24.7	42,400	23.5
Deciphering Market Reports	3,756	2.2	3,756	2.1
General Office & Salaries	25,472	14.5	26,758	14.8
TOTALS	$175,818	100.0%	$180,591	100.0%

Northwestern AP Revenue:	1872-1873b	
Membership Assessments	$23,973	93.7%
Outside Collections	1,602	6.3
TOTALS	$25,575	100.0%

Northwestern AP Expenses:		
Telegraph Tolls	$18,363	74.6
Western AP	4,279	17.4
General Office, Salaries & Misc.	1,987	8.0
TOTALS	$24,629	100.0%

II. New England, Western, and Trans-Mississippi APs, 1881-1884

	Expenses	Deficit	% to W.U.	% for News
New England Associated Press, May 1, 1883, to April 26, 1884:	$97,475	-$12	40.1	32.9% to NYAP
Western Associated Press, July 1, 1881, to June 30, 1882:	198,445	-$3,644	58.9	22.9% to NYAP
Trans-Mississippi AP, February 1, 1883, to January 31, 1884:	7,078	-$62	91.5	8.5% to WAP

a. Western AP's fiscal year at this time ran from June 1 to May 31.

b. Northwestern AP's fiscal year ran from March 31 to April 1.

c. This figure represents, in part, a reduction of $92,118.57 from 1874 caused by leasing and operating a wire between New York City and Washington, D.C., rather than relying on Western Union for a Washington circuit.

d. This figure includes $49,028.57 for the cost of a leased wire introduced in 1875 between New York City and Washington, D.C.

SOURCES: For Part I: William Henry Smith, "Annual Report of the New York Associated Press, for 1873," printed confidential circular, William Henry Smith Papers, Indiana Historical Society, Indianapolis; J. W. Simonton to D. M. Stone, January 29,
1876, Manton Marble Papers, Library of Congress, Washington, D.C.; Western Associated Press, *Proceedings* (1872), pp. 9, 12-13, and (1873), pp. 13-16; and Northwestern
Associated Press, *Seventh Annual Meeting* (n.p., [1873]), p. 2. For Part II: Handwritten "Statement of Receipts and Expenditures of the N.E. Associated Press, from May
1st, 1883, to April 26, 1884," New England Associated Press Papers, Baker Library,
Harvard University Graduate School of Business Administration, Boston; Western
Associated Press, *Proceedings* (1882), p. 7; and Trans-Mississippi Associated Press,
Articles of Incorporation, Constitution and Proceedings (Topeka, Kan.: Peerless,
1886), pp. 32-33, 35.

**Table 3. Western Associated Press Expenses and
Relations with Western Union, 1867-1892**

							Index of Expenses (1867 = 100)	
Period[a]	Tot. WAP Expenses	Surplus/ Deficit	% to NYAP	Tot. WAP Payment to W.U.	% of WAP Cost	% of W.U. Rev.	WAP Expenses	W.U. Expenses
1867-68	$151,972	$-1,675	n.a.	n.a.	–	–	100.0	100.0
1868-69	156,207	+3,445					102.8	103.9
1869-70	154,942	+2,134					102.0	117.7
1870-71	169,229	-69	26.3%	$97,568	57.7%	1.5%	111.4	122.9
1871-72	175,818	+12,124	24.7	103,090	58.6	1.4	115.7	125.1
1872-73	180,591	+6,721	23.5	107,677	59.6	1.3	118.8	150.5
1873-74	174,965	+7,265	n.a.	n.a.	–	–	115.1	176.2
1874-75	188,918	+453					124.3	160.7
1875-76	188,513	+4,164					124.0	164.1
1876-77	179,925	+3,618	23.3	108,101	60.1	1.2	118.4	165.1
1877-78	184,369	-691	22.8	112,877	61.2	1.3	121.3	153.2
1878-79	169,233	+17,808	24.8	97,786	57.8	1.1	111.4	141.9
1879-80	178,173	+7,233	23.6	105,867	59.4	1.0	117.2	158.8
1880-81	184,433	+2,714	22.8	110,456	59.9	1.0	121.4	206.6
1881-82	198,445	-3,644	22.9	116,844	58.9	0.8	130.6	244.7
1882-83	n.a.							284.1
1883-84	317,959	+61,631	n.a.	n.a.	–	–	209.2	325.3
1884-85	n.a.							298.6
1885-86	386,108	+5,627	19.2[b]	152,714	65.2	1.0	254.1	308.3
1886-87	436,063	-30,799	24.6	265,817[c]	61.0	1.7	286.9	325.5
1887-88	448,834	+18,350	17.4	301,757	67.2	1.7	295.3	365.4
1888-89	490,144	-17,924	15.4	338,934	69.1	1.8	322.5	360.9
1889-90	489,995	+614	16.1	335,947	68.6	1.7	322.4	371.0
1890-91	585,872	+55,296	n.a.	464,045	79.2	2.2	385.5	406.5
1891-92	647,901	-15,912	n.a.	550,115	84.9	2.5	426.3	404.2

NOTE: The above figures are taken from published Western Associated Press records
and proceedings. When the executive committee of the new Associated Press had
the Western AP records audited, a process lasting from the spring of 1892 to November 29, 1894, the auditors found a discrepancy between the books and the published

records of $112,709.79, the records showing a surplus of $33,098.45 and the books showing a deficit of $79,611.34. Moreover, the auditors, like the author, were unable to locate published records for 1882-83 and 1884-85. The auditors also noted uniformly larger receipts and expenses in the books than were published up to June 30, 1890, after which the books showed smaller receipts and expenses than the published records showed. The available records and documents failed to explain or resolve these discrepancies to the committee's satisfaction. See Victor F. Lawson, Charles W. Knapp, and Frederick Driscoll to William Henry Smith, December 6, 1894, and enclosures, William Henry Smith Papers, Indiana Historical Society, Indianapolis.

a. Western AP figures are for June 1 to May 31 through 1876 and for July 1 to June 30 beginning in 1876. Figures for June 1876 are not included above so that each line represents twelve months. Western Union figures are for January 1 to December 31 through 1875 and for July 1 to June 30 beginning in 1875. Figures for January to July 1875 are not included above.

b. While payments to New York AP continued at pre-1883 levels ($45,000 to $50,000 annually), additional payments, ordered by the Joint Executive Committee, appeared in 1885. The percentages after 1885 reflect both payments.

c. Beginning in 1886 Western AP statements break down payments to Western Union into "general" and "leased wire" categories. The leased wire proportion of Western AP's total payment to Western Union was 51.4% in 1886-87, 53% in 1887-88, 60.2% in 1888-89, 60.6% in 1889-90, 52.2% in 1890-91, and 55.5% in 1891-92. Included in the post-1886 "Payment to W.U." figures are Western AP expenses for operating the leased wires, which covered the agency's own telegraphers, equipment, etc., sums not actually going to Western Union.

SOURCES: Western Associated Press, *Proceedings* (1869), p. 15, (1870), pp. 10-11, (1871), pp. 13-14, (1872), pp. 9, 12-13, (1873), pp. 13-16, (1875), pp. 7, 13-15, (1876), pp. 11-12, (1877), p. 9, (1878), p. 14, (1879), p. 10, (1880), p. 11, (1881), p. 10, (1882), p. 7, (1887), p. 9, (1888), pp. 11-12, (1889), pp. 14-15, (1890), pp. 11-12, (1891), p. 24; [Western Associated Press], Special Auditing Committee, *(Private), Annual Report, 1886-87* (New York: Evening Post, [1887]); typed Western AP "Statement of Receipts and Expenditures, June 30th, 1890, to June 30th, 1892," and "Exhibit D" enclosed in Victor F. Lawson, Charles W. Knapp, and Frederick Driscoll to William Henry Smith, December 6, 1894, both in William Henry Smith Papers, Indiana Historical Society, Indianapolis; and U.S. Department of Commerce, Bureau of the Census, *Historical Statistics of the United States, Colonial Times to 1970*, 2 pts. (Washington, D.C.: Government Printing Office, 1975), p. 788.

Table 4. Associated Press and United Press Expenses, 1889-90, 1896, 1901-2

Expenditure	Western AP, 1889-90		AP, 1896		UP, [1896]		AP, 1901-02	
Telegraph:								
Tolls	$132,543	27.1%	$264,760	20.9%	$400,000	45.1%	$332,679	17.2%
Leased Wires	132,467	27.0	315,159	24.9	175,000	19.7	464,273	24.0
Leased Wire Operations	71,008	14.5	305,380	24.2	–	–	548,017	28.3
	336,018	68.6	885,299	70.0	575,000	64.8	1,344,969	69.5
Outside News Service:	78,674[a]	16.0	23,329[b]	1.8	140,000	15.8	17,120[b]	0.9
General Operations:	75,303	15.4	356,493	28.2	172,000	19.4	572,643	29.6
TOTALS:	$489,995	100.0%	$1,265,121	100.0 %	$887,000	100.0%	$1,934,732	100.0%

a. Includes $45,977 payment to New York Associated Press under contract and a $32,697 payment to Joint Executive Committee.

b. Largely, if not exclusively, the annual expense of the exclusive cartel contract with Reuters News Agency.

SOURCES: Western Associated Press, *Proceedings* (1890), pp. 11-12; Associated Press, *Annual Report* (1896), pp. 8-11, and (1901-2), pp. 6-9; and T[homas] B. Connery, "Great Business Operations—The Collection of News," *Cosmopolitan* 23 (May 1897): 25, 28.

Table 5. Associated Press Expenses and Comparison with Western Union and Gross National Product, 1894-1920

Period[a]	Total AP Expenses	Surplus/ Deficit	AP Expend. (1894 = 100)	WU Expend. (1894 = 100)	GNP (per capita) (1894 = 100)
1894	$1,126,095	$-133,747	100.0	100.0	100.0
1895	1,227,335	- 34,284	109.0	99.9	108.1
1896	1,265,121	- 37,302	112.3	104.4	101.6
1897	1,520,545	+ 85,321	135.0	105.1	109.2
1898	1,889,697	+ 16,028	167.8	109.9	113.5
1899	1,797,517	+138,279	159.6	111.5	125.9
1900[b]	1,395,663	+ 78,917	154.9[e]	114.7	–
1 9 0 0 - 1901[c]	1,440,575	+ 52,326	159.9[c]	121.8	133.0
1901-2	1,934,732	+142,958	171.8	128.3	144.3
1902-3	1,999,441	+133,644	177.6	130.5	147.6
1903-4	2,257,377	- 63,980	200.5	134.0	153.5
1904-5	2,321,577	- 43,279	206.2	137.0	150.8
1905-6	2,253,705	+110,454	200.1	147.9	161.6
1906-7	2,370,914	+114,940	210.5	167.1	181.6
1907[d]	1,378,921	- 94,708	244.9[e]	–	188.6
1908	2,605,657	+ 8,029	231.4	159.5	168.6
1909	2,697,157	- 57,405	239.5	144.7	199.5
1910	2,742,492	- 13,604	243.5	166.3	206.5
1911	2,846,812	- 54,186	252.8	188.5	206.5
1912	2,908,295	+ 49,735	258.3	236.0	223.2
1913	2,883,853	+209,556	256.1	286.7	220.0
1914	3,149,135	- 11,183	279.7	271.9	210.3
1915	3,197,412	- 26,002	283.9	276.3	215.1
1916	3,199,781	+ 41,647	284.1	n.a.	255.7
1917	3,383,960	+ 94,434	300.5		316.2
1918	3,940,766	-152,588	349.9		400.0
1919	4,449,898	+ 2,981	395.2		434.6
1920	5,191,143	+180,947	461.0		464.9

a. Associated Press figures are for calendar years, except between 1900 and 1907, when figures represent July 1 to June 30.

b. Figures are for January 1 to September 30, 1900, a nine-month period.

c. Figures are for October 1, 1900, to June 30, 1901, a nine-month period.

d. Figures are for July 1 to December 31, 1907, a six-month period.

e. Index number is based on an estimated twelve-month period derived from expenses for nine- or six-month periods.

SOURCES: Associated Press, *Annual Report* (1894), pp. 12-17, (1895), pp. 6-9, (1896), pp. 8-11, (1897), pp. 6-9, (1898), pp. 6-9, (1899), pp. 6-9, (1900), pp. 8-11, (1900-01), pp. 6-9, (1901-02), pp. 6-9, (1902-03), pp. 8-11, (1903-04), pp. 8-11, (1904-05), pp. 6-9, (1905-06), pp. 6-9, (1906-07), pp. 6-9, (1907), pp. 6-9, (1908), pp. 12-15, (1909), pp. 10-13, (1910), pp. 10-13, (1911), pp. 6-11, (1912), p. 9, (1913), p. 10, (1914), p. 8, (1915), p. 10, (1916), p. 10, (1917), p. 10, (1918), p. 11, (1919), p. 9, and (1920), p. 9; and U.S. Department of Commerce, Bureau of the Census, *Historical Statistics of the United States, Colonial Times to 1970*, 2 pts. (Washington, D.C.: Government Printing Office, 1975), pp. 224, 787-88.

Table 6. Western Associated Press Officials, 1865-83, 1884-92[a]

I. Directors of WAP

Yrs. as Dir.	Name, Newspaper,[b] Years on Board[c]
23	Walter N. Haldeman, *Louisville Courier-Journal,* 1867-83, 1884-90
22	Richard Smith, *Cincinnati Gazette,* 1867-69, 1870-83, 1884-90
13	D. M. Houser, *St. Louis Globe-Democrat,* 1870-72, 1877-83, 1884-88
12	Joseph Medill, *Chicago Tribune,* 1867-73, 1874-80
11	W. D. Bickham, *Dayton Joural,* 1869-74, 1884-90
8	I. F. Mack, *Sandusky* (Ohio) *Register,* 1875-83
	Joseph G. Siebeneck, Pittsburgh, 1869-70, 1872-74, 1875-77, 1880-83
	H. N. Walker, *Detroit Free Press,* 1867-75
6	Andrew J. Keller, *Memphis Avalanche,* 1874-80
	John Knapp, *St. Louis Republican,* 1867-70, 1874-77
4	W. W. Armstrong, *Cleveland Plain Dealer,* 1867-68, 1877-80
	H. H. Byram, *Pittsburgh Chronicle-Telegraph,* 1886-90
	Michel H. de Young, *San Francisco Chronicle,* 1886-89, 1891-92
	A. W. Fairbanks, *Cleveland Herald,* 1865-67, 1868-70
3	Victor F. Lawson, *Chicago Daily News,* 1889-92
	William Penn Nixon, *Chicago Inter Ocean,* 1880-83
	W. K. Sullivan, *Chicago Journal,* 1886-89
	Horace White, *Chicago Tribune,* 1865-67, 1873-74
2	A. J. Aikens, *Milwaukee Wisconsin,* 1870-72
	A. J. Barr, *Pittsburgh Post,* 1890-92
	Murat Halstead, *Cincinnati Commercial,* 1865-67
	Ira P. Jones, 1880-82
	George Knapp, *St. Louis Republican,* 1865-67
	J. A. Mann, *Kansas City Journal,* 1889-91
	Albert Roberts, *Nashville Republican-Banner,* 1882-83, 1885-86
	Melville E. Stone, *Chicago Daily News,* 1884-86
1	Jacob Barnes, *Detroit Free Press,* 1865-66
	A. H. Belo, *Galveston News,* 1884-85
	Alden J. Blethen, *Minneapolis Tribune,* 1890-91
	C. D. Brigham, *Pittsburgh Commercial,* 1866-67
	William A. Collier, *Memphis Avalanche,* 1891-92
	Frederick Driscoll. *St. Paul Pioneer Press,* 1891-92
	George W. Fishback, 1873-74
	J. W. Foster, *Evansville* (Ind.) *Journal,* 1867-68
	John Frew, *Wheeling* (W.Va.) *Intelligencer,* 1889-90
	W. R. Holloway, *Indianapolis Journal,* 1868-69
	William Hyde, *St. Louis Republican,* 1872-73
	Charles W. Knapp, *St. Louis Republic,* 1891-92
	Samuel E. Morss, *Indianapolis Sentinel,* 1890-91
	Morrison Munford, *Kansas City Times,* 1885-86
	John C. New, *Indianapolis Journal,* 1884-85
	Eugene H. Perdue, *Cleveland Leader,* 1891-92
	D. L. Phillips, 1874-75

II. Executive and Joint Executive Committee Members

Years on Com.		Name, Newspaper, Years WAP Executive Committee
Exec	Joint	
22	9	Richard Smith, *Cincinnati Gazette*, 1867-69, 1870-83, 1884-91
21	9	Walter N. Haldeman, *Louisville Courier-Journal*, 1869-83, 1884-91
12	–	Joseph Medill, *Chicago Tribune*, 1867-73, 1874-80
3	–	William Penn Nixon, *Chicago Inter Ocean*, 1880-83
3	–	W. K. Sullivan, *Chicago Journal*, 1886-89
2	1	Victor F. Lawson, *Chicago Daily News*, 1890-92
2	–	Melville E. Stone, *Chicago Daily News*, 1884-86
2	–	H. N. Walker, *Detroit Free Press*, 1868-70
2	–	Horace White, *Chicago Tribune*, 1866-67, 1873-74
1	–	H. H. Byram, *Pittsburgh Chronicle-Telegraph*, 1889-90
1	–	Murat Halstead, *Cincinnati Commercial*, 1866-67
1	1	Frederick Driscoll, *St. Paul Pioneer Press*, 1891-92
1	1	Charles W. Knapp, *St. Louis Republic*, 1891-92

III. Officers of Western AP[d]

Years as:			Name, Newspaper, Years in WAP Office
Pres.	V-P	Sec.	
–	–	26	H. E. Baker, *Detroit Advertiser & Tribune*, 1865-92
9	–	–	H. N. Walker, *Detroit Free Press*, 1866-75
7	1	–	Murat Halstead, *Cincinnati Commercial*, 1875-82, V-P 1874-75
5	2	–	I. F. Mack, *Sandusky* (Ohio) *Register*, 1886-91, V-P 1884-86
3	–	–	Joseph Medill, *Chicago Tribune*, 1882-83, 1884-86
1	–	–	William Penn Nixon, *Chicago Inter Ocean*, 1891-92
1	–	–	J. D. Osborne, *Louisville Journal*, 1865-66
–	4	–	James Phelan, *Memphis Avalanche*, 1886-90
–	3	–	John Knapp, *St. Louis Republican*, 1867-70
–	3	–	E. B. Martindale, 1877-80
–	2	–	H. W. Farrar, 1875-77
–	2	–	D. M. Houser, *St. Louis Globe-Democrat*, 1870-72
–	2	–	Joseph Pulitzer, *St. Louis Post-Dispatch*, 1880-82
–	1	–	W. W. Armstrong, *Cleveland Plain Dealer*, 1882-83
–	1	–	Samuel E. Morss, *Indianapolis Sentinel*, 1891-92
–	1	–	W. K. Sullivan, *Chicago Journal*, 1890-91

a. The one-year break in these lists of officers is caused by the absence of any record of the Western Associated Press election for the 1883-84 year.

b. Only infrequently did Western AP *Proceedings* give newspaper affiliations along with names. Newspaper names are supplied here wherever they could be ascertained.

c. The Western AP board consisted of five directors from 1865 to 1867 and seven directors from 1867 to 1892.

d. The Western AP president was an ex-officio member of the board but not a director except during the eight years between 1867 and 1875 when, because of a bylaw

APPENDIX

change, the president was also a director. No vice-president was elected in 1872 and 1873.

SOURCES: Western Associated Press, *Proceedings* (1867), pp. 8, 10, (1868), pp. 2-3, (1869), pp. 5, 7, (1870), pp. 5-6, (1871), pp. 4-5, (1872), pp. 5-6, (1873), pp. 3, 6, and handwritten notations in the copy of the *Proceedings* in the William Henry Smith Papers, Indiana Historical Society, Indianapolis, (1875), pp. 4, 6, (1876), pp. 3-4, 32, 35, (1877), pp. 3, 5, (1878), pp. 5, 7, (1879), p. 5, (1880), pp. 5, 7, (1881), pp. 5-6, (1882), pp. 4, 6, (1884), pp. 3, 5, (1885), pp. 4, 6, (1886), pp. 5, 7, (1887), pp. 7, 10, (1888), pp. 5, 8, (1889), pp. 5, 7, (1890), pp. 8-9, (1891), pp. 16, 30, and Western Associated Press letterhead, January 16, 1875, Smith Papers, IHS.

Table 7. Associated Press Officials, 1892-1920

I. Directors of the AP

Yrs. as Dir.	Name, Newspaper, Years on Board[c]
28½	*Victor F. Lawson, *Chicago Daily News*, 1892-1920 (WAP)[b]
26	*Frank B. Noyes, *Washington* (D.C.) *Star*, 1894-1920
24½	Charles W. Knapp, *St. Louis Republic*, 1892-1916 (WAP)
21	*William L. McLean, *Philadelphia Bulletin*, 1899-1920
20½	*Clark Howell, *Atlanta Constitution*, 1899-1900, 1901-20
	Albert J. Barr, *Pittsburgh Post*, 1892-1912 (WAP)
18½	Michel H. de Young, *San Francisco Chronicle*, 1892-1910 (WAP)
17	Thomas G. Rapier, *New Orleans Picayune*, 1895-98, 1900-1914
16	Herman Ridder, *New York Staats-Zeitung*, 1900-1916
15	*Adolph S. Ochs, *New York Times*, 1905-1920
11	Harvey W. Scott, *Portland Oregonian*, 1900-1911
10	*Charles Hopkins Clark, *Hartford Courant*, 1910-20
	*V. S. McClatchy, *Sacramento Bee*, 1910-20
	William R. Nelson, *Kansas City Star*, 1904-14
	*A. C. Weiss, *Duluth* (Minn.) *Herald*, 1910-20
9½	Charles H. Grasty, *Baltimore News*, 1900-1909
9	*W. H. Cowles, *Spokane Spokesman-Review*, 1911-20
8½	George Thompson, *St. Paul Dispatch*, 1900-1908
8	Frederick Driscoll, *St. Paul Pioneer Press*, 1892-1900 (WAP)
	*Charles A. Rook, *Pittsburgh Dispatch*, 1912-20
6	*R. M. Johnston, *Houston Post*, 1914-20
	Stephen O'Meara, *Boston Journal*, 1896-99, 1900-1903
5½	Charles H. Taylor, *Boston Globe*, 1906-12
5	Clayton McMichael, *Philadelphia North American*, 1894-99
	Whitelaw Reid, *New York Tribune*, 1900-1905
	*David E. Town, *Louisville Herald*, 1915-20
4½	Leopold Markbreit, *Cincinnati Volksblatt*, 1896-1900
4	*Elbert H. Baker, *Cleveland Plain Dealer*, 1916-20
	John Norris, *New York World*, 1896-1900
	Eugene H. Perdue, *Cleveland Leader*, 1892-96 (WAP)
	James E. Scripps, *Detroit Tribune & News*, 1892-96
3	Samuel Bowles, *Springfield* (Mass.) *Republican*, 1912-15

Albert P. Langtry, *Springfield* (Mass.) *Republican*, 1903-6

W. Y. Morgan, *Hutchinson* (Kan.) *News*, 1914-17

*John R. Rathom, *Providence Journal*, 1917-20

2¹/₂   S. S. Carvalho, *New York World*, 1894-96

Arthur Jenkins, *Syracuse Herald*, 1898-1900

2   William A. Collier, *Memphis Appeal-Avalanche*, 1892-94 (WAP)

*Frank P. MacLennan, *Topeka State Journal*, 1918-20

Charles P. Taft, *Cincinnati Times-Star*, 1900-1902

Oswald Garrison Villard, *New York Evening Post*, 1916-18

1¹/₂   Washington Hesing, (Chicago) *Illinois Staats-Zeitung*, 1892-94

1   William D. Brickell, *Columbus Dispatch*, 1902-3

E. H. Butler, *Buffalo Evening News*, 1894-95

Don C. Seitz, *New York World*, 1900-1

¹/₂   Edward P. Call, *New York Evening Post*, 1900

Frederick Roy Martin, *Providence Journal*, 1911-12

Edward Rosewater, *Omaha Bee*, 1900

II. Executive Committee Members

Yrs. on Com.	Name, Newspaper, Years on Committee
28¹/₂	Victor F. Lawson, *Chicago Daily News*, 1892-1920 (WAPE)ᶜ
26	Frank B. Noyes, *Washington* (D.C.) *Star*, 1894-1920
24¹/₂	Charles W. Knapp, *St. Louis Republic*, 1892-1916 (WAPE)
15	Adolph S. Ochs, *New York Times*, 1905-20
10	Charles Hopkins Clark, *Hartford Courant*, 1910-20
	William L. McLean, *Philadelphia Bulletin*, 1910-20
8	Frederick Driscoll, *St. Paul Pioneer Press*, 1892-1900 (WAPE)
	Charles A. Rook, *Pittsburgh Dispatch*, 1912-20
6	Charles H. Grasty, *Baltimore News*, 1903-9
4	Whitelaw Reid, *New York Tribune*, 1901-4
3	Charles McMichael, *Philadelphia North American*, 1896-99
2¹/₂	Charles H. Taylor, *Boston Globe*, 1909-12
2	S. S. Carvalho, *New York World*, 1894-96
	Stephen O'Meara, *Boston Journal*, 1901-3
	John R. Rathom, *Providence Journal*, 1918-20
	Oswald Garrison Villard, *New York Evening Post*, 1916-18
1¹/₂	Clark Howell, *Atlanta Constitution*, 1900, 1901-2
1	John Norris, *New York World*, 1899-1900
	Don C. Seitz, *New York World*, 1900-1901
¹/₂	Albert J. Barr, *Pittsburgh Post*, 1900
	Edward P. Call, *New York Evening Post*, 1900
	Frederick Roy Martin, *Providence Journal*, 1911-12

III. Officers of the Associated Press

Pres.	1st V-P	2nd Sec.	Name, Newspaper, Years in Office
20	–	–	Frank B. Noyes, *Washington* (D.C.) *Star*, 1900-1920
6	–	–	Victor F. Lawson, *Chicago Daily News*, 1894-1900[d]
2	–	–	William Penn Nixon, *Chicago Inter Ocean*, 1892-94[d]
$1/2$	–	–	Charles W. Knapp, *St. Louis Republic*, 1900
–	7	–	Horace White, *New York Evening Post*, 1894-99, 1901-3
–	4	–	Charles H. Taylor, *Boston Globe*, 1904-6, 1912-14
–	3	–	Charles Hopkins Clark, *Hartford Courant*, 1906-9
–	2	–	Ralph H. Booth, *Muskegon* (Mich.) *Chronicle*, 1917-19
–	2	–	R. M. Johnston, *Houston Post*, 1910-12
–	2	–	Charles P. Taft, *Cincinnati Times-Star*, 1892-94
–	1	–	Charles H. Grasty, *Baltimore News*, 1914-15
–	1	–	E. B. Haskell, *Boston Herald*, 1903-4
–	1	–	J. C. Hemphill, *Richmond Times-Dispatch*, 1909-10
–	1	–	Clark Howell, *Atlanta Constitution*, 1900-1901
–	1	–	A. N. McKay, *Salt Lake Tribune*, 1919-20
–	1	–	Stephen O'Meara, *Boston Journal*, 1899-1900
–	1	–	Joseph Pulitzer, Jr., *St. Louis Post-Dispatch*, 1916-17
–	$1/2$	–	Samuel Bowles, *Springfield* (Mass.) *Republican*, 1900
–	1	1	Daniel D. Moore, *New Orleans Times-Picayune*, 1914-16
–	$1/2$	1	Harrison Gray Otis, *Los Angeles Times*, 1899-1900
–	–	4	R. N. Rhodes, *Birmingham News*, 1905-9
–	–	2	E. P. Adler, *Davenport* (Iowa) *Times*, 1917-19
–	–	2	Crawford Hill, *Denver Republican*, 1912-14
–	–	2	Frank P. MacLennan, *Topeka State Journal*, 1910-12
–	–	2	William R. Nelson, *Kansas City Star*, 1901-3
–	–	2	Hoke Smith, *Atlanta Journal*, 1896-98
–	–	1	B. H. Anthony, *New Bedford* (Mass.) *Standard*, 1915-16
–	–	1	A. H. Belo, *Galveston News*, 1894-95
–	–	1	H. H. Cabaniss, *Augusta* (Ga.) *Chronicle*, 1904-5
–	–	1	William H. Dow, *Portland* (Maine) *Express & Advertiser*, 1916-17
–	–	1	J. H. Estill, *Savannah* (Ga.) *News*, 1903-4
–	–	1	J. H. Fahey, *Boston Traveler*, 1909-10
–	–	1	John R. McLean, *Cincinnati Enquirer*, 1895-96
–	–	1	Thomas M. Patterson, *Denver Rocky Mountain News*, 1900-1901
–	–	1	Thomas G. Rapier, *New Orleans Picayune*, 1898-99
–	–	1	J. L. Sturtevant, *Wausau* (Wis.) *Record-Herald*, 1919-20

*Continued as a director of AP after 1920.

a. The board consisted of nine directors from 1892 to 1894, eleven directors from 1984 to 1900, and fifteen directors from 1900 to 1937, when the board was expanded to eighteen directors. During the period under study the board had one vacancy during 1903-4 and 1908-9 and two vacancies during 1909-10.

b. "(WAP)" designates directors of the Illinois corporation who had served on the Western Associated Press boards prior to 1892. All seven of the 1891-92 Western AP board members were retained on the first board (1892-93) of the Illinois corporation.

c. "(WAPE)" designates executive committee members of the Illinois corporation who had served on the Western AP executive committee and the joint executive committee prior to 1892.

d. As in the preceding Western AP organization, Nixon was president of the Illinos AP corporation without being a director. Beginning with Lawson's tenure in 1894, the AP president was also a director.

SOURCES: Associated Press, *Annual Report* (1901, Illinois), pp. 288-95, and (1963), pp. 95-103.

NOTES

Preface

1. "Newsbroking" is used in this work to avoid the various implications of current terminology intended to signify Associated Press, United Press International, and their predecessors. The literature offers a variety of terms as labels for the subject of this book, but each term may carry possibly misleading political, economic, or technological connotations. "Press association" either emphasizes AP's cooperative structure or refers to various state or national organizations of publishers. "News-gathering agency" and "news service" also may refer to a variety of journalistic activities well beyond the scope of this study. The same is true of "news agency," which may also have the connotation of governmental news or propaganda activities. When this study began more than two decades ago, "wire service" seemed sufficiently unambiguous and, in light of trade press usage, widely accepted as an appropriate name for the subject of this book. Although the author used "wire service" in previous published work on this subject, growing satellite delivery of the "wires' " news reports begun in the early 1980s may render this term technologically obsolete in the near future. The author does not strive to introduce new or obscure terms to our lexicon, but the failure of available terms to avoid ambiguity leads to the adoption of "newsbroker," "newsbrokerage," and "newsbroking" as precise and unslanted labels for the subject of this book.

2. See the author's doctoral dissertation, completed in 1965 at the University of Illinois-Urbana. It was published as *The American Wire Services: A Study of Their Development as a Social Institution* (New York: Arno, 1979).

3. Victor Rosewater, *History of Cooperative News-Gathering in the United States* (New York: D. Appleton, 1930).

4. Oliver Gramling, *AP: The Story of News* (New York: Farrar & Rinehart, 1940).

5. Joe Alex Morris, *Deadline Every Minute: The Story of the United Press* (Garden City, N.Y.: Doubleday, 1957).

6. Biographical material on Rosewater and his family is from *Dictionary of American Biography*, s.v. "Rosewater, Victor"; "The Rosewaters and the 'Bee' of Omaha," *Review of Reviews* 13 (June 1896): 709–10; and Rosewater Family Papers, American Jewish Archives, Cincinnati, Ohio.

7. Schwarzlose, *American Wire Services*.

8. Walter J. Ong, *Interfaces of the Word: Studies in the Evolution of Consciousness and Culture* (Ithaca, N.Y.: Cornell University Press, 1977), p. 329.

9. Stuart Bruchey, *The Roots of American Economic Growth, 1607–1861: An Essay in Social Causation* (New York: Harper & Row, 1965), pp. 214–15.

Chapter 1

1. The following discussion is based on two studies by Peter R. Knights, *The Press Association War of 1866–1867,* Journalism Monographs, no. 6 (Austin, Texas: Association for Education in Journalism, December 1967), pp. 3–6, and " 'Competition' in the U.S. Daily Newspaper Industry, 1865–68,'' *Journalism Quarterly* 45 (Autumn 1968): 473–80.

2. George B. Prescott, *History, Theory, and Practice of the Electric Telegraph* (Boston: Ticknor & Fields, 1860), p. 385. A year earlier an AP card mentioned the same figure. *New York Times,* August 10, 1859.

3. D. H. Craig to Messrs. F. Hudson and S. H. Gay, Executive Committee, January 1, 1866, Manton Marble Papers, Library of Congress, Washington, D.C. A later Craig estimate of revenue for 1866 appears to exaggerate the payments by the outside press. See Daniel H. Craig, *Answer of Daniel H. Craig. . . to the Interrogatories of the U.S. Senate Committee on Education and Labor at the City of New York, 1883* (New York, 1883), p. 5.

4. Newspaper totals are from U.S. Bureau of the Census reports as published in Alfred McClung Lee's *The Daily Newspaper in America: The Evolution of a Social Instrument* (New York: Macmillan, 1937), p. 718. In listing "the cheap press of New York" City founded between 1833 and 1871, Frederic Hudson names six such foundings between 1851 and 1860 and twelve between 1866 and 1870, but not a single new penny paper starting in the city during the Civil War. *Journalism in the United States from 1690 to 1872* (New York: Harper, 1873), pp. 487–88.

5. Knights, " 'Competition,' " pp. 475–76.

6. Ibid., p. 476.

7. Ibid., p. 475.

8. The following account of the transcontinental telegraph is drawn from Robert Luther Thompson, *Wiring a Continent: The History of the Telegraph Industry in the United States, 1832-1866* (Princeton, N.J.: Princeton University Press, 1947), pp. 348–68, which should be consulted for numerous details omitted here.

9. See ibid. pp. 373–405.

10. Ibid., pp. 377, 379.

11. Among the many sources on the Atlantic cable and the *Great Eastern,* the author found the following most useful in this discussion: Alvin F. Harlow, *Old Wires and New Waves: The History of the Telegraph, Telephone, and Wireless* (New York: D. Appleton-Century, 1936), pp. 287–305; Cyrus W. Field, *Prospects of the Atlantic Telegraph* (New York, 1862); Philip B. McDonald, *A Saga of the Seas: The Story of Cyrus W. Field and the Laying of the First Atlantic Cable* (New York: Wilson-Erickson, 1937), esp. pp. 47–49, 142–43; and James Dugan, *The Great Iron Ship* (New York: Harper, 1953), esp. pp. 1–18, 166–88.

12. For the most detailed account of the abortive 1865 cable-laying expedition, see [Anglo-American Telegraph Company], *The Atlantic Telegraph, Its History from the Commencement of the Undertaking in 1854 to the Sailing of the "Great Eastern" in 1866* (London: Bacon, 1866), pp. 23–66, which relies on the "Diary of Events" by Dr. W. H. Russell that appeared in the *Times of London* on August 19, 1865.

13. Harlow, *Old Wires,* p. 299.

14. George Kennan, *Tent Life in Siberia and Adventures among the Koraks and Other Tribes in Kamtchatka and Northern Asia* (New York: Putnam, 1870), pp. 421–22. A popular account of the Russian-American overland project is Phillip H. Ault, "The (almost) Russian-American Telegraph," *American Heritage* 26 (June 1975): 12–15, 92–98.

15. The following discussion of consolidation relies on Thompson, *Wiring,* pp. 406–26.

16. Reported in ibid., p. 407.

17. The Southwestern and Illinois & Mississippi companies remained independent of the American and Western Union companies in 1865 as the only surviving United States members of the association, the Atlantic & Ohio and the New York, Albany & Buffalo companies having joined Western Union during the Civil War. The Montreal Telegraph Company was the seventh association member.

18. James D. Reid, *The Telegraph in America, Its Founders, Promoters, and Noted Men* (New York: Derby Brothers, 1879), pp. 519–20.

19. American's directors were Samuel F. B. Morse, Amos Kendall, Francis Morris, William M. Swain, John McKesson, Wilson G. Hunt, Hiram O. Aldren, Cambridge Livingston, Caleb A. Burgess, Marshall Lefferts, Cyrus W. Field, and James Gordon Bennett, Jr., with E. S. Sanford as president. Thompson, *Wiring,* p. 414. Swain was publisher of the *Philadelphia Public Ledger,* and Bennett was the heir to the *New York Herald,* an AP partner.

20. Ibid., p. 426, relying on the Western Union annual report for 1877.

21. George P. Sanger, ed., *Public Laws of the United States of America Passed at the First Session of the Thirty-ninth Congress, 1865–1866* (Boston: Little, Brown, 1866), pp. 221–22.

22. William Orton, *A Letter to the Postmaster-General Reviewing the Recommendations of his Annual Report in Favor of a Postal Telegraph* (New York, 1873), pp. 7–8.

23. Harlow, *Old Wires,* p. 339.

24. The literature on both sides of this debate is extensive and largely repetitive, varying only in the degree of vitriol and the substance of current proposals before Congress. The reader may first wish to consult William L. Scott and Milton P. Jarnagin, *A Treatise upon the Law of Telegraphs*...(Boston: Little, Brown, 1868), for a view of existing postwar statutes dealing with telegraphy in the various states, the United States, Canada, and England. Among many titles the author examined on the government ownership issue between the 1860s and the 1880s, the following are recommended.

    Those supporting continuation of private ownership are Western Union Telegraph Company, *The Proposed Union of the Telegraph and Postal Systems* (Cambridge, Mass.: Welch, Bigelow, 1869).; Abram P. Eastlake, "The Great Monopoly," *Lippincott's* 6 (October 1870): 362–71; William Orton, *Government Telegraphs: Argument of William Orton, President of the Western Union Telegraph Company, on the Bill to Establish Postal Telegraph Lines* (New York: Russells' American Steam Printing House, 1870); Western Union Telegraph Company, Committee of the Board of Directors, *Remonstrance of the Western Union Telegraph Company against the Postal Telegraph Bill (Senate Bill, No. 341)* (New York, 1872); David A. Wells, *The Relation of the Government to the Telegraph, or a Review of the Two Propositions Now Pending before Congress for Changing the Telegraphic Service of the Country* (New York, 1873), written at the request of Western Union's William Orton; Orton, *Letter;* E. B. Grant, *Is Governmental Control of the Telegraph Desirable?* (n.p., [1884]); and *Government Telegraph: Some Opinions of the Press in Opposition Thereto* (n.p., [1887]).

    Those favoring some form of government sponsored postal telegraph system are U.S. Congress, House Committee on the Post Office and Post Roads, *Postal Telegraph: Letter from the Postmaster General Transmitting a Report of G. G. Hubbard, Esq., of Boston Relative to the Establishment of a Cheap System of Postal Telegraph,* 40th Cong., 3rd sess., January 11, 1869, Ex. Doc. 35; "The Postal Telegraph and the Newspaper Press," *Printers' Circular* 4 (January 1870): 411-12; Gardiner G. Hubbard, *In the Matter of the Postal Telegraph Bill* (n.p., [1872]); Gardiner G. Hubbard, *The Proposed Changes in the Telegraphic System* (Boston: James R. Osgood, 1873), reprinted from the *North American Review* 117 (July 1873): 80-107; and Charles A. Sumner, *The Postal Telegraph: A Lecture by Charles A. Sumner Delivered at Dashaway Hall, San Francisco, Oct. 12th, 1875* (San Francisco: Bacon, 1879).

25. Western Union, *Proposed Union,* p. 8.

26. Western Associated Press, *Proceedings* (1873), pp. 10-11. (Hereafter cited as WAP, *Proceedings.* Year in parentheses denotes period covered by the contents and not the year of publication.)

27. Harlow, *Old Wires,* p. 332.

28. A measure of the postwar strength of the seven New York AP partners among the city's daily press is the city assessor's report of gross sales for 1869: *Herald,* $801,323; *World,* $689,040; *Tribune,* $514,207; *Times,* $445,211; *News,* $269,000; *Staats-Zeitung,* $217,250; *Sun,* $186,707; *Evening Post,* $100,435; *Journal of Commerce,* $99,500; *Express,* $99,472; *Democrat,* $77,265; *Commercial Advertiser,* $41,050; *New Yorker Journal,* $39,201; *Demokrat,* $26,511; and *Evening Telegram,* $10,108. Hudson, *Journalism,* p. 687. Daily papers in Hudson's list were identified with the help of Augustus Maverick, *Henry J. Raymond and the New York Press for Thirty Years: Progress of American Journalism from 1840 to 1870* (Hartford, Conn.: A. S. Hale, 1870), pp. 330–31.

29. Based on birth dates in the *Dictionary of American Biography,* the ages of AP's New York partners in 1865 were James Gordon Bennett, 70; James Brooks, 55; Horace Greeley, 54; Erastus Brooks, 50; David M. Stone, 48; Henry J. Raymond, 45; Moses S. Beach, 43; William Cowper Prime, 40; Manton Marble, 30. (Charles A. Dana, who would purchase the *Sun* in 1868, was 46 in 1865).

30. Elmer Davis, *History of the New York Times, 1851–1921* (New York: Times, 1921), p. 81. Raymond, who was forty-nine years old when he died, was one of the youngest first-generation AP publishers in New York City and a steady worker in the newsbrokerage's cause. As a congressman, Raymond regularly evaluated and criticized AP's congressional dispatches. Francis Brown, *Raymond of the Times* (New York: Norton, 1951), p. 288. At the time of his death in June 1869, he was engaged on behalf of the New York AP in complex negotiations with the Western AP over sharing cable news costs. WAP, *Proceedings* (1869), p. 11.

31. *Telegrapher* 1 (September 25, 1865): 165.

32. J. H. Wade to Messrs. D. M. Stone and Others, Committee New York Assd. Press, October 9, 1865, Horace Greeley Papers, Library of Congress, Washington, D.C.

33. C[ambridge] Livingston, Secy., to David M. Stone, S. H. Gay & Frederic Hudson, Special Committee of the Associated Press, October 20, 1865, Greeley Papers.

34. "Agreement," December 22, 1865, William Henry Smith Papers, Indiana Historical Society, Indianapolis (hereafter cited as Smith Papers, IHS).

35. Hudson, *Journalism,* pp. 341-42.

36. "A Free Telegraph and a Free Press," *The Spirit of the Times,* August 14, 1869, p. 408.

37. "Is the Press Free?" *The Spirit of the Times,* July 31, 1869, p. 376.

38. "Free Telegraph."

39. "Is the Press Free?"

40. "The Great Monopoly," *The Spirit of the Times,* July 17, 1869, p. 344.

41. Maverick, *Raymond,* p. 327.

42. James G. Bennett to The General News Association of the City of New York & the President and Executive Committee thereof, June 29, 1867, George E. Jones Papers, New York Public Library, New York City.

43. Candace Stone, *Dana and the Sun* (New York: Dodd, Mead, 1938), pp. 125-26; Harry W. Baehr, Jr., *The New York Tribune since the Civil War* (New York: Dodd, Mead, 1936), pp. 73-74; Bingham Duncan, *Whitelaw Reid, Journalist, Politician, Diplomat* (Athens: University of Georgia Press, 1975), pp. 38-39; and Hudson, *Journalism,* pp. 560-61, 682-84.

44. Duncan, *Reid,* p. 52.

45. J. W. Simonton to Whitelaw Reid, January 11, 1870; Reid to Simonton, January 24, 1870; Reid to George H. Stout, January 24, 1870; Reid to Simonton, January 28, 1870, and February 1, 1870; Simonton to Reid, February 2, 1870; Reid to Simonton, February 10, 1870; Simonton to Reid, February 14, 1870; Reid to Stout, February 18, 1870; and Stout to Reid, December 30, 1870, and September 11, 1871, all in Whitelaw Reid Papers, Library of Congress, Washington, D.C.

46. Reid to John Hasson, October 20, 1869, and Reid to George H. Stout, June 12, 1870, Reid Papers.

47. Details of the struggle for control of the *Tribune* after Greeley's death are beyond the scope of this narrative, except for the fact that one of the Colfax backers was Western Union president William Orton, who had been active in Republican politics since 1860, holding appointive offices in both the Lincoln and Johnson administrations. *Dictionary of American Biography,* s.v. "Orton, William." Sources of the account of Dana's involvement in AP affairs and the struggle to control the *Tribune* are Royal Cortissoz, *The Life of Whitelaw Reid,* 2 vols. (New York: Scribners, 1921), 1:147-48, 242-48; Charles J. Rosebault, *When Dana Was the Sun: A Story of Personal Journalism* (New York: Robert M. McBride, 1931), pp. 199-202; Duncan, *Reid,* pp. 38-39, 46-49, 51-52; Harlow, *Old Wires,* p. 337; and *Dictionary of American Biography,* s.v. "Colfax, Schuyler," "Brooks, James," and "Reid, Whitelaw."

48. Cortissoz, *Reid,* 2:87-88, quoting from a Reid letter to John Hay.

49. [New York Associated Press], General News Association of the City of New York, *Rules* (New York: L. H. Bridgham, 1874). The quotations

are from this document, which includes only those rules in force in 1874.

50. "The Business Side of Journalism," *The Nation,* October 20, 1870, p. 255.

51. Rosewater, *News-Gathering,* p. 382; and [NYAP], *Rules,* p. 4.

52. WAP, *Proceedings* (1867), p. 16.

53. Kansas and Missouri Associated Press, *Charter and By-Laws . . . Revised January 31, 1883* (Topeka, Kan.: Commonwealth, 1883), p. 9.

54. Northwestern Associated Press, *Records of Incorporation, By-laws, and Existing Contracts* (Springfield, Ill.: Illinois State Register, 1887), p. 17.

55. S. N. D. North, *History and Present Condition of the Newspaper and Periodical Press of the United States with a Catalogue of the Publications of the Census Year* (Washington, D.C.: Government Printing Office, 1884), p. 107.

56. Ibid. Another way of expressing this is that while 64.2 percent of AP's membership published in the morning field, only 45.1 percent of the nation's dailies published in the morning.

57. Northwestern AP, *Records,* p. 5.

58. Rosewater, *News-Gathering,* p. 199.

59. "Memorandum for Mr. Lawson" by William Henry Smith, October 1890, pp. 11-12, Smith Papers, IHS.

60. Illinois members were the *Alton Democrat* and *Telegraph, Bloomington Pantagraph, Freeport Journal, Galesburg Register, Jacksonville Journal, Peoria Taeglicher Demokrat* and *Transcript, Quincy Herald* and *Whig, Rock Island Argus* and *Union,* and Springfield *Illinois State Journal* and *Illinois State Register.* Iowa members were the *Burlington Gazette* and *Hawkeye, Council Bluffs Nonpareil, Davenport Democrat* and *Gazette, Des Moines State Register* and *Statesman, Dubuque Herald* and *Times, Keokuk Constitution* and *Gate City,* and *Muscatine Courier* and *Journal.* Nebraska members were the *Omaha Herald* and *Republican* and *Nebraska City Press.* Northwestern AP, *Records,* p. 5.

61. Among the twenty-five pre–Civil War papers the median founding date was August 21, 1852. The two Burlington papers were founded in the 1830s; papers in Bloomington, Keokuk, Springfield (Ill.), Quincy and Des Moines were founded in the 1840s. The five post-1860 newspapers were the *Council Bluffs Nonpareil* and *Rock Island Union,* founded in 1862; *Omaha Herald,* founded in 1865; *Jacksonville Journal,* founded in 1866; and the *Galesburg Register,* which converted to daily publication in 1870. Winifred Gregory, ed., *American Newspapers, 1821-1936: A Union List of Files Available in the*

United States and Canada (New York: H. W. Wilson, 1937), pp. 115-41, 167-79, 398-401.

62. Rosewater, *News-Gathering,* p. 132.

63. The other new member, Edward Rosewater's *Omaha Bee,* is discussed below. Northwestern AP, *Records,* pp. 6, 11.

64. Ibid., p. 6.

65. North, *Present Condition,* p. 109.

66. When the Northwestern AP issued stock to member newspapers in 1879, the *Herald* and *Republican* were the only purchasers in Omaha. As of 1887, however, the *Republican* was listed as having withdrawn from membership, and the *Herald* and *Bee* were Omaha's members. Northwestern AP, *Records,* pp. 5-6, 11.

67. Certificate for five shares of American Press Association stock, September 11, 1875, written for Edward Rosewater, Rosewater Family Papers.

68. Northwestern AP, *Records,* p. 17.

69. National Associated Press Company, *The National Associated Press Company (Limited)* (n.p., [1877]), p. 3.

70. Melville E. Stone, *Fifty Years a Journalist* (Garden City, N.Y.: Doubleday, Page, 1921), p. 64.

71. Charles H. Dennis, *Victor Lawson, His Time and His Work* (Chicago: University of Chicago Press, 1935), p. 64.

72. Lawson to John A. Johnson, June 18, 1878, quoted at ibid.

73. W. A. Swanberg, *Pulitzer* (New York: Scribners, 1967), p. 30; and Jim Allee Hart, *A History of the St. Louis Globe-Democrat* (Columbia: University of Missouri Press, 1961), pp. 113-14.

74. Swanberg, *Pulitzer,* p. 44.

75. Hudson, *Journalism,* p. 679.

76. *Dictionary of American Biography,* s.v. "Beach, Moses Sperry."

77. Hudson, *Journalism,* p. 679. See Frank M. O'Brien, *The Story of the Sun, New York, 1833-1928,* 2nd ed. (New York: D. Appleton, 1928), pp. 149-51; and James Harrison Wilson, *The Life of Charles A. Dana* (New York: Harper, 1907), pp. 380-403, for generally approving descriptions of Dana's transformation of the *Sun.*

78. U.S. Congress, Senate Committee on Post-Offices and Post-Roads, *Report to Accompany S. 651,* 43d Cong., 1st sess., 1874, S. Rept. 242, p. 75. Orton testified on January 22, 1874.

79. Craig, *Answer,* pp. 6, 23-24.

80. Western Associated Press, Executive Committee, *Circular. . . : Contract with the New York Associated Press and Western Union Telegraph Company* (Cincinnati, 1867), p. 2.

81. "The General Telegraph Office of the Western Union Company in New-York City," *Telegrapher* 3 (July 15, 1867): 250.

82. The *Graphic* was founded on March 4, 1873. Lee, *Daily Newspaper,* p. 129.

83. New York Daily Graphic, *The Press and the Telegraph: The Ramifications and Oppressions of Two Gigantic Monopolies* (n.p., [1874]), p. 6, a pamphlet reprint of a *Graphic* article appearing on September 15, 1874.

84. Ibid., p. 7.

85. Ibid., pp. 4-7.

86. Emerson David Fite, *Social and Industrial Conditions in the North during the Civil War* (New York: Macmillan, 1910), p. v.

87. *New York Sun,* March 24, 1865, quoted in ibid., pp. 151-52.

88. Joseph Dorfman, *The Economic Mind in American Civilization,* 5 vols. (New York: Viking, 1946–59), 3:34.

89. George Rogers Taylor, *The Transportation Revolution, 1815-1860,* vol. 4 of The Economic History of the United States (New York: Rinehart, 1951), p. 398. Taylor's views are reported more completely in the discussion section of chapter 6 in Volume 1 of this work.

90. [James Parton], "The New York Herald," *North American Review* 102 (April 1866): 378-79. Authorship of this unsigned article was determined from quoted passages from the article attributed to Parton by Frederic Hudson. Hudson, *Journalism,* p. 548.

Chapter 2

1. Walter Lippmann, *Public Opinion* (New York: Macmillan, 1922), p. 339.

2. *Telegrapher* 6 (August 6, 1870): 400. This is the so-called Ring Combination, an international news cartel formed among these three European news agencies, dividing the world into territories, each agency responsible to the other two for gathering news in its own territory but having exclusive rights to distribute the cartel's news within its own territory. North and South America were in Reuters and Havas territory, jointly or independently, the United States belonging to Reuters exclusively. Three AP organizations over the years covered the United States for Reuters and its two European cartel partners and secured the cartel's foreign news report through Reuters—New York Associated Press, 1870-93; Associated Press of Illinois, 1893-1900; and Associated Press of New York, 1900–34. See "News Agencies in Europe," *New York Times,* September 20, 1868; Robert W. Desmond, *The Information Process: World News Reporting to the Twentieth Century* (Iowa City: University of Iowa Press, 1978), pp.

158-68; Graham Storey, *Reuters' Century, 1851-1951* (London: Max Parrish, 1951), pp. 49-53; and Kent Cooper, *Barriers Down: The Story of the News Agency Epoch* (New York: Farrar & Rinehart, 1942), passim.

3. Southern Press Association, *Proceedings. . . 1869* (Macon, Ga.: J. W. Burke, 1869), p. 11; and Wilhelmus Bogart Bryan, *A History of the National Capital from Its Foundation through the Period of the Adoption of the Organic Act* (New York: Macmillan, 1914-16), 2:586. This is the same M. W. Barr who as an AP correspondent was arrested during the Civil War by federal authorities and held for over a year as a Confederate sympathizer before being released to the South. See Volume 1.

4. SPA, *Proceedings,* p. 16.

5. U.S. Congress, House, *To Connect the Telegraph with the Postal Service,* 42nd Cong., 3rd sess., 1872, H. Rept. 6, p. 23.

6. H. H. Fletcher to Victor Rosewater, July 15, 1927, Rosewater Family Papers.

7. Ibid.; Rosewater, *News-Gathering,* p. 136; and *Fourth Estate,* May 21, 1896, p. 1.

8. Matthews et al. v. Associated Press of the State of New York et al., 136 N.Y. (91 Sickels) 333, 336 (1893).

9. *Telegrapher* 1 (October 16, 1865): 175.

10. D. H. Craig to Messrs. F. Hudson and S. H. Gay, Executive Committee, January 1, 1866, Marble Papers. The author thanks Carol Smith of the University of Iowa for copying this document and calling it to his attention.

11. Rosewater, *News-Gathering,* pp. 195, 205.

12. Typescript notes for remarks by Adolph S. Ochs made at a banquet given for Ochs by "his associates in the management of the Associated Press" at the Lotos Club, New York City, October 4, 1921, Adolph S. Ochs Papers, American Jewish Archives, Cincinnati, Ohio.

13. North, *Present Condition,* p. 108, quoting an 1880 address by AP general agent James W. Simonton.

14. Simonton reports in 1880 that the New York AP gathered the system's news in New Jersey, Pennsylvania (outside of Pittsburgh, Erie, and the oil region), Delaware, and Maryland, among other areas. Ibid.

15. WAP, Executive Committee, *Circular,* p. 1; and WAP, *Proceedings* (1875), p. 6.

16. "Memorandum of an agreement between [WAP] and the Press Assn. of Texas. . . ," May 23, 1888, Smith Papers, IHS.

17. J[ames] W. Simonton, *The Associated Press: It Is Not a Monopoly. . .* (New York: John Polhemus, 1879), pp. 7-8, a reprint of Simonton's testimony before the U.S. Senate Railroad Committee, February 17, 1879; *Dictionary of American Biography,* s.v. "Simonton, James

William''; U.S. Congress, Senate Committee on Education and Labor, *Report of the Committee of the Senate upon the Relations between Labor and Capital and Testimony Taken by the Committee*, 5 vols. (4 vols. published), 48th Cong., 2nd sess., 1885, testimony of Henry George, 1:481-83; and John P. Young, *Journalism in California* (San Francisco: Chronicle, 1915), p. 129.

18. North, *Present Condition*, p. 108.

19. *The Journalist*, June 28, 1890, p. 7, reprinting an article from the *San Francisco Chronicle*.

20. Quoted in North, *Present Condition*, p. 108.

21. J. F. B. Livesay, *The Canadian Press, Its Birth and Development* (n.p., [1939]), pp. 2-3; M[ark] E. Nichols, *(CP): The Story of the Canadian Press* (Toronto: Ryerson, 1948), pp. 4-7; Carlton McNaught, *Canada Gets the News* (Toronto: Ryerson, 1940), pp. 51-52; W[ilfred] H. Kesterton, *A History of Journalism in Canada* (Toronto: McClelland & Stewart, 1967), pp. 159-60. The Canadian arrangement, therefore, required the NYAP to sell its news to one telegraph company and obtain its Canadian news from another telegraph company.

22. WAP, *Proceedings* (1867), pp. 11-12.

23. Ibid., p. 6.

24. Smith "Memorandum for Mr. Lawson," October 1890, Smith Papers, IHS.

25. Northwestern AP, *Records*, pp. 5, 8-9. The Northwestern AP originally formed on December 20, 1866, as a movement by which newspapers served by the Illinois and Mississippi Telegraph Company would adhere to the New York AP during the battle between the NYAP and WAP for newsbroking supremacy, described later in this chapter. *New York Times*, December 21, 1866. Within a month WAP's successful assertion of rights to control news distribution in Illinois, Iowa, and Nebraska converted the Northwestern AP into a WAP auxiliary.

26. Northwestern Associated Press, *Seventh Annual Meeting* (n.p., [1873]), pp. 6-7.

27. Kansas and Missouri AP, *Charter*, pp. 2-3; and Kenneth Kitch, "The Associated Press in Kansas: Its Background and Development" (Master's thesis, University of Kansas, 1937), p. 21.

28. Kansas and Missouri AP, *Charter*, pp. 14-15; Kitch, "Associated Press," p. 34; and Trans-Mississippi Associated Press, *Articles of Incorporation, Constitution and Proceedings . . .* (Topeka, Kan.: Peerless, 1886), p. 4.

29. WAP, *Proceedings* (1877), p. 17, and (1879), pp. 17-19.

30. Smith to R. C. Clowry, August 9, 1882, Letterbook 26, William Henry Smith Papers, Ohio HIstorical Society, Columbus, Ohio (hereafter cited as Smith Papers, OHS); and WAP, *Proceedings* (1882), pp. 5-6.

31. The major Smith manuscript collections are located at the Indiana Historical Society, Indianapolis, and at the Ohio Historical Society, Columbus. Twenty-three different Western AP *Proceedings* have been located, covering 1867 to 1891, excluding 1874 and 1883. The author believes that no *Proceedings* were published for 1865 and 1866 and a volume may not have been issued for 1883. Copies of the *Proceedings* were located in the Smith collection in Indianapolis, the Wisconsin State Historical Society, the University of Minnesota Library, the Detroit Public Library, and the Chicago Historical Society. The author thanks Peter R. Knights for providing photocopies of some of the *Proceedings* used in this project.

32. At the request of Western AP members, general agent Smith compiled an account of the "origin and organization" of the newsbrokerage as an appendix to the organization's *Proceedings* for 1876, pp. 25-81. It contains numerous extended quotations from correspondence, minutes, and documents detailing Western AP's beginnings and breach with the New York AP. Relying largely on newspaper files, Knights's *The Press Association War of 1866-1867* adds the perspective of diverse and widespread editorial comment. Rosewater's *News-Gathering*, pp. 113-30, offers a brief sketch of the war.

33. WAP, *Proceedings* (1872), p. 7.

34. *Chicago Tribune*, April 12, 1861.

35. St. Louis *Missouri Republican*, November 18, 1862.

36. Quoted in ibid.

37. WAP, *Proceedings* (1876), p. 28.

38. John Tebbel, *An American Dynasty* (Garden City, N.Y.: Doubleday, 1947), p. 28. Most sources agree that the meeting was held in 1862; see, for example, WAP, *Proceedings* (1872), p. 7. But Smith's history of the Western AP first says 1863 and then corrects it to read 1861. WAP, *Proceedings* (1876), pp. 28, 81.

39. Those attending, according to Smith, were Walter N. Haldeman, *Louisville Courier*; J. D. Osborne, *Louisville Journal*; George Knapp or John Knapp, St. Louis *Missouri Republican*; Joseph Medill, *Chicago Tribune*; H. N. Walker, *Detroit Free Press*; A. W. Fairbanks, *Cleveland Herald*; Edwin Cowles, *Cleveland Leader*; "probably" C. D. Brigham, *Pittsburgh Commercial*; W. D. Bickham, *Dayton Journal*; Richard Smith, *Cincinnati Gazette*; M. D. Potter, *Cincinnati Commercial*; and W. R. Holloway "and other representatives of the Indianapolis papers." WAP, *Proceedings* (1876), p. 28.

40. New York AP's increase was $12,000 per year in the aggregate to papers outside its own members; the telegraph companies' increases totaled "several thousands of dollars" a year. New York Associated Press, *Annual Report of the General Agent* (New York, 186[3]), p. 7.

41. Ibid.

42. "Contracts" and "Remarks by the Committee," a printed document dated Cincinnati, September 17, 1864, and signed by J. D. Osborn[e], Richard Smith, J. Medill, Committee W.A.P., Smith Papers, IHS.

43. Associated Press, *Annual Report* (1896), p. 157.

44. The newspapers represented at this organizational meeting were *Cincinnati Gazette* and *Commercial*, *Louisville Press* and *Journal*, *Nashville Republican-Banner* and *Union*, *St. Louis Democrat* and *Missouri Republican*, *Cleveland Herald* and *Leader*, *Detroit Free Press* and *Advertiser* and *Tribune*, *Chicago Tribune*, *Madison* (Ind.) *Courier*, and *New Albany* (Ind.) *Ledger*. WAP, *Proceedings* (1876), pp. 29-30.

45. WAP, *Proceedings* (1867), p. 13.

46. The first bylaws do not mention an executive committee, but one first appears in 1865. WAP, *Proceedings* (1876), p. 31. The annual report of the board was regularly signed by the executive committee from 1869 onward, and in two instances the board formally transferred its power to the executive committee. WAP, *Proceedings* (1872), p. 6, and (1875), p. 6.

47. WAP, *Proceedings* (1867), pp. 14-16.

48. WAP, *Proceedings* (1888), pp. 13-18.

49. Richard Smith to William Henry Smith, March 2, 1891, Smith Papers, IHS.

50. [Parton], "New York Herald," pp. 378-79.

51. WAP, *Proceedings* (1876), p. 58.

52. "New York Associated Press Agreement with Chicago Papers," a printed document, dated Cleveland, March 25, 1865, Smith Papers, IHS.

53. WAP, *Proceedings* (1876), p. 33.

54. Ibid., p. 34.

55. Ibid., pp. 35-36.

56. Craig, *Answer*, p. 7. Craig, it must be noted, is the only source for this view of the episode.

57. Simonton's background is discussed in chapter 3.

58. "Cards from the Associated Press," *Telegrapher* 3 (December 15, 1866): 87.

59. "D. H. Craig and the Associated Press," *Telegrapher* 3 (November 15, 1866): 59; and *New York Times*, November 7, 1866.

60. "Cards from the Associated Press."

61. *New York Tribune*, November 30, 1866, as quoted in Knights, *War*, p. 20.

62. WAP, *Proceedings* (1876), p. 37. In fact, Craig simply moved from the AP room to another room in the Western Union building. Knights, *War,* p. 25.

63. Knights, *War,* p. 25. The quote is from the *New York World,* December 26, 1866, which credits the *Rochester* (N.Y.) *Union & Advertiser,* December 10, 1866. Later, when Craig's bubble burst, Bradford and Learned resurfaced in the service of the Western AP for a while and then with the New England AP. Hasson, as we shall shortly see, later established the beginnings of a long string of competitors of AP.

64. WAP, *Proceedings* (1876), pp. 35–36. Horace White became the *Tribune's* representative in the Western AP when Joseph Medill stepped down from editorial direction of the paper in April 1865. Continuing to hold an interest in the paper and performing some editorial and advertising duties, Medill remained with the paper and assumed full control of the paper in 1874. Philip Kinsley, *The Chicago Tribune, Its First Hundred Years* (New York: Knopf, 1943; Chicago: Tribune, 1945–46), 3:xi. The often acrimonious relations among the managers and owners of the *Tribune* during this period are detailed by Lloyd Wendt in *Chicago Tribune: The Rise of a Great American Newspaper* (Chicago: Rand McNally, 1979), pp. 205–15.

65. *Cincinnati Commercial,* December 5, 1866, as quoted in Knights, *War,* p. 24.

66. Knights observes that Craig had announced on November 6 that he would begin his new service on November 26. But when White and Halsted appeared in New York City intending to hold their first meeting with the New York AP on the 25th, Craig started his service one day earlier than expected. Knights comments, "It seems plausible that [the Western AP's] hand would have been strengthened by the actual establishment of an opposition press association." Knights, *War,* pp. 21, 25.

67. Ibid., p. 26; and WAP, *Proceedings* (1876), p. 43. The latter source reprints Halstead's report of the negotiations to a special WAP membership meeting. He indicates that New York AP's representatives at the first meeting were Samuel Sinclair, *Tribune* publisher; George Jones, *Times* business manager; William Cowper Prime, *Journal of Commerce* editor and New York AP president; Moses S. Beach, *Sun* manager; and Manton Marble, *World* editor and owner. New Yorkers at the second meeting were the same, except that Marble was absent and Erastus Brooks, *Express* editor, was present.

68. WAP, *Proceedings* (1876), pp. 43–44.

69. Ibid., p. 44.

70. Ibid., p. 46.

71. Ibid., p. 47.

72. *New York Times,* November 23, 1866.

73. WAP, *Proceedings* (1876), p. 41.

74. Knights, *War,* p. 27, relying on the *Washington* (D.C.) *Star,* November 23, 1866, and *Chicago Tribune,* November 29, 1866.

75. WAP, *Proceedings* (1876), p. 41. Knights, studying sixteen "better known dailies," found that an editor below forty-five years of age "was more likely to have been a Craig man" but that editors over that age "in almost all cases supported the NYAP." Knights, *War,* pp. 29-30.

76. Knights in two places refers to a total of thirty-three Western AP members by late 1866. Knights, *War,* pp. 22, 30. Smith's history of the episode lists thirty-two members attending the special Western AP meeting in December 1866, but the author is aware of at least one other member, the *Illinois Staats-Zeitung,* which was not listed by Smith as attending. WAP, *Proceedings* (1876), pp. 55-56.

77. WAP, *Proceedings* (1876), p. 41.

78. Hudson, *Journalism,* p. 675.

79. George T. McJimsey, *Genteel Partisan: Manton Marble, 1834-1917* (Ames: Iowa State University Press, 1971), p. 99.

80. Ibid., p. 100.

81. WAP, *Proceedings* (1876), p. 41, and Knights, *War,* p. 35.

82. Knights, *War,* p. 33, quoting the *New York World,* December 3, 1866.

83. Ibid., p. 34; and McJimsey, *Marble,* pp. 100-101, relying on minutes of an AP meeting, December 4, 1866.

84. Hudson, *Journalism,* p. 675.

85. WAP, *Proceedings* (1876), pp. 50-51.

86. Ibid., pp. 69-71.

87. Ibid., pp. 75-76. For New York's version of this meeting, see "The Press, East and West," *New York Times,* December 19, 1866.

88. Knights, *War,* pp. 38-42.

89. *New York World,* December 11, 1866, as quoted in ibid., p. 43.

90. W. F. G. Shanks, "How We Get Our News," *Harper's Monthly* 34 (March 1867): 515.

91. Knights, *War,* pp. 47-48.

92. Ibid., pp. 50-52. Knights relies here on W. F. G. Shanks's comment two months later that "owing to the inability of the telegraph companies to transmit the two reports in time, a compromise was effected and the breach healed." Shanks, "Our News," p. 515.

93. WAP, *Proceedings* (1876), p. 77. (In text and footnotes here Richard Smith is referred to as "R. Smith" after initial mention to distinguish him from William Henry Smith, who is referred to as "Smith" on subsequent mentions.)

94. *New York Times,* January 11, 1867.

95. WAP, Executive Committee, *Circular,* p. 1.

96. "Within the lines connecting [and] including...Cleveland, Pittsburgh, Wheeling, along the Ohio River to Covington, Louisville, Cairo, up the Mississippi to St. Louis, then including the States of Missouri, Kansas, the city of Omaha in Nebraska, the States of Iowa, Minnesota, Wisconsin, Illinois, Indiana, Michigan, and so along the south shore of Lake Erie to Cleveland..." Ibid., p. 5.

97. Ibid., pp. 4-6.

98. These cities received the more expensive report. Papers in Wheeling; Zanesville; Columbus, Ohio; Dayton; Madison, and New Albany, Indiana; and Sandusky, Ohio, received a 1,500-word report filed at Cleveland and consisting of an abbreviation of the 4,000 words filed daily in the "morning," "noon," and "night" reports. Ibid., p. 7.

99. Ibid.

100. WAP, *Proceedings* (1876), p. 78.

101. Craig, *Answer,* p. 8. A card, dated April 1, 1867, and signed by Simonton, announced the completion of this NYAP–Western Union commercial news venture. *New York Times,* April 2, 1867. See also J. D. Reid, *Telegraph,* pp. 607-15, on the commercial news department and the Gold and Stock Telegraph Company, founded in 1867 and absorbed by Western Union,which combined it with its commercial news department in 1871.

102. William Aplin, "At the Associated Press Office," *Putnam's* 6 (July 1870): 29.

103. See various letters from Craig to Marshall Lefferts, during 1869-1874, Lefferts Family Papers, New York Historical Society, New York City; "Automatic Telegraphy," *Telegrapher* 6 (August 13, 1870): 408; and Harlow, *Old Wires,* pp. 325-26. See also the following article and pamphlets by Daniel H. Craig: "Automatic Telegraphy," *Scientific American* 24 (January 1, 1871): 4; *Craig's Manual of the Telegraph Illustrating the Electro-Mechanical System of the American "Rapid" Telegraph Co. of New York...* (New York: John Polhemus, 1879); *Startling Facts! Practical Machine Telegraphy...* (n.p.,[1888]); and *Machine Telegraphy of To-Day* (n.p., 1888, 1890, 1891).

104. Craig to Smith, April 14, 1894, Smith Papers, IHS.

105. R. G. Dun & Co. Collection, New York City series, vol. 376, p. 590, Baker Library, Harvard University Graduate School of Business Administration, Boston.

106. WAP, Executive Committee, *Circular,* pp. 8-9.

107. WAP, *Proceedings* (1870), p. 19, and (1871), p. 8. "Colonel" Charles A. Boynton was the younger brother of "General" Henry Van Ness Boynton, who was the Washington correspondent for Richard Smith's *Cincinnati Gazette* and its *Commercial Gazette* successor, replacing

Whitelaw Reid in the capital bureau by January 14, 1866, and continuing there until 1896. Charles A. Boynton was AP's Washington bureau chief between 1892 and 1908; his son, Charles H., was also an AP staffer. F[rederick] B. Marbut, *News from the Capital: The Story of Washington Reporting* (Carbondale: Southern Illinois University Press, 1971), pp. 146-47; Muriel Bernitt Drell, ed., "Letters by Richard Smith of the Cincinnati Gazette," *Mississippi Valley Historical Review* 26 (March 1940): 553; and J. W. (Bill) Davis, "Washington AP: World's Greatest and Most Productive News Team," *AP World* 16 (Autumn 1961): 4.

108. WAP, *Proceedings* (1870), p. 19.

109. WAP, *Proceedings* (1867), p. 6.

110. WAP, *Proceedings* (1870), p. 7. Moving WAP headquarters to Chicago reflected changes in both telegraphy and newsbroking. Telegraph first operated in Chicago on January 15, 1848, the first message arriving from the East on April 6. During the next fifteen years numerous independent short- and long-line telegraph companies operated out of Chicago, but most of them were eventually absorbed by Western Union, which established its central division headquarters in the city. In terms of news-gathering, Chicago was becoming the Midwest's New York City. Bessie Louise Pierce, *A History of Chicago* (New York: Knopf, 1937–57), 2:73-74. From WAP's viewpoint, moving the headquarters from Cleveland to Chicago represented a step toward independence from the NYAP. WAP's agent would no longer sit at the edge of NYAP's territory awaiting his daily allotment of news, but would occupy his own throne room, surrounded by his own news system.

111. WAP, *Proceedings* (1869), p. 12. Smith's background is discussed in chapter 3.

112. Ibid., pp. 9-10, 17.

113. Ibid. to WAP, *Proceedings* (1873), passim, and (1875), p. 12.

114. WAP, *Proceedings* (1869), p. 19, and (1875), p. 12.

115. During October 1869 WAP moved 260,716 words of news report (an average of 10,026.5 words per day). In October 1875 the WAP news report totaled 212,209 (an average of 8,161.9 words per day), the reduction credited to transmitting market reports in code. WAP, *Proceedings* (1869), p. 16, and (1875), p. 19.

116. Northwestern AP, *Records,* pp. 19-20.

117. Kansas and Missouri AP, *Charter,* p. 13.

118. Trans-Mississippi AP, *Articles,* p. 21.

119. Aplin reports that the headquarters included two rooms as offices for Simonton and his assistants; a conference room where representa-

tives of the seven New York City partners held monthly meetings; one room for the messengers who delivered the news dispatches to the city's newspapers; a large room where the news was received and duplicated, where the news reports were compiled, and where the various auxiliary agencies exchanged their dispatches; and a manifold room, where the several copies of the dispatches were scribbled longhand by manifold writers. Aplin, "Associated Press Office," p. 24.

120. These papers were the *Herald, Times, Tribune, World, Sun, Journal of Commerce, Express, Evening Post, Commercial Advertiser, Staats Zeitung, Brooklyn Union, Newark Advertiser,* and *Newark Courier.* Ibid., p. 25.

121. Aplin, without naming the inventor, says "Manifolding has been brought to an astonishing degree of perfection by the invention of a gentleman now seventy years old. For a quarter of a century he has supplied the Association with the very peculiar paper required for this service, and that he alone knows how to make it. With his paper thirty copies may be made easily." Ibid.

122. Ibid.

123. Western Union Telegraph Company, *Proposed Union,* p. 53.

124. Maverick, *Raymond,* p. 327.

125. Shanks, "Our News," p. 516.

126. Ibid., pp. 515-16.

127. Harlow, *Old Wires,* pp. 322, 324-25.

128. *Telegrapher* 2 (April 16, 1866): 95.

129. U.S. Congress, Senate Committee on Education and Labor, *Report,* 1:482.

130. Henry George, Jr., *The Life of Henry George* (1900; reprinted, New York: Robert Schalkenbach Foundation, 1960), p. 183.

131. J. D. Reid, *Telegraph,* pp. 615-17. (Reid's comment that Hasson's agency began in 1866 is unsupported by the evidence.)

132. U.S. Congress, Senate Committee on Education and Labor, *Report,* 1:481.

133. The account of George's travels and activities in opposition to the AP is from George, *George,* pp. 180-87.

134. Ibid., p. 207; and Lee, *Daily Newspaper,* p. 212.

135. The officers were president A.L. Train, *New Haven Palladium;* vice-president A. E. Burr, *Hartford Times;* secretary M. E. Osborn, *New Haven Register;* and treasurer John B. Carrington, *New Haven Journal* and *Courier.* "A New Press Association," *Telegrapher* 4 (February 8, 1868): 195, quoting the *New Haven Journal* for January 28, 1868.

136. This American Press Association is not to be confused with a newspaper feature syndicate of the same name founded August 17, 1882,

by Orlando Jay Smith, publisher of the *Chicago Express*. The APA *newsbrokerage* formed in 1870 was reorganized as the National Associated Press Company in the fall of 1876, and is discussed later. The ADA *feature syndicate* was purchased by the Western Newspaper Union in 1917. Frank Luther Mott, *American Journalism: A History, 1690-1960*, 3rd ed. (New York: Macmillan, 1962), p. 777. Feature syndicates, although beyond the scope of this study, parallel newsbrokerages with delivery of news specials, news features, a variety of feature material, and advertising. Some have been run as auxiliaries of newsbrokerages (e.g., AP News Features, United Features, King Features, and Universal Features); some have been separate agencies; and others have been controlled by single, or groups of, newspapers. Ansel Nash Kellogg is considered the originator of the independent feature syndicate, organizing the Kellogg Newspaper Company on August 19, 1865, as a supplier of printed, mat, and plate "insides" for small newspapers. For more on syndicates, see Elmo Scott Watson, *A History of Newspaper Syndicates in the United States, 1865-1935* (Chicago, 1936); "Origin of Auxiliary Printing," pp. 7-20, in A. N. Kellogg Newspaper Company, *Kellogg's Auxiliary Hand-Book* (Chicago: A. N. Kellogg, 1878); and Lee, *Daily Newspaper,* pp. 576-602. For a personalized view of a Hearst company syndicate, King Features, see M[oses] Koenigsberg, *King News: An Autobiography* (Philadelphia: F. A. Stokes, 1941).

137. Simonton to Reid, January 11, 1870, Reid Papers.

138. Reid to Simonton, January 28, 1870, Reid Papers.

139. Simonton to Reid, February 2, 1870, Reid Papers.

140. Stout to Reid, September 11, 1871, and flimsy of telegraphic circular to editors referring to December 1 of either 1870 or 1871, Reid Papers.

141. George, *George,* p. 212.

142. *The Journalist,* September 25, 1886, p. 11.

143. Walter P. Phillips, *The United Press...* (n.p., [1891]), p. 1. Joseph Howard, Jr., as Volume 1 explains, was among those responsible for foisting the "bogus draft proclamation" on New York AP members during the Civil War.

144. Ibid., pp. 1-2.

145. Handwritten copy of agreement between Atlantic and Pacific Telegraph Company and the American Press Association, June 1, 1870, Smith Papers, IHS.

146. The incorporators were Francis Wells, *Philadelphia Evening Bulletin;* G. Wharton Hamersly, *Germantown Chronicle;* Alexander Cummings, *Philadelphia Day;* W. J. Koontz, *Pittsburgh Evening Mail;* R. P. Nevin, *Pittsburgh Evening Leader;* Sidney Dean, *Providence Morning Star;* Robert Johnston, *New York Evening Mail;* Benjamin Wood, *New York News;* Joseph Howard, Jr., *New York Star;* Feodore Mierson, *New Yorker Journal;* Robert C. Dunham, *Boston Times;* Frederich Schwed-

ler, *New York Demokrat;* L. G. Matthews, *Louisville Ledger;* and James H. Lambert, *New York Democrat.* American Press Association, *Charter and By-laws* (Philadelphia: Sherman, 1872), pp. 9-11.

147. W. P. Phillips, *United Press,* p. 1.

148. APA, *Charter,* p. 11; and "The American Press Association, Organized under the Act of Incorporation," *American Newspaper Reporter,* July 3, 1871, p. 649, quoting the *New York News.* McLean had come to the United States during the American Civil War as the Reuters correspondent. When Reuters dismissed him in about 1870 for sensationalizing news, McLean established a transatlantic news service, specializing in sensational news. Storey, *Reuters' Century,* pp. 32, 108.

149. Hudson, *Journalism,* p. 617.

150. Simonton to Reid, February 14, 1870, Reid Papers. Emphasis in original.

151. WAP, *Proceedings* (1870), p. 25. Emphasis in original.

152. Ibid.

153. "The American Press Association" (see n. 148 above).

154. "How the Associated Press Is Beaten," *American Newspaper Reporter,* May 29, 1871, p. 494, quoting the *New York Evening Mail.*

155. James Morgan, *Charles H. Taylor, Builder of the Boston Globe* ([Boston, 1923]), p. 57.

156. An analysis of the fifty-one agenda items discussed at Western AP's annual and board meetings between 1867 and 1875 reveals that one-third (seventeen) of the items involved corporate matters (contracts, finances, and assessments), nine or 17.7 percent involved the size or quality of the news report or the deployment of bureaus and news personnel, and twenty-five, or 49 percent, involved admitting or dropping WAP members. WAP, *Proceedings* (1867-73, 1875), passim.

157. Thomas C. Cochran, *Business in American Life: A History* (New York: McGraw-Hill, 1972), p. 145.

158. [William Henry Smith], *Governmental Regulation of the Press...* (New York: Evening Post, 1884), pp. 10, 15.

159. Simonton, *Associated Press,* p. 17.

160. By 1866 press associations had appeared in only five states—Wisconsin, New York, New Jersey, Maine, and Kansas. In the ten years after 1865, however, thirteen state associations appeared—Illinois, Mississippi, Michigan, Minnesota, Missouri, Kentucky, Massachusetts, Tennessee, Alabama, Arkansas, Nebraska, North Carolina, and South Carolina. Another thirteen new state associations would not appear until twenty-five years had passed. George Spears, "Founding Dates of Press Associations," *The Newspaper: Everything*

You Need to Know to Make It in the Newspaper Business, edited by D. Earl Newsom (Englewood Cliffs, N.J.: Prentice-Hall, 1981), p. 237.

Chapter 3

1. Sketchy and somewhat contradictory biographical material on Simonton appears in the *Dictionary of American Biography;* Maverick, Raymond, pp. 104–7; and the *New York Times,* November 4, 1882. An extensive report of Simonton's 1857 exposé of congressional corruption and subsequent encounter with the House of Representatives is in L[awrence] A. Gobright, *Recollection of Men and Things at Washington during the Third of a Century,* 2nd ed. (Philadelphia: Claxton, Remsen & Haffelfinger, 1869), pp. 402-7.

2. [Benjamin Perley Poore], "Washington News," *Harper's Monthly* 48 (January 1874): 230.

3. Gobright, *Recollection,* p. 405.

4. *One of the Reasons for Telegraphic Reform: Power and Tyranny of the Associated Press: The Character of Its Manager, James W. Simonton* (n.p., 1873), pp. 3-4.

5. Arthur C. Carey surveys the extent of national and international news in the *San Francisco Evening Bulletin, Los Angeles Star,* and *Sacramento Union* in response to the appearance of the pony express and transcontinental telegraph. His emphasis on column inches, however, gives no clue as to the origins of, or possible similarities among, the nonlocal news dispatches in these three papers between 1860 and 1862. Arthur C. Carey, "Effects of the Pony Express and the Transcontinental Telegraph upon Selected California Newspapers," *Journalism Quarterly* 51 (Summer 1974): 320-23.

6. R. G. Dun & Co. Collection, New York City series, vol. 412, p. 175. This entry is dated September 25, 1866.

7. Simonton to Reid, August 5, 1870, Reid Papers.

8. Simonton to Reid, August 8, 1870, Reid Papers.

9. Simonton to Reid, October 14, 1873, Reid Papers.

10. Simonton to Samuel Sinclair, November 10, 1868, Horace Greeley Papers, Library of Congress, Washington, D.C.

11. Biographical material on William Henry Smith is drawn principally from the *Dictionary of American Biography;* Smith to Francis F. Browne, December 28, 1887, Smith Papers, OHS; Edgar Laughlin Gray, "The Career of William Henry Smith, Politician-Journalist" (Ph.D. diss., Ohio State university, 1951); Whitelaw Reid's "Introduction" to Smith's *A Political History of Slavery . . .* (New York: Putnam, 1903); and *New York Tribune,* July 28, 1896.

12. Halstead's *Commercial* and Richard Smith's *Gazette* merged in 1883, two long-standing Republican competitors, feeling pressure from the

Democratic *Cincinnati Enquirer.* Halstead became editor-in-chief of the new *Commercial Gazette,* and Richard Smith was vice-president. (In text and footnotes Richard Smith is referred to as R. Smith after initial mention, to distinguish him from William Henry Smith, who is referred to as Smith in all subsequent mentions.)

13. Reid in W. H. Smith, *Political History,* 1:xiii.

14. Stephenson to Smith, December 20, 24, and 31, 1867, Smith Papers, OHS.

15. Stephenson to Smith, December 20 and 24, 1867, Smith Papers, OHS; Gray, "Smith," p. 56; Lee, *Daily Newspaper,* p. 166; and WAP, *Proceedings* (1871), pp. 3-4.

16. Smith to Reid, November 27, 1868, Reid Papers.

17. Reid to Smith, telegram November 30, 1868, and Reid to Smith, December 1, 1868, Smith Papers, OHS.

18. Smith to Reid, January 26, 1869, Reid Papers; and D. Blakely to R. H. Stephenson and Smith, December 14, 1868, Smith Papers, OHS.

19. Gray, "Smith," p. 56.

20. WAP, *Proceedings* (1869), pp. 7, 14.

21. A report to the stockholders of the National Telegraph Company, but probably intended for wide circulation as a promotional pamphlet, was issued on December 1, 1869. It contained letters from Craig and Hicks supporting the feasibility of an automatic telegraph system developed by George Little. Craig, who had an interest in the Little system, was correctly identified as a former general agent of the NYAP, but Hicks was identified as general agent of the Western AP. The document claims that Hicks was commissioned by a WAP committee to investigate the Little device. See National Telegraph Company, Executive Committee, *Report of the Executive Committee of the National Telegraph Co. to Subscribers of Its Capital Stock, on Little's Automatic System of Fast Telegraphy . . .* (New York: Fisher & Field, 1869).

22. Gray, "Smith," pp. 60-61.

23. R. Smith to Reid, February 5, 1871, Reid Papers.

24. *World Almanac & Book of Facts, 1975* (New York: Newspaper Enterprise Association, 1974), p. 791; and Richard B. Morris, ed., *Encyclopedia of American History,* 2nd ed. (New York: Harper & Row, 1970), p. 250.

25. Wendt, *Tribune,* pp. 233-34.

26. Smith to Reid, October 20, 1871, Reid Papers. Gen. Anson Stager was then general manager of Western Union. (It might be noted that Smith addressed Reid as "My Dear Agate," Reid's Civil War pen name, until the time Reid acquired control of the New York Tribune Company in late 1872, when Smith began addressing him "My dear Whitelaw.")

27. WAP, *Proceedings* (1872), pp. 4, 14-16.

28. R. G. Dun & Co. Collection, New York City series, vol. 412, p. 175.

29. Charles Sanford Diehl, *The Staff Correspondent...* (San Antonio, Texas: Clegg, 1931), p. 159.

30. William Henry Smith, ed., *The St. Clair Papers*, 2 vols. (Cincinnati, Ohio: R. Clarke, 1882).

31. W. H. Smith, *Political History.*

32. Charles Richard Williams, *The Life of Rutherford Birchard Hayes*, 2 vols. (Boston: Houghton Mifflin, 1914). Williams then edited *Diary and Letters of Rutherford Birchard Hayes*, 5 vols. (Columbus: Ohio State Archaeological and Historical Society, 1922-26).

33. "A Familiar Talk about Monarchists and Jacobins," *Ohio Archaeological and Historical Quarterly* 2 (June 1888): 180-205, reprinted in *Ohio Archaeological and Historical Publications* (Columbus, Ohio: Fred J. Heer, 1900); "The Pelham Papers—Loss of Oswego," in vol. 4 of *American Historical Association Papers* (New York: Putnam, 1890), pp. 367-79; "The Press as a News Gatherer," *Century* 42 (August 1891): 524-36; and "The First Fugitive Slave Case of Record in Ohio," in *American Historical Association Annual Report, 1893* (Washington, D.C.: Government Printing Office, 1894), pp. 91-100.

34. As noted in chapter 2, Henry George testified before a Senate committee in 1883 that Simonton had told him in 1869, "I hold this position at a salary of $5,000 a year; I would not work for $5,000 a year; I am simply here to keep yours and any other paper from getting the news." U.S. Congress, Senate Committee on Education and Labor, *Report,* 1:482.

35. Smith to Hayes, October 26, 1871, William Henry Smith Papers, Rutherford B. Hayes Library, Fremont, Ohio (hereafter cited as Smith Papers, Hayes Library).

36. *The Journalist,* July 26, 1884, p. 2.

37. Medill to Smith, March 11, 1870, Smith Papers, OHS.

38. WAP, *Proceedings* (1872), pp. 10, 22.

39. J. D. Reid, *Telegraph,* pp. 568-69.

40. Ibid., pp. 572-73. AP's address thus became 197 Broadway in 1875 and so continued until 1879, when it changed to 195 Broadway (another entrance to the Western Union building). Letterheads on various correspondence from Simonton and *Wilson's Business Directory of New York City* (1874 and after), s.v. "New York Associated Press" and "James W. Simonton" under the heading of "News Agents."

41. Smith to Medill, January 16, 1875, and copy of [Smith] to Murat Halstead, January 30, 1875, Smith Papers, IHS; and Smith to Reid, February 3, 1875, Reid Papers.

42. Smith to Reid, February 11, 1875, enclosing a copy of Medill to Jones, February 9, 1875, Reid Papers.

43. Smith to Reid, February 3, 11, and 26, 1875, the latter enclosing a copy of Stone to Medill, February 15, 1875, Reid Papers.

44. R. Smith to Medill, April 13, 1875, Smith Papers, IHS. Emphasis in original.

45. WAP, *Proceedings* (1975), p. 7.

46. R. Smith told Medill, after visiting New York, "There is a growing feeling against Simonton. The Herald and Tribune are dead against him; the Times half and the World 3/4." R. Smith to Medill, April 13, 1875. Smith Papers, IHS. Meanwhile William Henry Smith was soliciting the support of the *Tribune's* Whitelaw Reid in the quarrel over rooms in the new building and in the possible termination of the 1867 NYAP-WAP contract. Smith to Reid, telegram, February 3, 1875, and letters, February 11 and 26, 1875, Reid Papers.

47. Smith to Reid, October 7 and 20, 1871, Reid Papers.

48. Boynton to Smith, June 23, 1873, Smith Papers, IHS.

49. Simonton to Reid, March 13, 1876, Reid Papers.

50. Simonton to Smith, July 11, 1876, Smith Papers, IHS.

51. WAP, *Proceedings* (1876), p. 21, quoting a Simonton letter to Smith dated July 15, 1876.

52. Ibid., pp. 18-22.

53. Simonton to Smith, July 12, 1876, Smith Papers, IHS.

54. This California episode is necessarily abbreviated here, but it represents a continuing, at times significant, separate vignette in AP history. An excellent summary of California AP history is given in Charles S. Diehl to William Henry Smith, April 22, and June 14, 1893, Smith Papers, IHS.

55. WAP, *Proceedings* (1876), pp. 17-18.

56. Simonton to Smith, June 1, 5, and 6, 1876, Smith Papers, IHS.

57. WAP, *Proceedings* (1876), p. 18.

58. WAP, *Proceedings* (1879), p. 18.

59. Ibid.

60. Smith to Medill, July 15, 1879, Smith Papers, IHS.

61. Erastus Brooks to Medill, July 11 and 25 and August 4, 1879, Smith Papers, IHS.

62. Smith to Medill, July 15, 1879, Smith Papers, IHS.

63. Halstead to Medill, February 1, 1880, Smith Papers, OHS.

64. Jones to Medill, December 30, 1879, Smith Papers, OHS.

65. WAP, *Proceedings* (1879), p. 19.

66. William Henry Smith, "Memorandum for Mr. Lawson," October 1890, pp. 7, 14, Smith Papers, IHS.

67. Major sources relied on for telegraph and telephone developments during this period are Harlow, *Old Wires,* pp. 322-434; John George Glover and William Bouck Cornell, eds., *The Development of American Industries, Their Economic Significance,* 3rd ed. (New York: Prentice-Hall, 1951), pp. 864-95; N. R. Danielian, *A. T. & T.: The Story of Industrial Conquest* (New York: Vanguard, 1939), pp. 3-18; Horace Coon, *American Tel & Tel: The Story of a Great Monopoly* (New York: Longmans, Green, 1939), pp. 31-68; Matthew Josephson, *The Robber Barons: The Great American Capitalists, 1861-1901* (Boston: Harcourt, Brace, 1934), pp. 192-215; Trumbull White, *The Wizard of Wall Street and His Wealth. . .* (Chicago: Mid-continent, 1892); Murat Halstead and J. Frank Beale, Jr., *Life of Jay Gould: How He Made His Millions* (Philadelphia: Edgewood, 1892); Robert Irving Warshow, *Jay Gould: The Story of a Fortune* (New York: Greenberg, 1928); Richard O'Connor, *Gould's Millions* (Garden City, N.Y.: Doubleday, 1962); Edwin P. Hoyt, *The Goulds: A Social History* (New York: Weybright & Talley, 1969); George S. Bryan, *Edison, The Man and His Work* (New York: Knopf, 1926), esp. pp. 61-70; Frank Lewis Dyer and Thomas Commerford Martin, *Edison, His Life and Inventions,* 2 vols. (New York: Harper, 1929), esp. 1:139-69; and George B. Prescott, *Electricity and the Electric Telegraph,* 8th ed., 2 vols. (New York: D. Appleton, 1892).

68. Two such companies included Daniel H. Craig, deposed NYAP general agent, among their guiding spirits—the National Telegraph Company, formed in 1869, and the American Rapid Telegraph Company, formed in 1879. Neither, despite claims of having superior high-speed telegraphic instruments, survived to challenge or be purchased by Western Union. Harlow, *Old Wires,* pp. 323-34, 415-16.

69. W. P. Phillips, *United Press,* p. 2.

70. *New York Tribune,* October 2, 1876.

71. Ibid.

72. NAP, *National Associated Press,* pp. 5-7, 11.

73. W. P. Phillips, *United Press,* p. 2.

74. The 1877-78 NAP board included: president James H. Goodsell, *New York Graphic;* vice-president W. L. Leonard, *Cincinnati Star;* treasurer William Mayer, *New York Allegemeine-Zeitung;* secretary Ralph Bagaley, *Pittsburgh Telegraph;* E. M. Bacon, *Boston Globe;* Sidney Dean, *Providence Press;* George Bartholemew, *New York News;* Melville E. Stone, *Chicago Daily News;* and Edward Rosewater, *Omaha Bee.* Bacon, Bartholemew, and Stone made up the NAP executive committee. NAP, *National Associated Press,* p. 3.

75. Based on raw figures supplied by James D. Reid, the two telegraph companies' portions of the total United States–Canadian telegraph system in 1877 were as follows:

	A&P	W.U.
Offices	4.1%	59.1%
Employees	3.9	59.9
Miles of Poles	7.0	61.1
Miles of Wire	7.8	69.7

    Reid, *Telegraph,* pp. 813-15.

76. WAP, *Proceedings* (1878), p. 20.

77. WAP, *Proceedings* (1879), p. 8.

78. WAP, *Proceedings* (1878), pp. 3-4. Emphasis added.

79. WAP, *Proceedings* (1879), p. 5.

80. Ibid., pp. 9-10.

81. Ibid., p. 14.

82. "Confidential Memorandum," typed and bearing William Henry Smith's handwritten notation "Confidential statement made by Mr. Reid to Mr. Bennett in the winter, and first seen by me June 30, 1891," Smith Papers, OHS.

83. M. E. Stone, *Journalist,* p. 209.

84. E. B. Wight to W. W. Clapp, May 24, 1879, William Warland Clapp Papers, Library of Congress, Washington, D.C.

85. Somerville to Smith, April 6 and July 5, 1876, Smith Papers, IHS.

86. WAP, *Proceedings* (1879), p. 9.

87. Josephson, *Robber Barons,* p. 195.

88. The new NYAP–Western Union contract, signed April 10, 1877, prohibited Western Union from delivering news to NYAP competitors in New York City, a protection which, although written into WAP's 1867 contract with Western Union, the telegraph company now chose to ignore because of the revenue it could realize from the NAP business it inherited in the merger with the Atlantic and Pacific company. By the 1877 NYAP contract Western Union gave up only the NAP business to New York City NAP papers. Western Associated Press, William Henry Smith, *(Confidential)* (Chicago, 1877), which is a copy of the NYAP–Western Union contract printed for the benefit of WAP's board of directors, "obtained after due diligence, and the exaction of a pledge that it would not be permitted to go into hands other than" WAP members. Smith Papers, IHS. A supplemental contract to this agreement, signed on the same day and included in this printed copy, is in the Jones Papers.

89. The French cable, the third to link Europe and the United States, after Field's two cables in 1866, was completed on July 23, 1869.

90. *Correspondence Relating to the Proposed Joint Purse Arrangement between the Direct U.S. Cable Co. and the Anglo-American Telegraph Company* (n.p., [1876]); and [S. F. Van Choate], *Statement of Facts and Argument of the [American Cable] Company before the Committees on Foreign Affairs of the Forty-fifth Congress of the United States* (n.p., 1877).

91. Cyrus W. Field to Henry J. Raymond, two letters on June 26, 1867, Jones Papers. See also [James W. Simonton], *Atlantic Cable Mismanagement: Correspondence between J. W. Simonton and Cyrus W. Field and Others* (New York: Union Printing House, 1871). *New York Tribune* correspondent George W. Smalley, who arrived in London to cover the Austro-Prussian war about the time the cable went into operation, describes some of the arbitrary rules and a cable rate at the start of nearly $500 for a news dispatch of about one hundred words. See Smalley's *Anglo-American Memories*, 2 vols. (London: Duckworth, 1911-12), 1:144-49.

92. Field to Raymond, June 26, 1867, Jones Papers.

93. U.S. Department of Commerce, Bureau of the Census, *Historical Statistics of the United States, Colonial Times to 1970*, 2 pts. (Washington, D.C.: Government Printing Office, 1975), p. 791.

94. James Grant, *The Newspaper Press: Its Origin, Progress, and Present Position*, 3 vols. (London: Tinsley Brothers, 1871–72), 2:341; and Desmond, *Information*, p. 246.

95. L. J. Jennings, "Mr. Raymond and Journalism," *Galaxy* 9 (April 1870): 473.

96. Reid, *Telegraph*, p. 838.

97. Eckert to Reid, July 19, 1880, Reid Papers.

98. Gould's ownership of this NYAP newspaper is discussed later in this chapter.

99. Six years later the Bell company spawned the American Telephone and Telegraph Company, at first a subsidiary of Bell but later assuming the parental role in the Bell system. Since only the Bell company had promised Western Union that it would stay out of telegraphy, AT & T was free to operate in both communication media. In fact, in 1909 Western Union became a subsidiary of AT & T; it was returned to independent status in 1913 only under threat of an antitrust suit from the federal government.

100. The proposed named was undoubtedly intended to suggest to other APs the potentialities of a WAP alliance with the competing newsbrokerage if this proposal were rejected.

101. Those attending the New York meeting were George E. Jones, Erastus Brooks, and James W. Simonton, all of the NYAP; Murat Halstead, Joseph Medill, Richard Smith, and William Henry Smith, of the WAP; Royal M. Pulsifer, George W. Danielson, and a Mr. Waters, of the New

England AP; Carroll E. Smith of the New York State AP; Clayton Mc-Michael and a Mr. McLoughlin of the Philadelphia AP. *New York Tribune,* November 27, 1879.

102. Brooks, Halstead, Pulsifer, William Henry Smith, and McMichael formed the group meeting in Philadelphia. McMichael to Halstead, January 5, 1880, Smith Papers, OHS.

103. "Meeting of Press Organizations," *Printers' Circular* 14 (February 1880): 277.

104. Brooks and Jones to Medill, January 10, 1880, Smith Papers, OHS.

105. WAP, *Proceedings* (1880), p. 9.

106. Ibid.; and WAP, *Proceedings* (1881), passim.

107. Mackay and Bennett, both heavy users of Gould's cable monopoly (Mackay to stay in touch with his wife, who lived in Europe, and expatriate Bennett to stay in touch with his newspaper and to deliver foreign news to the *Herald),* were attracted to a transatlantic project by the profits promised by cable competition. It was the only instance in which Bennett deviated from his rule of having no business interests other than his newspapers. Don C. Seitz, *The James Gordon Bennetts, Father and Son, Proprietors of the New York Herald* (Indianapolis: Bobbs-Merrill, 1928), p. 363; and Richard O'Connor, *The Scandalous Mr. Bennett* (Garden City, N.Y.: Doubleday, 1962), p. 172.

108. George Abel Schreiner, *Cables and Wireless and Their Role in the Foreign Relations of the United States* (Boston: Stratford, 1924), pp. 20, 100.

109. Ibid., pp. 100-101.

110. White, *Wizard,* p. 152.

111. Alvin F. Harlow estimates that during the 1880s and 1890s the ratio was ten articles favoring government ownership to one opposing it. Although the subject had never completely disappeared, Gould's new commanding presence in telegraphy spurred a new flurry of articles and monographs. A representative sampling of this new wave of publications includes Norvin Green, "The Government and the Telegraph," *North American Review* 137 (November 1883): 422-34, reprinted as part of Green's *Statement Submitted to the Senate Committee on Post-Offices and Post-Roads* (n.p., [1884]), pp. 12-20; Gardiner G. Hubbard, "Government Control of the Telegraph," *North American Review* 137 (December 1883): 521-35; D. McG. Means, "Government Telegraphy," *North American Review* 139 (July 1884): 51-66; Cyrus W. Field, "Government Telegraphy," *North American Review* 142 (March 1886): 227-29; William A. Phillips, "Should the Government Own the Telegraph?" *North American Review* 143 (July 1886): 35-41; Shelby M. Cullom, "The Government and the Telegraph," *Forum* 4 (February 1888): 561-72; Richard T. Ely, "The Telegraph Monopoly," *North American Review* 149 (July 1889): 44-53;

Norvin Green, *Postal Telegraphs: Statements. . . to the Committee on Post Offices and Post Roads of the House of Representatives. . .* (n.p., [1890]); Bronson C. Keeler, "Public Control of the Telegraph," *Forum* 9 (June 1890): 450-60; and Frank Parsons, *The Telegraph Monopoly* (Philadelphia: C. F. Taylor, 1899), the definitive statement of the pro-government ownership position, portions of which appeared in *Arena* during 1896 and 1897. A helpful guide to the postal telegraph literature, focusing on the 1900-1914 period, is Katharine B. Judson, comp., *Selected Articles on Government Ownership of Telegraph and Telephone* in the Debaters' Handbook Series (White Plains, N.Y.: H. W. Wilson, 1914).

112. The U.S. Senate Committee on Education and Labor took testimony touching on newsbroking from Henry George on August 22, 1883, and from Daniel H. Craig on October 2, 1883. U.S. Congress, Senate Committee on Education and Labor, *Report,* 1:480–89 and 2:1265–83. Craig's testimony was privately published as *Answer of Daniel H. Craig. . . to the Interrogatories of the U.S. Senate Committee on Education and Labor at the City of New York, 1883* (New York, 1883). The U.S. Senate Committee on Post-Offices and Post-Roads, considering postal telegraph legislation, heard Walter P. Phillips on February 22, 1884, and William Henry Smith on March 7, 1884. U.S. Congress, Senate Committee on Post-Offices and Post-Roads, *Testimony, Statements, etc., Taken. . . in Reference to Postal Telegraph,* 48th Cong., 1st sess., 1884, S. Rept. 577, pt. 2, pp. 165-84, 287-316. Smith's testimony was also privately published as *Governmental Regulation of the Press. . .* (New York: Evening Post, 1884).

113. *New York Tribune,* January 13, 1877.

114. [Benjamin F. Butler], "The Despot of To-day," *Old and New* 11 (January 1875): 15. (The *Old and New* editor identifies the anonymous author of this article as a "careful student," who was requested to prepare this piece for the magazine. Large sections of the article are verbatim or slightly rewritten passages from a report by Congressman Benjamin F. Butler submitted on February 4, 1875, on behalf of the House Judiciary Committee. See *New York Tribune,* February 25, 1875, for coverage of the Butler report.)

115. Ibid., p. 14.

116. This characterization of the *Times* is from Mott, *American Journalism,* p. 429.

117. Swanberg, *Pulitzer,* p. 67.

118. *New York Times,* November 26, 1886.

119. The *Evening Mail,* it will be recalled, had gathered enough American Press Association stock by the fall of 1876 to necessitate dissolving the APA and creating the National Associated Press, whose reports the *Mail* presumably received.

120. Samuel Carter III, *Cyrus Field, Man of Two Worlds* (New York: Putnam, 1968), p. 329.

121. It is uncertain whether Reid bowed to Gould's wishes because of the editor's financial obligation to the financier or because their similar political viewpoints made them natural allies. Harry W. Baehr, Jr., suggests that the Gould burden was lifted from Reid and the paper soon after the editor's marriage to Elizabeth Mills on April 26, 1881, when the bride's father, Darius Ogden Mills, purchased Gould's *Tribune* stock for himself and his daughter. Baehr, *Tribune*, pp. 201, 237; and *Dictionary of American Biography*, s.v. "Reid, Whitelaw."

122. Vernon Parrington, *The Beginnings of Critical Realism in America, 1860-1920*, vol. 3 in Main Currents in American Thought (New York: Harcourt, Brace & World, 1930), pp. 44-46.

123. Josephson, *Robber Barons*, p. 208.

124. Gustavus Myers, *History of the Great American Fortunes* (1909; reprinted in 1 vol., New York: Modern Library, 1936), p. 493.

125. Smith to Victor F. Lawson, January 9, 1891, Letterbook 31, Smith Papers, OHS.

126. James Creelman, "James Gordon Bennett," *Cosmopolitan* 33 (May 1902): 46.

127. E. Davis, *Times*, pp. 99-100.

128. *New York Tribune*, September 17, 1881; diary transcript, September 15, 188[1], Edwin M. Hood Papers, Library of Congress, Washington, D.C.; *New York Times*, November 4, 1882; *Dictionary of American Biography*, s.v. "Simonton, James William"; and R. G. Dun & Co. Collection, New York City series, vol. 412, p. 175.

129. T[homas] B. Connery, "Great Business Operations—The Collection of News," *Cosmopolitan* 23 (May 1897): 27.

130. *New York Times*, October 12, 1893. "Hueston" is the correct spelling of his name, according to his obituary and several references in contemporary letters, despite Oliver Gramling's and Victor Rosewater's use of "Huston." Gramling, *AP*, pp. 89-90, and Rosewater, *News-Gathering*, p. 116.

131. Smith to R. Smith, June 6, 1882, Letterbook 28, Smith Papers, OHS. By "the three fellows who run" the NYAP, Smith probably meant Hueston and the executive committee of Jones and Brooks.

132. WAP, *Proceedings* (1891), p. 28.

133. Smith to Haldeman, June 6, 1882, Letterbook 28, Smith Papers, OHS.

134. Haldeman to Smith, June 8, 1882, Smith Papers, IHS.

135. WAP, *Proceedings* (1891), p. 28.

136. Smith to Haldeman, June 6, 1882, Letterbook 28, Smith Papers, OHS; W. P. Phillips, *United Press*, pp. 2, 4; United Press (1882-97), *The*

United Press (New York: Evening Post, 1884), pp. 3-4; and [W. B. Somerville] to Smith, telegram, July 8, 1882, and John W. Strong to R. C. Clowry, July 27 and 31, 1882, Smith Papers IHS. This United Press, which died in 1897, is not related to the United Press Associations established by E. W. Scripps in 1907.

137. Copy of E. D. Morgan and Jay Gould to David M. Stone, June 2, 1882, and R. Smith to Smith, telegram, May 29, 1882, Smith Papers, IHS.

138. Copy of Smith to Gould, June 10, 1882, Smith Papers, IHS.

139. Smith to R. Smith, June 16, 1882, Smith Papers, IHS.

140. Western Union to Smith, note, June 23, 1882, Eckert to Smith, telegram, June 26, 1882, David M. Stone to William Henry Hurlbert, July 8, 1882, and copy of Erastus Brooks to Norvin Green, July 18, 1882, in Eckert to Smith, July 21, 1882, Smith Papers, IHS; and Smith to Reid, July 6, 1882, Reid Papers; and Letterbook 29, Smith Papers, OHS.

141. Smith to Reid, July 6, 1882, Reid Papers; and Letterbook 29, Smith Papers, OHS.

142. Stone to Hurlbert, July 8, 1882, Smith Papers, IHS.

143. Hurlbert to Stone, July 11, 1882, Smith Papers, IHS.

144. Copy of Stone to Hurlbert, July 13, 1882, sent by Eckert to Smith, Smith Papers, IHS.

145. Eckert to Smith, telegram, July 8, 1882, Smith Papers, IHS.

146. Copy of Brooks to Green, July 17, 1882, copy of Green to Brooks, July 17, 1882, and copy of Brooks to Green, July 18, 1882, all sent by Eckert to Smith, Smith Papers, IHS.

147. Smith, "Memorandum for Mr. Lawson," October 1890, pp. 15-16, Smith Papers, IHS.

148. Eckert to Smith, telegrams, August 12 and 15, 1882, Smith Papers, IHS; and Smith to Murat Halstead, August 28, 1882, Letterbook 26, Smith Papers, OHS.

149. Smith notes for telegram to Eckert, ca. August 15, 1882, Smith Papers, IHS.

150. Smith to Haldeman, August 26, 1882, Letterbook 26, and printed Smith circular to WAP members, August 26, 1882, Smith Papers, OHS.

151. Smith to Haldeman, August 26, 1882, Letterbook 26, Smith Papers, OHS.

152. [New York and Western] Associated Press, *Resolutions Adopted by the Western Associated Press in Convention at Detroit, 1882* (New York: Republic, 1891), pp. 3-4.

153. Ibid., p. 4.

154. *New York Times*, September 23, 1882.

155. Dana to Jones, September 29, 1882, Jones Papers.

156. Smith to Haldeman and Smith to Medill, September 25, 1882, Letterbook 28, Smith to Hurlbert, October 2, 1882, Letterbook 29, and Hurlbert to Smith, telegram, October 6, 1882, Smith Papers, OHS; and Hurlbert to Smith, September 29, 1882, Smith Papers, IHS.

157. Reid to Smith, Hurlbert to Smith, and Eckert to Smith, all telegrams of October 7, 1882, Smith Papers, IHS; and Smith to Hurlbert, October 9, 1882, Letterbook 26, Smith Papers, OHS.

158. Hurlbert to Smith, September 29 and October 10, 1882, Smith Papers, IHS.

159. [NY and W] AP, *Resolutions Adopted*, pp. 1-2; and WAP, *Proceedings* (1882), pp. 3-4.

160. Smith to R. Smith and Smith to Eckert, October 20, 1882, Letterbook 26, Smith Papers, OHS.

161. [NY and W] AP, *Resolutions Adopted*, pp. 4-8.

162. Ibid., pp. 9-10.

163. Ibid., pp. 11-12. The *Herald* and *Times* abstained from voting for joint committee members, and Stone voted for the *Evening Mail and Express* as chairman and for the *Times* and *Herald* as members.

164. Ibid., p. 10.

165. "Confidential Memorandum," typed and bearing William Henry Smith's handwritten notation "Confidential statement made by Mr. Reid to Mr. Bennett in the winter, and first seen by me June 30, 1891," Smith Papers, OHS.

166. Copy of Hurlbert to Smith, June 3, 1891, Smith Papers, IHS; and Letterbook 31, Smith Papers, OHS.

167. Handwritten, unsigned minutes of November 15, 1882, meeting, Smith Papers, IHS.

168. Simonton had died two weeks earlier in Napa, California.

169. Typed, unsigned minutes of November 16, 1882, meeting, Smith Papers, IHS.

170. Smith to D. M. Houser, November 28, 1882, Letterbook 26, Smith Papers, OHS.

171. A memorandum of understanding, signed by Western Union president Norvin Green on November 16, 1882, extended existing rates for AP news reports until February 1, 1883, while a new contract was being written. Smith Papers, IHS.

172. Western Union hastened negotiations to determine "the exact functions of the two associations [and] dispose of the question of the New

York agency," the latter referring to the company's disapproval of Erastus Brooks's desire to stay on as agent. Eckert to Smith, December 6, 1882, Smith Papers, IHS.

173. U.S. Congress, Senate Committee on Post-Offices and Post-Roads, *Testimony, Statements,* pp. 317-20.

174. R. Smith to Medill, January 26, 1883, Smith Papers, IHS.

175. Ibid.

176. Although correspondence early in 1883 referred to the position by the old name of "general agent," Smith and the AP soon after changed the name to "general manager," a title retained by AP up to the 1980s.

177. R. Smith to Smith, December 7 and 9, 1882, Smith Papers, IHS.

178. Hurlbert to Smith, December 6, 1882, Smith Papers, IHS; and Reid to Smith, December 8, 1882, Smith Papers, OHS.

179. *New York Times,* October 12, 1893. After leaving the NYAP Hueston practiced law, serving as counsel for the Baltimore and Ohio Railroad. An "enthusiastic" Democrat, he worked in the South for Grover Cleveland's election in 1884 and 1888. He died October 10, 1893, at the age of fifty-one.

180. Reid to Smith, January 10, 1883, Smith Papers, OHS.

181. Smith to Mrs. William Henry Smith, May 5, 1883, Smith Papers, IHS.

182. Copy of Smith to Rutherford B. Hayes, March 1, 1886, Smith Papers, OHS.

183. *Lakeside Directory of the City of Chicago* (1876-77 to 1883), s.v. "Associated Press" and "Neef, Walter W."; and Associated Press, *Service Bulletin,* June 1, 1905, pp. 2-3.

184. [New York and Western] Associated Press, *(Private Circular), The Associated Press* (n.p., [1883]), p. where all of Smith's major lieutenants beginning in 1882 are listed. The reader will get an intimate look at the operations of the WAP and the relationship between Smith and his secretary by perusing Smith's letterbooks during 1882-83. See especially July 3 to November 29, 1882, in Letterbook 26 and from January 1883, onward in Letterbook 27, Smith Papers, OHS.

185. Diehl, *Correspondent,* p. 159.

186. McKee became Washington bureau chief on May 12, 1882, during the Hueston-Brooks regime. Diary transcript, May 26, 188[2], Hood Papers. McKee was AP's third Washington chief. Chapter 4 discusses the succession in that post as a factor in Walter P. Phillips's career.

187. Boynton left New York for Washington on February 1, 1883. Boynton to Smith, June 11, 1894, Smith Papers, IHS.

188. J. W. Davis, "Washington AP," p. 4.

189. Reid to Smith, January 10, 1883, Smith Papers, OHS; and copy of Smith to C. E. Dekker, February 9, 1883, Smith Papers, IHS.

190. Reid to Smith, January 10, 1883, Smith Papers, OHS.

191. R. Smith to Medill, January 26, 1883, Smith Papers, IHS.

192. WAP, *Proceedings* (1886), p. 6.

193. Ibid., pp. 3, 5-6.

194. WAP, *Proceedings* (1884), p. 4, and (1885), p. 5.

195. Thomas C. Cochran and William Miller, *The Age of Enterprise: A Social History of Industrial America* (New York: Macmillan, 1942), p. 151.

196. Henry Watterson, *The Compromises of Life and Other Lectures and Addresses* (New York: Fox, Duffield, 1903), pp. 225-26.

Chapter 4

1. "The Mystery of the Associated Press," *Printers' Circular* 4 (April 1869): 49-51.

2. "Journalism as a Career," April 4, 1872, at the University of the City of New York; "The Practical Issues in a Newspaper Office," June 17, 1879, to the Editorial Association of New York at Rochester; and "Recent Changes in the Press," February 25, 1901, and "Journalistic Duties and Opportunities," February 28, 1901, the first and second Bromley Lectures, Yale University. All are reprinted in Whitelaw Reid, *American and English Studies,* 2 vols. (1913; reprint ed., Freeport, N.Y.: Books for Libraries Press, 1968), 2:193-344. The 1879 address, also delivered to the Ohio Editorial Association, is reprinted as Reid, *Some Newspaper Tendencies* (New York: Henry Holt, 1879).

3. W. Reid, *Studies,* 2:233, 254.

4. Ibid., 2:254-55.

5. Ibid., 2:288-89.

6. U.S. Department of Commerce, Bureau of the Census, *Historical Statistics,* p. 788.

7. Western Union's traffic growth rate slightly exceeded the physical growth of its system. Based on 1867 operations, the company's message traffic had grown tenfold by 1890–91 and its miles of wire had grown tenfold by 1897–98, the lag in mileage due to duplex and quadruplex transmission and to heavy loads on some well established routes. Ibid., pp. 787-88.

8. Magnetic Telegraph Company, *Articles of Association and Charter from the State of Maryland of the Magnetic Telegraph Company Together with the Office Regulations and the Minutes of the Meetings of Stockholders and Board of Directors* (New York: Chatterton & Christ, [1852]), pp. 236-37.

9. John Van Horne to Whitelaw Reid, December 17, 1876, Reid Papers.

10. Don McNicol, "Phillips Code, Telegraphers' 'Short-Hand,' " *Dots and Dashes* 6 (September-October 1969): 3. The author wishes to thank Joseph B. Milgram for calling this article to his attention. Victor Rosewater in 1930 suggests that AP's first leased wire opened in 1879, but by 1934, in a biographical sketch of Walter P. Phillips, he was dating the first leased wire in 1875. Cf. Rosewater's *News-Gathering,* p. 175; and *Dictionary of American Biography,* s.v. "Phillips, Walter Polk." See also "SDX Historic Site Ceremonies Hail AP First Leased Wire," *The Quill* 56 (January 1968): 23.

11. J. W. Simonton to D. M. Stone, January 29, 1876, Marble Papers.

12. Walter P. Phillips, *The Phillips Telegraphic Code for the Rapid Transmission by Telegraph of Press Reports, Commercial and Private Telegrams and All Other Matter Sent by Wire or Cable* (Washington, D.C.: Gibson Brothers, 1879).

13. Quoted in McNicols, "Phillips Code."

14. Diary transcript, Hood Papers.

15. M. E. Stone, *Journalist,* p. 212. An example of Stone's view is AP's Phillips, who in 1876 had enough telegraphic experience to publish a widely acclaimed collection of short sketches about and for telegraphers using the pseudonym John Oakum. See *Oakum Pickings: A Collection of Sketches and Paragraphs Contributed from Time to Time to the Telegraphic and General Press* (New York: W. J. Johnston, 1876). A *Cincinnati Enquirer* article on December 26, 1886, lists as former telegraphers "who have stepped up and out of the ranks" in Washington four UP staffers—P. V. DeGraw, Walter P. Phillips, W. W. Burhams, and James Thurston—and one AP staffer, F. T. Bickford. Reprinted in *The Journalist,* January 8, 1887, p. 12-13.

16. WAP, *Proceedings* (1887), p. 9.

17. Ibid., p. 4.

18. U.S. Congress, Senate Committee on Post-Offices and Post-Roads, *Testimony of Walter P. Phillips...on Postal Telegraph before the Committee on Post-Offices and Post-Roads of the United States Senate, February 22, 1884,* printed for the use of the committee (Washington, D.C.: Government Printing Office, 1884), pp. 3, 5 and 8. Phillips's testimony is also available in U.S. Congress, Senate Committee on Post-Offices and Post-Roads, *Testimony, Statements,* pp. 165-84.

19. *The Journalist,* May 22, 1886, pp. 10-11.

20. George Grantham Bain, "The Telegraphic Service of News," *Newspaperdom,* April 23, 1896, p. 1.

21. WAP, *Proceedings* (1871), pp. 29, 31. One source estimated that before the automatic repeater was introduced, a message from Boston to

San Francisco had to be retransmitted by operators at eight or ten way-offices. [Butler], "Despot," p. 9.

22. [Butler], "Despot," p. 8. WAP's William Henry Smith first took public notice of the press possibilities of duplex in his annual report of mid-1872, observing that duplex "cannot but prove interesting to the members of the Press, now more than ever dependent on the telegraph for the successful prosecution of the business of journalism." WAP, *Proceedings* (1872), p. 28.

23. The value of quadruplex to telegraphic traffic may be grasped from the following 1875 description: "[W]hile messages are being exchanged between Boston and New York, two more can be sent on the same wire between Boston and Worcester, two between Worcester and Springfield, and two between Springfield and New Haven, or New York—eight messages, in all, passing over the same wire at the same time." [Butler], "Despot," p. 8.

24. *The Journalist,* October 23, 1886, pp. 12-13, reprinting an undated article from the *New York Times.*

25. McNicol, "Phillips Code"; W. F. Carter, "AP Seems To Be Going 'Electronic' in a Big Way; Blant Kimbell Heads New Technical Triumvirate," *AP World* 16 (Winter 1961-62): 17; Diehl, *Correspondent,* pp. 164-65; and John L. Given, *Making a Newspaper* (New York: Henry Holt, 1907), pp. 226-27.

26. L. E. Beard to W. W. Clapp, January 25, 1887, William W. Clapp Collection, New England Associated Press Papers, Baker Library, Harvard University, Graduate School of Business Administration, Boston (hereafter cited as NEAP Papers).

27. WAP, *Proceedings* (1891), p. 20.

28. Cf. descriptions of AP operations in [William H. Rideing], "The Metropolitan Newspaper," *Harper's Monthly* 56 (December 1877): esp. 55-58; and William Henry Smith, "The Press as a News Gatherer," *Century* 42 (August 1891): esp 531-32; or Charles R. Williams, *The Associated Press* (n.p., 1890), a reprint of an address at Princeton College, May 7, 1890.

29. William Henry Smith to Delavan Smith, December 17, 1890, Smith Papers, OHS.

30. The rate for ten words or less transmitted between New York City and Chicago was in 1866, $1.85; 1869, $2.05; 1870, $1; 1873, $1; 1875, 25 cents; 1876, 50 cents; 1877, 60 cents; 1883, 50 cents; 1888, 50 cents; 1890, 40 cents; and 1908, 50 cents. U. S. Department of Commerce, Bureau of the Census, *Historical Statistics,* p. 790.

31. The contracted service was for a six-day week. These per-word rates are based on a 313-day year.

32. WAP, Executive Committee, *Circular,* p. 4; and WAP, *Proceedings* (1869), pp. 17, 19, (1872), p. 9, (1879), p. 22, and (1881), p. 8.

33. "Contract between the Western Union Telegraph Company and the Associated Press," in U.S. Congress, Senate Committee on Post-Offices and Post-Roads, *Testimony, Statements,* pp. 317-18.

34. Smith to Clapp, September 24, 1890, NEAP Papers.

35. WAP, *Proceedings* (1891), p. 26.

36. WAP, *Proceedings* (1881), p. 18.

37. [New York] Associated Press. *Annual Report of the General Manager for the Year 1891 . . .* (Chicago: J. M. W. Jones, 1893), p. 12.

38. Ibid., pp. 5-6.

39. Ibid., p. 5.

40. Ibid., p. 20.

41. Marbut, *News,* p. 135.

42. For a brief discussion of the trends in Washington reporting between 1866 and 1900, see ibid., pp. 133-37.

43. [NY]AP, *Annual Report,* p. 20.

44. Hood lists the AP Capitol Hill reporters as himself, F. T. Bickford, Henry G. Hayes, Charles J. Hayes, Charles M. Merillat, and John Gross. Those in the "Downtown" offices and departments were McKee, Charles A. Boynton, A. J. Clarke, J. J. Wilber, William Dwyer, and reporters named Holton, Mudd, and George Kennan. Diary transcript, May 8, 1888, Hood Papers, and other sources available to the author.

45. WAP, *Proceedings* (1876), p. 10.

46. W. H. Smith, "News Gatherer," p. 532.

47. WAP, *Proceedings* (1876), p. 10.

48. Smith to Clapp, June 11, 1888, NEAP Papers.

49. Although his breakdown does not equal his total, Smith's figures are illuminating: Republican convention in Minneapolis, $2,082.65; Democratic convention in Chicago, $1,205.17; People's Party convention in Omaha, $134.56; Prohibition convention in Cincinnati, $38.25; and overtime for telegraph operators at various points, $256.88. "Costs of National Conventions," [1892], Smith Papers, IHS.

50. Susan R. Brooker-Gross, "Timeliness: Interpretations from a Sample of 19th Century Newspapers," *Journalism Quarterly* 58 (Winter 1981): 594-98.

51. See telegrams between H. H. Fletcher and O'Rielly, April 1, 7, 9, 12, 14, and 18, 1890, NEAP Papers.

52. WAP, *Proceedings* (1891), p. 66.

53. Ibid., p. 26.

54. Printed circular by E. L. Beard, "To the Agents of the Associated Press," October 1, 1883, NEAP Papers.

55. "Instructions of the Associated Press to its Correspondents," quoted in John Palmer Gavit, *The Reporter's Manual: A Handbook for Newspaper Men* (n.p., 1903), p. 77.

56. Oliver Knight records very little direct AP or UP activity in the coverage of the Indian Wars, in comparison with newspaper specials. See Oliver Knight, *Following the Indian Wars: The Story of the Newspaper Correspondents among the Indian Campaigners* (Norman: University of Oklahoma Press, 1960).

57. M. E. Stone, *Journalist,* pp. 211-12. See also Gramling, *AP,* pp. 102-4.

58. Gramling, *AP,* pp. 96-97.

59. Henry Watterson, *"Marse Henry": An Autobiography,* 2 vols. (New York: George H. Doran, 1919), 1:252.

60. All three comments appear in the *New York Times,* July 26, 1872.

61. With the exception of the 1840 and 1844 elections, in which nearly 80 percent of the voters cast ballots, the period of 1856 to 1900 saw voter participation running higher than in any other time, with turnouts regularly above 70 percent. From 1912 to 1970, voter turnout slumped to between 48 and 65 percent. U. S. Department of Commerce, Bureau of the Census, *Historical Statistics,* pp. 1071-72.

62. Harry Barnard, *Rutherford B. Hayes and His America* (Indianapolis: Bobbs-Merrill, 1954), p. 278.

63. Malcolm Moos, *The Republicans: A History of Their Party* (New York: Random House, 1956), p. 151.

64. James E. Pollard, *The Presidents and the Press* (New York: Macmillan, 1947), p. 456.

65. F[rancis] C[olburn] Adams, *President Hayes' Professional Reformers: The Two Smiths, Tommie and William Henry, Men after Hayes' Own Heart, How He Rewarded Them* (Washington, D.C.: Judd & Detweiler, 1880), p. 20.

66. The evidence of Smith's involvement in Hayes's campaign strategy and selection of a cabinet is clear from Smith's correspondence. See letters during 1876 and 1877 by Smith in Letterbook 22, Smith Papers, OHS.

67. Smith to Hayes, May 18, 1877, Smith Papers, Hayes Library.

68. Barnard, *Hayes,* pp. 486-87.

69. Tenures of WAP officers indicated here are for the duration of the agency, not just up to the 1876 campaign. See table 6 in the Appendix for a complete list of WAP officers.

70. Barnard's biography of Hayes gives the most detailed account of WAP editors' involvement, based on extensive research. See Barnard,

Hayes, esp. pp. 284-86 and 359-62. For general treatments of this election, see Moos, *Republicans,* pp. 145-52. A sense of Smith's intimate relationship with Hayes may be gained from *Hayes: The Diary of a President, 1875-1881,* edited by T. Harry Williams (New York: McKay, 1964), pp. 34-35, 39-40, 79, 133, and 295; and *Diary and Letters of Rutherford Birchard Hayes,* edited by Charles Richard Williams, 5 vols. (Columbus: Ohio State Archaeological and Historical Society, 1922–26), esp. 4:111-12.

71. This relationship may, of course, be reversed. The Western AP may also be described as the creation of a group of Midwestern publishers with similar Republican views and with the nucleus of a Cincinnati faction that rallied around the Liberal Republican standard in 1872 and Hayes in 1876. Properly, however, it may be supposed that the WAP grew out of both journalism and regional Republicanism.

72. Hayes to Smith, November 13, 1876, Smith Papers, OHS.

73. Hayes, *Diary and Letters,* 4:358.

74. Medill to Smith, August 4, 1877, Smith Papers, OHS.

75. Smith to Hayes, May 9 and 18, 1877, and Hayes to Smith, May 13, June 24, and September 4, 1877, Smith Papers, Hayes Library.

76. Clippings enclosed in Smith to Hayes, September 12, 1877, Smith Papers, Hayes Library.

77. Smith to "The Business Men of Chicago," December 12, 1881, Letterbook 25, Smith Papers, OHS.

78. O'Connor, *Gould's Millions,* pp. 238-39, which is the source of the *New York World* quote.

79. Smith to Pulitzer, July 16, 1884, Joseph Pulitzer Papers, Columbia University Library, New York City (hereafter cited as Pulitzer Papers, CU).

80. Smith to Pulitzer, October 8, 1884, Pulitzer Papers, CU.

81. Smith to Pulitzer and W. H. French to Pulitzer, November 28, 1884, Pulitzer Papers, CU.

82. Smith to Clapp, November 29, 1884, NEAP Papers. The Dana-Haldeman report is reprinted in its entirety in *The Journalist,* November 29, 1884, p. 4.

83. *The Journalist,* August 16, 1884, p. 6; November 8, 1884, p. 5; and November 29, 1884, p. 4.

84. *Dictionary of American Biography,* s.v. "Phillips, Walter Polk."

85. Phillips to Reid, March 18, 1878, Reid Papers.

86. WAP, *Proceedings* (1878), pp. 23-24.

87. Diary transcript, July 8, 1878, Hood Papers.

88. *Printers' Circular* 14 (August 1879): 137.

89. *New York Times,* May 15, 1881, and diary transcript, May 17, 1881, Hood Papers.

90. Phillips to Reid, May 25, 1882 (enclosing copies of Phillips to Hueston, April 30, 1882, Hueston to Phillips, May 8, 1882, Phillips to Hurlbert, May 19, 1882, and Hurlbert to Phillips, May 22, 1882), and Phillips to Reid, two letters on May 31, 1882, Reid Papers; and diary transcript, May 26, 188[2], Hood Papers.

91. Diary transcript, January 7, 1883, Hood Papers.

92. Phillips to Smith, September 27, 1882, Smith Papers, IHS; and Smith to Phillips, November 21, 1882, Letterbook 26, Smith Papers, OHS.

93. UP, *United Press,* pp. 3-4.

94. *The Journalist,* April 12, 1884, p. 9.

95. U.S. Congress, Senate Committee on Post-Offices and Post-Roads, *Testimony of . . . Phillips,* pp. 3-4, 9.

96. Phillips to O'Meara, March 31, 1890, NEAP Papers.

97. H. H. Fletcher to Victor Rosewater, July 15, 1927, Rosewater Family Papers.

98. Morgan, *Taylor,* p. 91. Morgan joined UP as a telegrapher in 1882; he was assigned to UP's bureau in the *Globe* office, taking the UP report for the *Globe* and filing New England news to UP in New York City; but he soon joined the *Globe's* staff, commencing a sixty-year career as a political journalist. Louis M. Lyons, *Newspaper Story: One Hundred Years of the Boston Globe* (Cambridge, Mass.: Belknap Press of Harvard University, 1971), p. 46.

99. Oswald Garrison Villard, *Some Newspapers and Newspaper-Men,* 2nd ed. (New York: Knopf, 1926), p. 98.

100. Mott, *American Journalism,* p. 467.

101. UP's directors in 1884 consisted of young or maverick newspaper editors, principally from the East: Charles H. Taylor, *Boston Globe;* William L. Brown, *New York News;* Robert S. Davis, *Philadelphia Call;* James W. Scott, *Chicago Herald;* Isaac Dinkelspiel, *Louisville Commercial;* Arthur Jenkins, *Syracuse Herald;* James E. Scripps, *Detroit Evening News;* John H. Farrell, *Albany Press and Knickerbocker;* George H. Sandison, *New York Star;* E. H. Butler, *Buffalo Evening News;* C. R. Baldwin, *Waterbury* (Conn.) *American;* Max Marckhoff, *New York Volks Zeitung;* and William J. Kline, *Amsterdam Democrat* (New York City). Taylor was president, Butler was vice-president, and Baldwin was treasurer. On the 1886 board William C. Bryant, of the *Brooklyn Times;* Samuel D. Lee, *Rochester Herald;* Samuel S. Blood, no affiliation listed; and Walter P. Phillips had replaced Dinkelspiel, Sandison, Marckhoff, and Kline. The entire board was reelected in 1887, and William M. Laffin, *New York Evening Sun,* replaced Blood

in 1888. The 1888 board was still intact in 1890. UP, *United Press,* p. 1; and *The Journalist,* January 15, 1887, p. 6; June 30, 1888, p. 16; March 23, 1889, p. 16 and January 11, 1890, p. 9.

102. In 1884, UP's headquarters were at 187 Broadway; AP's were at 195 Broadway. *Wilson's Business Directory of New York City* (1884).

103. Smith to Medill, January 24, 1883, Smith Papers, IHS.

104. Reid to Smith, August 25, 1883, Smith Papers, OHS, and W. H. French to Smith, August 25, 1883, Smith Papers, IHS.

105. [NY]AP, *Annual Report,* p. 13.

106. Smith to Reid, March 14, 1893, Smith Papers, IHS.

107. Watterson, *"Marse Henry,"* 2:104.

108. Joseph Frazier Wall, *Henry Watterson, Reconstructed Rebel* (New York: Oxford University Press, 1956), p. 181.

109. Watterson, *"Marse Henry,"* 2:104-5. The 1918 ruling, International News Service v. Associated Press, 248 U.S. 215, is discussed in chapter 7.

110. WAP board approval came on February 28, 1883, well after the joint executive committee began its work. And even later did the WAP membership approve the actions of its board, although back in the fall of 1882 WAP had granted the board broad powers to act. WAP, *Proceedings* (1882), pp. 3-4, and (1890), p. 17.

111. [NY and W] AP, *Resolutions Adopted,* pp. 12-15; and WAP, *Proceedings* (1887), p. 5.

112. "Extracts from minutes of Joint Executive Committee, November 2, 1887," Smith Papers, IHS.

113. Dana to Smith, January 28, 1888, Reid Papers.

114. "The Boston Herald," *Bay State Monthly, New England Magazine* 2 (October 1884): 29; and Mott, *American Journalism,* pp. 452-53.

115. Smith to Walter Allen, January 17, 1885, Reid Papers.

116. North, *Present Condition,* p. 106.

117. Pulsifer to W. W. Clapp, November 17, 1884, and Phillips to Clapp, December 17, 1884, NEAP Papers.

118. Henry W. Farnam to Pulsifer, March 25, April 4, April 19, April 25, April 26, and June 7, 1884, and telegram April 24, 1884, NEAP Papers.

119. N. G. Osborn to S. A. Hubbard, April 9, 1884, NEAP Papers.

120. Hubbard to Pulsifer, April 6, 1884, NEAP Papers. Emphasis in original.

121. L. L. Morgan to E. L. Beard, September 23, 1884, NEAP Papers.

122. Alex Troup to S. A. Hubbard, July 2, 1884, NEAP Papers.

123. Samuel Bowles to Clapp, March 3, 1887, NEAP Papers.

124. Smith to Walter Allen, January 17, 1885, Reid Papers.

125. Reid to Clapp, March 16, 1885, William Warland Clapp Papers, Houghton Library, Harvard University, Cambridge, Massachusetts, (hereafter cited as Clapp Papers, HL).

126. Charles H. Taylor to Smith, June 18, 1885, Smith Papers, OHS.

127. Smith to Reid, May 28, 1885, Reid Papers.

128. Western Associated Press, Special Committee of Conference, *Report* (Detroit, 1891), p. 5.

129. Smith to Phillips, May 29, 1886, Letterbook 30, Smith Papers, OHS.

130. "To The New England Associated Press," an undated committee report, and Benjamin Kimball to Clapp, March 5, 1887, NEAP Papers.

131. *The Journalist,* March 16, 1889, p. 3.

132. AP-UP contract, May 28, 1888, Smith Papers, IHS.

133. Smith to Clapp, April 16 and 18, 1887, NEAP Papers.

134. John S. Baldwin to Clapp, May 6, 1887, NEAP Papers.

135. S. A. Hubbard to Beard, April 22, 1887, NEAP Papers.

136. Morgan, *Taylor,* p. 115.

137. Dana to Reid, February 18, 1886, enclosing Smith to Jno. Van Horne, January 28, 1886, and Van Horne to Smith, January 29, 1886, Reid Papers; Smith to Richard Smith, March 20, 1886, Letterbook 30, Smith Papers, OHS; and Smith to D. H. Bates, October 6, 1887, and R. Smith to Smith, October 7, 1887, Smith Papers, IHS.

138. WAP, *Proceedings* (1887), p. 5.

139. Dennis, *Lawson,* p. 76.

140. Richard Smith, Jr., to Smith, May 13, 1891, Smith Papers, IHS.

141. "Statement of Mr. Haldeman," undated typed transcript of interrogation by Victor F. Lawson, Frederick Driscoll, Elliott F. Shepard, William L. Davis, and a Mr. Smith, Victor F. Lawson Papers, Newberry Library, Chicago.

142. WAP, Special Committee, *Report,* pp. 5, 20-22. The fifth member of the joint executive committee, James Gordon Bennett, Jr., did not participate in the stock pool. In fact, Bennett "never attended any meetings of the committee." R. Smith to Smith, June 10, 1891, Smith Papers, IHS. He was so little involved in AP affairs that during one of his rare visits to New York City, Bennett, under the mistaken impression that the *Herald* and not he was the committee member, had to be corrected by Dana. Bennett to Dana and Dana to Bennett, October 18, 1887, enclosed in Dana to Reid, October 18, 1887, Reid Papers. It should also be noted that when these various AP-UP arrangements were discovered, Whitelaw Reid, as a committee member, wrote a

four-page typed confidential memorandum to Bennett, the often-absent committee member, explaining the background and substance of these arrangements. See "Confidential Memorandum," typed and bearing William Henry Smith's handwritten notation "Confidential statement made by Mr. Reid to Mr. Bennett in the winter, and first seen by me June 30, 1891," Smith Papers, OHS.

143. WAP, Special Committee, *Report,* pp. 6-7, 23-24.

144. R. Smith to Reid, February 18, 1888, Reid Papers.

145. Smith to Reid, February 8, 1888, Reid Papers.

146. Smith to Clapp, March 30, 1888, NEAP Papers.

147. Phillips to Smith, September 20, 1887, Smith Papers, IHS.

148. Copies of the working contract are in Smith Papers, IHS; and in WAP, Special Committee, *Report,* pp. 2-4. See also typed minutes of meeting in which the contract was executed, dated May [?], 1888, Smith Papers, IHS.

149. Theodore Dreiser, *A Book about Myself* (New York: Boni & Liveright, 1922), p. 38.

150. T. C. Cochran, *Business,* p. 153.

151. Joseph M. Webb, "Historical Perspective on the New Journalism," *Journalism History* 1 (Summer 1974): 38-39.

152. Susan Ruth [Brooker-]Gross, "Spatial Organization of the News Wire Services in the Nineteenth Century United States" (Ph.D. diss., University of Illinois, 1977), p. 162.

153. H[arold] A. Innis, *The Press, A Neglected Factor in the Economic History of the Twentieth Century* (London: Oxford University Press, 1949), pp. 36-37.

154. Ida M. Tarbell, *The Nationalizing of Business, 1878-1898,* vol. 9 of A History of American Life, edited by Arthur M. Schlesinger and Dixon Ryan Fox (New York: Macmillan, 1936), p. 267.

Chapter 5

1. Victor Rosewater's discussion of this episode in AP history relies almost exclusively on published accounts and documents in the annual reports for the Western AP and the AP of Illinois. As such it is a partial account that emphasizes formal and overt maneuvers, but is unable to sketch the covert intrigues and the clashes of personalities and philosophies. See Rosewater's *News-Gathering,* pp. 182-246.

2. In his explanation to Bennett early in 1891, Whitelaw Reid wrote, "The success of this scheme depended absolutely on its secrecy, and its being confined to the individuals who had the power to enforce it." Reid, "Confidential Memorandum" seen by Smith June 30, 1891, Smith Papers, OHS. Numerous references in the Smith Papers in Indi-

ana and Ohio indicate that UP was expected to rewrite the news stories it received from AP.

3. Frank R. O'Neil to Pulitzer, August 23, 1887, Pulitzer Papers, CU.

4. WAP, Special Committee, *Report,* p. 28.

5. WAP, *Proceedings* (1888), p. 10, and (1889), pp. 7-10.

6. Felix Agnus to Smith, July 9, 1891, Smith Papers, OHS.

7. Mott, *American Journalism,* p. 449.

8. WAP, Special Committee, *Report,* p. 28; WAP, *Proceedings* (1889), p. 12; and O'Brien, *Sun,* p. 242.

9. WAP, *Proceedings* (1889), p. 12.

10. WAP, *Proceedings* (1890), p. 6.

11. Ibid., p. 8.

12. H. E. Baker to Smith, August 6, 1890, Smith Papers, IHS. Emphasis in original.

13. WAP, *Proceedings* (1890), p. 14.

14. Reid to Smith, June 25, 1891, Smith Papers, OHS.

15. Robert Lloyd Tree, "Victor Fremont Lawson and His Newspapers, 1890-1900: A Study of the Chicago Daily News and the Chicago Record" (Ph.D. diss., Northwestern University, 1959), p. 29.

16. Lawson's 243,619 daily circulation for the *Daily News* and *Record* was exceeded only by the *New York World's* total morning and evening circulation of 374,741 in 1892. Mott, *American Journalism,* p. 507.

17. Wendt, *Tribune,* p. 342.

18. Joseph Medill to Smith, May 7, 1888, Smith Papers, IHS.

19. Richard Smith, Jr., to Smith, May 13, 1891, Smith Papers, IHS.

20. Letterbook 39, Regular Series, Lawson Papers. Lawson at this time was preoccupied with planning and erecting the new building for his newspapers.

21. Lawson to Driscoll, January 30, 1891, Letterbook 40, Regular Series, Lawson Papers.

22. Lawson to Driscoll, January 6, 1891, Letterbook 39, Regular Series, Lawson Papers.

23. I. F. Mack to Smith, January 22, 1894, Smith Papers, IHS.

24. R. Smith to Smith, September 18, 1890, Smith Papers, IHS. The AP "crisis" was only part of Richard Smith's worries at this time. After the merger of his *Cincinnati Gazette* with Murat Halstead's *Cincin-*

nati Commercial in 1883, the resulting *Commercial Gazette* steadily fell behind the *Cincinnati Enquirer,* owned by John R. McLean. A desperate need for cash to pay old debts caused Halstead unexpectedly in late October 1890 to deliver three hundred shares of the paper's stock and a promise of control of the paper to a broker with ties to McLean. William Henry Smith observed that Halstead's actions stemmed from Richard Smith's refusal to allow Halstead's son, Marshall, to become managing editor of the *Commercial Gazette.* After reading the documents regarding the affair, Smith concluded "that Mr. Halstead is verging on insanity. This is the opinion of others." Halstead soon after this left Cincinnati to become editor of the *Brooklyn Standard-Union,* R. Smith and his friends regained control of the paper, and within nine months R. Smith was attempting to interest William Henry Smith in joining the paper's staff. Mott, *American Journalism,* p. 459; Donald W. Curl, *Murat Halstead and the Cincinnati Commercial* (Boca Raton: University Presses of Florida, 1980), pp. 128-35; Smith to Delavan Smith, October 29, 1890, Smith Papers, OHS; and R. Smith to Smith, June 10, 1891, Smith Papers, IHS.

25. See pages 1-7 of Letterbook 40, Regular Series, Lawson Papers, for a summary of this correspondence from numerous WAP papers in thirteen Midwestern and Western cities.

26. "Memorandum for Mr. Lawson," October 1890, Smith Papers, IHS.

27. Lawson to Smith, two letters, January 6, 1891, Smith Papers, IHS.

28. Smith to Lawson, January 9, 1891, Letterbook 31, Smith Papers, OHS.

29. Smith to Lawson, February 16, 1891, Letterbook 31, Smith Papers, OHS.

30. Smith to Lawson and Driscoll, February 19, 1891, Letterbook 29, Smith Papers, OHS.

31. Swanberg, *Pulitzer,* p. 69; and S. Carter, *Field,* p. 350.

32. Smith to Reid, July 6, 1891, Letterbook 31, Smith Papers, OHS.

33. The previous discussion of conditions within NYAP is gleaned from R. Smith to Smith, March 2, 10, and 16, 1891, Nicholson to Smith, March 16, 1891, and Richard Smith, Jr., to Smith, May 13, 1891, Smith Papers, IHS; Reid to Smith, May 15, 1891, Smith Papers, OHS; and Nicholson to Reid, May 15, 1891, Reid Papers.

34. Smith to Lawson, January 9, 1891, Letterbook 31, Smith Papers, OHS.

35. Ibid., Smith to Delavan Smith, February 2, 1891, and Smith to Walter Neef, April 24, 1891, Letterbook 31, Smith Papers, OHS.

36. Smith to Reid, May 5, 1891, Letterbook 31, Smith Papers, OHS.

37. Smith to Neef, April 24, 1891, Letterbook 31, Smith Papers, OHS.

38. "Proceedings of a Joint Conference...May 13, 1891," and Richard Smith, Jr., to Smith, two letters, May 13, 1891, Smith Papers, IHS.

39. Smith to Lawson, June 4, 1891, Letterbook 31, Smith Papers, OHS.

40. "Memorandum of Conversation with Victor F. Lawson," June 4, 1891, Letterbook 31, Smith Papers, OHS; also found in rough draft form on personal stationery in Smith Papers, IHS, and Smith to Reid, June 9, 1891, Reid Papers, and Letterbook 31, Smith Papers, OHS.

41. R. Smith to Smith, telegram, June 4, 1891, Lawson Papers. An earlier R. Smith reply on the same date is in the Smith Papers, IHS.

42. Haldeman to Smith, telegram, June [5], 1891, Smith Papers, IHS.

43. Smith to Lawson, June 4, 1891, Lawson Papers.

44. Smith to Reid, June 9, 1891, Letterbook 31, Smith Papers, OHS, and also in Reid Papers. Emphasis in original.

45. Letterbook 40, Regular Series, Lawson Papers.

46. The regular annual meeting was scheduled, as prescribed in the by-laws, for August 19, 1891. The old hands wished to hold the director elections, a fixture of the annual meetings, before Lawson's report could be heard. They hoped to push the Lawson report off to a special meeting in the fall, but Lawson prevailed, in part because R. Smith did not want to give him further grievances. Lawson's report was thus scheduled for a special meeting the day before the annual meeting. Copy of Lawson to Haldeman, June 26, 1891, and R. Smith to Smith, June 20, 1891, Smith Papers, IHS.

47. "To the Proprietor of. . .," printed letter, dated August 8, 1891, signed Lawson, Driscoll, and Patterson, in Smith Papers, OHS. Emphasis in original.

48. R. Smith to Smith, July 13, 1891, Smith Papers, IHS.

49. See WAP, Special Committee, *Report.*

50. WAP, *Proceedings* (1891), pp. 11-12.

51. Ibid., pp. 12-13; and WAP, Special Committee, *Report,* pp. 17-19.

52. WAP, *Proceedings* (1891), pp. 13-14.

53. The actual number of new directors elected each year was four in 1884, two in 1885, three in 1886, none in 1887 and 1888, and three each in 1889 and 1890.

54. WAP, *Proceedings* (1891), pp. 7-8, 12, 15-16.

55. Lawson to H. N. McKinney, August 21, 1891, quoted in Dennis, *Lawson,* p. 189.

56. Among several letters to Smith, see esp. Nixon to Smith, July 11, 1891, Smith Papers, OHS.

57. W. H. Smith, "News Gatherer," p. 532.

58. Smith to Reid, August 20, 1891, Letterbook 29, Smith Papers, OHS.

59. Ibid.

60. Smith to Dana, August 20, 1891, Letterbook 29, Smith Papers, OHS.

61. Notably WAP, *Proceedings* (1891), passim; Smith to William Walter Phelps, January 28, 1893, Smith Papers, IHS; and AP, *Annual Report* (1892-93), passim.

62. AP, *Annual Report* (1892-93), pp. 3-5.

63. WAP, *Proceedings* (1891), p. 50.

64. R. Smith to Smith, January 13, 1892, Smith Papers, IHS.

65. Copy of R. Smith to William Penn Nixon, April 25, 1892, Smith Papers, IHS.

66. Haldeman to Nixon, January 14, 1892, reprinted in WAP, *Proceedings* (1891), pp. 73-74.

67. *The Journalist,* December 19, 1891, p. 3.

68. William Penn Nixon to Smith, October 3, 1891, Smith Papers, OHS; and William A. Collier to Smith, November 9, 1891, Smith Papers, IHS.

69. Smith to Phelps, January 28, 1893, Smith Papers, IHS.

70. Evan P. Howell et al., representing the Southern AP, to Smith, April 21, 1892, and Adolph S. Ochs to Smith, July 14, 1892, Smith Papers, IHS.

71. Typed minutes of October 12, 1892, meeting of Southern AP committee, Smith Papers, IHS.

72. Smith to John R. Walsh, November 12, 1891, and copy of R. Smith and Haldeman to John R. Walsh, December 11, 1891, Smith Papers, IHS.

73. WAP, *Proceedings* (1891), pp. 88-89. The proposal was dated June 14, 1892, and the board accepted it the following day.

74. AP, *Annual Report* (1892-93), p. 13.

75. Smith to Phelps, January 28, 1893, Smith Papers, IHS.

76. Smith to W. W. Clapp, June 30, 1891, Clapp Papers, HL.

77. W. H. Smith, *Political History.*

78. W. H. Johnson, ''The Slavery Controversy in America,'' review of *A Political History of Slavery . . .* by William Henry Smith, *The Dial,* July 16, 1903, pp. 33-34.

79. Hayes, *Diary and Letters.*

80. Williams, *Hayes.*

81. Gardiner G. Howland to Smith, November 18, 1892, Smith Papers, IHS.

82. Smith to Addison P. Russell, July 19, 1887, Letterbook 29, Smith Papers, OHS.

83. Entry for September 6, 1894, in Smith's ''Memoirs,'' Smith Papers, Hayes Library.

84. Copy of Smith to Reid, January 3, 1892, Smith Papers, IHS.

85. Charles A. Dana, *The Art of Newspaper Making: Three Lectures* (1895; New York: D. Appleton, 1900), p. 244.

86. *The Journalist,* September 24, 1892, p. 8.

87. Smith to Phelps, January 28, 1893, Smith Papers, IHS.

88. Ibid.; Nicholson to Smith, December 16, 1892, Smith Papers, IHS; and W. P. Phillips, *United Press,* p. 1.

89. Diehl, *Correspondent,* p. 244.

90. AP, *Annual Report* (1892-93), pp. 7, 13, 74, 76, and (1894), p. 3; and M.E. Stone, *Journalist,* p. 216.

91. Circular from Smith and Stone to Proprietor . . . , April 12, 1893, Smith Papers, IHS.

92. The original sixty-two AP members were the *St. Louis Westliche Post, Post-Dispatch, Republic, Globe-Democrat, Anzeiger des Westens,* and *Amerika; Cleveland Leader* and *Plain Dealer; Chicago Daily News, Staats-Zeitung, Inter Ocean, Journal, Times,* and *Tribune; Cincinnati Volksblatt, Enquirer, Commerical Gazette, Times-Star,* and *Volksfreund; Toledo Blade* and *Commercial; Minneapolis Journal* and *Tribune; Pittsburgh Chronicle-Telegraph, Dispatch, Post,* and *Commercial Gazette; Oil City* (Pa.) *Derrick; Kansas City Journal* and *Times; St. Paul Pioneer Press* and *Globe; Portland Oregonian; Sandusky* (Ohio) *Register; Seattle Post-Intelligencer; Terre Haute* (Ind.) *Express* and *Gazette;* Springfield *Illinois State Journal; Indianapolis Sentinel, News,* and *Journal; Columbus Dispatch* and *Ohio State Journal; Milwaukee Herold, Sentinel,* and *Wisconsin; Wheeling* (W.Va.) *Intelligencer* and *Register; Galveston News; Memphis Appeal* and *Avalanche; Detroit Tribune* and *Free Press; Dayton Journal; Louisiville Courier-Journal; Denver Times, Republican,* and *News; Evansville* (Ind.) *Journal-News; Omaha Bee; Nashville American;* and *San Francisco Chronicle.* AP, *Annual Report* (1892-93), pp. 52-53.

93. Ibid., pp. 13-14.

94. AP, *Annual Report* (1895), pp. 207-10, 213-22. Membership figures are for May 13, Series A figures are for May 20, and stockholder figures are for May 10, all in 1896.

95. The following account is drawn from several sources: AP, *Annual Report* (1892-93), pp. 7-17; Smith to Reid, February 23 and March 14, 1893, Letterbook 32, Smith Papers, OHS; Smith to Lawson, February 3, 1893, and a copy of Walter P. Phillips to R. Smith, with enclosures, August 23, 1893, Smith Papers, IHS.

96. Smith to Reid, March 14, 1893, Letterbook 32, Smith Papers, OHS.

97. Neef to Smith, October 27, 1890, and December 13, 1892, Smith Papers, IHS.

98. Lawson to Neef, February 17, 1893, reprinted in AP, *Annual Report* (1892-93), pp. 64-65.

99. Neef to Smith, February 21, 1893, Smith Papers, IHS.

100. AP, *Annual Report* (1892-93), pp. 10, 76-81; and M. E. Stone, *Journalist,* p. 216.

101. Storey, *Reuters' Century,* p. 116.

102. Copy of Phillips to R. Smith, August 23, 1893, Smith Papers, IHS.

103. Haldeman to Stone, August 23, 1893, reprinted in AP, *Annual Report* (1892-93), p. 11.

104. AP, *Annual Report* (1892-93), p. 12.

105. Ibid., p. 13.

106. Ibid., pp. 14-15, and M. E. Stone, *Journalist,* p. 217.

107. See Diehl, *Correspondent,* pp. 244-48.

108. Dairy transcript, Hood Papers.

109. AP, *Annual Report* (1894), p. 3, and (1895), pp. 279-83.

110. AP, *Annual Report* (1894), pp. 4-5.

111. Phillips to Dana, Reid, Gardiner G. Howland, and George F. Spinney, March 5, 1894, Reid Papers.

112. Copy of Phillips to Dana, July 22, 1894, Reid Papers.

113. AP, *Annual Report* (1894), pp. 6, 10.

114. AP, *Annual Report* (1895), pp. 111-28, 134-38; and [United Press (1882-97)], *Joint Conference Committee Representing the Associated Press and United Press: Proceedings, Minutes, Correspondence and Addendum* (New York, 1895), which contains an addendum of pro-UP comment.

115. *Fourth Estate,* May 16, 1895, p. 1, May 23, 1895, p. 1, and May 30, 1895, pp. 1, 8-11.

116. [United Press (1882-97)], *Facts vs. Lies, with an incidental forecast as to the outcome of the contest between the Press Associations* (New York: Evening Post, [1895]); [United Press (1882-97)], *The United Press, Scope of Service and Business Methods: Interviews with General Manager Phillips* (n.p., [1895]); United Press (1882-97), *By-laws in Force July 1, 1895* (n.p., [1895]); [UP], *Joint Conference;* and an open printed letter "To Stockholding Members of The Associated Press," signed by AP member V. S. McClatchy, dated June 20, 1895, and including reprints of antagonistic correspondence from McClatchy to AP's board, Reid Papers.

117. "An Open Letter to the Daily Newspapers of the Country," signed Victor F. Lawson, dated July 11, 1895, Reid Papers, and reprinted in AP, *Annual Report* (1895), pp. 32-39.

118. AP, *Annual Report* (1895), p. 3.

119. Ibid., p. 5.

120. Associated Press v. United States, 326 U.S. 1 (1945).

121. Reid to Smith, October 21, 1893, Smith Papers, IHS.

122. E. W. Scripps's "The United Press Association," an undated type-script, Negley D. Cochran Papers, Toledo Public Library, Toledo, Ohio. Cochran calls these Scripps's "autobiographical notes" in his *E. W. Scripps* (New York: Harcourt, Brace, 1933), p. 82; they are similar to portions of Chapter 19, "I Buck the A. P.," in Edward Wyllis Scripps, *Damned Old Crank: A Self-Portrait of E. W. Scripps,* edited by Charles R. McCabe (New York: Harper, 1951).

123. Printed circular from Walter P. Phillips, dated July 27, 1896, Reid Papers.

124. Phillips to Dana, Howland or Bennett, Nicholson or Reid, C. R. Miller or Alfred Ely, March 5 and June 4, 1896, and Howland to Reid, September 5, 1896, Reid Papers.

125. Copies of telegrams from someone at the *Herald* to Bennett, July 22, 1896, and Bennett's telegraphed reply, July 23, 1896, Reid Papers. Such sentiments reached public print as gossip early in 1897. *Fourth Estate,* January 21, 1897, p. 1.

126. Howland to Reid, July 27, 1896, Reid Papers; and Alfred Bates to John Norris, July 28, 1896, Joseph Pulitzer Papers, Library of Congress, Washington, D.C. (hereafter cited as Pulitzer Papers, LC).

127. Howland to Reid, July 27, 1896, Reid Papers.

128. E. Davis, *Times,* p. 241.

129. *Newspaperdom,* March 4, 1897, p. 4.

130. Handwritten copy of notice in *New York Sun,* February 19, 1897, Reid Papers.

131. AP, *Annual Report* (1896), p. 4; *Fourth Estate,* March 25, 1897, p. 1, and April 1, 1897, p. 1; and *Newspaperdom,* April 1, 1897, p. 1.

132. AP, *Annual Report* (1897), p. 169.

133. Ibid., p. 171.

134. Ibid., pp. 180-81. The *New York Evening Mail and Express* had returned to the AP in early October 1896 in reaction to UP's granting to Hearst's *New York Evening Journal* a full UP franchise, such as the *Evening Mail and Express* was denied when the NYAP partners moved into the UP in 1892. *Fourth Estate,* October 8, 1896, p. 1; and *Newspaperdom,* October 15, 1896, p. 1.

135. AP, *Annual Report* (1896), p. 3.

136. Diehl, *Correspondent,* p. 253.

137. Connery, "Operations," pp. 21-32. This article is recommended not only as a snapshot of the two newsbrokerages in 1896, but also for the many photographs accompanying it of the men engaged in this struggle.

138. Dennis, *Lawson,* p. 225.

139. Ibid., p. 208.

140. Ibid., p. 219.

141. M. E. Stone, *Journalist,* pp. 215-16.

142. AP, *Annual Report* (1897), p. 272.

143. Ibid., p. 264.

144. Ibid., pp. 273-307.

145. See ibid., pp. 480-502.

146. Diehl, *Correspondent,* p. 254.

147. AP, *Annual Report* (1897), p. 483.

148. Ibid., pp. 493-94.

149. [W. H. Smith], *Governmental Regulation,* p. 10.

Chapter 6

1. M. E. Stone, *Journalist,* pp. 215, 235.

2. More than 30 percent of Victor Rosewater's book concerns itself with the post-1897 period, a period of which Rosewater had personal knowledge. See his *News-Gathering,* pp. 260-279. Briefer, but adequate treatments are in Lee, *Daily Newspaper,* pp. 520-40; Mott, *American Journalism,* pp. 591-92; and Edwin Emery and Michael Emery, *The Press and America: An Interpretive History of the Mass Media,* 5th ed. (Englewood Cliffs, N.J.: Prentice-Hall, 1984), pp. 338-42.

3. *Appletons' Cyclopaedia of American Biography,* s.v. "Smith, Richard"; AP, *Annual Report* (1893), p. 12; and Mott, *American Journalism,* pp. 459-60. The author has been unable to discover when Smith died.

4. *Who Was Who in America: Historical Volume, 1607-1896,* 2nd ed. (1967), s.v. "Haldeman, Walter Newman"; AP, *Annual Report* (1893), p. 11, and (1895), pp. 279-83; and Associated Press, *Preliminary Proceedings* (1900), p. 77 (hereafter cited as AP, *Proceedings* [1900]).

5. *Dictionary of American Biography,* s.v. "Phillips, Walter Polk"; and Walter P. Phillips [John Oakum], *Sketches Old and New* (1897; reprint ed., New York: J. H. Bunnell, 1902), pp. ii-xiv.

6. Various letters from Richard Smith, Jr., to William Henry Smith, 1891-92, Smith Papers, IHS; AP, *Annual Report* (1894), p. 21; and *New York Times,* September 4, 1922.

7. J. W. Davis, "Washington AP," p. 4.

8. "Obituary, Walter Neef," in AP, *Service Bulletin,* June 1, 1905, pp. 2-3.

9. *Lakeside Directory of the City of Chicago,* various numbers; AP, *Annual Report* (1894), p. 23; and Charles Edward Kloeber, Jr., "The American Newspaper: IX. The Press Association," *Bookman* 20 (November 1904): 200.

10. Diehl, *Correspondent,* pp. 43, 59-60, 69, 94ff.

11. Ibid., pp. 154, 204, 234-35, 241.

12. M. E. Stone, *Journalist,* pp. 1-52.

13. Dennis, *Lawson,* p. 14.

14. M. E. Stone, *Journalist,* pp. 179-82.

15. Ibid., pp. 194-96.

16. Ibid., pp. 214-15.

17. Ibid., p. 216.

18. W. H. England to Edward Rosewater, October 27, 1892, Rosewater Family Papers.

19. Printed circular from American Press Association, dated March 15, 1893, Smith Papers, IHS.

20. Boynton to Smith, March 15, 1893, Smith Papers, IHS.

21. Lawson to Charles W. Knapp, June 11, 1898, AP Letterbook, Lawson Papers.

22. Lawson telegram to Stanton, July 22, 1898, Regular Letterbook, Lawson Papers.

23. Dennis, *Lawson.* p. 264. In 1901 Lawson transferred the service from the *Record* to the *Chicago Daily News,* where it stayed until the latter's death in 1978. In addition to Dennis's detailed account of the Daily News Service, see Lawson's account reprinted from *Editor & Publisher* in Jason Rogers, *Newspaper Building: Application of Efficiency to Editing, to Mechanical Production, to Circulation and Advertising* (New York: Harper, 1918), pp. 145-52.

24. Andrew Long, "The Federated Press," *Survey,* October 23, 1920, pp. 126-27; Upton Sinclair, *The Brass Check: A Study of American Journalism* (Pasadena, Calif.: the author, 1920), pp. 444-45; and Lee, *Daily Newspaper,* p. 541.

25. I. Garland Penn, *The Afro-American Press and Its Editors* (Springfield, Mass.: Willey, 1891), pp. 112, 114.

26. Ibid., pp. 544, 546.

27. Articles of organization quoted in ibid., p. 538.

28. Ibid., pp. 539ff.

29. Frederick G. Detweiler, *The Negro Press in the United States* (Chicago: University of Chicago Press, 1922), p. 28.

30. Associated Negro Press, *The Service of the Associated Negro Press, 1919-1920: Annual,* edited by Nahum Daniel Brascher (n.p., [1920]), p. 3.

31. Ibid., back cover.

32. Ibid., p. 1.

33. For later history and additional information on the Associated Negro Press, see Roland E. Wolseley, *The Black Press, U.S.A.* (Ames: Iowa State University Press, 1971), pp. 269-71; Linda J. Evans, "Claude A. Barnett and the Associated Negro Press," *Chicago History* 12 (Spring 1983): 44-56; Richard L. Beard and Cyril E. Zoerner II, "Associated Negro Press: Its Founding, Ascendency and Demise," *Journalism Quarterly* 46 (Spring 1969): 47-52; Thomas De Baggio and Julia Aldridge, "Black News Services: Dying of Neglect?" *Columbia Journalism Review* 13 (July-August 1974): 48-49; Lawrence D. Hogan, *A Black National News Service: The Associated Negro Press and Claude Barnett, 1919-1945* (Cranbury, N.J.: Associated University Presses, 1984); and the Claude A. Barnett Papers, Chicago Historical Society, Chicago, which include ANP's working correspondence and news dispatches from 1928 to 1964.

34. Melville E. Stone, "Newspapers in the United States, Their Functions, Interior Economy, and Management," *Self Culture* 5 (July 1897): 306. Reprinted in *Newspaperdom,* July 24, 1897, pp. 1-2, 6.

35. AP, *Annual Report* (1896), pp. 4-5.

36. AP, *Annual Report* (1897), p. 3.

37. Ibid., p. 4.

38. Minnesota Tribune Company v. Associated Press, 83 F. 350 (1897); and AP, *Annual Report* (1897), pp. 128-32.

39. Ohio State Journal v. Associated Press, decision of the Court of Common Pleas, Franklin County, Ohio, reprinted in AP, *Annual Report* (1897), pp. 142-43.

40. Missouri ex rel. The Sayings Company v. Associated Press, 159 Mo. 410, 456, 457 (1898), quoted in "Corporations, other than trading and producing, so far (July 11, 1903) investigated with a view to ascertaining whether they are under the jurisdiction of the Department of Commerce and Labor—News-Gathering Companies," U.S. Department of Commerce and Labor, Record Group no. 122, National Archives, Washington, D.C.

41. Quoted in Associated Press, *Law of the Associated Press,* 2 vols. (New York: Associated Press, 1914-19), 1:484-85.

42. Quoted in ibid., 1:485-87.

43. Lee, *Daily Newspaper,* pp. 212-13.

44. Letter from E. W. Scripps to Roy W. Howard, September 27, 1912, reprinted in Edward Wyllis Scripps, *I Protest: Selected Disquisitions of*

E. W. Scripps, edited by Oliver Knight (Madison: University of Wisconsin Press, 1966), pp. 294-95.

45. Ibid., p. 295.

46. Ibid., p. 296.

47. Scripps, *Old Crank, p. 199.*

48. Scripps, *I Protest,* p. 296.

49. AP, *Annual Report* (1897), pp. 318-20.

50. Ibid., pp. 150, 320-22.

51. Ibid., pp. 350-51.

52. Ibid., p. 365.

53. Scripps, *I Protest,* p. 297.

54. Ibid.

55. Typescript, "The United Press Association," Cochran Papers.

56. Scripps, *I Protest,* p. 297. The Scripps-McRae Press Association first surfaced 1½ months before Scripps's rejection by the AP board, when the trade press reported incorporation of the agency under Ohio law. *Fourth Estate,* March 18, 1897, p. 1.

57. Typescript, "The United Press Association," Cochran Papers.

58. "The Story of Scripps-Howard: A Study in Personality, Policy and Achievement in Journalism," a special ed. of *Scripps-Howard News* (September 1929), p. 13.

59. Scripps, *I Protest,* p. 298.

60. Typescript, "The United Press Association," Cochran Papers.

61. Ibid.

62. Ibid.; and *Fourth Estate,* March 16, 1899, pp. 1-2.

63. AP, *Annual Report* (1903-4), p. 35.

64. The PPA subscribers on its first day were the *New York News, New York Evening Journal, Brooklyn Citizen, Brooklyn Standard-Union, Brooklyn Times, Philadelphia Call, Philadelphia Gazette, Cleveland World, Pittsburgh Press, McKeesport* (Pa.) *News, Allegheny* (Pa.) *Record, Zanesville* (Ohio) *Signal, Wheeling* (W. Va.) *News, Elizabeth Journal, Columbus* (Ohio) *Press* and *Post, Chicago Dispatch, Buffalo Enquirer, Syracuse Journal, St. Louis Star, Rochester* (N.Y.) *Post-Express,* and *Springfield* (Ohio) *News. Fourth Estate,* April 8, 1897, pp. 1-2; May 6, 1897, p. 1; and June 10, 1897, p. 1.

65. AP, *Annual Report* (1897), p. 388.

66. AP, *Annual Report* (1898), p. 204, see Art. XIV, sec. 6.

67. Ibid., p. 203, see Art XIV, sec. 1.

68. AP, *Annual Report* (1897), p. 140. Peckham's entire opinion is reprinted on pp. 137-41.

69. Benjamin F. Wright, *The Growth of American Constitutional Law* (Chicago: University of Chicago Press, 1942), p. 173.

70. Lochner v. New York, 198 U.S. 45 (1905).

71. Robert G. McCloskey, *The American Supreme Court* (Chicago: University of Chicago Press, 1960), p. 154.

72. The earliest mention of the *Inter Ocean's* affiliation with the Associated Press is in William Henry Smith's 1876 history of the Western AP, showing that the paper was represented at a WAP meeting on December 12-13, 1866, in Chicago when it was still called the *Republican.* WAP, *Proceedings* (1876), p. 56.

73. Chicago Inter Ocean, *Centennial History of the City of Chicago, Its Men and Institutions* [2nd ed.] (Chicago: Inter Ocean, 1905), pp. 82-83. Between May 1891 and May 3, 1894, a controlling block of Nixon's stock in the *Inter Ocean* was held by Herman H. Kohlsaat. For a well-researched history of the newspaper, see Walter E. Ewert, "The History of the Chicago Inter Ocean, 1872-1914" (master's thesis, Northwestern University, 1940), esp. pp. 107-16 for the paper's confrontation with AP.

74. Inter Ocean, *Centennial History,* p. 83.

75. Ibid.; Emmett Dedmon, *Fabulous Chicago,* 2nd ed. (New York: Atheneum, 1981), pp. 259-61; and *Dictionary of American Biography,* s.v. "Nixon, William Penn."

76. "Antagonism" between the *Inter Ocean* and other Chicago newspapers, beyond the requirements of AP bylaws, is suggested by David Paul Nord's study of newspaper editorial policy in relation to the municipal reform movement from 1890 to 1900. Viewed in this context, the issue of the *Inter Ocean's* violation of an AP bylaw is an aspect of a broader and persistent editorial contest between Yerkes and the rest of Chicago newspaper journalism. David Paul Nord, *Newspapers and New Politics: Midwestern Municipal Reform, 1890-1900* (Ann Arbor, Mich.: UMI Research Press, 1981), esp. pp. 93, 103-08.

77. Munn v. Illinois, 94 U.S. 113 (1877).

78. AP, *Annual Report* (1893), p. 4.

79. Inter Ocean Publishing Co. v. Associated Press, 184 Ill. 438 (1900), quoted in AP, *Annual Report* (1899), pp. 48-52. Quotation is from p. 50.

80. Ibid.

81. Ibid., pp. 51-52. This decision and subsequent antitrust cases involving the AP are discussed exhaustively in William F. Swindler, "The AP Anti-Trust Case in Historical Perspective," *Journalism Quarterly* 23 (March 1946): 40-57.

82. As of February 24, 1900, when previous declarations of antagonism were rescinded, AP held the following organizations antagonistic to AP: Scripps-McRae Press Association, *Cleveland Press, Cincinnati Post, St. Louis Chronicle, Kansas City World,* Covington *Kentucky Post,* Inter Ocean News Bureau, *Chicago Inter Ocean,* the Sun Printing and Publishing Association in New York City, the Laffan News Bureau, and the Publishers' Press Association. AP, *Annual Report* (1900), p. 152.

83. *Newspaperdom,* March 1, 1900, p. 8.

84. *Fourth Estate,* March 3, 1900, p. 5.

85. "Victor F. Lawson to The Members of the Associated Press," printed circular dated February 24, 1900, Reid Papers.

86. AP, *Annual Report* (1899), p. 56.

87. AP, *Annual Report* (1900), p. 193.

88. Ibid., pp. 183-84.

89. Ibid., p. 192.

90. Such votes were also tallied by shares of stock. In this case 841 shares were voted to reject the recommendations, 16 shares to accept them, and 185 shares to abstain. By stock, the majority was 80.7 percent of the total represented at the meeting. Ibid., p. 193.

91. Ibid., p. 182.

92. Quoted in *Newspaperdom,* May 17, 1900, p. 5.

93. *New York Sun,* June 7, 1900, clipping in Reid Papers.

94. Stone to Edward Rosewater, June 7, 1900, Rosewater Family Papers.

95. AP, *Proceedings* (1900), p. 1.

96. AP, *Annual Report* (1901), p. 42.

97. Ibid.; and AP, *Proceedings* (1900), pp. 1-18.

98. AP, *Annual Report* (1900), pp. 198, 200.

99. Ibid., pp. 185-86.

100. The six directors of both APs were Albert J. Barr, *Pittsburgh Post;* Victor F. Lawson, *Chicago Daily News;* Charles W. Knapp, *St. Louis Republic;* Michel H. de Young, *San Francisco Chronicle;* William L. McLean, *Philadephia Bulletin;* and Frank B. Noyes, *Washington* (D.C.) *Star.*

101. See table 7 in the Appendix for sources of directors' tenures.

102. See numerous notes, correspondence, and minutes of meetings between June 9 and September 8, 1900, Reid Papers.

103. James Martin to Reid, June 19, 1900, Reid Papers.

104. *Fourth Estate,* June 16, 1900, p. 2.

105. C. S. Burch to George G. Booth, June 19, 1900, George Gough Booth Papers, Michigan Historical Collections, Bentley Library, Ann Arbor, Mich. The author is grateful to John D. Stevens for calling this correspondence to his attention.

106. "Suggested Defects in By-Laws of the (New) Associated Press...," printed circular dated June 15, 1900, Reid Papers.

107. Stone to Seitz, June 11, 1900, Pulitzer Papers, CU.

108. "Charles W. Knapp and Charles S. Diehl to the Stockholders of The Associated Press," printed call for a stockholders' meeting, dated September 1, 1900, Reid Papers.

109. AP, *Annual Report* (1900), p. 240.

110. Ibid., pp. 240-46.

111. Ibid., p. 249.

112. Ibid., p. 259.

113. Ibid., p. 260.

114. An earlier version of this motion authorized the board to arrange expressly with the new AP in New York, but objection to specifying the New York corporation caused an amendment. Ibid., pp. 265-66.

115. The committee consisted of chairman Harvey W. Scott, *Portland Oregonian;* Fred E. Whiting, *Boston Herald;* Florence D. White, *New York World;* H. J. Ford, *Pittsburgh Chronicle-Telegraph;* M. D. Munn, *St. Paul Dispatch;* Herman H. Kohlsaat, *Chicago Times-Herald;* John Hicks, *Oshkosh* (Wis.) *Northwestern;* D. A. Tompkins, *Charlotte* (N.C.) *Observer;* Thomas G. Rapier, *New Orleans Picayune;* Frank B. Noyes, *Washington* (D.C.) *Star;* V. S. McClatchy, *Sacramento Bee;* E. C. Hughes, *Seattle Post-Intelligencer;* and P. H. Lannan, *Salt Lake Tribune.* "Report of Committee of the Associated Press Newspaper Publishers," printed circular dated September 21, 1900, and typed telegraphic dispatch entitled "Confidential Communication to Publishers," dated September 20, 1900, both in Reid Papers.

116. "Confidential Communication to Publishers," September 20, 1900, Reid Papers.

117. The New York City papers thus applying were the *Tribune, Herald, Evening Telegram, Evening Post, World, Evening World, Journal and Advertiser, Brooklyn Daily Eagle, Times, Press, Evening Mail and Express, Staats Zeitung, Abendblatt der Staats Zeitung,* and *Commercial Advertiser,* according to attendance at the meeting. Typed minutes of meeting, September 21, 1900, Reid Papers. Other New York City papers qualifying for membership at the end of September were *Courrier des Etats Unis, New Yorker Herold & Revue, Journal of Commerce,* and *Gross New Yorker Zeitung.* AP, *Proceedings* (1900), p. 79.

118. AP, *Annual Report* (1900–1901), pp. 55-58, 60.

119. Tabulations combined from separate lists of members and protest rights in AP, *Proceedings* (1900), pp. 74-144.

120. Based on crude bar graphs published in mid-1917 by AP, the following are AP's total membership and the percentages of evening papers at the end of each year: 1900, 612, 58.3%; 1901, 612, 58.3%; 1902, 621, 59.6%; 1903, 652, 60.6%; 1904, 680, 61%; 1905, 715, 61.4%; 1906, 740, 60.7%; 1907, 800, 61.25%; 1908, 800, 61.25%; 1909, 800, 61.25%; 1910, 820, 62.2%; 1911, 825, 62.9%; 1912, 850, 62.4%; 1913, 885, 62.4%; 1914, 910, 62.7%; 1915, 910, 62.7%; 1916, 949, 61.5%; and 1917, 1,036, 62.7%. Associated Press, *Traffic Bulletin,* July 1, 1917, pp. 8-9.

121. Lee, *Daily Newspaper,* pp. 719-20.

122. AP, *Annual Report* (1904-5), p. 67.

123. Associated Press v. United States, 326 U.S. 1, 20 (1945).

Chapter 7

1. Oswald Garrison Villard, *Some Weaknesses of Modern Journalism* (Lawrence: University of Kansas *News-Bulletin,* November 2, 1914).

2. AP, *Annual Report* (1897), p. 487.

3. "Social institution" is used in this book in its common meaning: a structured, enduring pattern of human behavior and relationships designed to cope with specific sociocultural problems.

4. Lee, *Daily Newspaper,* p. 537; and *Fourth Estate,* May 19, 1898, p. 1.

5. J. A. Morris, *Deadline,* p. 23.

6. Ibid., p. 19.

7. Table 1 in the Appendix; and AP, *Traffic Bulletin,* July 1, 1917, p. 9.

8. AP, *Proceedings* (1900), p. 14, see Art. VIII, sec. 7.

9. In fact, AP's board on February 20, 1901, decided that "the placing of an operator of any other news gathering or distributing association in the office of an [AP] paper is a step which establishes a condition which will be likely to permit [AP's] news. . .to be disclosed to unauthorized persons. . . ." AP, *Annual Report* (1900-1901), p. 80.

10. The petition, answer, and decision are reprinted in AP, *Annual Report* (1903-4), pp. 35-45.

11. This would, as we shall see, be a greater problem for Hearst, many of whose papers took both AP and his own International News Service after 1909. But it would also become a problem for Scripps, who, in the course of expanding his chain, might purchase an AP paper and

introduce United Press service. The *Toledo News-Bee,* an AP paper, acquired for the Scripps-McRae chain in 1903, is a case in point. To avoid AP's preoccupation with the "inviolability" of its news report, the Scripps news wire was installed in an adjoining building. The *News-Bee,* however, then ran afoul of another AP bylaw prohibiting members from supplying news of its territory to outside newbro-kerages. See various letters and memoranda during 1909, especially a copy of H. N. Rickey to Philip R. Dillon, March 23, 1909, in Cochran Papers.

12. "The United Press Association," Cochran Papers.

13. Milton A. McRae, *Forty Years in Newspaperdom: The Autobiography of a Newspaper Man* (New York: Brentano's, 1924), p. 122.

14. J. A. Morris, *Deadline Every Minute,* p. 19; and Frank R. Ford, ed., *A Handbook of Scripps-Howard,* 2nd ed. (Cincinnati, 1967), p. 73.

15. "The United Press Association," Cochran Papers; and McRae, *Forty Years,* p. 122.

16. "The United Press Association," Cochran Papers.

17. Ibid.; and J. A. Morris, *Deadline Every Minute,* pp. 19, 23, 25. Al-though incorporated in the plural form, Scripps's new newsbrokerage was usually referred to as United Press Associations, or simply United Press.

18. Biographical material on Howard is drawn from *Current Biography, 1940,* s.v. "Howard, Roy Wilson"; Forrest Davis, "Press Lord," *Saturday Evening Post,* March 12, 1938, pp. 5-7, 30, 32, 34, reprinted in [Saturday Evening Post], *Post Biographies of Famous Journalists,* edited by John E. Drewry (Athens: University of Georgia Press, 1942), pp. 167-86; Ford, *Handbook,* pp. 69-77; *Scripps-Howard News,* "Story of Scripps-Howard," pp. 24-27; and J. A. Morris, *Deadline Every Minute,* pp. 23-128 passim.

19. Scripps, *Old Crank,* pp. 219, 221.

20. Hugh Baillie, *High Tension: The Recollections of Hugh Baillie* (New York: Harper, 1959), p. 34.

21. Stephen Vincent Benet, "The United Press," *Fortune* 7 (May 1933): 70-71.

22. F. Davis, "Press Lord," pp. 6, 30.

23. Youth was for many years a trademark of UP staffers. Plucky young reporters barely into their twenties from small-town newspapers and Scripps-McRae (later Scripps-Howard) newspaper staffs went careen-ing from bureau to bureau in UP in a whirlwind tour of the nation or globe, some being lifted into administrative duty well before their thirtieth birthdays. Even as late as 1933, one and a half years in a bu-reau for a young news person was average and three years was a long

time. The oldest man in UP in 1933 was fifty-six years of age and the rest were between twenty-two and forty-five. Benet, "United Press," p. 104.

24. Jack Alexander, "Rip-roaring Baillie," *Saturday Evening Post*, June 1, 1946, p. 39, reprinted in [Saturday Evening Post], *More Post Biographies*, edited by John E. Drewry (Athens: University of Georgia Press, 1947), pp. 1-34.

25. Following details of UP's early operations are from J. A. Morris, *Deadline Every Minute*, pp. 23, 25, 29, 39, and a typed publicity release, dated November 18, 1938, Kenneth Smith Papers, United Press International, New York.

26. AP, *Annual Report* (1908), p. 143; and J. A. Morris, *Deadline Every Minute*, pp. 36, 167.

27. J. A. Morris, *Deadline Every Minute*, pp. 33-34; and Kent Cooper, *Kent Cooper and the Associated Press: An Autobiography* (New York: Random House, 1959), pp. 32-36.

28. Cooper, *Kent Cooper*, p. 42.

29. J. A. Morris, *Deadline Every Minute*, p. 32.

30. Ibid., pp. 36, 56.

31. William G. Shepherd, *Confessions of a War Correspondent* (New York: Harper, 1917), pp. 18-19.

32. J. A. Morris, *Deadline Every Minute*, pp. 118-20; and "United Press," a typed publicity release, dated November, 1932, Kenneth Smith Papers.

33. J.A. Morris, *Deadline Every Minute*, pp. 50, 64, 76, 118.

34. The AP-Reuters contract was to expire in 1913, and the Reuters man in New York City, S. Levy Lawson, was so impressed with UP's early success that as early as 1909 he was recommending that his employer shift his contract to the UP. Howard and Lawson both traveled to London in 1912 to discuss a possible contract, but Howard broke off talks, preferring to see UP develop as an independent worldwide news-gathering and distributing agency. It had in 1911 established a news-supply contract with the Nippon Dempo Tsushin-sha, Japan's newsbrokerage, which in turn served several large Japanese news-papers. Ibid., pp. 54-55, 102; "Memorandum re United Press," typed publicity release, dated June 21, 1939, Kenneth Smith Papers; and Robert W. Desmond, *Windows on the World: The Information Process in a Changing Society, 1900-1920* (Iowa City: University of Iowa Press, 1980), p. 126.

35. For more detailed accounts of these South American affairs, see J. A. Morris, *Deadline Every Minute*, pp. 102-9; Cooper, *Kent Cooper*, pp. 65-67, 81-82; and Cooper, *Barriers Down*, pp. 4-6, 15-18, 34-80.

36. J. A. Morris, *Deadline Every Minute*, pp. 76-77.

37. Ibid., pp. 24, 127-28; and *Scripps-Howard News,* "Story of Scripps-Howard," pp. 28-29.

38. M. E. Stone, *Journalist,* p. 330.

39. [Associated Press], *"M.E.S.", His Book*...(New York: Harper, 1918), p. v.

40. M. E. Stone, *Journalist,* p. 332.

41. AP, *Annual Report* (1908), p. 80.

42. Cooper, *Kent Cooper,* p. 36.

43. AP, *Annual Report* (1921), p. 52. Uncharacteristically, Stone in his autobiography misreports his retirement as coming in 1919. M. E. Stone, *Journalist,* p. 361.

44. Among numerous sources on Stone's death, see especially [Associated Press], *"M.E.S." In Memoriam*... (New York, 1929).

45. Quoted in [Richard Edes Harrison], "(AP)," *Fortune* 15 (February 1937): 158.

46. Oswald Garrison Villard, *The Disappearing Daily: Chapters in American Newspaper Evolution* (New York: Knopf, 1944), p. 54.

47. Author's interviews with Philip G. Reed, September 3, 1970, and Kenneth Smith, September 1, 1970, both in New York City.

48. J. Richard Cote, "A Study of Accuracy of Two Wire Services," *Journalism Quarterly* 47 (Winter 1970): 660-66.

49. Frank B. Noyes, "The Associated Press," *North American Review* 197 (May 1913): 701-2.

50. Karl A. Bickel, "Bickel Reviews History of United Press," *Editor & Publisher,* April 30, 1927, pp. 31, 53.

51. AP, *Annual Report* (1893), p. 74.

52. AP, *Annual Report* (1894), p. 140.

53. W. A. Swanberg, *Citizen Hearst: A Biography of William Randolph Hearst* (New York: Scribners, 1961), pp. 75-76.

54. *Fourth Estate,* October 1, 1896, pp. 1-2.

55. Ferdinand Lundberg, *Imperial Hearst: A Social Biography* (New York: Equinox Cooperative Press, 1936), p. 53; *Fourth Estate,* April 8, 1897, p. 1; and *Newspaperdom,* April 8, 1897, p. 5.

56. AP, *Annual Report* (1897), p. 170.

57. AP, *Proceedings* (1900), pp. 74-144.

58. AP, *Annual Report* (1906-7), p. 115.

59. AP, *Annual Report* (1900-1901), pp. 3-4, and (1903-4), p. 6.

60. AP, *Annual Report* (1906-7), p. 3. The court's decision is reprinted on pp. 115-19.

61. AP, *Annual Report* (1902-3), p. 5. Quotation is from the board's annual report, dated September 10, 1902.

62. Cooper, *Kent Cooper,* pp. 198-99.

63. AP, *Annual Report* (1924), p. 99. For an example of Hearst's lobbying effort in this battle, see the large and impressive volume, [Hearst Corporation], *Shall the Individual Rights of Associated Press Franchise Holders Be Upheld?. . .* [(New York: Davidson], 1924). This, of course, did not end the animosity between Hearst and the AP directors. The next round of the fight is described, with a Hearstian slant, in Koenigsberg, *King News,* pp. 458-67.

64. Cooper, *Kent Cooper,* p. 199.

65. Ibid., pp. 196-97.

66. Ibid., pp. 138, 195.

67. AP, *Annual Report* (1902-3), pp. 92-93, and (1903-4), pp. 48-49.

68. AP, *Annual Report* (1909), p. 95.

69. Koenigsberg, *King News,* p. 434.

70. Lee, *Daily Newspaper,* pp. 538-39; "I N S," publicity release hand-dated 1938, "Highlights in the History and Development of I.N.S." an undated post-1937 chronology, "International News Service," publicity release dated November 30, 1946, and "From United Press International," publicity release hand-dated July 10, 1958, all from Kenneth Smith Papers; and Reed and Smith interviews.

71. Koenigsberg, *King News,* pp. 453-54.

72. Ibid., p. 456.

73. UP and INS figures generally were rounded off and reported in contexts that gave them public relations value for the agencies. AP reported its totals more precisely in the annual reports of the general manager or board of directors, and those totals were occasionally buttressed by published lists of members. For a fragmentary comparison of the agencies' own figures between 1892 and 1964, see the author's *American Wire Services,* pp. 396-97.

74. Lee, *Daily Newspaper,* pp. 722-23.

75. The total membership recorded in n. 123 of this chapter represents the following percentages of total U.S. dailies: 1900, 27.7%; 1901, 27.6%; 1902, 27.2%; 1903, 28.3%; 1904, 29%; 1905, 30.7%; 1906, 31.1%; 1907, 33.4%; 1908, 33.1%; 1909, 33.3%; 1910, 33.7%; 1911, 34.1%; 1912, 34.9%; 1913, 36.2%; 1914, 37.0%; 1915, 37.2%; 1916, 38.6%; 1917, 43%. Ibid.; and AP, *Traffic Bulletin,* July 1, 1917, pp. 8-9.

76. Figures used in this table are drawn from the author's "Trends in U.S. Newspapers' Wire Service Resources, 1934-66," *Journalism Quarterly* 43 (Winter 1966): 627-38; and Judith Sobel and Edwin Emery, "U.S. Dailies' Competition in Relation to Circulation Size: A Newspaper

Data Update," *Journalism Quarterly* 55 (Spring 1978): 145-49. Both studies relied on Editor & Publisher's *International Year Book*s for total dailies and dailies' newsbroker affiliations.

77. Carter Brooke Jones, "Journalist and Journalese," chap. 18 in *Dateline Washington: The Story of National Affairs Journalism in the Life and Times of the National Press Club,* edited by Cabell Phillips (New York: Doubleday, 1949), pp. 291-92.

78. Salvatore Cortesi, *My Thirty Years of Friendships* (New York: Harper, 1927), p. 16.

79. Baillie, *High Tension,* p. 71.

80. George Murray, *The Madhouse on Madison Street* (Chicago: Follett, 1965), p. 159, where the *Harper's* quote also appears. The article referred to here was H. D. Wheeler's "At the Front with Willie Hearst," *Harper's Weekly,* October 9, 1915, pp. 340-42.

81. International News Service v. Associated Press, 248 U.S. 215 (1918). Volume 2 of AP's *Law of the Associated Press,* published in 1919, is devoted to reprinting the opinions and filings in the case. For AP's view of the case, see M. E. Stone, *Journalist,* pp. 354-61; [AP], *"M.E.S.", His Book,* pp. 66-75. For an interesting view of the decision from INS's perspective, see Koenigsberg, *King News,* pp. 454-55; and Barry Faris, "The Role of the Wire Services," *Quill* 47 (December 1959): 16. A balanced discussion of the decision is Paul W. Sullivan's *News Piracy: Unfair Competition and the Misappropriation Doctrine.* Journalism Monographs, no. 56 (Lexington, Ky.: Association for Education in Journalism, 1978), pp. 4-8.

82. International News Service, *INS: The Story of International News Service* (n.p., [1955]), p. 1.

83. The quote is from J. A. Morris, *Deadline Every Minute,* p. 72. "Hellbox" was a receptacle in a newspaper composing room where used and leftover lead type was thrown for remelting.

84. Each newsbrokerage had its own favorite death-of-a-Pope story. AP was the first to report the death of Leo XIII in 1902. Gramling, pp. 168-69. UP claimed scoops on the deaths of Pius X in 1914 and Benedict XV in 1922. J. A. Morris, *Deadline Every Minute,* pp. 73-75.

85. The basic literature on this famous journalistic blunder includes Arthur Hornblow, Jr., "The Amazing Armistice: Inside Story of the Premature Peace Report," *Century* 103 (November 1921): 90-99; Roy Howard, "Premature Armistice," chap. 7 in Webb Miller, *I Found No Peace: The Journal of a Foreign Correspondent* (New York: Simon & Schuster, 1936), pp. 90-108; "Three Stages of a 24-Hour Wonder," *Fourth Estate,* November 9, 1918, p. 2; "Armistice Blunder to Get Coat of Oblivion," *Fourth Estate,* November 16, 1918, p. 2; Josephus Daniels, *The Wilson Era: Years of War and After, 1917-1923* (Chapel Hill: University of North Carolina, 1946), chap. 32, esp. pp. 338-43;

J. A. Morris, *Deadline Every Minute,* pp. 94-101; and Gramling, *AP,* pp. 277-81.

86. AP was premature with the Reims Armistice in Europe in 1945, and UP ended the Pacific phase of World War II too early. See J. C. Oestreicher, *The World Is Their Beat* (New York: Duell, Sloan & Pearce, 1945), pp. 13-14.

87. The Spanish-American War has attracted considerable literary attention: Charles H. Brown, *The Correspondents' War: Journalists in the Spanish-American War* (New York: Scribners, 1967); Joseph E. Wisan, *The Cuban Crisis as Reflected in the New York Press (1895-1898)* (New York: Columbia University Press, 1934); and Marcus M. Wilkerson, *Public Opinion and the Spanish-American War: A Study of War Propaganda* (Baton Rouge: Louisiana State University Press, 1932). Of special interest on newsbroking's involvement in the war are M. E. Stone, *Journalist,* pp. 228-30; and Diehl, *Correspondent,* pp. 256-91. Diehl, AP's assistant general manager at the time, directed the agency's coverage of the war.

88. M. E. Stone, *Journalist,* p. 228.

89. Diehl, *Correspondent,* p. 291.

90. AP, *Annual Report* (1902-3), p. 4, (1903-4), p. 4, (1904-5), pp. 3-4, and (1905-6), p. 3.

91. Villard, *Disappearing Daily,* p. 52. Elsewhere Villard discloses the committee's careful wording of this charge against Stone: His "social relations. . . with the individuals prominent in powerful financial circles, and likewise his acceptance of decorations from foreign governments without objection from the board of directors, had not unnaturally aroused unjust suspicion of the independence and impartiality of his administration of the news service." The committee was convinced that Stone had not been influenced by these relations, but it commented that AP's general manager should "by his personal conduct and relations give no ground for a suspicion of his independence and incorruptibility as the agent and representative of the press." Oswald Garrison Villard, *Fighting Years: Memoirs of a Liberal Editor* (New York: Harcourt, Brace, 1939), p. 251.

92. AP, *Annual Report* (1902-3), p. 3. John L. Given in 1907 compared contemporary foreign news coverage with that of just a few years earlier, observing that "plenty of newspaper workers. . . can remember the time when the appearance of a half-column long cablegram called for wide comment." He notes that at times one-fifth of AP's daily 50,000-word report consisted of foreign news in 1907. Given, *Making a Newspaper,* pp. 219-21.

93. Pollard, *Presidents,* pp. 571-72.

94. Roosevelt provided White House space for a press room after noticing a handful of reporters standing in the rain buttonholing visitors for news as they left the White House. Associated Press reporter William

W. Price reportedly was the first to keep the vigil outside the White House gate. Ibid., p. 574.

95. AP, *Annual Report* (1909), pp. 2-3.

96. Villard, *Disappearing Daily,* p. 6.

97. Rollo Ogden, "The Press and Foreign News," *Atlantic* 86 (September 1900): 390-91, where Lowell is also quoted. Emphasis in original.

98. Lippmann, *Public Opinion,* pp. 339, 341.

99. See esp. Shanks, "News," pp. 511-22; Aplin, "Associated Press Office," pp. 23-30; and [Rideing], "Metropolitan Newspaper," pp. 43-59.

100. W. H. Smith, "News Gatherer," pp. 524-36.

101. M. E. Stone, "Newspapers," reprinted in *Newspaperdom,* June 24, 1897.

102. Kloeber, "Press Association."

103. Melville E. Stone, "The Associated Press," *Century* 69 (April 1905): 888-95, 70 (May 1905): 143-51, (June 1905): 299-310, (July 1905): 379-86, and (August 1905): 504-10, also reprinted in [AP], *"M.E.S.", His Book,* pp. 91-173.

104. " 'Mensur' and 'Kriegsherr'," *The Nation,* May 17, 1906, p. 406; "The Associated Press and Germany," *The Nation,* May 31, 1906, p. 447; and "The Associated Press and Germany," *The Nation,* June 21, 1906, p. 509.

105. "Faked Cable News," *Independent,* November 1, 1906, pp. 1068-69.

106. William Kittle, "The Making of Public Opinion," *Arena* 41 (July 1909): 433-50.

107. "The Secretary of War: A Victim of Fake Journalism," *Outlook,* October 5, 1912, p. 236, and "The Associated Press and Fake Journalism," *Outlook,* October 19, 1912, pp. 328-29.

108. Max Sherover, *Fakes in American Journalism,* 3rd ed. (Brooklyn, N.Y.: Free Press League, 1916), p. 72.

109. The bylaw that threatened expulsion for members who permitted non-AP operators and wires into their news rooms, thus threatening the inviolability of the AP news report, was rescinded in 1915 in response to the attorney general's opinion. The AP board, despite a long record of hearings and threats to members on the basis of the bylaw, insisted that "the powers reserved under that By-law have never been used," adding that in practice "this By-law has been a dead letter." AP, *Annual Report* (1914), p. 5, with the attorney general's opinion reprinted on pp. 119-23. The entire proceeding is reprinted in AP, *Law of the Associated Press,* 1:644-725.

110. "The Associated Press as a Trust," *Literary Digest,* February 21, 1914, p. 364.

111. "The Associated Press under Fire" and "The 'Sun's' Complaint," *Outlook,* February 28, 1914, pp. 426-27.

112. Gregory Mason, "The Associated Press: I—A Criticism," and George Kennan, "The Associated Press, II—A Defense," *Outlook,* May 30, 1914, pp. 237-40, 249-50.

113. "The Associated Press," *Outlook,* July 18, 1914, pp. 631-32.

114. Will Irwin, "What's Wrong with the Associated Press?" *Harper's Weekly,* March 28, 1914, pp. 10-12.

115. Will Irwin, "The United Press," *Harper's Weekly,* April 25, 1914, pp. 6-8.

116. "Is There a News Monopoly?" *Collier's,* June 6, 1914, p. 16.

117. Melville E. Stone, "The Associated Press," a letter to the editor, *Collier's,* July 11, 1914, pp. 28-29. The exchange is also reprinted in pamphlet form, entitled *The Associated Press: Criticism and Reply* (n.p., [1914]), and appears in [AP], *"M.E.S.", His Book,* pp. 279-85.

118. Robert V. Hudson provides an insightful account of Irwin's activities as a free-lance writer and muckraker, noting that the Harper's articles on AP and UP "extended his reputation as a critic of the daily press" established by his "The American Newspaper" series in *Collier's* in 1911. See Hudson's *The Writing Game: A Biography of Will Irwin* (Ames: Iowa State University Press, 1982), esp. pp. 68-77.

119. An Observer, "The Problem of the Associated Press," *Atlantic* 114 (July 1914): 132-37.

120. Melville E. Stone, *Letter to the Editor, Atlantic Monthly* (n.p., 1914), also appearing in [AP], *"M.E.S.", His Book,* pp. 273-79. There is no evidence that *Atlantic* published this reply by Stone.

121. See, for example: Sinclair, *Brass Check;* Silas Bent, *Ballyhoo: The Voice of the Press* (New York: Boni & Liveright, 1927), and *Strange Bedfellows: A Review of Politics, Personalities, and the Press* (New York: Horace Liveright, 1928), esp. pp. 209-17; George Seldes, *Freedom of the Press* (Indianapolis: Bobbs-Merrill, 1935), esp. pp. 171-93; and Villard, *Disappearing Daily,* esp. pp. 40-69, 172-74, 201-03.

122. AP, *Service Bulletin,* February 1924, pp. 1-2.

123. See Barbara W. Tuchman's *The Zimmermann Telegram,* 2nd ed. (New York: Macmillan, 1966).

124. AP, *Annual Report* (1936), pp. 3-4.

125. Cooper, *Kent Cooper,* pp. 75-76.

126. Ibid., p. 188.

127. Schwarzlose, *American Wire Services,* pp. 136-58.

128. "Batten Confident of AP's Role in Industry's Future," *AP Log,* May 2, 1983, pp. 1-2.

129. The author finds the earliest consideration of an INS-UP merger made by Hearst people in 1926 during one of Hearst's battles with the AP hierarchy. See Koenigsberg, *King News,* pp. 463-65. A reasonably detailed account of the merger in 1957 is in Lindsay Chaney and Michael Cieply, *The Hearsts, Family and Empire: The Later Years* (New York: Simon & Schuster, 1981), pp. 194-99. A post-merger Spanish-language edition of Joe Alex Morris's UP history contains a brief account of the merger. See Morris, *Hora de Cierre a Cada Minuto: Historia de la United Press* (Buenos Aires: Ediciones Gure, 1959), pp. 373-75.

130. UPI, *UPI Reporter,* June 17, 1982.

131. Much is being published about the future of teletext and videotext as this volume is being completed, but for an overview with historical perspective, see Anthony Smith, *Goodbye, Gutenberg: The Newspaper Revolution of the 1980s* (New York: Oxford University Press, 1980). For AP's recent brush with a threatened AT & T takeover of news service, see Lawrence G. Blasko, "The Cat, the Burglar, and Santa," *Quill* 71 (April 1983): 22-25, and portions of accompanying articles. For opinions on the consent decree which, among other things, limits AT & T's news activities, see United States v. American Telephone and Telegraph, 8 Med. L. Rptr. 1574, 2118 (DC, DC, 1982).

BIBLIOGRAPHY

Comment

Anyone even casually acquainted with journalism history knows that escaping the Associated Press's prominence is impossible if one's research is anywhere in the general regions of news reporting, writing, and technology. Even though the modern AP dates from 1893, the name was affixed to news-gathering from the late 1840s. Most of the pre-1893 literature and primary source material deals with the AP, and well over half of the post-1893 material focuses on AP.

The author took this state of affairs as a challenge to uncover as much evidence as possible describing Abbot & Winans, the United States Associated Press, the independent news room, the Press Association of the Confederacy, Hasson's News Association, American Press Association, National Associated Press Company, the first United Press, Laffan News Service, Publishers' Press Association, Scripps-McRae Press Association, Scripps News Service, United Press Associations, Hearst's various news agencies, and United Press International. To the limit allowed by his feeble success in this endeavor, the author has attempted to give proper perspective to these agencies in the two volumes of this work. The fact remains, however, that winners, especially if they are self-styled cooperatives of newspapers scattered throughout the nation, are more likely to print and preserve their records, more likely to be written about, and more likely to write about themselves.

From a bibliographic standpoint, the history of newsbroking may be divided into three periods. In the first, extending up to 1865, the student relies on widely scattered and diverse sources for glimpses and mere suggestions about news-gathering activity. Most of the time devoted to this research was spent on following hunches and promising leads in quest of bits of pre-1865 information, not the least of which being some indication of the moment of creation of the New York City Associated Press. Some headway was made here in correcting previously reported misinformation and misimpressions and in bringing additional evidence to the subject. But the modest results of that effort reported in the first volume of this research, *The Nation's Newsbrokers: The Formative Years, from Pre-*

329

telegraph to 1865, came from scouring telegraphy's literature, city directories, newspaper files, and the sparse manuscript collections bearing on newsbroking up to 1865.

The second bibliographic period, from 1865 to 1900, is characterized by a gold mine of detailed and broad-based evidence arising from many manuscript collections bearing in some way on newsbroking. Once again AP dominates the source material, with the largest and most significant collections of papers being those of William Henry Smith, Whitelaw Reid, Joseph Pulitzer, and Victor F. Lawson. Smith's two enormous collections in Indianapolis and Columbus, Ohio, provide the student with an intimate study of daily operations, negotiations, economics, and politics for ten years at the head of the Western AP and for another ten years at the top of AP's national system. Meanwhile, the AP's growing propensity for cooperation and openness generated a meaty published literature of annual and special reports. AP's competitors, of course, were responding with their versions of newsbroking affairs. Thanks to this wealth of evidence, this volume traverses previously uncharted waters of journalism as a business in the last third of the nineteenth century. Whereas Volume 1 sets the record straight on numerous points and fleshes out the procedural and news report skeleton offered by its predecessors, Volume 2 offers fresh material and insights about a complicated chapter in American journalism history.

The third period, from 1900 to the present, consists increasingly of popular materials of sanitized comment and laundered description. Since the author's purpose in this research is to trace newsbroking's development to institutional status, which occurs roughly by the end of World War I, these volumes have successfully avoided having to deal with most of the thin and syrupy depictions of wire services in the twentieth century.

Listed on the following pages are the roughly 370 sources cited in the text, notes, and Appendix of this Volume 2. The first volume of this work contains its own bibliography of cited sources.

Manuscript Collections

Barnett, Claude A., Papers, 1919–67. Chicago Historical Society, Chicago.

Booth, George Gough, Papers, 1892–1926. Michigan Historical Collections, Bentley Library, Ann Arbor, Mich.

Clapp, William Warland, Papers, 1834–91. Houghton Library, Harvard University, Cambridge, Mass.

Clapp, William Warland, Papers, 1856–1911. Library of Congress, Washington, D.C.

Clapp, William W., Collection, New England Associated Press Papers, 1874–90. Baker Library, Harvard University Graduate School of Business Administration, Boston.

Cochran, Negley D., Papers, 1890–1940. Toledo Public Library, Toledo, Ohio.

Dun, R. G. & Co. Collection, New York City Series. Baker Library, Harvard University Graduate School of Business Administration, Boston.

Greeley, Horace, Papers, 1826–1928. Library of Congress, Washington, D.C.

Hood, Edwin M., Papers, 1875–1935. Library of Congress, Washington, D.C.

Jones, George E., Papers, 1845–94. New York Public Library, New York.

Lawson, Victor F., Papers, 1873–1925. Newberry Library, Chicago.

Lefferts Family Papers, 1849–1925. New York Historical Society, New York.

Marble, Manton, Papers, 1852–1916. Library of Congress, Washington, D.C.

Ochs, Adolph S., Papers, 1893–1939. American Jewish Archives, Cincinnati, Ohio.

Pulitzer, Joseph, Papers, 1880–1924. Library of Congress. Washington, D.C.

Pulitzer, Joseph, Papers, 1883–1911. Columbia University Library, New York.

Reed, Philip G., interview with author, September 3, 1970, New York.

Reid, Whitelaw, Papers, 1861–1912. Library of Congress, Washington, D.C.

Rosewater Family Papers, 1841–1940. American Jewish Archives, Cincinnati.

Smith, Kenneth, Papers. Privately held collection, United Press International, New York.

Smith, Kenneth, interviews with author, July 24, 1967, and September 1, 1970, New York.

Smith, William Henry, Papers, 1756–1907. Indiana Historical Society, Indianapolis.

Smith, William Henry, Papers, 1800–96. Ohio Historical Society, Columbus.
Smith, William Henry, Papers, 1864–95. Rutherford B. Hayes Library, Fremont, Ohio.
U.S. Department of Commerce and Labor. Record Group no. 122. National Archives, Washington, D.C.

Newspapers

Chicago Tribune
New York Sun
New York Times
New York Tribune
New York World
St. Louis *Missouri Republican*

Periodicals

American Newspaper Reporter
Atlantic
Collier's
Editor & Publisher
Fourth Estate
Harper's Monthly
Harper's Weekly
Independent
The Journalist
Literary Digest
The Nation
Newspaperdom
Outlook
Printers' Circular
The Quill
The Spirit of the Times
Telegrapher

Cases

Associated Press v. United States, 326 U.S. 1 (1945).
International News Service v. Associated Press, 248 U.S. 215 (1918).
Inter Ocean Publishing Co. v. Associated Press, 184 Ill. 438, 56 N.E. 822 (1900).

Lochner v. New York, 198 U.S. 45 (1905).

Matthews et al. v. Associated Press of the State of New York et el., 136 N.Y. (91 Sickels) 333 (1893).

Minnesota Tribune Company v. Associated Press, 83 F. 350 (1897).

Missouri ex rel. The Sayings Company v. Associated Press, 159 Mo. 410 (1898).

Munn v. Illinois, 94 U.S. 113 (1877).

Ohio State Journal v. Associated Press, Court of Common Pleas, Franklin County, Ohio, reprinted in Associated Press, *Annual Report* (1897), pp. 142-43.

United States v. American Telephone and Telegraph, 8 Med. L. Rptr. 1574, 2118 (DC, DC, 1982).

Books and Articles

Adams, F[rancis] C[olburn]. *President Hayes' Professional Reformers: The Two Smiths, Tommie and William Henry, Men after Hayes' Own Heart, How He Rewarded Them.* Washington, D.C.: Judd & Detweiler, 1880.

Alexander, Jack. "Rip-roaring Baillie." *Saturday Evening Post,* June 1, 1946, pp. 9ff, and June 8, 1946, pp. 20ff.

American Press Association. *Charter and By-laws.* Philadelphia: Sherman, 1872.

[Anglo-American Telegraph Company]. *The Atlantic Telegraph, Its History from the Commencement of the Undertaking in 1854 to the Sailing of the "Great Eastern" in 1866.* London: Bacon, 1866.

Aplin, William. "At the Associated Press Office." *Putnam's* 6 (July 1870): 23-30.

Appletons' Cyclopaedia of American Biography. Edited by James Grant Wilson and John Fiske. 7 vols. New York: D. Appleton, 1894-1900.

Associated Negro Press. *The Service of the Associated Negro Press, 1919-1920: Annual.* Edited by Nahum Daniel Brascher. N.p., [1920].

Associated Press. *Annual Report.* Chicago & New York: annual, 1893-.

———. *AP Log.* New York: weekly.

———. *AP World.* New York: quarterly, 1945-.

———. *Law of the Associated Press.* 2 vols. New York: Associated Press, 1914-19.

[———]. *"M.E.S.", His Book: A Tribune and a Souvenir of the Twenty-five Years, 1893-1918, of the Service of Melville E. Stone as General Manager of the Associated Press.* New York: Harper, 1918.

[———]. *"M.E.S.", In Memoriam: A Tribute to the Life and Accomplishments of Melville E. Stone, 1848–1929, General Manager of The Associated Press, 1892–1921.* New York, 1929.

———. *Preliminary Proceedings.* New York, 1900.

———. *Service Bulletin.* New York: irregular, 1904–.

———. *Traffic Bulletin.* New York: irregular, 1916–.

Ault, Phillip H. "The (almost) Russian-American Telegraph." *American Heritage* 26 (June 1975): 12ff.

Ayer, N. W., & Son. *American Newspaper Annual.* New York, 1880–1920.

Baehr, Harry W., Jr. *The New York Tribune since the Civil War.* New York: Dodd, Mead, 1936.

Baillie, Hugh. *High Tension: The Recollections of Hugh Baillie.* New York: Harper, 1959.

Bain, George Grantham. "The Telegraphic Service of News." *Newspaperdom,* April 23, 1896, p. 1.

Barnard, Harry. *Rutherford B. Hayes and His America.* Indianapolis: Bobbs-Merrill, 1954.

Beard, Richard L., and Cyril E. Zoerner II. "Associated Negro Press: Its Founding, Ascendency and Demise." *Journalism Quarterly* 46 (Spring 1969): 47-52.

Benet, Stephen Vincent. "The United Press." *Fortune* 7 (May 1933): 67ff.

Bent, Silas. *Ballyhoo: The Voice of the Press.* New York: Boni & Liveright, 1927.

———. *Strange Bedfellows: A Review of Politics, Personalities, and the Press.* New York: Horace Liveright, 1928.

Bickel, Karl A. "Bickel Reviews History of United Press." *Editor & Publisher,* April 30, 1927, pp. 31, 53.

Blasko, Lawrence G. "The Cat, the Burglar, and Santa." *Quill* 71 (April 1983): 22-25.

"The Boston Herald." *Bay State Monthly (New England Magazine)* 2 (October 1884): 22-35.

[Brooker-]Gross, Susan Ruth. "Spatial Organization of the News Wire Services in the Nineteenth Century United States." Ph.D. dissertation, University of Illinois, 1977.

———. "Timeliness: Interpretations from a Sample of 19th Century Newspapers." *Journalism Quarterly* 58 (Winter 1981): 594-98.

Brown, Charles H. *The Correspondents' War: Journalists in the Spanish-American War.* New York: Scribners, 1967.

Brown, [Ernest] Francis. *Raymond of the Times.* New York: Norton, 1951.

Bruchey, Stuart. *The Roots of American Economic Growth, 1607–1861: An Essay in Social Causation.* New York: Harper & Row, 1965.

Bryan, George S. *Edison, The Man and His Work.* New York: Knopf, 1926.

Bryan, Wilhelmus Bogart. *A History of the National Capital from Its Foundation through the Period of the Adoption of the Organic Act.* 2 vols. New York: Macmillan, 1914–16.

[Butler, Benjamin F.] "The Despot of To-day." *Old and New* 11 (January 1875): 7-18.

Carey, Arthur C. "Effects of the Pony Express and the Transcontinental Telegraph upon Selected California Newspapers." *Journalism Quarterly* 51 (Summer 1974): 320-23.

Carter, Samuel, III. *Cyrus Field, Man of Two Worlds.* New York: Putnam, 1968.

Carter, W. F. "AP Seems To Be Going 'Electronic' in a Big Way; Blant Kimbell Heads New Technical Triumvirate." *AP World* 16 (Winter 1961–62): 2ff.

Chaney, Lindsay, and Michael Cieply. *The Hearsts, Family and Empire: The Later Years.* New York: Simon & Schuster, 1981.

Chicago Inter Ocean. *Centennial History of the City of Chicago, Its Men and Institutions.* [2nd ed.] Chicago: Inter Ocean, 1905.

Cochran, Negley D. *E. W. Scripps.* New York: Harcourt, Brace, 1933.

Cochran, Thomas C. *Business in American Life: A History.* New York: McGraw-Hill, 1972.

Cochran, Thomas C., and William Miller. *The Age of Enterprise: A Social History of Industrial America.* New York: Macmillan, 1942.

Connery, T[homas] B. "Great Business Operations—The Collection of News." *Cosmopolitan* 23 (May 1897): 21-32.

Coon, Horace. *American Tel & Tel: The Story of a Great Monopoly.* New York: Longmans, Green, 1939.

Cooper, Kent. *Barriers Down: The Story of the News Agency Epoch.* New York: Farrar & Rinehart, 1942.

———. *Kent Cooper and the Associated Press: An Autobiography.* New York: Random House, 1959.

Correspondence Relating to the Proposed Joint Purse Arrangement between the Direct U.S. Cable Co. and the Anglo-American Telegraph Company. N.p., [1876].

Cortesi, Salvatore. *My Thirty Years of Friendships.* New York: Harper, 1927.

Cortissoz, Royal. *The Life of Whitelaw Reid.* 2 vols. New York: Scribners, 1921.

Cote, J. Richard. "A Study of Accuracy of Two Wire Services." *Journalism Quarterly* 47 (Winter 1970): 660-66.

Craig, Daniel H. *Answer of Daniel H. Craig, Organizer and Manager of the New York Associated Press, 1850 to 1867, [sic] and Originator and Promoter of Machine or Rapid Telegraphing, to the Interrogatories of the U.S. Senate Committee on Education and Labor at the City of New York, 1883.* New York, 1883.

——. "Automatic Telegraphy." *Scientific American* 24 (January 1, 1871): 4.

——. *Craig's Manual of the Telegraph Illustrating the Electro-Mechanical System of the American "Rapid" Telegraph Co. of New York Designed for Use in Schools, Business Colleges, Counting Rooms and the Home Circle.* New York: John Polhemus, 1879.

——. *Machine Telegraph of To-day.* N.p., 1888, 1890, 1891.

——. *Startling Facts! Practical Machine Telegraphy: One Thousand Words per Minute.* N.p., [1888].

Creelman, James. "James Gordon Bennett." *Cosmopolitan* 33 (May 1902): 44-47.

Cullom, Shelby M. "The Government and the Telegraph." *Forum* 4 (February 1888): 561-72.

Curl, Donald W. *Murat Halstead and the Cincinnati Commercial.* Boca Raton: University Presses of Florida, 1980.

Current Biography. New York: H. W. Wilson, 1940–.

Dana, Charles A. *The Art of Newspaper Making: Three Lectures.* 1895. New York: D. Appleton, 1900.

Danielian, N[oobar] R[etheos]. *A. T. & T.: The Story of Industrial Conquest.* New York: Vanguard, 1939.

Daniels, Josephus. *The Wilson Era: Years of War and After, 1917–1923.* Chapel Hill: University of North Carolina Press, 1946.

Davis, Elmer. *History of the New York Times, 1851–1921.* New York: Times, 1921.

Davis, Forrest. "Press Lord." *Saturday Evening Post,* March 12, 1838, pp. 5ff.

Davis, J. W. (Bill). "Washington AP: World's Greatest and Most Productive News Team." *AP World* 16 (Autumn 1961): 3-13.

De Baggio, Thomas, and Julia Aldridge. "Black News Services: Dying of Neglect?" *Columbia Journalism Review* 13 (July-August 1974): 48-49.

Dedmon, Emmett. *Fabulous Chicago.* 2nd ed. New York: Atheneum, 1981.

Dennis, Charles H. *Victor Lawson, His Time and His Work.* Chicago: University of Chicago Press, 1935.

Desmond, Robert W. *The Information Process: World News Reporting to the Twentieth Century.* Iowa City: University of Iowa Press, 1978.

———. *Windows on the World: The Information Process in a Changing Society, 1900-1920.* Iowa City: University of Iowa Press, 1980.

Detweiler, Frederick G. *The Negro Press in the United States.* Chicago: University of Chicago Press, 1922.

Dictionary of American Biography. 22 vols. New York: Scribners, 1928–44.

Diehl, Charles Sanford. *The Staff Correspondent: How the News of the World Is Collected and Dispatched by a Body of Trained Press Writers.* San Antonio, Texas: Clegg, 1931.

Dorfman, Joseph. *The Economic Mind in American Civilization.* 5 vols. New York: Viking, 1946–59.

Dreiser, Theodore. *A Book about Myself.* New York: Boni & Liveright, 1922.

Drell, Muriel Bernitt, ed. "Letters by Richard Smith of the Cincinnati Gazette." *Mississippi Valley Historical Review* 26 (March 1940): 535-54.

Dugan, James. *The Great Iron Ship.* New York: Harper, 1953.

Duncan, Bingham. *Whitelaw Reid, Journalist, Politician, Diplomat.* Athens: University of Georgia Press, 1975.

Dyer, Frank Lewis, and Thomas Commerford Martin. *Edison, His Life and Inventions.* 2 vols. New York: Harper, 1929.

Eastlake, Abram P. "The Great Monopoly." *Lippincott's* 6 (October 1870): 362-71.

Ely, Richard T. "The Telegraph Monopoly." *North American Review* 149 (July 1889): 44-53.

Emery, Edwin, and Michael Emery. *The Press and America: An Interpretive History of the Mass Media.* 5th ed. Englewood Cliffs, N.J.: Prentice-Hall, 1984.

Evans, Linda J. "Claude A. Barnett and the Associated Negro Press." *Chicago History* 12 (Spring 1983): 44-56.

Ewert, Walter E. "The History of the Chicago Inter Ocean, 1872-1914." Master's thesis, Northwestern University, 1940.

Faris, Barry. "The Role of the Wire Services." *Quill* 47 (December 1959): 15-16.

Field, Cyrus W. "Government Telegraphy." *North American Review* 142 (March 1886): 227-29.

———. *Prospects of the Atlantic Telegraph.* New York, 1862.

Fite, Emerson David. *Social and Industrial Conditions in the North during the Civil War.* New York: Macmillan, 1910.

Ford, Frank R., ed. *A Handbook of Scripps-Howard.* 2nd ed. Cincinnati, 1967.

Gavit, John Palmer. *The Reporter's Manual: A Handbook for Newspaper Men.* N.p., 1903.

George, Henry, Jr. *The Life of Henry George.* 1900. New York: Robert Schalkenbach Foundation, 1960.

Given, John L. *Making a Newspaper.* New York: Henry Holt, 1907.

Glover, John George, and William Bouck Cornell, eds. *The Development of American Industries, Their Economic Significance.* 3rd ed. New York: Prentice-Hall, 1951.

Gobright, L[awrence] A. *Recollection of Men and Things at Washington during the Third of a Century.* 2nd ed. Philadelphia: Claxton, Remsen & Haffelfinger, 1869.

Government Telegraph: Some Opinions of the Press in Opposition Thereto. N.p., [1887].

Gramling, Oliver. *AP: The Story of News.* New York: Farrar & Rinehart, 1940.

Grant, E. B. *Is Governmental Control of the Telegraph Desirable?* N.p., [1884].

Grant, James. *The Newspaper Press: Its Origin, Progress, and Present Position.* 3 vols. London: Tinsley Brothers, 1871–72.

Gray, Edgar Laughlin. "The Career of William Henry Smith, Politician-Journalist." Ph.D. dissertation, Ohio State University, 1951.

Green, Norvin. "The Government and the Telegraph." *North American Review* 137 (November 1883): 422-34.

———. *Postal Telegraphs: Statements of Dr. Norvin Green, President, Western Union Telegraph Company, to the Committee on Post Offices and Post Roads of the House of Representatives,*

Washington, D.C., February 28th, May 20th and June 9th, 1890. N.p., [1890].

———. *Statement Submitted to the Senate Committee on Post-Offices and Post-Roads.* N.p., [1884].

Gregory, Winifred, ed. *American Newspapers, 1821–1936: A Union List of Files Available in the United States and Canada.* New York: H. W. Wilson, 1937.

Halstead, Murat, and J. Frank Beale, Jr. *Life of Jay Gould: How He Made His Millions.* Philadelphia: Edgewood, 1892.

Harlow, Alvin F. *Old Wires and New Waves: The History of the Telegraph, Telephone, and Wireless.* New York: D. Appleton-Century, 1936.

[Harrison, Richard Edes]. "(AP)." *Fortune* 15 (February 1937): 88ff.

Hart, Jim Allee. *A History of the St. Louis Globe-Democrat.* Columbia: University of Missouri Press, 1961.

Hayes, Rutherford Birchard. *Diary and Letters of Rutherford Birchard Hayes.* Edited by Charles Richard Williams, 5 vols. Columbus: Ohio State Archaeological and Historical Society, 1922–26.

———. *Hayes: The Diary of a President, 1875–1881.* Edited by T. Harry Williams. New York: McKay, 1964.

[Hearst Corporation]. *Shall the Individual Rights of Associated Press Franchise Holders Be Upheld? Prepared on Behalf of the Baltimore News and the Rochester Journal and Post Express in Defense of Their Exclusive Membership Rights in the Associated Press, and Opposed to the Granting of Membership to the Baltimore Evening Sun and the Rochester Times-Union.* [New York: Davidson Press], 1924.

Hogan, Lawrence D. *A Black National News Service: The Associated Negro Press and Claude Barnett, 1919–1945.* Cranbury, N.J.: Associated University Presses, 1984.

Hornblow, Arthur, Jr. "The Amazing Armistice: Inside Story of the Premature Peace Report." *Century* 103 (November 1921): 90-99.

Hoyt, Edwin P. *The Goulds: A Social History.* New York: Weybright & Talley, 1969.

Hubbard, Gardiner G. "Government Control of the Telegraph." *North American Review* 137 (December 1883): 521-35.

———. *In the Matter of the Postal Telegraph Bill.* N.p., [1872].

———. *The Proposed Changes in the Telegraphic System.* Boston: James R. Osgood, 1873.

Hudson, Frederic. *Journalism in the United States from 1690 to 1872*. New York: Harper, 1873.

Hudson, Robert V. *The Writing Game: A Biography of Will Irwin*. Ames: Iowa State University Press, 1982.

Innis, Harold A. *The Press, A Neglected Factor in the Economic History of the Twentieth Century*. London: Oxford University Press, 1949.

International News Service. *INS: The Story of International News Service*. N.p., [1955].

Irwin, Will. "The United Press." *Harper's Weekly,* April 25, 1914, pp. 6-8.

———. "What's Wrong with the Associated Press?" *Harper's Weekly,* March 28, 1914, pp. 10-12.

Jennings, L. J. "Mr. Raymond and Journalism." *Galaxy* 9 (April 1870): 466-74.

Johnson, W. H. "The Slavery Controversy in America." Review of *A Political History of Slavery . . .* by William Henry Smith. *The Dial,* July 16, 1903, pp. 33-34.

Josephson, Matthew. *The Robber Barons: The Great American Capitalists, 1861–1901*. Boston: Harcourt, Brace, 1934.

Judson, Katharine B., comp. *Selected Articles on Government Ownership of Telegraph and Telephone*. In the Debaters' Handbook Series. White Plains, N.Y.: H. W. Wilson, 1914.

Kansas and Missouri Associated Press. *Charter and By-Laws of the Kansas and Missouri Associated Press, Revised January 31, 1883*. Topeka, Kan.: Commonwealth, 1883.

Keeler, Bronson, C. "Public Control of the Telegraph." *Forum* 9 (June 1890): 450-60.

Kellogg Newspaper Company, A. N. *Kellogg's Auxiliary Hand-Book*. Chicago: A. N. Kellogg, 1878.

Kennan, George. "The Associated Press, II—A Defense." *Outlook,* May 30, 1914, pp. 240ff.

———. *Tent Life in Siberia and Adventures among the Koraks and Other Tribes in Kamtchatka and Northern Asia*. New York: Putnam, 1870.

Kesterton, W[ilfred] H. *A History of Journalism in Canada*. Toronto: McClelland & Stewart, 1967.

Kinsley, Philip. *The Chicago Tribune, Its First Hundred Years*. 3 vols. New York: Knopf, 1943; Chicago: Tribune, 1945–46.

Kitch, Kenneth. "The Associated Press in Kansas: Its Background and Development." Master's thesis, University of Kansas, 1937.

Kittle, William. "The Making of Public Opinion." *Arena* 41 (July 1909): 433-50.

Kloeber, Charles Edward, Jr. "The American Newspaper: IX. The Press Association." *Bookman* 20 (November 1904): 196-212.

Knight, Oliver. *Following the Indian Wars: The Story of the Newspaper Correspondents among the Indian Campaigners.* Norman: University of Oklahoma Press, 1960.

Knights, Peter R. " 'Competition' in the U.S. Daily Newspaper Industry, 1865–68." *Journalism Quarterly* 45 (Autumn 1968): 473-80.

———. *The Press Association War of 1866–1867.* Journalism Monographs, no. 6. Austin, Texas: Association for Education in Journalism, 1967.

Koenigsberg, M[oses]. *King News: An Autobiography.* Philadelphia: F. A. Stokes, 1941.

Lakeside Directory of the City of Chicago. Chicago: Lakeside Press, 1876/77–83.

Lee, Alfred McClung. *The Daily Newspaper in America: The Evolution of a Social Instrument.* New York: Macmillan, 1937.

Lippmann, Walter. *Public Opinion.* New York: Macmilllan, 1922.

Livesay, J. F. B. *The Canadian Press, Its Birth and Development.* N.p., [1939].

Long, Andrew. "The Federated Press." *Survey,* October 23, 1920, pp. 126-27.

Lundberg, Ferdinand. *Imperial Hearst: A Social Biography.* New York: Equinox Cooperative Press, 1936.

Lyons, Louis M. *Newspaper Story: One Hundred Years of the Boston Globe.* Cambridge, Mass.: Belknap Press of Harvard University, 1971.

McCloskey, Robert G. *The American Supreme Court.* Chicago: University of Chicago Press, 1960.

McDonald, Philip B. *A Saga of the Seas: The Story of Cyrus W. Field and the Laying of the First Atlantic Cable.* New York: Wilson-Erickson, 1937.

McJimsey, George T. *Genteel Partisan: Manton Marble, 1834–1917.* Ames: Iowa State University Press, 1971.

McNaught, Carlton. *Canada Gets the News.* Toronto: Ryerson, 1940.

McNicol, Don. "Phillips Code, Telegraphers' 'Short-Hand.' " *Dots and Dashes* 6 (September-October 1969): 3.

McRae, Milton A. *Forty Years in Newspaperdom: The Autobiography of a Newspaper Man.* New York: Brentano's, 1924.

Magnetic Telegraph Company. *Articles of Association and Charter from the State of Maryland of the Magnetic Telegraph Company*

Together with the Office Regulations and the Minutes of the Meetings of Stockholders and Board of Directors. New York: Chatterton & Crist, [1852].

Marbut, F[rederick] B. *News from the Capital: The Story of Washington Reporting.* Carbondale: Southern Illinois University Press, 1971.

Mason, Gregory. "The Associated Press: I—A Criticism." *Outlook,* May 30, 1914, pp. 237-40.

Maverick, Augustus. *Henry J. Raymond and the New York Press for Thirty Years: Progress of American Journalism from 1840 to 1870.* Hartford, Conn.: A. S. Hale, 1870.

Means, D. McG. "Government Telegraphy." *North American Review* 139 (July 1884): 51-66.

Miller, Webb. *I Found No Peace: The Journal of a Foreign Correspondent.* New York: Simon & Schuster, 1936.

Moos, Malcolm. *The Republicans: A History of Their Party.* New York: Random House, 1956.

Morgan, James. *Charles H. Taylor, Builder of the Boston Globe.* [Boston, 1923].

Morris, Joe Alex. *Deadline Every Minute: The Story of the United Press.* Garden City, N.Y.: Doubleday, 1957.

———. *Hora de Cierre a Cada Minuto: Historia de la United Press.* Buenos Aires: Ediciones Gure, 1959.

Morris, Richard B., ed. *Encyclopedia of American History.* 2nd ed. New York: Harper & Row, 1970.

Mott, Frank Luther. *American Journalism: A History, 1690–1960.* 3rd ed. New York: Macmillan, 1962.

Murray, George. *The Madhouse on Madison Street.* Chicago: Follett, 1965.

Myers, Gustavus. *History of the Great American Fortunes.* 3 vols. 1909. Reprint (3 vols. in 1). New York: Modern Library, 1936.

National Associated Press Company. *The National Associated Press Company (Limited).* N.p., [1877].

National Telegraph Company, Executive Committee. *Report of the Executive Committee of the National Telegraph Co. to Subscribers of Its Capital Stock on Little's Automatic System of Fast Telegraphy, with Letters from D. H. Craig, Esq., General Agent of the New York Associated Press from 1848 to 1867, [sic] and Geo. B. Hicks, General Agent of the Western Associated Press.* New York: Fisher & Field, 1869.

Newsom, D. Earl, ed. *The Newspaper: Everything You Need to Know to Make It in the Newspaper Business.* Englewood Cliffs, N.J.: Prentice-Hall, 1981.

New York Associated Press. *Annual Report of the General Agent.* New York, 186[3].

———. *Annual Report of the General Manager for the Year 1891 Made to the President of the New York Associated Press.* Chicago: J. M. W. Jones, 1893.

[———]. General News Association of the City of New York. *Rules.* New York: L. H. Bridgham, 1874.

[New York and Western] Associated Press. *(Private Circular), The Associated Press.* N.p., [1883].

———. *Resolutions Adopted by the Western Associated Press in Convention at Detroit, 1882.* New York: Republic, 1891.

New York Graphic. *The Press and the Telegraph: The Ramifications and Oppressions of Two Gigantic Monopolies.* N.p., [1874].

Nichols, M[ark] E. *(CP): The Story of the Canadian Press.* Toronto: Ryerson, 1948.

Nord, David Paul. *Newspapers and New Politics: Midwestern Municipal Reform, 1890–1900.* Studies in American History and Culture, no. 27. Ann Arbor, Mich.: UMI Research Press, 1981.

North, S. N. D. *History and Present Condition of the Newspaper and Periodical Press of the United States with a Catalogue of the Publications of the Census Year.* Washington, D.C.: Government Printing Office, 1884.

Northwestern Associated Press. *Records of Incorporation, By-laws and Existing Contracts.* Springfield, Ill.: Illinois State Register, 1887.

———. *Seventh Annual Meeting.* N.p., 1873.

Noyes, Frank B. "The Associated Press." *North American Review* 197 (May 1913): 701-10.

O'Brien, Frank M. *The Story of The Sun, New York, 1833–1928.* 2nd ed. New York: D. Appleton, 1928.

O'Connor, Richard. *Gould's Millions.* Garden City, N.Y.: Doubleday, 1962.

———. *The Scandalous Mr. Bennett.* Garden City, N.Y.: Doubleday, 1962.

Oestreicher, J[ohn] C. *The World Is Their Beat.* New York: Duell, Sloan & Pearce, 1945.

Ogden, Rollo. "The Press and Foreign News." *Atlantic* 86 (September 1900): 390-93.

One of the Reasons for Telegraphic Reform: Power and Tyranny of the Associated Press: The Character of Its Manager, James W. Simonton. N.p., 1873.

Ong, Walter J. *Interfaces of the Word: Studies in the Evolution of Consciousness and Culture.* Ithaca, N.Y.: Cornell University Press, 1977.

Orton, William. *Government Telegraphs: Argument of William Orton, President of the Western Union Telegraph Company, on the Bill to Establish Postal Telegraph Lines.* New York: Russells' American Steam Printing House, 1870.

———. *A Letter to the Postmaster-General Reviewing the Recommendations of his Annual Report in Favor of a Postal Telegraph.* New York, 1873.

Parrington, Vernon L. *The Beginnings of Critical Realism in America, 1860–1920.* Vol. 3 in Main Currents in American Thought. New York: Harcourt, Brace & World, 1930.

Parsons, Frank. *The Telegraph Monopoly.* Philadelphia: C. F. Taylor, 1899.

[Parton, James]. "The New York Herald." *North American Review* 102 (April 1866): 373-419.

Penn, I[rvine] Garland. *The Afro-American Press and Its Editors.* Springfield, Mass.: Willey, 1891.

Phillips, Cabell, ed. *Dateline Washington: The Story of National Affairs Journalism in the Life and Times of the National Press Club.* New York: Doubleday, 1949.

Phillips, Walter P. *The Phillips Telegraphic Code for the Rapid Transmission by Telegraph of Press Reports, Commercial and Private Telegrams and All Other Matter Sent by Wire or Cable.* Washington, D.C.: Gibson Brothers, 1879.

———. *The United Press: Address upon the Opening of the New Offices of the United Press in 'The World' Building, January 1, 1891.* N.p., [1891].

———[John Oakum]. *Oakum Pickings: A Collection of Sketches and Paragraphs Contributed from Time to Time to the Telegraphic and General Press.* New York: W. J. Johnston, 1876.

———[John Oakum]. *Sketches Old and New.* 1897. New York: J. H. Bunnell, 1902.

Phillips, William A. "Should the Government Own the Telegraph?" *North American Review* 143 (July 1886): 35-41.

Pierce, Bessie Louise. *A History of Chicago.* 3 vols. New York: Knopf, 1937-57.

Pollard, James E. *The Presidents and the Press.* New York: Macmillan, 1947.

[Poore, Benjamin Perley]. "Washington News." *Harper's Monthly* 48 (January 1874): 225-36.

Prescott, George B. *Electricity and the Electric Telegraph.* 8th ed. 2 vols. New York: D. Appleton, 1892.

———. *History, Theory, and Practice of the Electric Telegraph.* Boston: Ticknor & Fields, 1860.

Reid, James D. *The Telegraph in America, Its Founders, Promoters, and Noted Men.* New York: Derby Brothers, 1879.

Reid, Whitelaw. *American and English Studies.* 2 vols. 1913. Freeport, N.Y.: Books for Libraries Press, 1968.

———. *Some Newspaper Tendencies.* New York: Henry Holt, 1879.

[Rideing, William H.] "The Metropolitan Newspaper." *Harper's Monthly* 56 (December 1877): 43-59.

Rogers, Jason. *Newspaper Building: Application of Efficiency to Editing, to Mechanical Production, to Circulation and Advertising.* New York: Harper, 1918.

Rosebault, Charles J. *When Dana Was the Sun: A Story of Personal Journalism.* New York: Robert M. McBride, 1931.

Rosewater, Victor. *History of Cooperative News-Gathering in the United States.* New York: D. Appleton, 1930.

"The Rosewaters and the 'Bee' of Omaha." *Review of Reviews* 13 (June 1896): 709-10.

Sanger, George P., ed. *Public Laws of the United States of America Passed at the First Session of the Thirty-ninth Congress, 1865–1866.* Boston: Little, Brown, 1866.

[Saturday Evening Post]. *More Post Biographies.* Edited by John E. Drewry. Athens: University of Georgia Press, 1947.

[———]. *Post Biographies of Famous Journalists.* Edited by John E. Drewry. Athens: University of Georgia Press, 1942.

Schreiner, George Abel. *Cables and Wireless and Their Role in the Foreign Relations of the United States.* Boston: Stratford, 1924.

Schwarzlose, Richard A. *The American Wire Services: A Study of Their Development as a Social Institution.* 1965. New York: Arno, 1979.

———. "Trends in U.S. Newspapers' Wire Service Resources, 1934–66." *Journalism Quarterly* 43 (Winter 1966): 627-38.

Scott, William L., and Milton P. Jarnagin. *A Treatise upon the Law of Telegraphs with an Appendix Containing the General Statutory Provisions of England, Canada, the United States, and the*

States of the Union upon the Subject of Telegraphs. Boston: Little, Brown, 1868.

Scripps, Edward Wyllis. *Damned Old Crank: A Self-Portrait of E. W. Scripps.* Edited by Charles R. McCabe. New York: Harper, 1951.

——. *I Protest: Selected Disquisitions of E. W. Scripps.* Edited by Oliver Knight. Madison: University of Wisconsin Press, 1966.

Scripps-Howard Newspapers. "The Story of Scripps-Howard: A Study in Personality, Policy and Achievement in Journalism." A special ed. of *Scripps-Howard News* (September 1929).

Seitz, Don C. *The James Gordon Bennetts, Father and Son, Proprietors of the New York Herald.* Indianapolis: Bobbs-Merrill, 1928.

Seldes, George. *Freedom of the Press.* Indianapolis: Bobbs-Merrill, 1935.

Shanks, W. F. G. "How We Get Our News." *Harper's Monthly* 34 (March 1867): 511-22.

Shepherd, William G. *Confessions of a War Correspondent.* New York: Harper, 1917.

Sherover, Max. *Fakes in American Journalism.* 3rd ed. Brooklyn, N.Y.: Free Press League, 1916.

Simonton, J[ames] W. *The Associated Press: It Is Not a Monopoly but an Independent Cooperative Union of Newspaper Publishers and Only a Private Business; Congress Has No Rightful Power to Interfere with Its Affairs.* New York: John Polhemus, 1879.

[——]. *Atlantic Cable Mismanagement: Correspondence between J. W. Simonton and Cyrus W. Field and Others.* New York: Union Printing House, 1871.

Sinclair, Upton. *The Brass Check: A Study of American Journalism.* Pasadena, Calif.: the author, 1920.

Smalley, George W. *Anglo-American Memories.* 2 vols. London: Duckworth, 1911–12.

Smith, Anthony. *Goodbye, Gutenberg: The Newspaper Revolution of the 1980s.* New York: Oxford University Press, 1980.

Smith, William Henry. "A Familiar Talk about Monarchists and Jacobins." *Ohio Archaeological and Historical Quarterly* 2 (June 1888): 180-205.

——. "The First Fugitive Slave Case of Record in Ohio." In *American Historical Association Annual Report, 1893.* Washington, D.C.: Government Printing Office, 1894.

[——]. *Governmental Regulation of the Press: Testimony Taken Before the Senate Committee on Post-Offices and Post-Roads, March 7, 1884.* New York: Evening Post, 1884.

——. "The Pelham Papers—Loss of Oswego." In vol. 4 of *American Historical Association Papers*. New York: Putnam, 1890.

——. *A Political History of Slavery, Being an Account of the Slavery Controversy from the Earliest Agitations in the Eighteenth Century to the Close of the Reconstruction Period in America*. 2 vols. New York: Putnam, 1903.

——. "The Press as a News Gatherer." *Century* 42 (August 1891): 524-36.

——, ed. *The St. Clair Papers*. 2 vols. Cincinnati: R. Clarke, 1882.

Sobel, Judith, and Edwin Emery. "U.S. Dailies' Competition in Relation to Circulation Size: A Newspaper Data Update." *Journalism Quarterly* 55 (Spring 1978): 145-49.

Southern Press Association. *Proceedings of the Southern Press Association at the Session Held in Mobile, Alabama, February 17th, 18th, 19th and 20th, 1869*. Macon, Ga.: J. W. Burke, 1869.

Stone, Candace. *Dana and the Sun*. New York: Dodd, Mead, 1938.

Stone, Melville E. "The Associated Press." Five-part series in *Century* 69 (April 1905): 888-95, 70 (May 1905): 143-51, (June 1905): 299-310, (July 1905): 379-86, and (August 1905): 504-10.

——. "The Associated Press." Letter to the editor of *Collier's*, July 11, 1914, pp. 28-29.

——. *The Associated Press: Criticism and Reply*. N.p., [1914].

——. *Fifty Years a Journalist*. Garden City, N.Y.: Doubleday, Page, 1921.

——. *Letter to the Editor, Atlantic Monthly*. N.p., 1914.

——. "Newspapers in the United States, Their Functions, Interior Economy, and Management." *Self Culture* 5 (July 1897): 300-309.

Storey, Graham. *Reuters' Century, 1851-1951*. London: Max Parrish, 1951.

Sullivan, Paul W. *News Piracy: Unfair Competition and the Misappropriation Doctrine*. Journalism Monographs, no. 56. Lexington, Ky.: Association for Education in Journalism, 1978.

Sumner, Charles A. *The Postal Telegraph: A Lecture by Charles A. Sumner Delivered at Dashaway Hall, San Francisco, Oct. 12th, 1875*. San Francisco: Bacon, 1879.

Swanberg, W[illiam] A[ndrew]. *Citizen Hearst: A Biography of William Randolph Hearst*. New York: Scribners, 1961.

——. *Pulitzer*. New York: Scribners, 1967.

Swindler, William F. "The AP Anti-Trust Case in Historical Perspective." *Journalism Quarterly* 23 (March 1946): 40-57.

Tarbell, Ida M. *The Nationalizing of Business, 1878–1898.* Vol. 9 of A History of American Life, edited by Arthur M. Schlesinger and Dixon Ryan Fox. New York: Macmillan, 1936.

Taylor, George Rogers. *The Transportation Revolution, 1815–1860.* Vol. 4 of The Economic History of the United States. New York: Rinehart, 1951.

Tebbell, John. *An American Dynasty.* Garden City, N.Y.: Doubleday, 1947.

Thompson, Robert Luther. *Wiring a Continent: The History of the Telegraph Industry in the United States, 1832–1866.* Princeton, N.J.: Princeton University Press, 1947.

Trans-Mississippi Associated Press. *Articles of Incorporation, Constitution and Proceedings of the Trans-Mississippi Associated Press.* Topeka, Kan.: Peerless, 1886.

Tree, Robert Lloyd. "Victor Fremont Lawson and His Newspapers, 1890–1900: A Study of the Chicago Daily News and the Chicago Record." Ph.D. dissertation, Northwestern University, 1959.

Tuchman, Barbara W. *The Zimmermann Telegram.* 2nd ed. New York: Macmillan, 1966.

United Press (1882–97). *By-laws in Force July 1, 1895.* N.p., [1895].

[———]. *Facts vs. Lies, With an incidental forecast as to the outcome of the contest between the Press Associations.* New York: Evening Post, [1895].

[———]. *Joint Conference Committee Representing the Associated Press and United Press: Proceedings, Minutes, Correspondence and Addendum.* New York, 1895.

———. *The United Press.* New York: Evening Post, 1884.

[———]. *The United Press, Scope of Service and Business Methods: Interviews with General Manager Phillips.* N.p., [1895].

United Press International. *UPI Reporter.* New York: weekly.

U.S. Congress, House. *To Connect the Telegraph with the Postal Service.* 42nd Cong., 3rd sess., 1872, H. Rept. 6.

U.S. Congress, House Committee on the Post Office and Post Roads. *Postal Telegraph: Letter from the Postmaster General Transmitting a Report of G. G. Hubbard, Esq., of Boston Relative to the Establishment of a Cheap System of Postal Telegraph.* 40th Cong. 3rd sess., January 11, 1869, Ex. Doc. 35.

U.S. Congress, Senate Committee on Education and Labor. *Report of the Committee of the Senate upon the Relations between Labor* and Capital and Testimony Taken by the Committee. 5 vols. (4 vols. published). 48th Cong., 2nd sess., 1885.

U.S. Congress, Senate Committee on Post-Offices and Post-Roads. *Report to Accompany S. 651*. 43d Cong., 1st sess., 1874, S. Rept. 242.

U.S. Congress, Senate Committee on Post-Offices and Post-Roads. *Testimony of Walter P. Phillips . . . on Postal Telegraph before the Committee on Post-Offices and Post-Roads of the United States Senate, February 22, 1884*. Printed for the Use of the Committee. Washington, D.C.: Government Printing Office, 1884.

U.S. Congress, Senate Committee on Post-Offices and Post-Roads. *Testimony, Statements, etc., Taken by the Committee on Post-Offices and Post-Roads, United States Senate in Reference to Postal Telegraph*. 48th Cong., 1st sess., 1884, S. Rept. 577, pt. 2.

U.S. Department of Commerce, Bureau of the Census. *Historical Statistics of the United States, Colonial Times to 1970*. 2 pts. Washington, D.C.: Government Printing Office, 1975.

[Van Choate, S. F.] *Statement of Facts and Argument of the* [American Cable] *Company before the Committees on Foreign Affairs of the Forty-fifth Congress of the United States*. N.p., 1877.

Villard, Oswald Garrison. *The Disappearing Daily: Chapters in American Newspaper Evolution*. New York: Knopf, 1944.

———. *Fighting Years: Memoirs of a Liberal Editor*. New York: Harcourt, Brace, 1939.

———. *Some Newspapers and Newspaper-Men*. 2nd ed. New York: Knopf, 1926.

———. *Some Weaknesses of Modern Journalism*. Lawrence: University of Kansas *News-Bulletin*, November 2, 1914.

Wall, Joseph Frazier. *Henry Watterson, Reconstructed Rebel*. New York: Oxford University Press, 1956.

Warshow, Robert Irving. *Jay Gould: The Story of a Fortune*. New York: Greenberg, 1928.

Watson, Elmo Scott. *A History of Newspaper Syndicates in the United States, 1865–1935*. Chicago, 1936.

Watterson, Henry. *The Compromises of Life and Other Lectures and Addresses*. New York: Fox, Duffield, 1903.

———. *"Marse Henry": An Autobiography*. 2 vols. New York: George H. Doran, 1919.

Webb, Joseph M. "Historical Perspective on the New Journalism." *Journalism History* 1 (Summer 1974): 38-42, 60.

Wells, David A. *The Relation of the Government to the Telegraph, or a Review of the Two Propositions Now Pending before Congress for Changing the Telegraphic Service of the Country.* New York, 1873.

Wendt, Lloyd. *Chicago Tribune: The Rise of a Great American Newspaper.* Chicago: Rand McNally, 1979.

Western Associated Press. *Proceedings.* Detroit: annual, 1867–91.

Western Associated Press, Executive Committee. *Circular from the Executive Committee of the Western Associated Press: Contract with the New York Associated Press and Western Union Telegraph Company.* Cincinnati, 1867.

[Western Associated Press], Special Auditing Committee. *(Private), Annual Report, 1886–87.* New York: Evening Post, [1887].

Western Associated Press, Special Committee of Conference. *Report.* Detroit, 1891.

Western Associated Press, William Henry Smith. *(Confidential).* Chicago, 1877.

Western Union Telegraph Company. *The Proposed Union of the Telegraph and Postal Systems: Statement of the Western Union Telegraph Co.* Cambridge, Mass.: Welch, Bigelow, 1869.

Western Union Telegraph Company, Committee of the Board of Directors. *Remonstrance of the Western Union Telegraph Company against the Postal Telegraph Bill (Senate Bill, No. 341).* New York, 1872.

Wheeler, H. D. "At the Front with Willie Hearst." *Harper's Weekly,* October 9, 1915, pp. 340-42.

White, Trumbull. *The Wizard of Wall Street and His Wealth, or the Life and Deeds of Jay Gould.* Chicago: Mid-continent, 1892.

Who Was Who in America: Historical Volume, 1607–1896: A Component Volume of Who's Who in American History. 2nd ed. Chicago: A. N. Marquis, 1967.

Wilkerson, Marcus M. *Public Opinion and the Spanish-American War: A Study in War Propaganda.* Baton Rouge: Louisiana State University Press, 1932.

Williams, Charles Richard. *The Life of Rutherford Birchard Hayes.* 2 vols. Boston: Houghton Mifflin, 1914.

———. *The Associated Press.* N.p., 1890.

Wilson, James Harrison. *The Life of Charles A. Dana.* New York: Harper, 1907.

Wilson's Business Directory of New York City. Henry Wilson, comp. New York: John F. Trow, 1849–89.

Wisan, Joseph E. *The Cuban Crisis as Reflected in the New York Press (1895–1898).* New York: Columbia University Press, 1934.

Wolseley, Roland E. *The Black Press, U.S.A.* Ames: Iowa State University Press, 1971.

World Almanac & Book of Facts, 1975. New York: Newspaper Enterprise Association, 1974.

Wright, Benjamin F. *The Growth of American Constitutional Law.* Chicago: University of Chicago Press, 1942.

Young, John P. *Journalism in California.* San Francisco: Chronicle, 1915.

INDEX

Abbot & Winans, 210, 329
Adscititious Report, 196–97
Agnus, Felix, 152
Albany (N.Y.) *Times-Union*, 215
American News Association proposal, 94–95
American Newspaper Publishers Association, 144
American News Service, 229
American Press Association (1870–76), x, 24, 28, 56, 61, 75, 133, 188, 329; officers of, 278 n.135, 279 n.146; origins and operations of, 57–59; suspension of, 79–80
American Press Association (1882–1917), 188–89, 278 n.136
American Rapid Telegraph Company, 52
American Speaking Telephone Company, 84
American Telegraph Company, 4–7, 10–11, 15–16; officers of, 263 n.19
American Telephone & Telegraph Company, 246
American Union Telegraph Company, 82–83, 85, 86
Associated Correspondents of Race Newspapers, 190
Associated Negro Press, 191
Associated Press (in general and 1882–93), 125, 329, 330; addresses of, 27, 53, 73–74, 301 n.102; and 1883 contract with Western Union, 101, 118; and 1888 working contract with UP, 143–44, 149–50, 154, 156–57, 166; finances of, 2, 51, 52–53, 83, 134; franchises of, 2, 21–26, 30, 95, 107, 151–52, 179, 210,

242–43; joint executive committee of, 97–101, 102–3, 105–7, 132, 134, 135–36, 137–43, 145, 151, 154, 156, 157–66, 180, 184, 252; leased wires of, 111–12, 114–15, 116–17; membership statistics of, 22–23; 107, 136, 248–49; news report of, 51, 83, 117–30; regional organizations of, 34–39, 60; and stock pool with UP, 140–43, 145, 149–50, 154, 156–60, 162, 165, 166; structure, officers and operations of, 53–54, 117, 297 n.44; and tripartite agreement, 138–39, 149, 150, 154; and UP, 135–45, 149–62, 164–65; and Western Union, 1, 3, 12–14, 26–28, 30, 43–44, 50–51, 60–61, 87–88, 90, 92–96, 105–6, 107, 124, 129–30, 139–40. *See also* Associated Press of Illinois; Associated Press of New York; Baltimore Associated Press; California Associated Press; Colorado Associated Press; Kansas and Missouri Associated Press; New England Associated Press; New York Associated Press; New York State Associated Press; Northern Associated Press; Northwestern Associated Press; Philadelphia Associated Press; Smith, William Henry; Southern Associated Press; Texas Associated Press; Trans-Mississippi Associated Press; Western Associated Press
Associated Press Managing Editors Association, 244
Associated Press of Illinois (1893–1900), x, 150, 164, 165; *Annual*